DENMARK
5th Edition

**Where to Stay and Eat
for All Budgets**

**Must-See Sights
and Local Secrets**

Ratings You Can Trust

Fodor's Travel Publications   New York, Toronto, London, Sydney, Auckland
www.fodors.com

FODOR'S DENMARK

Editors: Sarah Sper, Carissa Bluestone

Editorial Production: Tom Holton
Editorial Contributors: Bruce Bishop, Nima Adl
Maps: David Lindroth, *cartographer;* Rebecca Baer and Bob Blake, *map editors*
Design: Fabrizio La Rocca, *creative director;* Guido Caroti, *art director;* Moon Sun Kim, *cover designer;* Melanie Marin, *senior picture editor*
Production/Manufacturing: Colleen Ziemba
Cover Photo (detail of a house facade, Copenhagen): DIOMEDIA/Alamy

AN IMPORTANT TIP & AN INVITATION

Although all prices, opening times, and other details in this book are based on information supplied to us at press time, changes occur all the time in the travel world, and Fodor's cannot accept responsibility for facts that become outdated or for inadvertent errors or omissions. So **always confirm information when it matters,** especially if you're making a detour to visit a specific place. Your experiences—positive and negative—matter to us. If we have missed or misstated something, **please write to us.** We follow up on all suggestions. Contact the Denmark editor at editors@fodors.com or c/o Fodor's at 1745 Broadway, New York, NY 10019.

PRINTED IN THE UNITED STATES OF AMERICA

10 9 8 7 6 5 4 3 2 1

Be a Fodor's Correspondent

Your opinion matters. It matters to us. It matters to your fellow Fodor's travelers, too. And we'd like to hear it. In fact, we *need* to hear it.

When you share your experiences and opinions, you become an active member of the Fodor's community. That means we'll not only use your feedback to make our books better, but we'll publish your names and comments whenever possible. Throughout our guides, look for "Word of Mouth," excerpts of your unvarnished feedback.

Here's how you can help improve Fodor's for all of us.

Tell us when we're right. We rely on local writers to give you an insider's perspective. But our writers and staff editors—who are the best in the business—depend on you. Your positive feedback is a vote to renew our recommendations for the next edition.

Tell us when we're wrong. We're proud that we update most of our guides every year. But we're not perfect. Things change. Hotels cut services. Museums change hours. Charming cafés lose charm. If our writer didn't quite capture the essence of a place, tell us how you'd do it differently. If any of our descriptions are inaccurate or inadequate, we'll incorporate your changes in the next edition and will correct factual errors at fodors.com *immediately.*

Tell us what to include. You probably have had fantastic travel experiences that aren't yet in Fodor's. Why not share them with a community of like-minded travelers? Maybe you chanced upon a beach or bistro or B&B that you don't want to keep to yourself. Tell us why we should include it. And share your discoveries and experiences with everyone directly at fodors.com. Your input may lead us to add a new listing or highlight a place we cover with a "Highly Recommended" star or with our highest rating, "Fodor's Choice."

Give us your opinion instantly at our feedback center at www.fodors.com/feedback. You may also e-mail editors@fodors.com with the subject line "Denmark Editor." Or send your nominations, comments, and complaints by mail to Denmark Editor, Fodor's, 1745 Broadway, New York, NY 10019.

You and travelers like you are the heart of the Fodor's community. Make our community richer by sharing your experiences. Be a Fodor's correspondent.

Bon rejse! (Or simply: Happy traveling!)

Tim Jarrell, Publisher

CONTENTS

ABOUT THIS BOOK

Our Ratings

Sometimes you find terrific travel experiences and sometimes they just find you. But usually the burden is on you to select the right combination of experiences. That's where our ratings come in.

As travelers we've all discovered a place so wonderful that its worthiness is obvious. And sometimes that place is so experiential that superlatives don't do it justice: you just have to be there to know. These sights, properties, and experiences get our highest rating, **Fodor's Choice**, indicated by orange stars throughout this book.

Black stars highlight sights and properties we deem **Highly Recommended**, places that our writers, editors, and readers praise again and again for consistency and excellence.

By default, there's another category: any place we include in this book is by definition worth your time unless we say otherwise. And we will.

Disagree with any of our choices? Care to nominate a place or suggest that we rate one more highly? Visit our feedback center at www.fodors.com/feedback.

Budget Well

Hotel and restaurant price categories from ¢ to $$$$ are defined in the opening pages of each chapter. For attractions, we always give standard adult admission fees; reductions are usually available for children, students, and senior citizens. Want to pay with plastic? **AE, D, DC, MC, V** following restaurant and hotel listings indicate if American Express, Discover, Diner's Club, MasterCard, and Visa are accepted.

Restaurants

Unless we state otherwise, restaurants are open for lunch and dinner daily. We mention dress only when there's a specific requirement and reservations only when they're essential or not accepted—it's always best to book ahead.

Hotels

Hotels have private bath, phone, TV, and air-conditioning and operate on the European Plan (aka EP, meaning without meals), unless we specify that they use the Continental Plan (CP, with a Continental breakfast), Breakfast Plan (BP, with a full breakfast), or Modified American Plan (MAP, with breakfast and dinner) or are all-inclusive (including all meals and most activities). We always

list facilities but not whether you'll be charged an extra fee to use them, so when pricing accommodations, find out what's included.

Many Listings	
★	Fodor's Choice
★	Highly recommended
✉	Physical address
✛	Directions
⌂	Mailing address
☎	Telephone
🖷	Fax
⊕	On the Web
✉	E-mail
💷	Admission fee
☉	Open/closed times
►	Start of walk/itinerary
Ⓜ	Metro stations
▭	Credit cards
Hotels & Restaurants	
🏨	Hotel
⌁	Number of rooms
⚇	Facilities
❍	Meal plans
✕	Restaurant
⌁	Reservations
🏛	Dress code
⚲	Smoking
ⱓ	BYOB
✕🏨	Hotel with restaurant that warrants a visit
Outdoors	
⛳	Golf
⛺	Camping
Other	
♨	Family-friendly
🖪	Contact information
⇨	See also
✉	Branch address
☞	Take note

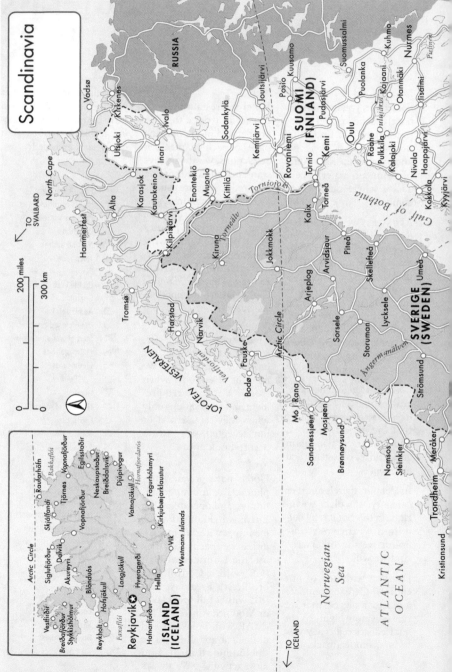

Scandinavia

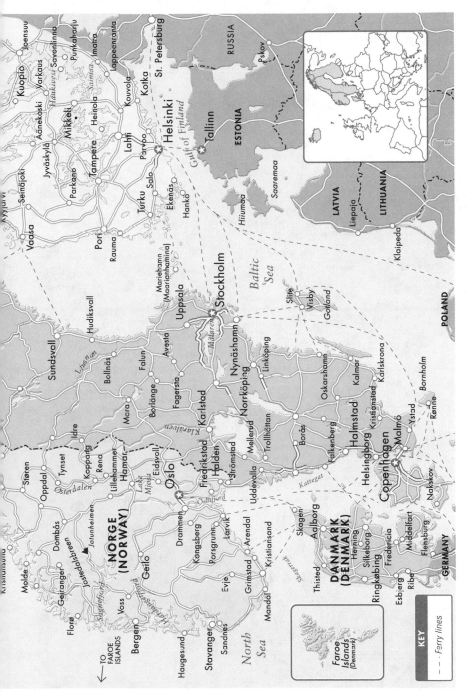

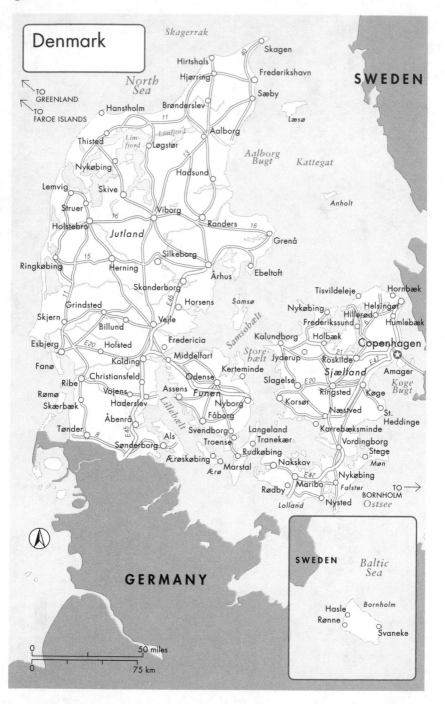

WHAT'S WHERE

COPENHAGEN

Europeans love Copenhagen, and judging from the number of other international visitors, the Danish capital is on many must-see lists. And why not? Copenhagen is cool, literally and figuratively. Restaurants in all price ranges are plentiful; it's extremely safe and walkable; history blends effortlessly with modernity; and locals are naturally friendly, maybe because they're so happy to be residents of such a livable city.

This is Scandinavia's largest city (population 1.5 million), incorporating the easternmost reaches of Zealand and the northern part of adjacent Amager island. For almost 600 years Copenhagen has been the seat of the oldest kingdom in the world, and grandeur finds its expression in the city's royal residences. Glancing over the skyline, you'll see towers and turrets, domes and decks, all glinting in the northern sun.

If coziness is a Danish trait, then Copenhagen is most certainly Danish. Bicycles roll alongside cars in the narrow streets, and a handful of skyscrapers are tucked away amid cafés, canals, and quaint old homes. But don't let the low-slung skyline fool you: downtown Copenhagen is a sophisticated cultural hub with a wealth of attractions. Strøget, Copenhagen's main pedestrian shopping avenue, packs in the best in Danish design from furniture to flatware; street performers, sidewalk cafés, and pastry shops beckon outdoors. There are minor irritants: smoking is still allowed in every bar and virtually every restaurant (unless forbidden by the chef); taxis and liquor can be terribly expensive by North American standards; and place names will not sound the way that they are spelled.

This is a youthful city, where all ages seem to truly enjoy the best Copenhagen can offer. Certainly the best-known attraction is Tivoli Gardens, a bewitching blend of blooming gardens, funfair rides, pantomime theater, stylish restaurants, and concerts. There aren't too many capital cities that can lay claim to a similar venue in the heart of the metropolis.

ZEALAND & ITS ISLANDS

If it's necessary to "escape" from Copenhagen, then the island of Zealand, the largest of the Danish isles, is the country's most convenient and popular bit of countryside. North of the city are royal castles (including Helsingør's Kronborg of Hamlet fame), ritzy beach towns, and top-notch museums. The modern-art museum Louisiana has a spectacular seaside perch on Zealand's northeastern coast and a superb collection of modern European and American art, from Warhol to Gia-cometti. The only drawback here might be the fact that bar-gains of any kind are scarce: this was and is an enclave to the well heeled, much like Skagen in north Jutland.

To the west, Roskilde holds relics of medieval Denmark; it also hosts Northern Europe's largest music festival, usually at the end of June, which draws over 75,000 revelers who come to groove to rock, pop, jazz, and folk music. And to the west and south, rural towns and farms edge up to beach communities and fine white beaches, often surrounded by forests. On the southeast island of Møn, 75-million-year-old chalk cliffs plunge dramatically to the sea.

FUNEN & THE CENTRAL ISLANDS	Fyn (Funen), the smaller of the country's two main islands, is the site of Denmark's third-largest city, Odense, the birth-place of Hans Christian Andersen. In 2005 it was H. C. Andersen 24 hours a day, seven days a week, as everyone was celebrating his 200th birthday. The infatuation continues, so don't be surprised if seemingly every innkeeper or restaura-teur tells you Andersen stayed or ate at that establishment. It's no wonder this area inspired many fairy tales: 1,120 km (700 mi) of coastline and lush stretches of vegetable and flower gar-dens are punctuated by manor houses, beech glades, castles, swan ponds, and thatch-roof houses. In the south is the Egeskov Slot, a well-preserved Renaissance castle that even has a moat. Myriad islands speckle the sea south of Funen, including ver-dant Ærø, called the Jewel of the Archipelago. In the island's friendly port town of Ærøskøbing, narrow cobbled streets wind among beautifully preserved half-timber houses. Artists have flocked here for decades, which always makes for a slightly more bohemian, fun atmosphere.
SOUTH JUTLAND	Jutland, Denmark's western peninsula, shares its southern border with Germany, its northern end jutting sharply toward the coast of Sweden. South Jutland's people and geography are quite different from the north; it's in the center of the penin-sula where tastes and traditions seem to converge. South Jut-land is pastoral, with smaller, quiet beaches on the eastern side and a super-Danish patriotism running throughout the re-gion. Danish flags fly everywhere and on everything, as this was where the Germans invaded in World War II and on pre-

vious occasions of annexation. South Jutland is also a bit of "the road less traveled," and small hotels and restaurants are commonplace, with very good prices to match. On the western coast is the vacation island of Rømø, but if given the choice, further north is the island of Fanø, which is more historic and interesting, but with the same incredibly broad expanses of beach. To get there, you'll have to take the ferry from Esbjerg, which, comparatively speaking, is one of the country's newer settlements. It is a busy port, and with that comes sailors on leave looking for a place to party. Some people may not enjoy the noisemakers downtown at night.

CENTRAL JUTLAND	Central Jutland is home to lively Århus in the east; charming Randers and Viborg to the north; Silkeborg's quiet beauty; and Ringkøbing to the west. The hub of central Jutland would have to be Billund, a small town with a huge employer—Legoland and the Lego toy company—responsible for most of the jobs in the area as well as for the construction of an international airport there.
NORTH JUTLAND	In North Jutland, Aalborg is the biggest city and one with lots of vitality, taking some of the shine off Århus. At the northernmost point stands Skagen, a luminous, dune-covered site that attracts art lovers, artists and those seeking a quieter, more genteel approach to seaside vacations.
BORNHOLM	The island of Bornholm, 177 km (110 mi) southeast of Zealand, sits off the coast of Sweden and has a temperate climate that distinguishes it from the rest of Denmark. Its old-fashioned towns and exuberant natural beauty have earned it the title of Pearl of the Baltic. Gardens, forests, and dune grasses sprout up in a patchwork of verdure, and active cod and herring fisheries reap similar abundance from the surrounding Baltic waters. This is another off-the-beaten-path destination, so you may not find as many amenities here as you would in Jutland or on Zealand.

QUINTESSENTIAL DENMARK

Danish Design

While many people may think of Danish design as simply being cool-looking chairs that were sold around the world in the 1960s, it actually encompasses many facets of Danish life, like lighting, electronics, and everyday household items. Even the local grocery store will impress you with "Made in Denmark" kitchen items that somehow look so much better than the fare sold back home. The Danish design aesthetic itself is simple and inventive, marked by clean lines. Design is so ingrained in life here that many young Danes could tell you the names of their favorite Danish furniture and industrial designers (perhaps Hans Wegner or Arne Jacobsen) as readily as their favorite rock stars (whose CDs they might be playing on their sleek Bang & Olufsen player).

Gardens

Gardens reach into the very soul of a Dane and abound all over Denmark. Though space is at a premium in this small country, Danes have ensured that everyone has access to natural beauty. There are over 62,000 federally protected gardens scattered throughout the country. They're inexpensive and popular, and many contain small weekend cottages, beautiful flowerbeds, and the Danish flag—*Dannebrog*—flying at the top of the flagpole on Sundays. People living in apartments and cities flock to these retreats. There's even a "visual pollution" law that bans billboards from being erected along roads and highways.

Beer & Aquavit

There's a renewed interest in the Danish national drink: beer (or øl in Danish). Danes are rarely short of an excuse for a beer celebration. Microbreweries have

If you want to get a sense of contemporary Danish culture, and indulge in some of its pleasure, start by familiarizing yourself with the rituals of daily life. These are a few highlights.

popped up all over the country, and even in Copenhagen, where Carlsberg beer was founded in the early 19th century, loyalty to that stalwart is wavering in favor of newer flavors and brands. Independent microbreweries in Copenhagen alone include Nørrebro Bryghus, Bryggeriet Apollo, Brøckhouse, and Færgekroen (in Tivoli). Denmark now has more breweries per capita than any other European country.

Akvavit, or aquavit, is a Scandinavian liquor of about 40% alcohol by volume. Its name comes from aqua vitae (Latin for "water of life"). Like other liquors made in Norway and Sweden, it is distilled from potatos or grains and is flavored with herbs such as caraway seeds, cumin, dill, fennel, or coriander. Akvavit is an acquired taste. It's usually drunk as a shot, or as the Danes say, a *snaps*, during meals—especially during the appetizer course—along with a chaser of beer.

Hygge (coziness)

Though you may have trouble saying *hygge* ("euoooh-ga" is the probably the closest you'll get), if you manage to get it out, it's one of the highest compliments you can pay a home, restaurant, hotel, party, or any kind of place or situation. Hygge is the singularly Danish way of describing a warm feeling of contentment—a coziness without cutesiness. Order, synergy, symmetry, and comfort all mixed together are hygge. While driving through a small rural town on any given morning you may notice that candles have been lit in some apartment windows or homes. The candles, even at 10 am, make these domiciles just a little more hygge. Enjoying a dinner with new Danish friends is definitely hygge. Even the Danish nature, never boastful or ostentatious, seems to facilitate this good feeling.

IF YOU LIKE

Biking

Denmark was designed for the cyclist. It's primarily a flat country, and there is a national bicycle routing system, allowing as many bike paths as is humanly possible. The paths may share pavement with sidewalks, which some (tourist) pedestrians may not notice, or they may be separate paved paths that follow the highways and byways of the country. Cycle routes are signposted everywhere with a symbol depicting a white bike on a blue background. This symbol, used together with a number, name, or logo, marks each route.

Most tourist offices will have bike maps available for free or for a small fee. One of the more recently posted routes follows the German-Danish border in South Jutland, allowing you to effectively see both sides of a geographic coin. These same tourism offices can help you book a biking holiday, where everything you need, including a bicycle and hotel reservations, is waiting for you upon arrival.

Bicycle stands are ubiquitous and handy to everything. You'll see every age group represented on a bike, from toussle-haired kids to grandmothers to students, some with an ever-present cigarette dangling from their mouths.

Check out www.trafikken.dk for an overview of the country's bike paths.

At lunchtime, go for the smørrebrød. Modest, family-run restaurants have the best, most traditional sampling of these open-face sandwiches, and they focus on generous portions and artful presentation.

Castles & Churches

Denmark's small geographical area and efficient train and highway system makes getting around to visit restored castles and proud churches a breeze. What will amaze even the most jaded visitor are how well churches and castles have been kept over the centuries. Copenhagen has a multitude of churches and castles, and one you shouldn't miss is Amalienborg, King Christian VIII's palace (it's also known as the Royal Residence). A tour takes you through recreations of the royal family's private apartments from the past 150 years—the actual interiors of the apartments were moved here from other mansions and arranged in exactly the same way the king or queen had them. At Christiansborg, where the current Queen lives, you can visit some of the rooms she uses for official receptions. Roskilde Domkirke, the sepulchral chapel of Danish kings and queens, is a fantastic example of church architecture over the past 800 years. In Jutland you may want to see the restored Koldinghus castle in Kolding, a magnificent feat of interior engineering that restored a fortress ravaged by fire. There are so many castles (ranging from modest to spectacular) and rural and city churches from as far back as the 13th century that you may never see all of them.

Note that opening and closing hours are nothing if not confusing, and although we do our best to provide them, it doesn't hurt to ask at the local tourist office or give the property a quick phone call.

Hans Christian Andersen

No one can dispute that the best-known (and arguably, the best-loved) Dane is Hans Christian Andersen (1805–1875), known worldwide for his children's fairy tales. Almost everyone in the English-speaking world has heard of "The Ugly Duckling," "The Emperor's New Clothes," "The Princess and the Pea," and certainly "The Little Mermaid." (The latter fable was apparently a symbolic tale of his infatuation with Edward Collin, a friend who did not return Andersen's love.)

Andersen was also a poet, and is considered by his countrymen to be the world's first tourist in the modern sense of the word. He visited Jutland twice, battling seasickness to get there when no one else traveled to the peninsula for pleasure. He coined the phrase, "To travel is to live." Your must-see spot to visit is his hometown of Odense, where he was born in 1805, but the Hans Christian Andersen Museum in Copenhagen is also a worthy way to perform a pilgrimage or satisfy simple curiosity.

Danish Cuisine

From the hearty meals of Denmark's fishing heritage to the inspired creations of a new generation of chefs, Danish cuisine combines the best of tradition and novelty. Though the country has long looked to the French as a beacon of gastronomy, chefs have proudly returned to the Danish table, emphasizing fresh, local ingredients and combining them with fusion trends. Many of Denmark's young up-and-coming chefs have completed all their training locally at the country's expanding list of superb, internationally recognized restaurants.

At lunchtime, go for the *smørrebrød*. Modest, family-run restaurants have the best, most traditional sampling of these open-face sandwiches, and they focus on generous portions and artful presentation. Look for tender mounds of roast beef topped with pickles or baby shrimp piled high on a slice of French bread. If you like what's billed as "Danish pastry" at home, don't leave the country without tasting a *wienerbrød* at a local bakery—*this* is the real thing. An excellent fresh fish to try is the European flatfish plaice. It's caught off the Scandinavian coast, and its mild meat goes well with many types of sauces.

As for beer, you can't do better than to stick with the ubiquitous Danish brands Carlsberg and Tuborg, which complement the traditional fare better than high-priced wine. If you go for the harder stuff, try the famous *snaps,* the aquavit savored with cold food. For an evening tipple, have a taste of Gammel Dansk, a Danish bitters.

GREAT ITINERARIES

DENMARK CLASSIC

Day 1

Start off an ideal week-long itinerary of Denmark in magical Copenhagen. The city is safe, walkable, historic, and pretty. You can get oriented by traipising around on your own or taking a guided walking or bus tour. Make time to people-watch in the Tivoli gardens.

Day 2

Today, continue to explore Copenhagen. Feel like royalty at Christiansborg Slot, where you can don slippers and tour the Royal Reception Chambers (be sure to check the complicated opening hours before making a visit). Or go antiestablishment and head out to Christiania, a fascinating anarchists' commune in Christianshavn. In the evening, indulge in Danish cuisine at one of Copenhagen's cutting-edge restaurants, such as noma.

Day 3

On your third day, head to the top of the country: take a one-hour flight to Aalborg, and then drive or take the train to Skagen (pronounced Skane). Here you find immense skies, fantastic sunsets, and a lovely, seaside ambience that has been attracting Danes and other savvy travelers for years. Spend the rest of the day exploring the town, whether it's ambling along the pebble beaches or ducking into the Skagen Museum, which shows broad impressionist canvases from talented 19th-century Danish artists.

Day 4

Take the morning and early afternoon to finish soaking up Skagen. You could meander around on a bike or see the famous Danish artists Michael and Anna Ancher's House, which includes Anna's studio. Head back to Aalborg late in the day via car or train. The nightlife scene is pretty good here, if you decide to stay overnight; otherwise, have a bite to eat, and then drive or take the train to Billund, home to Legoland.

Day 5

Today, it's all about toys: you're off to Legoland. The whimsical display of meticulous miniature cities and villages from around the world is a must-see, even if you aren't traveling with children. Take a train back to Copenhagen this evening to catch your flight home tomorrow.

ALTERNATIVE: If you'd rather have a taste of the Danish rural countryside, head south to Kolding instead of Legoland. This town has a little of everything, including a wonderful modern art museum, good shopping, and country inns. The train ride back to Copenhagen from here is a little over two hours, and allows you a chance to see the countryside before you get back to the big city.

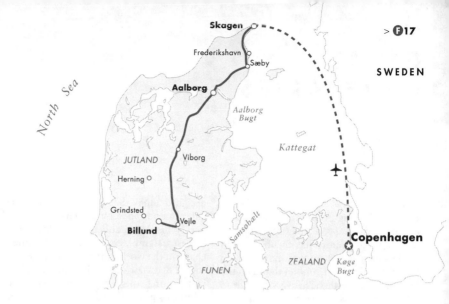

TIPS

❶ This itinerary assumes that you're here to sample as much of Denmark as possible in a short amount of time. If you want to spend more time relaxing, pick just one of the suggested side trips and split your time between that town and Copenhagen. A good idea would be to spend two to three days in Copenhagen, and two to three days in another town, with the last day reserved for traveling back to Copenhagen for your flight home. One note: There's not much in Billund, where Legoland is located, so if you're planning on making your one sidetrip to Legoland, do a day in Legoland and then head to nearby Vejle.

GREAT ITINERARIES

DESIGN

Day 1

Between Kolding in Jutland, and Copenhagen in Zealand, you'll be seeing the best of design the country has to offer. Begin in Copenhagen, where you may want to stay at the Skt. Petri, a hotel that uses the Danish design aesthetic in everything from the guest rooms to the restaurants. Although it's not inexpensive, design reigns supreme here, and enthusiasts appreciate the attention to detail.

As you tour the city, you should definitely make a stop at the Danish Design Center, where the agenda is to increase the use of design in Danish companies, brand Danish design worldwide, and raise design awareness among the general public. Exhibits from the DDC have appeared at the MoMA in New York and have been shown in connection with EXPO 2005 in Japan.

Day 2

Make your way to the Danish Museum of Art & Design in Copenhagen, which has both permanent and special collections for the discerning design aficianado. This contemporary museum for Danish and international crafts and design is among the premier exhibition venues in Scandinavia. You'll want at least a half-day to browse through the collections, archives, and library.

Day 3

Make the two-hour drive out to Kolding, via Highways E20 and E45, to get to the Trapholt Museum for Modern Art. It's perhaps the best modern-art museum outside of Copenhagen, due to its focus on Danish design. A true highlight is the Danish Furniture Museum, housed in a specially designed annex that is accessed via a circular ramp topped by a skylight. The superbly displayed collection includes the largest assemblage of Danish-designed chairs in the world, offering a unique historical overview of the birth and popularization of Danish furniture design. In addition, prolific and famous designer Arne Jacobsen's summer cottage has been relocated here, to the delight of many.

Day 4

Today, back in Copenhagen, shop some of the best spots for arts, crafts, and design in Europe. Check out the Danish Design Centre's Web site for a list of over 25 suggested shops (www.ddc.dk/ddcnet/shopping). Don't miss Paustian, where the building is as much an attraction as the furniture for sale, or Tage Anderson, which has such fabulous displays that they actually charge an admission for browsers.

ALTERNATIVE: If Kolding and its Trapholt Musem cast their spell on you, spend an extra day here soaking it all up. Then return to Copenhagen on Day 5 for some shopping.

SWEDEN

Aalborg Bugt

Kattegat

North Sea

Viborg

JUTLAND

Grindsted

Billund

Bramming

Samsøbælt

✈ **Copenhagen**

Ribe

Vojens

FUNEN

ZEALAND

Køge Bugt

Vojens

Tønder

Åbenrå

Sønderborg

GERMANY

TIPS

❶ For simple, inexpensive design souve-
niers, you can find "Made in Denmark"
kitchen tools, such as corkscrews, coasters, and mugs, at the local grocery
store.

❷ Don't miss the Trapholt Museum's gift
shop. You can find items done by some
of Denmark's best designers and carried
exclusively by the museum.

THE FAMILY

Day 1

What better way to start off a family vacation in Denmark than to first arrive in Billund, home to world-famous Legoland? You'll fly into the international, squeaky-clean new Billund airport from Copenhagen (or elsewhere) and check into the Legoland Hotel for the ultimate family experience. You'll want to spend the day here, and the morning of the next day (ask for a late check-out).

Day 2

Take the kids and the train to Ribe, reported to be the country's oldest city. Stay at Ribe Byferie, where you'll have a two-bedroom townhouse to make you feel at home. (Or, you could stay at the Danhostel, which is less expensive.) The kids will love wandering around the old town and checking out the Viking Center and the Viking Museum. In inclement weather, there's a large indoor swimming pavilion to keep them occupied.

Day 3

Rent a car and make your way to Sønderborg, still in South Jutland, and stay overnight at Ballebro Færgekro. Take the ferry next to the hotel for a five-minute ride

with your car to Als and the nearby Danfoss Universe, a new theme park where you'll be as inspired as your children in discovering scientific and human attributes through outdoor games, computers, and visual attractions. There are no white-knuckle rides here; it's educational and fun.

Day 4

Finally, make you way back to Copenhagen for at least one full day there. Make the obligatory stop to see the *Little Mermaid,* but try to allot most of your time to Tivoli Gardens or one of the museums (the National Museum is especially good for kids).

TIPS

❶ Extend this itinerary by spending an extra day in Ribe or Sønderborg, and another in Copenhagen. Beyond Danfoss Universe, Sønderborg has castles to explore, and Ribe's medieval atmosphere just may bewitch your kids.

❷ If you stay at Ribe Byferie, you can stock up on groceries and make use of the townhouse's kitchen.

WHEN TO GO

Summertime—when the lingering sun of June, July, and August brings out the best in the climate and the Danes—is the best time to visit. In July most Danes flee to their summer homes or go abroad. If you do go in winter, the weeks preceding Christmas are a prime time to explore Tivoli. Although the experience is radically different from the flower-filled summertime park, the winter park has a charm all its own. Much of Tivoli is closed during these weeks, but you can still experience some of the shops, restaurants, a handful of rides, an "elf house," and some Danish theater.

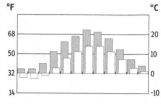

Climate

Mainland Denmark and its surrounding islands have a cool maritime climate with mild to warm summers and cold (but not frigid) winters. Late summer and early fall is the rainiest season, but even then, precipitation is rarely heavy. In summer Bornholm tends to stay warmer and sunnier longer than elsewhere. Skagen, in North Jutland, receives more sunny days than any other place in the country, although temperatures may not be so high. Winter is dark and misty, but it's a great time to visit museums, libraries, and the countless atmospheric meeting places in which the Danes take refuge.

Forecasts **Weather Channel Connection** ☎ 900/932–8437 95¢ per minute ⊕ www.weather.com.

ON THE CALENDAR

Denmark's top seasonal events are listed below, and any one of them could provide the stuff of lasting memories. You'll want to book tickets and plan ahead for the crowded Roskilde Festival. The summer jazz festivals in Copenhagen and Århus, as well as the early-fall Århus Festival, are also well-attended. The Danish Tourist Board's Web site, ⊕ www.visitdenmark.com, also has information about events.

WINTER Late November–Late December	The **Christmas Market** at Tivoli Gardens has lots of decorations, gift ideas, and seasonal treats.
SPRING April 16	The **Queen's Birthday** is celebrated with the royal guard in full ceremonial dress as the royal family appears before the public on the balcony of Amalienborg.
Late May	The **Aalborg Carnival** draws 100,000 visitors to the Jutland city for two days of festivities, which include fireworks, outdoor concerts, and parades of costumed revelers. ☎ *98/13–72–11* ⊕ *www.karnevaliaalborg.dk.*
Late May–Early June	The **Copenhagen Carnival** includes boat parades in Nyhavn and costumed revelers in the streets. Various musical and dance performances take place throughout the city. ☎ *26/73–24–00* ⊕ *www.karneval.dk.*
SUMMER Early June	The **Aalborg Jazz & Blues Festival**, though not as large as its Copenhagen counterpart, fills the city with four days of indoor and outdoor concerts, many of them free. ⊕ *www.denblaafestival.dk.*
Mid-June	The **International Kite Festival in Fanø**, an island off the western coast of Jutland, attracts thousands of kite enthusiasts who fill the skies above with their diving and soaring kites. ⊕ *www.kitefliersmeetingfanoe.de/index.htm.* The **Riverboat Jazz Festival** draws jazz fans to Silkeborg for the four-day celebration featuring local international bands. ☎ *86/80–16–17* ⊕ *www.riverboat.dk.* The **Round Sjælland Regatta**, one of the largest yachting events in the world, starts and ends in Helsingør. ☎ *49/21–15–67* ⊕ *www.has-sejlklub.dk.*
June 21	On **Midsummer's Night**, Danes celebrate the longest day of the year with bonfires and picnics in the countryside.

Late June– Early July	The **Roskilde Festival**, the largest rock concert in northern Europe, attracts dozens of premier rock, pop, and hip-hop groups, and more than 75,000 fans. ☎ 46/36–66–13 ⊕ *www.roskilde-festival. dk/*.
Late June	The **Skagen Festival**, brings the northern tip of Jutland to its liveliest, showcasing international and local folk music. ☎ 98/44–40–94 ⊕ *www.skagenfestival.dk/*.
July	The **Copenhagen Jazz Festival**, one of Europe's largest jazz-music events, gathers international and Scandinavian jazz greats for a week of concerts, many of them free. ☎ 33/93–20–13 ⊕ *www. jazzfestival.dk*.
July 4	The **Fourth of July** celebration in Rebild Park, near Aalborg, represents the only American Independence Day festivities outside the United States. ⊕ *www.visitaalborg.com*.
Mid-July	The **Århus International Jazz Festival** gathers world-renowned names for indoor and outdoor concerts. ☎ 86/12–13–12 ⊕ *www.jazzfest. dk*. The family-friendly **Samsø Festival** gets underway on the island of Samsø, Jutland, with music performed by Danish and international acts. ☎ 86/59–18–15 ⊕ *www.samfest.dk*.
Mid-August	The **Mermaid Pride Parade** is a gay pride event that navigates the streets of Copenhagen, which has a sizeable gay and lesbian community. ⊕ *www.mermaidpride.dk/*.
Late August	The **Tønder Festival**, held in this town in southern Jutland since 1974, brings in folk, bluegrass, and gospel artists, as well as folk-music lovers from around the world. ☎ 74/72–46–10 ⊕ *www. tf.dk*.
FALL Early September	The 10-day **Århus Festival**, Denmark's most comprehensive fête, fills the city with exhibits, concerts, sporting events, and theater. ☎ 89/40–91–91 ⊕ *www.aarhusfestuge.dk*.
September	The **Golden Days Festival** in Copenhagen celebrates Denmark's 19th-century cultural blossoming through exhibits, readings, and performances. ☎ 35/42–14–32 ⊕ *www.goldendays.dk*.

Late October	On **Culture Night** in Copenhagen, which falls on the third Friday of October, the city's museums and cultural centers stay open, some by candlelight, into the wee hours of the morning. Over 100,000 Copenhageners and tourists take advantage of this opportunity to mill about the streets and check out the readings, exhibitions, and performances that take place at more than 700 venues. ☎ *33/25–74–00* ⊕ *www.kulturnatten.dk/en.*
November	The **Musikhøst (Music Harvest)** in Odense holds performances of new and avant-garde concert music throughout the city. The festival keeps to a different sub-genre each year. ☎ *66/11–06–63* ⊕ *www.musikhost.dk.*

SMART TRAVEL TIPS

Finding out about your destination before you leave home means you won't spend time organizing everyday minutiae once you've arrived. You'll be more streetwise when you hit the ground as well, better prepared to explore the aspects of Denmark that drew you here in the first place. The organizations in this section can provide information to supplement this guide; contact them for up-to-the-minute details, and consult the A to Z sections that end each chapter for facts on the various topics as they relate to the country's many regions. Happy landings!

AIR TRAVEL

BOOKING

When you book, look for nonstop flights and remember that "direct" flights stop at least once. Try to avoid connecting flights, which require a change of plane. Two airlines may operate a connecting flight jointly, so ask whether your airline operates every segment of the trip; you may find that the carrier you prefer flies you only part of the way. To find more booking tips and to check prices and make online flight reservations, log on to www.fodors.com.

CARRIERS

Nearly all international air service to Denmark flies into Copenhagen Airport. SAS, the main carrier, makes nonstop flights to the capital from Chicago, Newark, and Seattle. British Airways offers connecting flights via London from Atlanta, Baltimore, Boston, Charlotte, Chicago, Dallas, Denver, Detroit, Houston, Los Angeles, Miami, New York, Orlando, Philadelphia, Phoenix, Pittsburgh, San Diego, San Francisco, Seattle, Tampa, and Washington, D.C. Icelandair has connecting flights to Copenhagen via Reykjavík from Baltimore, Fort Lauderdale, New York, and Orlando. Finnair has service through Helsinki from Miami, New York, and—from May to September—San Francisco and Toronto. At this writing, Delta planned to begin nonstop service from Atlanta and Continental planned nonstop service from Newark, both starting May 2006.

British Airways flies nonstop to Copenhagen from London (Heathrow and Gatwick), Birmingham, and Manchester. SAS Scandinavian Airlines flies nonstop from London, Manchester, and Glasgow, and also from London to Århus. Aer Lingus flies from Dublin, connecting in London; the flights are operated by British Airways. Mærsk Air flies nonstop from Gatwick to Billund and Copenhagen. Easyjet has cheap flights between London's Stansted airport and Copenhagen. Virgin Airlines is also inexpensive and flies between London's Gatwick and Stansted airports via Brussels to Copenhagen. Air France also flies out of Copenhagen.

In Jutland, Billund Airport is Denmark's second-largest airport. Mærsk Air flies to Billund from Amsterdam, Bergen, Brussels, the Faroe Islands, Frankfurt, London, Manchester, Nice, Oslo, Stockholm, and Paris. Sunair serves Århus, Billund, Göteborg, Oslo, and Stockholm. Several domestic airports, including Aalborg, Århus, and Esbjerg, are served by Mærsk and SAS, both of which have good connections to Copenhagen. Cimber Air links Sønderborg, just north of the German border, with Copenhagen.

Cimber Air makes several daily flights to Bornholm from Copenhagen, and flies also from Berlin. Lufthansa flies to Bornholm from Berlin and Hamburg.

⒎ Air France ☏ 800/237-2747 in North America, 82/33-27-01 in Denmark ⊕ www.airfrance.com/dk. **Air Greenland** ☏ 299/34-34-34 in Greenland, 32/31-40-88 in Denmark ⊕ www.airgreenland.gl. **Aer Lingus** ☏ 800/474-7424 in North America, 0161/832-5771 in Ireland ⊕ www.aerlingus.com. **British Airways** ☏ 0207/491-4989 in the U.K., 800/247-9297 in North America, 80/20-80-22 in Denmark ⊕ www.britishairways.com. **Cimber Air** ☏ 74/42-22-77, 56/95-11-11 in Bornholm ⊕ www.cimber.dk. **Continental** ☏ 800/525-0280 ⊕ www.continental.com. **Delta** ☏ 800/221-1212 ⊕ www.delta.com. **Easyjet** ☏ 0870/600-0000 in the U.K., 70/12-43-21 in Denmark ⊕ www.easyjet.com. **Finnair** ☏ 800/950-5000 in North America, 32/50-45-10 in Denmark ⊕ www.finnair.fi. **Icelandair** ☏ 354/505-0300 in Iceland, 0207/874-1000 in the U.K., 800/223-5500 in North America, 33/70-22-00 in Denmark ⊕ www.icelandair.com. **Lufthansa**

☏ 33/37-73-33 ⊕ www.lufthansa.com. **Mærsk Air** ☏ 0207/333-0066 in the U.K., 32/31-44-44 or 70/10-74-74 in Denmark ⊕ www.maersk-air.dk. **SAS Scandinavian Airlines** ☏ 0207/706-8832 in the U.K., 800/221-2350 in North America, 32/32-00-00 in Denmark ⊕ www.scandinavian.net. **Sunair** ☏ 75/33-16-11 ⊕ www.sunair.dk/uk/html/index1.html. **Virgin Airlines** ☏ 01293/450-150 in the U.K., 800/862-8621 in North America ⊕ www.virginatlantic.com.

CHECK-IN & BOARDING

Always **find out your carrier's check-in policy.** Plan to arrive at the airport about 2 hours before your scheduled departure time for domestic flights and 2½ to 3 hours before international flights. You may need to arrive earlier if you're flying from one of the busier airports or during peak air-traffic times.

To avoid delays at airport-security checkpoints, try not to wear any metal. Jewelry, belt and other buckles, steel-toe shoes, barrettes, and underwire bras are among the items that can set off detectors.

Assuming that not everyone with a ticket will show up, airlines routinely overbook planes. When everyone does, airlines ask for volunteers to give up their seats. In return, these volunteers usually get a several-hundred-dollar flight voucher, which can be used toward the purchase of another ticket, and are rebooked on the next available flight out. If there are not enough volunteers, the airline must choose who will be denied boarding. The first to get bumped are passengers who checked in late and those flying on discounted tickets, so get to the gate and check in as early as possible, especially during peak periods.

Always **bring a government-issued photo ID** to the airport; even when it's not required, a passport is best.

CUTTING COSTS

Intra-Scandinavian air travel is usually expensive. If you want to economize, look into the **SAS Visit Scandinavia/Europe Air Pass** offered by SAS. One coupon costs between $84 and $97, but they vary depending on routing and destination. The coupons are valid for destinations within Denmark, Norway, and Sweden, and also to Finland (for

$97). They are sold only in the United States and only to non-Scandinavians. Coupons can be used year-round for a maximum of three months and must be purchased in conjunction with trans-atlantic flights. SAS also provides family fares—children between 2 and 17 and a spouse can receive 50% off the full fare of business-class tickets with the purchase of one full-fare business-class ticket. Contact SAS for information.

The least expensive airfares to Denmark are often priced for round-trip travel and must usually be purchased in advance. Airlines generally allow you to change your return date for a fee; most low-fare tickets, however, are nonrefundable. It's smart to call a number of airlines and check the Internet; when you are quoted a good price, book it on the spot—the same fare may not be available the next day, or even the next hour. Always check different routings and look into using alternate airports. Also, price off-peak flights and red-eye, which may be significantly less expensive than others. Travel agents, especially low-fare specialists (➪ Discounts & Deals), are helpful.

Consolidators are another good source. They buy tickets for scheduled flights at reduced rates from the airlines, then sell them at prices that beat the best fare available directly from the airlines. (Many also offer reduced car-rental and hotel rates.) Sometimes you can even get your money back if you need to return the ticket. Carefully read the fine print detailing penalties for changes and cancellations, purchase the ticket with a credit card, and confirm your consolidator reservation with the airline.

🛈 Consolidators **AirlineConsolidator.com** ☎ 888/468-5385 ⊕ www.airlineconsolidator.com; for international tickets. **Best Fares** ☎ 800/880-1234 ⊕ www.bestfares.com; $59.90 annual membership. **Cheap Tickets** ☎ 800/377-1000 or 800/652-4327 ⊕ www.cheaptickets.com. **Expedia** ☎ 800/397-3342 or 404/728-8787 ⊕ www.expedia.com. **Hotwire** ☎ 866/468-9473 or 920/330-9418 ⊕ www.hotwire.com. **Now Voyager Travel** ☎ 212/459-1616 ⊕ www.nowvoyagertravel.com. **Onetravel.com** ⊕ www.onetravel.com. **Orbitz** ☎ 888/656-4546 ⊕ www.orbitz.com. **Priceline.com** ⊕ www.priceline.com. **Travelocity** ☎ 888/709-5983, 877/282-2925 in Canada, 0870/111-7061 in the U.K. ⊕ www.travelocity.com.

ENJOYING THE FLIGHT
State your seat preference when purchasing your ticket, and then repeat it when you confirm and when you check in. For more legroom, you can request one of the few emergency-aisle seats at check-in, if you're capable of moving obstacles comparable in weight to an airplane exit door (usually between 35 pounds and 60 pounds)—a Federal Aviation Administration requirement of passengers in these seats. Seats behind a bulkhead also offer more legroom, but they don't have underseat storage. Don't sit in the row in front of the emergency aisle or in front of a bulkhead, where seats may not recline. SeatGuru.com has more information about specific seat configurations, which vary by aircraft.

Ask the airline whether a snack or meal is served on the flight. If you have dietary concerns, request special meals when booking. These can be vegetarian, low-cholesterol, or kosher, for example. It's a good idea to pack some healthful snacks and a small (plastic) bottle of water in your carry-on bag. On long flights, try to maintain a normal routine, to help fight jet lag. At night, get some sleep. By day, eat light meals, drink water (not alcohol), and **move around the cabin** to stretch your legs. For additional jet-lag tips consult *Fodor's FYI: Travel Fit & Healthy* (available at bookstores everywhere).

Smoking policies vary from carrier to carrier. Most airlines prohibit smoking on all of their flights; others allow smoking only on certain routes or certain departures. Ask your carrier about its policy.

FLYING TIMES
The flight from London to Copenhagen takes 1 hour, 55 minutes. From New York, flights to Copenhagen take 7 hours, 40 minutes. From Chicago, they take 9 hours, 30 minutes. From Seattle and Los Angeles the flight time is about 10 hours, 55 minutes. Flight times within the country are all less than 1 hour.

HOW TO COMPLAIN
If your baggage goes astray or your flight goes awry, complain right away. Most carriers require that you **file a claim immediately.**

The Aviation Consumer Protection Division of the Department of Transportation publishes *Fly-Rights,* which discusses airlines and consumer issues and is available online. You can also find articles and information on mytravelrights.com, the Web site of the nonprofit Consumer Travel Rights Center.

✈ Airline Complaints **Aviation Consumer Protection Division** ✉ U.S. Department of Transportation, Office of Aviation Enforcement and Proceedings, C-75, Room 4107, 400 7th St. SW, Washington, DC 20590 ☎ 202/366-2220 ⊕ http://airconsumer.ost. dot.gov. **Federal Aviation Administration Consumer Hotline** ✉ For inquiries: FAA, 800 Independence Ave. SW, Washington, DC 20591 ☎ 800/322-7873 ⊕ www.faa.gov.

RECONFIRMING
Check the status of your flight before you leave for the airport. You can do this on your carrier's Web site, by linking to a flight-status checker (many Web booking services offer these), or by calling your carrier or travel agent. Always confirm international flights at least 72 hours ahead of the scheduled departure time.

AIRPORTS
Kastrup International Airport (CPH) is the hub of Scandinavian and international air travel in Denmark, 10 km (6 mi) from the center of Copenhagen. Jutland has regional hubs in Aalborg (AAL), Århus (AAR), and Billund (BLL), which handle mainly domestic and some European traffic. Rønne (RNN) is the main airport in Bornholm.

✈ Airport Information **Kastrup International Airport** ☎ 32/31-32-31 ⊕ www.cph.dk.

BIKE TRAVEL
Biking is a way of life in Denmark, with more people biking to work than driving. Biking vacations in Denmark are popular and they are easy for all ages due to the flat landscape and about 9,600 km (6,000 mi) of mapped and signposted bike paths throughout the country. Most towns have rentals, but check with local tourism offices for referrals.

"Inclusive" cycling trips, offered by many organizations in Denmark, are just that—these trips include everything from bike rental to ferry tickets to maps to overnight accommodations. Note that bikes are the standard Danish variety; you can bring your own bike, which will also reduce the price of the trip. Routes are determined by local experts, ensuring that less-trafficked, more scenic roads are chosen.

If you want to do it yourself, there is a nationwide labeling scheme for cyclists which allows you to find the best offers and experiences during your vacation. The national quality logo—a white silhouette of a bike with an orange star in the background—indicates accommodations that are amenable to cyclists, fulfilling their extra needs (such as toolboxes, places to dry clothing, secure bike parking, and hearty breakfasts). For more information, contact the Danish Cyclist Federation. The Danish Tourist Board publishes helpful bicycle maps and brochures.

Danish State Railways (DSB) allows cyclists to check their bikes as luggage on most of their train routes, but only if there is room. S-trains that serve the suburbs of Copenhagen don't permit bikes during rush hour (7 AM–8:30 AM and 3:30 PM–5 PM). Bicycles can also be carried onto most trains and ferries; contact the DSB travel office for information; a bicycle ticket usually costs from DKr 10 to DKr 60, depending on the distance traveled. Taxis are required to take bikes and are equipped with racks, though they add a modest fee of DKr 10.

From May to October, you'll also see *by-cykler* (city bikes) parked at special bike stands placed around the center of Copenhagen and Århus. Deposit DKr 20 and pedal away. The bikes are often dinged and dented, but they do function. Your deposit will be returned when you return the bike.

✈ **Danmarks Turistråd** (Danish Tourist Board) ✉ Vesterbrog. 6D, Vesterbro, DK-1620 Copenhagen ☎ 33/11-14-15 ✉ 33/93-14-16 ⊕ www. visitdenmark.com. **Dansk Cyklist Forbund** (Danish Cyclist Federation) ✉ Rømersg. 7, Downtown, DK-1362 Copenhagen ☎ 33/32-31-21 ✉ 33/32-76-83 ⊕ www.dcf.dk. **DSB** ☎ 70/13-14-15 ⊕ www.dsb.dk.

BIKES IN FLIGHT
Most airlines accommodate bikes as luggage, provided they are dismantled and

boxed; check with individual airlines about packing requirements. Some airlines sell bike boxes, which are often free at bike shops, for about $20 (bike bags can be considerably more expensive). International travelers often can substitute a bike for a piece of checked luggage at no charge; otherwise, the cost is about $100. Most U.S. and Canadian airlines charge $40–$80 each way.

BOAT & FERRY TRAVEL

Once upon a time, ferries were an indispensable mode of transport in and around the many islands of Denmark. This is changing as more people drive or take trains over new bridges spanning the waters. However, ferries are still a good way to explore Denmark and Scandinavia, especially if you have a rail pass.

Scandinavian Seaways Ferries (DFDS) sail from Harwich in the United Kingdom to Esbjerg (20 hours) on Jutland's west coast. Schedules in both summer and winter are highly irregular. DFDS also connects Denmark with the Baltic States, Belgium, Germany, the Netherlands, Norway, Poland, Sweden, and the Faroe Islands. There are many discounts, including 20% for senior citizens and travelers with disabilities, and 50% for children between the ages of 4 and 16.

Mols-Linien links up Jutland and Zealand, while Scandlines services the southern islands as well as Germany, Sweden, and the Baltic countries. The island of Bornholm, Denmark's farthest outpost to the East and a popular domestic tourist destination, is reachable with Bornholms Trafikken.

The ScanRail Pass, for travel anywhere within Scandinavia (Denmark, Sweden, Norway, and Finland), and the Interail and Eurail passes are valid on some ferry crossings. Call the DSB Travel Office for information.

CAR FERRIES

Vehicle-bearing hydrofoils operate between Funen's Ebeltoft or Århus to Odden on Zealand; the trip takes about 1 hour. You can also take the slower (2 hours, 40 minutes), but less expensive, car ferry from Århus to Kalundborg on Zealand. From there, Route 23 leads to Copenhagen. Make reservations for the ferry in advance through Mols-Linien. Scandlines services the southern islands. (*Note:* During the busy summer months, passengers without reservations for their vehicles can wait hours.)

Some well-known international vehicle and passenger ferries run between Helsingør, Denmark, and Helsingborg, Sweden, and between Copenhagen and Göteborg, Sweden. The Helsingør/ Helsingborg ferry (Scandlines) takes only 20 minutes; taking a car costs between €32 and €67 (about $39–$81) one-way. 🛈 **Boat & Ferry Information Bornholms Trafikken** ✉ Havnen, DK-3700 Rønne ☎ 56/95-18-66 🖷 56/ 91-07-66 ⊕ www.bornholmstrafikken.dk. **DSB** 🖷 70/ 13-14-15 ⊕ www.dsb.dk. **Mols-Linien** ☎ 70/10-14-18 🖷 89/52-52-90 ⊕ www.molslinien.dk. **Scandinavian Seaways Ferries (DFDS)** ✉ Skt. Annæ Pl. 30, DK-1295 Copenhagen ☎ 33/42-33-42 🖷 33/ 42-33-41 ⊕ www.dfds.com. **Scandlines** ☎ 33/ 15-15-15 🖷 35/29-02-01 ⊕ www.scandlines.dk.

BUSINESS HOURS

BANKS & OFFICES

Banks in Copenhagen are open weekdays 9:30 to 4 and Thursdays until 6. Several *bureaux de change,* including the ones at Copenhagen's central station and airport, stay open until 10 PM. Outside Copenhagen, banking hours vary.

MUSEUMS & SIGHTS

A number of Copenhagen's museums hold confounding hours, so always call first to confirm. As a rule, however, most museums are open 10 to 3 or 11 to 4 and are closed Monday. In winter, opening hours are shorter, and some museums close for the season, especially on the smaller islands, including Bornholm, Ærø, and Fanø. Check the local papers or ask at tourist offices for current schedules.

SHOPS

Though many Danish stores are expanding their hours, sometimes even staying open on Sunday, most shops still keep the traditional hours: weekdays 10 to 5:30, until 7 or 8 on Friday, and until 1 or 2 on Saturday—though the larger department stores stay open until 5. Everything except bakeries, kiosks, flower shops, and a handful of grocers are closed Sunday. The first Saturday of every month is a Long Saturday, when even the smaller shops, especially in large cities, stay open until 4 or 5. Grocery stores stay open until 8 on weekdays, and kiosks until much later.

BUS TRAVEL

Although not particularly comfortable or fast, bus travel is inexpensive. Eurolines departs from London's Victoria Station on Saturday at 2:30 PM, crossing the North Sea on the Dover–Calais ferry, and arrives in Copenhagen about 22 hours later. With its many other routes, Eurolines links the principal Danish cities to a network of service that includes major European cities. Säfflebussen is the other main bus company with international routes to Denmark. The company offers regular trips between Copenhagen and Berlin, Göteborg, Karlstad, Stockholm, and Oslo.

To encourage travelers to make full use of Denmark's domestic transportation services, private bus operators and Danish State Railways (DSB) have collaborated to create Bus/Tog Samarbejde. This useful resource consolidates schedule and route information for the country's trains and buses.

Domestic bus companies include Thinggaard, which has regular routes between Zealand and Jutland, and Abildskou, which offers service from Århus to Copenhagen and Ebeltoft, as well as between Roskilde and the Copenhagen airport. Bus tickets are usually sold on board the buses immediately before departure. Ask about discounts for children, senior citizens and groups.

🛈 Abildskou ✉ Graham Bellsvej 40, DK-8200 Århus ☎ 70/21-08-88 ⊕ www.abildskou.dk. **Bus/ Tog Samarbejde** ⊕ www.rejseplan.dk. **Eurolines** ✉ 52 Grosvenor Gardens, SW1 London ☎ 0207/ 730-8235 ✉ Reventlowsg. 8, DK-1651 Copenhagen ☎ 70/10-00-30 ⊕ www.eurolines.com. **Säffle- bussen** ✉ Halmtorvet 5, DK-1700 Copenhagen ☎ 33/23-54-20 ⊕ www.safflebussen.se. **Thing- gaard Ekspres** ✉ Jyllandsg. 6, DK-9000 Aalborg ☎ 70/10-00-20 ⊕ www.thinggaard-bus.dk.

CUTTING COSTS

Eurolines offers 15-, 30-, and 40-day passes for unlimited travel between Stock-

holm, Copenhagen, and Oslo and more than 35 destinations throughout Europe.

CAMERAS & PHOTOGRAPHY

The *Kodak Guide to Shooting Great Travel Pictures* (available at bookstores everywhere) is loaded with tips.
🛈 Photo Help Kodak Information Center ☎ 800/ 242-2424 ⊕ www.kodak.com.

EQUIPMENT PRECAUTIONS

Don't pack film or equipment in checked luggage, where it is much more susceptible to damage. X-ray machines used to view checked luggage are extremely powerful and therefore are likely to ruin your film. Try to ask for hand inspection of film, which becomes clouded after repeated exposure to airport X-ray machines, and keep videotapes and computer disks away from metal detectors. Always keep film, tape, and computer disks out of the sun. Carry an extra supply of batteries, and be prepared to turn on your camera, camcorder, or laptop to prove to airport security personnel that the device is real.

FILM & DEVELOPING

Most bigger towns in Denmark have a photo shop with one-hour or 24-hour developing. A roll of 36-exposure color film usually costs between 35 DKr and 60 DKr, depending on its quality.

VIDEOS

While VHS videotapes and players are common, Denmark, like other European countries, uses a different video system than the one used in the United States. This means you won't be able to play the videotapes you bring from home on Danish equipment, and tapes purchased in Denmark won't work in an American VCR.

CAR RENTAL

Rental rates in Copenhagen begin at DKr 550 a day and DKr 2,220 a week. This does not include an additional per-kilometer fee and any insurance you choose to purchase; there is also a 25% tax on car rentals.
🛈 Major Agencies Alamo ☎ 800/522-9696 ⊕ www.alamo.com. **Avis** ☎ 800/331-1084, 800/ 879-2847 in Canada, 0870/606-0100 in the U.K., 02/

9353-9000 in Australia, 09/526-2847 in New Zealand ⊕ www.avis.com. **Budget** ☎ 800/527-0700 ⊕ www.budget.com. **Dollar** ☎ 800/800-6000, 0800/085-4578 in the U.K. ⊕ www.dollar.com. **Hertz** ☎ 800/654-3001, 800/263-0600 in Canada, 0870/844-8844 in the U.K., 02/9669-2444 in Australia, 09/256-8690 in New Zealand ⊕ www.hertz.com. **National Car Rental** ☎ 800/227-7368 ⊕ www.nationalcar.com.
🚹 Wholesalers Auto Europe ☎ 207/842-2000 or 800/223-5555 🖷 207/842-2222 ⊕ www.autoeurope.com. **Destination Europe Resources (DER)** ✉ 9501 W. Devon Ave., Rosemont, IL 60018 ☎ 800/782-2424 🖷 800/282-7474. **Europe by Car** ☎ 212/581-3040 or 800/223-1516 🖷 212/246-1458 ⊕ www.europebycar.com. **Kemwel** ☎ 877/820-0668 or 800/678-0678 🖷 207/842-2124 or 866/726-6726 ⊕ www.kemwel.com.

INSURANCE

When driving a rented car you are generally responsible for any damage to or loss of the vehicle. Collision policies that car-rental companies sell for European rentals typically do not cover stolen vehicles. Before you rent—and purchase collision or theft coverage—see what coverage you already have under the terms of your personal auto-insurance policy and credit cards

REQUIREMENTS & RESTRICTIONS

Ask about age requirements. Several countries require drivers to be over 20 years old, but some car-rental companies require that drivers be at least 25.

SURCHARGES

Before you pick up a car in one city and leave it in another, ask about drop-off charges or one-way service fees, which can be substantial. Also inquire about early-return policies; some rental agencies charge extra if you return the car before the time specified in your contract, while others give you a refund for the days not used. Most agencies note the tank's fuel level on your contract; to avoid a hefty refueling fee, return the car with the same tank level. If the tank was full, refill it just before you turn in the car, but be aware that gas stations near the rental outlet may overcharge. It's almost never a deal to buy a tank of gas with the car when you rent

it; the understanding is that you'll return it empty, but some fuel usually remains.

CAR TRAVEL

The only part of Denmark that is connected to the European continent is Jutland, via the E45 highway from Germany. The E20 highway then leads to Middelfart on Funen and east to Nyborg. The Storebæltsbro bridge connects Funen and Zealand via the E20 highway; the E20 then continues east, over the Lillebæltsbro bridge, to Copenhagen. The bridges have greatly reduced the driving time between the islands. You can reach many of the smaller islands via toll bridges. In some locations car ferries are still in service; for ferry information, see Boat & Ferry Travel.

In Scandinavia your own driver's license is acceptable for a limited time; check with the Danish Tourist Board before you go. International driving permits (IDPs) are available from the American and Canadian automobile associations and, in the United Kingdom, from the Automobile Association and Royal Automobile Club. These international permits, valid only in conjunction with your regular driver's license, are universally recognized; having one may save you a problem with local authorities.

EMERGENCY SERVICES

Members of organizations affiliated with Alliance International de Tourisme (AIT) can get technical and legal advice from the Danish Motoring Organization, open 10-4 weekdays. All highways have emergency phones, and you can call the rental company for help. If you cannot drive your car to a garage for repairs, the rescue corps Falck can help anywhere, anytime. In most cases they do charge for assistance. In the event of an emergency, call 112.
🚹 Falck ✉ Polititorvet, DK-1780 Copenhagen ☎ 70/10-20-30 for emergencies, 70/33-33-11 for headquarters 🖷 33/14-41-73 ⊕ www.falck.dk. **Forenede Danske Motorejere** (Danish Motoring Organization) ✉ Firskovvej 32, DK-2800 Lyngby ☎ 70/13-30-40 🖷 45/27-09-93 ⊕ www.fdm.dk.

GASOLINE

Gasoline costs about DKr 10 per liter (¼ gallon). Stations are mostly self-service and open from 6 or 7 AM to 9 PM or later.

PARKING

You can usually park on the right-hand side of the road, though not on main roads and highways. Signs reading PARKERING/ STANDSNING FORBUNDT mean no parking or stopping, though you are allowed a three-minute grace period for loading and unloading. In town, parking disks are used where there are no automated ticket-vending machines. Get disks from gas stations, post offices, police stations, or tourist offices, and set them to show your time of arrival. For most downtown parking you must buy a ticket from an automatic vending machine and display it on the dash. Parking costs about DKr 10 or more per hour.

ROAD CONDITIONS

Roads in Denmark are in good condition and largely traffic-free (except for the manageable traffic around Copenhagen).

RULES OF THE ROAD

To drive in Denmark you need a valid adult driver's license, and if you're using your own car it must have a certificate of registration and national plates. A triangular hazard-warning sign is compulsory in every car and is provided with rentals. No matter where you sit in a car, you must wear a seat belt, and cars must have low beams on at all times. Motorcyclists must wear helmets and use low-beam lights as well. Talking on the phone while operating a car, bicycle, or any other kind of vehicle is illegal.

Bicyclists have equal rights on the road, and a duty to signal moves and observe all traffic regulations. Be especially careful when making turns. Check for bicyclists, who have the right of way if they are going straight and a car is turning.

Drive on the right and give way to traffic—*especially to bicyclists*—on the right. A red-and-white YIELD sign or a line of white triangles across the road means you must yield to traffic on the road you are entering. Do not turn right on red unless there is a green arrow indicating that this is allowed. Speed limits are 50 kph (30 mph) in built-up areas; 100 kph (60 mph) on highways; and 80 kph (50 mph) on other roads. If you are towing a trailer,

you must not exceed 70 kph (40 mph). Speeding and, especially, drinking and driving are punished severely, even if no damage is caused. The consumption of one or two beers might lead to a violation, and motorists traveling across the Øresund Bridge must remember that Sweden has an even lower legal limit for blood-alcohol levels. It is therefore possible to drive legally out of Denmark and illegally into Sweden. Americans and other foreign tourists must pay all fines on the spot.

CHILDREN IN DENMARK

In Denmark children are to be seen *and* heard and are genuinely welcome in most public places. Most restaurants, pubs, stores, waiting rooms, and shopping malls will have a play area for children.

If you are renting a car, don't forget to arrange for a car seat when you reserve. For general advice about traveling with children, consult *Fodor's FYI: Travel with Your Baby* (available in bookstores everywhere).

DISCOUNTS

Children are entitled to discount tickets (often as much as 50% off) on buses, trains, and ferries throughout Denmark, as well as reductions on special City Cards. With the ScanRail Pass (⇨ Train Travel)— good for rail journeys throughout Scandinavia—children under age 4 (on lap) travel free; those ages 4–11 pay half fare and those ages 12–25 can get a ScanRail Youth Pass, providing a 25% discount off the adult fare.

Youngsters receive a discount at most museums and attractions, but the age limits vary. Check at the gate for information about youth or family discounts.

FLYING

Children under age 12 pay 75% of the adult fare and children under age 2 pay 10% on SAS round-trips. There are no restrictions on children's fares when booked in economy class. "Family fares," only available in business class, are also worth looking into (⇨ Cutting Costs *in* Air Travel).

If your children are two or older, ask about children's airfares. As a general rule, infants under two not occupying a seat fly at greatly reduced fares or even for free. But if you want to guarantee a seat for an infant, you have to pay full fare. Consider flying during off-peak days and times; most airlines will grant an infant a seat without a ticket if there are available seats. When booking, confirm carry-on allowances if you're traveling with infants. In general, for babies charged 10% to 50% of the adult fare you are allowed one carry-on bag and a collapsible stroller; if the flight is full, the stroller may have to be checked or you may be limited to less.

Experts agree that it's a good idea to use safety seats aloft for children weighing less than 40 pounds. Airlines set their own policies: if you use a safety seat, U.S. carriers usually require that the child be ticketed, even if he or she is young enough to ride free, because the seats must be strapped into regular seats. And even if you pay the full adult fare for the seat, it may be worth it, especially on longer trips. Do **check your airline's policy about using safety seats during takeoff and landing.** Safety seats are not allowed everywhere in the plane, so get your seat assignments as early as possible.

When reserving, request children's meals or a freestanding bassinet (not available at all airlines) if you need them. But note that bulkhead seats, where you must sit to use the bassinet, may lack an overhead bin or storage space on the floor.

LODGING
Most hotels in Denmark allow children under a certain age to stay in their parents' room at no extra charge, but others charge for them as extra adults; be sure to find out the cutoff age for children's discounts.

SIGHTS & ATTRACTIONS
Places that are especially appealing to children are indicated by a rubber-duckie icon (🐥) in the margin.

CONSUMER PROTECTION
Whether you're shopping for gifts or purchasing travel services, **pay with a major credit card** whenever possible, so you can cancel payment or get reimbursed if there's a problem (and you can provide documentation). If you're doing business with a particular company for the first time, contact your local Better Business Bureau and the attorney general's offices in your state and (for U.S. businesses) the company's home state as well. Have any complaints been filed? Finally, if you're buying a package or tour, always consider travel insurance that includes default coverage (⇨ Insurance).

🛈 BBBs Council of Better Business Bureaus ✉ 4200 Wilson Blvd., Suite 800, Arlington, VA 22203 ☎ 703/276-0100 🖷 703/525-8277 ⊕ www.bbb.org.

CUSTOMS & DUTIES
When shopping abroad, keep receipts for all purchases. Upon reentering the country, **be ready to show customs officials what you've bought.** Pack purchases together in an easily accessible place. If you think a duty is incorrect, appeal the assessment. If you object to the way your clearance was handled, note the inspector's badge number. In either case, first ask to see a supervisor. If the problem isn't resolved, write to the appropriate authorities, beginning with the port director at your point of entry.

IN AUSTRALIA
Australian residents who are 18 or older may bring home A$900 worth of souvenirs and gifts (including jewelry), 250 cigarettes or 250 grams of cigars or other tobacco products, and 2.25 liters of alcohol (including wine, beer, and spirits). Residents under 18 may bring back A$450 worth of goods. If any of these individual allowances are exceeded, you must pay duty for the entire amount (of the group of products in which the allowance was exceeded). Members of the same family traveling together may pool their allowances. Prohibited items include meat products. Seeds, plants, and fruits need to be declared upon arrival.

🛈 Australian Customs Service 🏛 Customs House, 10 Cooks River Dr., Sydney International Airport, Sydney, NSW 2020 ☎ 02/6275-6666 or 1300/363-263, 02/8334-7444 or 1800/020-504 quarantine-inquiry line 🖷 02/8339-6714 ⊕ www.customs.gov.au.

IN CANADA
Canadian residents who have been out of Canada for at least seven days may bring

in C$750 worth of goods duty-free. If you've been away fewer than seven days but more than 48 hours, the duty-free allowance drops to C$200. If your trip lasts 24 to 48 hours, the allowance is C$50; if the goods are worth more than C$50, you must pay full duty on all of the goods. You may not pool allowances with family members. Goods claimed under the C$750 exemption may follow you by mail; those claimed under the lesser exemptions must accompany you. Alcohol and tobacco products may be included in the seven-day and 48-hour exemptions but not in the 24-hour exemption. If you meet the age requirements of the province or territory through which you reenter Canada, you may bring in, duty-free, 1.5 liters of wine *or* 1.14 liters (40 imperial ounces) of liquor *or* 24 12-ounce cans or bottles of beer or ale. Also, if you meet the local age requirement for tobacco products, you may bring in, duty-free, 200 cigarettes, 50 cigars or cigarillos, and 200 grams of tobacco. You may have to pay a minimum duty on tobacco products, regardless of whether or not you exceed your personal exemption. Check ahead of time with the Canada Border Services Agency or the Department of Agriculture for policies regarding meat products, seeds, plants, and fruits.

You may send an unlimited number of gifts (only one gift per recipient, however) worth up to C$60 each duty-free to Canada. Label the package UNSOLICITED GIFT—VALUE UNDER $60. Alcohol and tobacco are excluded.

Canada Border Services Agency ⊠ Customs Information Services, 191 Laurier Ave. W, 15th fl., Ottawa, Ontario K1A 0L5 ☎ 800/461-9999 in Canada, 204/983-3500, 506/636-5064 ⊕ www.cbsa.gc.ca.

IN DENMARK

If you are 16 or older, have purchased goods in a country that is a member of the European Union (EU), and pay that country's value-added tax (V.A.T.) on those goods, you may import duty-free 1½ liters of liquor and 300 cigarettes or 150 cigarillos or 75 cigars or 400 grams of tobacco. If you are entering Denmark from a non-EU country or if you have purchased your goods on a ferryboat or in an airport not

taxed in the EU, you must pay Danish taxes on any amount of alcoholic beverages greater than 1 liter of liquor or 2 liters of strong wine, plus 2 liters of table wine. For tobacco, the limit is 200 cigarettes or 100 cigarillos or 50 cigars or 250 grams of tobacco. You are also allowed 50 grams of perfume. Other articles (including beer) are allowed up to a maximum of DKr 1,350.

Non-EU citizens can save 20% (less a handling fee) off the purchase price if they shop in one of the hundreds of stores throughout Denmark displaying the TAX-FREE SHOPPING sign. The purchased merchandise must value more than DKr 300 and the taxes will be refunded after submitting the application with customs authorities at their final destination before leaving the EU.

Told og Skat (Toll and Taxes) ⊠ Tagensvej 135, DK-2200 Copenhagen ☎ 35/87-73-00 🖷 35/85-90-94 ⊕ www.toldskat.dk.

IN NEW ZEALAND

All homeward-bound residents may bring back NZ$700 worth of souvenirs and gifts; passengers may not pool their allowances, and children can claim only the concession on goods intended for their own use. For those 17 or older, the duty-free allowance also includes 4.5 liters of wine or beer; one 1,125-ml bottle of spirits; and either 200 cigarettes, 250 grams of tobacco, 50 cigars, *or* a combination of the three up to 250 grams. Meat products, seeds, plants, and fruits must be declared upon arrival to the Agricultural Services Department.

New Zealand Customs ⊠ Head office: The Customhouse, 17–21 Whitmore St., Box 2218, Wellington ☎ 0800/428-786 or 09/300-5399 ⊕ www.customs.govt.nz.

IN THE U.K.

If you are a U.K. resident and your journey was wholly within the European Union, you probably won't have to pass through customs when you return to the United Kingdom. If you plan to bring back large quantities of alcohol or tobacco, check EU limits beforehand. In most cases, if you bring back more than 200 cigars,

3,200 cigarettes, 400 cigarillos, 3 kilo-grams of tobacco, 10 liters of spirits, 110 liters of beer, 20 liters of fortified wine, and/or 90 liters of wine, you have to de-clare the goods upon return.

🛈 HM Customs and Excise ✉ Portcullis House, 21 Cowbridge Rd. E, Cardiff CF11 9SS ☎ 0845/010-9000 or 0208/929-0152 advice service, 0208/929-6731 or 0208/910-3602 complaints ∰ www.hmce. gov.uk.

IN THE U.S.

U.S. residents who have been out of the country for at least 48 hours may bring home, for personal use, $800 worth of for-eign goods duty-free, as long as they haven't used the $800 allowance or any part of it in the past 30 days. This exemp-tion may include 1 liter of alcohol (for travelers 21 and older), 200 cigarettes, and 100 non-Cuban cigars. Family members from the same household who are traveling together may pool their $800 personal ex-emptions. For fewer than 48 hours, the duty-free allowance drops to $200, which may include 50 cigarettes, 10 non-Cuban cigars, and 150 ml of alcohol (or 150 ml of perfume containing alcohol). The $200 al-lowance cannot be combined with other in-dividuals' exemptions, and if you exceed it, the full value of all the goods will be taxed. Antiques, which U.S. Customs and Border Protection defines as objects more than 100 years old, enter duty-free, as do origi-nal works of art done entirely by hand, in-cluding paintings, drawings, and sculptures. This doesn't apply to folk art or handicrafts, which are in general dutiable.

You may also send packages home duty-free, with a limit of one parcel per ad-dressee per day (except alcohol or tobacco products or perfume worth more than $5). You can mail up to $200 worth of goods for personal use; label the package PER-SONAL USE and attach a list of its contents and their retail value. If the package con-tains your used personal belongings, mark it AMERICAN GOODS RETURNED to avoid pay-ing duties. You may send up to $100 worth of goods as a gift; mark the package UNSO-LICITED GIFT. Mailed items do not affect your duty-free allowance on your return.

To avoid paying duty on foreign-made high-ticket items you already own and will take on your trip, register them with a local customs office before you leave the country. Consider filing a Certificate of Registration for laptops, cameras, watches, and other digital devices identified with se-rial numbers or other permanent markings; you can keep the certificate for other trips. Otherwise, bring a sales receipt or insur-ance form to show that you owned the item before you left the United States.

For more about duties, restricted items, and other information about international travel, check out U.S. Customs and Border Protection's online brochure, *Know Before You Go.* You can also file complaints on the U.S. Customs and Border Protection Web site, listed below.

🛈 U.S. Customs and Border Protection ✉ For in-quiries and complaints, 1300 Pennsylvania Ave. NW, Washington, DC 20229 ☎ 877/227-5551, 202/354-1000 ∰ www.cbp.gov.

DISABILITIES & ACCESSIBILITY

Facilities for travelers with disabilities in Denmark are generally good, and most of the major tourist offices offer special book-lets and brochures on travel and accommo-dations. Note that several older hotels have very small elevators or none at all. Perhaps the most comprehensive of these booklets for those with disabilities is from West Jut-land. Contact: www.visithandicap.com. Notify and make all local and public trans-portation and hotel reservations in advance to ensure a smooth trip.

LODGING

Best Western offers properties with wheel-chair-accessible rooms just outside Copen-hagen. If wheelchair-accessible rooms on other floors are not available, ground-floor rooms are provided.

🛈 Best Western ☎ 800/780-7234 in North Amer-ica, 800/109-88 (toll-free) in Denmark ∰ www. bestwestern.com.

RESERVATIONS

When discussing accessibility with an oper-ator or reservations agent, ask hard ques-tions. Are there any stairs, inside *or* out? Are there grab bars next to the toilet *and* in the shower/tub? How wide is the doorway to the room? To the bathroom? For the most extensive facilities meeting the latest legal specifications, opt for newer accommodations. If you reserve through a toll-free number, consider also calling the hotel's local number to confirm the information from the central reservations office. Get confirmation in writing when you can.

SIGHTS & ATTRACTIONS

Although most major attractions in Copenhagen present no problems, winding cobblestone streets in the older sections of cities (for example, the very old cities of Ribe and Ringkøbing) may be challenging for travelers with disabilities.

TRANSPORTATION

The U.S. Department of Transportation Aviation Consumer Protection Division's online publication *New Horizons: Information for the Air Traveler with a Disability* offers advice for travelers with a disability, and outlines basic rights. Visit DisabilityInfo.gov for general information.

With advance notice, most airlines, buses, and trains can arrange assistance for those requiring extra help with boarding. Contact each individual company at least one week in advance, or ideally at the time of booking.

Confirming ahead is especially important when planning travel to less populated regions. The smaller planes and ferries often used in such areas are not all accessible.

🚹 Information & Complaints **Aviation Consumer Protection Division** (⇨ Air Travel) for airline-related problems; ⊕ http://airconsumer.ost.dot.gov/publications/horizons.htm for airline travel advice and rights. **Departmental Office of Civil Rights** ⊠ For general inquiries, U.S. Department of Transportation, S-30, 400 7th St. SW, Room 10215, Washington, DC 20590 ☎ 202/366-4648, 202/366-8538 TTY 🖀 202/366-9371 ⊕ www.dotcr.ost.dot.gov. **Disability Rights Section** ⊠ NYAV, U.S. Department of Justice, Civil Rights Division, 950 Pennsylvania Ave. NW, Washington, DC 20530 ☎ 800/514-0301, 202/514-0301 ADA information line, 800/514-0383 TTY, 202/514-0383 TTY ⊕ www.ada.gov. **U.S. Department of Transportation Hotline** ☎ 800/778-4838 or 800/455-9880 TTY for disability-related air-travel problems.

TRAVEL AGENCIES

In the United States, the Americans with Disabilities Act requires that travel firms serve the needs of all travelers. Some agencies specialize in working with people with disabilities.

🚹 Travelers with Mobility Problems **Access Adventures/B. Roberts Travel** ⊠ 1876 East Ave., Rochester, NY 14610 ☎ 800/444-6540 ⊕ www.brobertstravel.com, run by a former physical-rehabilitation counselor. **CareVacations** ⊠ No. 5, 5110-50 Ave., Leduc, Alberta, Canada, T9E 6V4 ☎ 780/986-6404 or 877/478-7827 🖀 780/986-8332 ⊕ www.carevacations.com, for group tours and cruise vacations. **Flying Wheels Travel** ⊠ 143 W. Bridge St., Box 382, Owatonna, MN 55060 ☎ 507/451-5005 🖀 507/451-1685 ⊕ www.flyingwheelstravel.com.

DISCOUNTS & DEALS

Be a smart shopper and compare all your options before making decisions. A plane ticket bought with a promotional coupon from travel clubs, coupon books, and direct-mail offers or purchased on the Internet may not be cheaper than the least expensive fare from a discount ticket agency. And always keep in mind that what you get is just as important as what you save.

DISCOUNT RESERVATIONS

To save money, look into discount reservations services with Web sites and toll-free numbers, which use their buying power to get a better price on hotels, airline tickets (⇨ Air Travel), even car rentals. When booking a room, always **call the hotel's local toll-free number** (if one is available) rather than the central reservations number—you'll often get a better price. Always ask about special packages or corporate rates.

When shopping for the best deal on hotels and car rentals, look for guaranteed exchange rates, which protect you against a falling dollar. With your rate locked in, you won't pay more, even if the price goes up in the local currency.

🚹 Hotel Rooms **Accommodations Express** ☎ 800/444-7666 or 800/277-1064. **Hotels.com** ☎ 800/246-8357 ⊕ www.hotels.com. **Steigenberger Reservation Service** ☎ 800/223-5652

⊕ www.srs-worldhotels.com. **Turbotrip.com**
☎ 800/473-7829 ⊕ www.turbotrip.com.

PACKAGE DEALS

Don't confuse packages and guided tours.
When you buy a package, you travel on
your own, just as though you had planned
the trip yourself. Fly/drive packages, which
combine airfare and car rental, are often a
good deal. In cities, ask the local visitor's
bureau about hotel and local transportation packages that include tickets to major
museum exhibits or other special events. If
you **buy a rail/drive pass,** you may save
on train tickets and car rentals. All Eurail-
Pass holders get a discount on Eurostar
fares through the Channel Tunnel and
often receive reduced rates for buses, hotels, ferries, sightseeing cruises, and car
rentals. Also check rates for a ScanRail
Pass (⇨ Train Travel).

EATING & DRINKING

Denmark's major cities have a good selection of restaurants serving both traditional
Danish and international cuisines. The
restaurants we list are the cream of the
crop in each price category. Properties indicated by an ✕⌂ are lodging establishments whose restaurant warrants a
special trip.

CATEGORY	MAIN CITIES	ELSEWHERE
$$$$	over 200	over 180
$$$	151–200	141–180
$$	121–150	121–140
$	90–120	90–120
¢	under 90	under 90

*Prices are for a main course at dinner and are
given in Danish kroner.*

CUTTING COSTS

You can reduce the cost of food by planning. Breakfast is often included in your
hotel bill; if not, you may wish to buy
fruit, sweet rolls, and a beverage for a picnic breakfast. Bakeries abound and offer
all the fixings for breakfast, except coffee
or tea. In recent years many corner convenience stores have begun to sell hot drinks.
Opt for a restaurant lunch instead of dinner, since the latter tends to be significantly more expensive. Instead of beer or
wine, drink tap water—liquor can cost
four times the price of the same brand in a

store—but do specify tap water, as the
term "water" can refer to soft drinks and
bottled water, which are also expensive.

MEALTIMES

Danes start the workday early, which
means they generally eat lunch at noon
and consume their evening meal on the
early side. Make sure you make your dinner reservations for no later than 9 PM.
Bars and cafés stay open later, and most
offer at least light fare. Unless otherwise
noted, the restaurants listed in this guide
are open daily for lunch and dinner.

RESERVATIONS & DRESS

Reservations are always a good idea; we
mention them only when they're essential
or not accepted. Book as far ahead as you
can, and reconfirm as soon as you arrive.
(Large parties should always call ahead to
check the reservations policy.) We mention
dress only when men are required to wear
a jacket or a jacket and tie, which is quite
unusual; even in the most chic establishments the tone is elegantly casual.

WINE, BEER & SPIRITS

Restaurants' markup on alcoholic beverages is often very high in Denmark: as
much as four times that of a standard retail price.

ELECTRICITY

To use electric-powered equipment purchased in the United States or Canada,
bring a converter and adapter. The electri-
cal current in Denmark is 220 volts, 50 cy-
cles alternating current (AC); wall outlets
take Continental-type plugs, with two
round prongs.

If your appliances are dual-voltage, you'll
need only an adapter. Don't use 110-volt
outlets marked FOR SHAVERS ONLY for high-
wattage appliances such as blow-dryers.
Most laptops operate equally well on
110 and 220 volts and so require only
an adapter.

EMBASSIES

New Zealanders should contact the U.K.
embassy for assistance.
🇦🇺 Australia ⊠ Dampfærgevej 26, 2nd. fl., Østerbro, DK-2100 Copenhagen ☎ 70/26-36-76 🖷 70/
26-36-86 ⊕ www.denmark.embassy.gov.au.

F Canada ⊠ Kristen Bernikows G. 1, Downtown, DK-1105 Copenhagen ☎ 33/48-32-00 ⊟ 33/48-32-20 ⊕ www.canada.dk.

F Ireland ⊠ Østbaneg. 21, Østerbro, DK-2100 Copenhagen ☎ 35/42-32-33 ⊟ 35/43-18-58.

F South Africa ⊠ Gammel Vartov Vej 8, DK-2900 Hellerup ☎ 39/18-01-55 ⊟ 39/18-40-06 ⊕ www.southafrica.dk.

F United Kingdom ⊠ Kastelsvej 36-40, Østerbro, DK-2100 Copenhagen ☎ 35/44-52-00 ⊟ 35/44-52-93 ⊕ www.britishembassy.dk.

F United States ⊠ Dag Hammarskjölds Allé 24, Østerbro, DK-2100 Copenhagen ☎ 33/41-71-00 ⊟ 35/43-02-23 ⊕ www.usembassy.dk.

EMERGENCIES

The general 24-hour emergency number throughout Denmark is 112.

ETIQUETTE & BEHAVIOR

When greeting others, Danes shake hands. Good friends and relatives kiss on the cheek.

In July and August, it isn't common to conduct heavy business affairs as this may be seen as being inconsiderate.

Social public nudity in the summer months isn't that uncommon and there are no laws against being nude on a beach or in a park unless you are bothering someone near you.

Table manners in Denmark are formal. Don't toast your host or anyone senior to you in rank or age until they toast you first. Don't begin to drink until the "Skoal!" (Cheers!) is said by the host. On truly formal occasions, if you are seated to the left of your hostess you can propose a toast during dessert. If you're on her right, you may be expected to deliver a short speech of appreciation. If you fill your plate from a buffet table, be sure to finish the food that you've taken for yourself.

GAY & LESBIAN TRAVEL

Denmark has a liberal and accommodating attitude toward gays and lesbians. The Danish government grants to same-sex couples the same or nearly the same rights as heterosexual married couples. Copenhagen has an active, although not large, gay community.

F Gay- & Lesbian-Friendly Travel Agencies **Different Roads Travel** ⊠ 1017 N. LaCienega Blvd.,

Suite 308, West Hollywood, CA 90069 ☎ 800/429-8747 or 310/289-6000 (Ext. 14 for both) ⊟ 310/855-0323 ✆ lgernert@tzell.com. **Kennedy Travel** ⊠ 130 W. 42nd St., Suite 401, New York, NY 10036 ☎ 800/237-7433 or 212/840-8659 ⊟ 212/730-2269 ⊕ www.kennedytravel.com. **Now, Voyager** ⊠ 4406 18th St., San Francisco, CA 94114 ☎ 800/255-6951 or 415/626-1169 ⊟ 415/626-8626 ⊕ www.nowvoyager.com. **Skylink Travel and Tour/Flying Dutchmen Travel** ⊠ 1455 N. Dutton Ave., Suite A, Santa Rosa, CA 95401 ☎ 800/225-5759 or 707/546-9888 ⊟ 707/636-0951; serving lesbian travelers.

HEALTH

The healthcare network in Denmark is advanced and well socialized, so you shouldn't have trouble receiving healthcare if you need it. Because all Danes receive English-language instruction when in school, almost everyone has a good working knowledge of the language.

HOLIDAYS

All Scandinavian countries celebrate New Year's Eve and Day, Good Friday, Easter and Easter Monday, Midsummer Eve and Day (late June), and Christmas (as well as Christmas Eve and Boxing Day, the day after Christmas).

In addition, Denmark has the following holidays: Holy/Maundy Thursday, Common Prayer (May), Ascension (40 days after Easter), Constitution Day (June 5; shops close at noon), and Whitsun/Pentecost (Sunday and Monday 10 days after Ascension).

Schools close for a week in fall, normally the third week in October. The tradition goes back to the days when youngsters were called upon to help with the harvest, so the occasion is sometimes referred to as the "potato holiday." Many lodging and travel-related prices are hiked up significantly during this week.

On major holidays such as Christmas, most shops close or operate on a Sunday schedule. On the eves of such holidays, many shops are also closed all day or are open with reduced hours.

Although May Day (May 1) is not an official holiday, many offices and some merchants close up shop, and the cities are full of celebrations and parades. For Midsummer Day at the end of June, locals flock to the lakes and countryside to celebrate the beginning of long summer days with bonfires and other festivities.

INSURANCE

The most useful travel-insurance plan is a comprehensive policy that includes coverage for trip cancellation and interruption, default, trip delay, and medical expenses (with a waiver for preexisting conditions). Without insurance you'll lose all or most of your money if you cancel your trip, regardless of the reason. Default insurance covers you if your tour operator, airline, or cruise line goes out of business—the chances of which have been increasing. Trip-delay covers expenses that arise because of bad weather or mechanical delays. Study the fine print when comparing policies.

If you're traveling internationally, a key component of travel insurance is coverage for medical bills incurred if you get sick on the road. Such expenses aren't generally covered by Medicare or private policies. U.K. residents can buy a travel-insurance policy valid for most vacations taken during the year in which it's purchased (but check preexisting-condition coverage). British and Australian citizens need extra medical coverage when traveling overseas.

Always **buy travel policies directly from the insurance company**; if you buy them from a cruise line, airline, or tour operator that goes out of business you probably won't be covered for the agency or operator's default, a major risk. Before making any purchase, review your existing health and home-owner's policies to find what they cover away from home.

🛈 Travel Insurers In the United States: **Access America** ✉ 2805 N. Parham Rd., Richmond, VA 23294 ☎ 800/284-8300 🖷 800/346-9265 or 804/673-1469 🌐 www.accessamerica.com. **Travel Guard International** ✉ 1145 Clark St., Stevens Point, WI 54481 ☎ 800/826-1300 or 715/345-1041 🖷 800/955-8785 or 715/345-1990 🌐 www.travelguard.com. 🛈 In Australia: **Insurance Council of Australia** ✉ Level 3, 56 Pitt St., Sydney, NSW 2000 ☎ 02/9253-5100 🖷 02/9253-5111 🌐 www.ica.com.au. In Canada: **RBC Insurance** ✉ 6880 Financial Dr., Mississauga, Ontario L5N 7Y5 ☎ 800/387-4357 or 905/

816-2559 🖷 888/298-6458 🌐 www.rbcinsurance.com. In New Zealand: **Insurance Council of New Zealand** ✉ Level 7, 111-115 Customhouse Quay, Box 474, Wellington ☎ 04/472-5230 🖷 04/473-3011 🌐 www.icnz.org.nz. In the United Kingdom: **Association of British Insurers** ✉ 51 Gresham St., London EC2V 7HQ ☎ 020/7600-3333 🖷 020/7696-8999 🌐 www.abi.org.uk.

LANGUAGE

Danish is a difficult tongue for foreigners—except those from Norway and Sweden—to understand, let alone speak. Danes are good linguists, however, and almost everyone, except perhaps elderly people in rural areas, speaks English. In Sønderjylland, the southern region of Jutland, most people speak or understand German. If you are planning to visit the countryside or the small islands, it would be a good idea to bring a phrase book.

Difficult-to-pronounce Danish characters include the "ø," pronounced a bit like a very short "er," similar to the French "eu"; "æ," which sounds like the "a" in "ape" but with a glottal stop, or the "a" in "cat," depending on the region; and the "å" (also written "aa"), which sounds like "or." The important thing about these characters isn't that you pronounce them correctly—foreigners usually can't—but that you know to look for them in the phone book at the very end. Mr. Søren Åstrup, for example, will be found after "Z;" Æ and Ø follow.

LODGING

Assume that hotels operate on the European Plan (EP, with no meals) unless we specify that they use the Continental Plan (CP, with a Continental breakfast), Breakfast Plan (BP, with a full breakfast), Modified American Plan (MAP, with breakfast and dinner), or the Full American Plan (FAP, with all meals).

The lodgings we list are the cream of the crop in each price category. We always list the facilities that are available—but we don't specify whether they cost extra: When pricing accommodations, always ask what's included and what costs extra.

In the larger cities, lodging ranges from first-class business hotels run by SAS,

Sheraton, and Scandic; to good-quality tourist-class hotels, such as RESO, Best Western, and Scandic Budget; to a wide variety of single-entrepreneur hotels. In the countryside look for independently run inns and motels called *kroer.*

Before you leave home, **ask your travel agent about discounts,** including summer hotel checks for Best Western and Scandic, and enormous year-round rebates at SAS hotels for travelers over 65. All EuroClass (business class) passengers can get discounts of at least 10% at SAS hotels when they book through SAS.

Two things about hotels usually surprise North Americans: the relatively limited dimensions of Scandinavian beds and the generous size of Scandinavian breakfasts. Scandinavian beds are often about 60 inches wide or slightly less, close in size to the U.S. queen size. King-size beds (72 inches wide) are difficult to find and, if available, require special reservations.

Older hotels may have some rooms described as "double," which in fact have one double bed plus one fold-out sofa big enough for two people. This arrangement is occasionally called a combi-room but is being phased out.

Make reservations whenever possible. Even countryside inns, which usually have space, are sometimes packed with vacationing Europeans.

CATEGORY	MAIN CITIES	ELSEWHERE
$$$$	over 1,700	over 1,500
$$$	1,400–1,700	1,200–1,500
$$	1,000–1,400	1,000–1,200
$	700–1,000	700–1,000
¢	under 700	under 700

Prices, listed in Danish kroner, are for two people in a standard double room, including service charge and tax.

APARTMENT & VILLA RENTALS
Each year many Danes choose to rent out their summer homes in the verdant countryside and along the coast. Typically, a simple house accommodating four persons costs from DKr 1,000 weekly up to 10 times that amount in summer. You should book well in advance. A group of Danes who regularly rent out their holiday

houses have formed the Association of Danish Holiday House Letters (ADHHL). You can also contact DanCenter and Lejrskolebureauet for information. Homes for You lists fully furnished homes and apartments.

🚹 International Agents Hideaways International ✉ 767 Islington St., Portsmouth, NH 03801 ☎ 800/843–4433 or 603/430–4433 🖶 603/430–4444 ⊕ www.hideaways.com, annual membership $185. **🚹 Local Agents DanCenter** ✉ Lyngbyvej 20, Østerbro, DK–2100 Copenhagen ☎ 70/13–16–16 🖶 70/13–70–73 ⊕ www.dancenter.com. **Feriehusudlejernes Brancheforeningen (ADHHL)** ✉ Obels Have 32, DK–9000 Aalborg ☎ 96/30–22–44 🖶 96/30–22–45 ⊕ www.fbnet.dk. **Homes for You** ✉ Vimmelskaftet 49, Downtown, DK–1161 Copenhagen ☎ 33/33–08–05 🖶 33/32–08–04 ⊕ www.hay4you.dk. **Lejrskolebureauet (LSB)** ✉ Nordlævej 13, DK–3250 Gilleleje ☎ 48/30–14–88 🖶 48/30–14–66.

BED & BREAKFASTS
Contact Dansk Bed & Breakfast to order their B&B catalog for the whole of Denmark. Odense Tourist Bureau maintains its own list for the Funen and the Central Islands region.

🚹 Reservation Services Dansk Bed & Breakfast ✉ Bernstorffsvej 71a, DK–2900 Hellerup ☎ 39/61–04–05 🖶 39/61–05–25 ⊕ www.bedandbreakfast.dk. **Odense Tourist Bureau** ✉ Rådhuset,, DK–5000 Odense ☎ 66/12–75–20 🖶 66/12–75–86 ⊕ www.bed-breakfast-fyn.dk.

CAMPING
If you plan to camp in one of Denmark's 500-plus approved campsites, you'll need an International Camping Carnet or Danish Camping Pass (available at any campsite and valid for one year). Call Campingrådet for information.

🚹 Campingrådet ✉ Mosedalsvej 15, DK–2500 Valby ☎ 39/27–88–44 🖶 39/27–80–44 ⊕ www.campingraadet.dk.

FARM VACATIONS & HOMESTAYS
A farm vacation is perhaps the best way to experience the Danish countryside, sharing meals with your host family and perhaps helping with the chores. Bed-and-breakfast packages are about DKr 200, whereas half board—an overnight with breakfast and

one hot meal—runs around DKr 280. Full board, including an overnight with three square meals, can also be arranged. The minimum stay is three nights. Contact Landboferie for details.

If you aren't necessarily looking for a pastoral experience but would still like to get an insider's view of Danish society, you might want to consider a homestay. Meet the Danes helps travelers find accommodation in Danish homes. The informative local hosts can give you invaluable tips regarding sightseeing, shopping, dining, and nightlife.

🔁 Landboferie (Holiday in the Country) ✉ Ceresvej 2, DK 8410 Rønde ☎ 86/37-39-00 🖷 86/37-35-50 ⊕ www.bondegaardsferie.dk. **Meet the Danes** ✉ Ravnsborgg. 2, 2nd fl., Nørrebro DK-2200 Copenhagen ☎ 33/46-46-46 🖷 33/46-46-47 ⊕ www.meetthedanes.dk.

HOME EXCHANGES

If you would like to exchange your home for someone else's, join a home-exchange organization, which will send you its updated listings of available exchanges for a year and will include your own listing in at least one of them. It's up to you to make specific arrangements.

🔁 Exchange Clubs HomeLink USA ✉ 2937 N.W. 9th Terr., Wilton Manors, FL 33311 ☎ 800/638-3841 or 954/566-2687 🖷 954/566-2783 ⊕ www. homelink.org; $75 yearly for a listing and online access; $45 additional to receive directories. **Intervac U.S.** ✉ 30 Corte San Fernando, Tiburon, CA 94920 ☎ 800/756-4663 🖷 415/435-7440 ⊕ www. intervacus.com; $128 yearly for a listing, online access, and a catalog; $68 without catalog.

HOSTELS

No matter what your age, you can save on lodging costs by staying at hostels. In some 4,500 locations in more than 70 countries around the world, Hostelling International (HI), the umbrella group for a number of national youth-hostel associations, offers single-sex, dorm-style beds and, at many hostels, rooms for couples and family accommodations. Membership in any HI national hostel association, open to travelers of all ages, allows you to stay in HI-affiliated hostels at member rates; one-year membership is about $28 for adults (A$52 in Aus-

tralia, C$35 for a two-year minimum membership in Canada, NZ$40 in New Zealand, £15 in the United Kingdom); hostels charge about $10–$30 per night. Members have priority if the hostel is full; they're also eligible for discounts around the world, even on rail and bus travel in some countries.

Youth hostels in Denmark are open to everyone regardless of age. If you have an International Youth Hostels Association card (it costs DKr 160 to obtain in Denmark), the rate is roughly DKr 115 for a single bed, DKr 150–DKr 575 for a private room accommodating up to four people. Without the card, there's a surcharge of about DKr 30 per person. Prices don't include breakfast.

The hostels fill up quickly in summer, so make your reservations early. Most hostels are sympathetic to students and will usually find them at least a place on the floor. Bring your own linens or sleep sheet, though these can usually be rented at the hostel. Sleeping bags are not allowed. Contact Danhostel Danmarks Vandrerhjem—the organization charges for information, but you can get a free brochure, *Camping/Youth and Family Hostels*, from the Danish Tourist Board.

🔁 Organizations Danhostel Danmarks Vandrerhjem ✉ Vesterbrog. 39, Vesterbro, DK-1620 Copenhagen ☎ 33/31-36-12 🖷 33/31-36-26 ⊕ www.danhostel.dk. **Hostelling International–Canada** ✉ 205 Catherine St., Suite 400, Ottawa, Ontario K2P 1C3 ☎ 800/663-5777 or 613/237-7884 🖷 613/237-7868 ⊕ www.hihostels.ca. **Hostelling International–USA** ✉ 8401 Colesville Rd., Suite 600, Silver Spring, MD 20910 ☎ 301/495-1240 🖷 301/495-6697 ⊕ www.hiusa.org. **YHA Australia** ✉ 422 Kent St., Sydney, NSW 2001 ☎ 02/9261-1111 🖷 02/9261-1969 ⊕ www.yha.com.au. **YHA England and Wales** ✉ Trevelyan House, Dimple Rd., Matlock, Derbyshire DE4 3YH, U.K. ☎ 0870/870-8808, 0870/770-8868, 0162/959-2600 🖷 0870/770-6127 ⊕ www.yha.org.uk. **YHA New Zealand** ✉ Level 1, Moorhouse City, 166 Moorhouse Ave., Box 436, Christchurch ☎ 0800/278-299 or 03/379-9970 🖷 03/365-4476 ⊕ www.yha.org.nz.

HOTELS

All hotels listed have private bath unless otherwise noted. Many Danes prefer a shower to a bath, so if you particularly want a bath, ask for it, but be prepared to pay more. Taxes are usually included in prices, but check when making a reservation. As time goes on, it appears that an increasing number of hotels are eliminating breakfast from their room rates; even if it is not included, breakfast is usually well worth its price. Many of Denmark's larger hotels, particularly those that cater to the conference crowd, offer discounted rates on weekends, so inquire when booking. (Oddly, these are the hotels where breakfast is usually not included in the price of the room.) Try www.danishhotels. dk for listings not included in this book.

The Scandinavian countries offer Inn Checks, or prepaid hotel vouchers, for accommodations ranging from first-class hotels to country cottages. These vouchers, which must be purchased from travel agents or from the Scandinavian Tourist Board (⊕ www.goscandinavia.com) before departure, are sold individually and in packets for as many nights as needed and offer savings of up to 50%. Most countries also offer summer bargains for foreign tourists; winter bargains can be even greater. For further information about Scandinavian hotel vouchers, contact the Scandinavian Tourist Board.

ProSkandinavia checks can be used in 400 hotels across Scandinavia for savings up to 50%, for reservations made usually no earlier than 24 hours before arrival, although some hotels allow earlier bookings. One check costs about $40. Two checks will pay for a double room at a hotel, one check for a room in a cottage. The checks can be bought at many travel agencies in Scandinavia or directly from ProSkandinavia.

The old stagecoach *kroer* (inns) scattered throughout Denmark can be cheap yet charming alternatives to standard hotel rooms. You can cut your costs by contacting Danske Kroer & Hoteller to invest in a book of Inn Checks, valid at 83 participating inns and hotels throughout the country. Each check costs about DKr 690 per couple and entitles you to an overnight stay in a double room including breakfast. Family checks for three (DKr 790) and four (DKr 890) are also available. Order

a free catalog from Danske Kroer & Hoteller, but choose carefully; the organization includes a few chain hotels bereft of the charm you might be expecting. Some of the participating establishments tack on a DKr 150 surcharge.

🛪 Reservation Services **Danske Kroer & Hoteller** ⊠ Vejlevej 16, DK-8700 Horsens ☎ 75/64-87-00 🖷 75/64-87-20 ⊕ www.krohotel.dk. **ProSkandinavia** ⊠ Akersgt. 11, N-0158 Oslo, Norway 🖷 47/22-41-13-13 ⊕ www.proskandinavia.no.

RESERVING A ROOM

Make your reservations well in advance, especially in resort areas near the coasts. Many places offer summer reductions to compensate for the slowdown in business travel and conferences. The very friendly staff at the hotel booking desk at Wonderful Copenhagen (see Visitor Information, below) can help find rooms in hotels, hostels, and private homes, or even campsites in advance of a trip. If you find yourself in Copenhagen without a reservation, head for the tourist office's hotel booking desk, which is open May through August, Monday to Saturday 9–8 and Sunday 10–8; September through April, weekdays 10–4:30 and Saturday 10–1:30. Note that hours of the hotel booking desk can be fickle, and change from year to year depending on staff availability; in the low season they are often closed weekends. Young travelers looking for a room should head for Use It, the student and youth budget travel agency.

Reservations should be made two months in advance, but last-minute (as in same-day) hotel rooms booked at the tourist office can save you 50% off the normal price.

🛪 Local Reservation Services **Hotel booking desk** ⊠ Bernstorffsg. 1, Vesterbro, DK-1577 Copenhagen ☎ 70/22-24-42 ⊕ www.visitcopenhagen.com. **Use It** ⊠ Rådhusstr. 13, Downtown, DK-1466 Copenhagen ☎ 33/73-06-20 🖷 33/73-06-49 ⊕ www. useit.dk.

🛪 Toll-Free Numbers **Best Western** ☎ 800/528-1234 ⊕ www.bestwestern.com. **Choice** ☎ 800/424-6423 ⊕ www.choicehotels.com. **Clarion** ☎ 800/424-6423 ⊕ www.choicehotels.com. **Comfort Inn** ☎ 800/424-6423 ⊕ www.choicehotels.com. **Hilton** ☎ 800/445-8667 ⊕ www.hilton.com. **Holiday Inn** ☎ 800/465-4329 ⊕ www.ichotelsgroup.com. **Qual-**

ity Inn ☎ 800/424-6423 ⊕ www.choicehotels.com.
Radisson ☎ 800/333-3333 ⊕ www.radisson.com.

MAIL & SHIPPING
POSTAL RATES
Airmail letters and postcards to non-EU countries cost DKr 6.50 for 50 grams. Airmail letters and postcards within the EU cost DKr 5.50. Length, width, and thickness all influence the postage price. Letters must be marked with an "A." Contact Copenhagen's main post office for more information. You can buy stamps at post offices or from shops selling postcards.

RECEIVING MAIL
You can arrange to have your mail sent general delivery, marked *poste restante,* to any post office, hotel, or inn. If no post office is specified, the letter or package is automatically sent to the main post office in Copenhagen.

SHIPPING PARCELS
🔁 Copenhagen Main Post Office ✉ Tietgensg. 37, Vesterbro, DK-1566 Copenhagen ☎ 80/20-70-30 ⊕ www.postdanmark.dk.

MONEY MATTERS
Denmark's economy is stable, and inflation remains reasonably low. On the other hand, the Danish cost of living is quite high, even for Europe. In some areas prices are comparable to other European capitals, while other goods or services tend to be higher. As in all of Scandinavia, prices for alcoholic beverages and tobacco products are steep due to heavy taxation. Prices are highest in Copenhagen, lower elsewhere in the country. Some sample prices: cup of coffee, DKr 20–DKr 30; bottle of beer, DKr 30–DKr 35; soda, DKr 20–DKr 25; ham sandwich, DKr 35–DKr 45; 1½-km (1-mi) taxi ride, about DKr 55.

Prices throughout this guide are given for adults. Substantially reduced fees are almost always available for children, students, and senior citizens. For information on taxes, *see* Taxes.

ATMS
Automatic Teller Machines/ATMs are located around most towns and cities. Look for the red signs for KONTANTEN/DANKORT AUTOMAT. You can use Visa, Plus, MasterCard/Eurocard, Eurochequecard, and sometimes JCB cards to withdraw cash. Many, but not all, machines are open 24 hours. Check with your bank about daily withdrawal limits before you go.
🔁 ATM Locations MasterCard/Cirrus ☎ 800/424-7787 ⊕ www.mastercard.com.

CREDIT CARDS
Most major credit cards are accepted in Denmark, though it's wise to inquire about American Express and Diners Club beforehand. Throughout this guide, the following abbreviations are used: **AE,** American Express; **DC,** Diners Club; **MC,** MasterCard; and **V,** Visa.
🔁 Reporting Lost Cards American Express ✉ Amagertorv 18, DK-1146 Copenhagen ☎ 33/11-50-05. Diners Club ✉ H. J. Holst Vej 5, DK-2605 Brøndby ☎ 36/73-73-73. MasterCard ☎ 44/89-27-50. Visa ☎ 44/89-29-29.

CURRENCY
The monetary unit in Denmark is the krone (DKr), divided into 100 øre. Even though Denmark has not adopted the euro, the Danish krone is firmly bound to it at about DKr 7.5 to 1€, with only minimal fluctuations in exchange rates.

At this writing, the krone stood at 7.46 to the euro, 4.71 to the Australian dollar, 11.07 to the British pound, 5.26 to the Canadian dollar, 4.31 to the New Zealand dollar, 0.96 to the South African rand, and 6.14 to the U.S. dollar.

CURRENCY EXCHANGE
For the most favorable rates, **change money through banks.** Although ATM transaction fees may be higher abroad than at home, ATM rates are excellent because they're based on wholesale rates offered only by major banks. You won't do as well at exchange booths in airports or rail and bus stations, in hotels, in restaurants, or in stores. To avoid lines at airport exchange booths, get a bit of local currency before you leave home.
🔁 Exchange Services International Currency Express ✉ 427 N. Camden Dr., Suite F, Beverly Hills, CA 90210 ☎ 888/278-6628 orders ⊞ 310/278-6410

⊕ www.foreignmoney.com. **Travel Ex Currency Services** ☎ 800/287-7362 orders and retail locations ⊕ www.travelex.com.

TRAVELER'S CHECKS

Do you need traveler's checks? It depends on where you're headed. If you're going to rural areas and small towns, go with cash; traveler's checks are best used in cities. Lost or stolen checks can usually be replaced within 24 hours. To ensure a speedy refund, buy your own traveler's checks—don't let someone else pay for them: irregularities like this can cause delays. The person who bought the checks should make the call to request a refund. Traveler's checks can be cashed at banks and at many hotels, restaurants, and shops.

PACKING

Bring a folding umbrella and a lightweight raincoat, as it is common for the sky to be clear at 9 AM, rainy at 11 AM, and clear again in time for lunch. Pack casual clothes, as Scandinavians tend to dress more casually than their Continental brethren. Even in summer it's wise to bring a sweater or a jacket, because temperatures can really drop off with an on-shore breeze or a sudden cloudburst. If you have trouble sleeping when it is light or are sensitive to strong sun, bring an eye mask and dark sunglasses; in summer the sun rises as early as 4 AM in some areas, and the far-northern latitude causes it to slant at angles unseen elsewhere on the globe. Bring bug repellent if you plan to venture away from the capital cities; large mosquitoes can be a real nuisance on summer evenings throughout Scandinavia.

In your carry-on luggage pack an extra pair of eyeglasses or contact lenses and enough of any medication you take to last a few days longer than the entire trip. You may also ask your doctor to write a spare prescription using the drug's generic name, as brand names may vary from country to country. In luggage to be checked, **never pack prescription drugs, valuables, or undeveloped film.** And don't forget to carry with you the addresses of offices that handle refunds of lost traveler's checks. Check *Fodor's How to Pack* (available at online retailers and bookstores everywhere) for more tips.

To avoid customs and security delays, carry medications in their original packaging. Don't pack any sharp objects in your carry-on luggage, including knives of any size or material, scissors, nail clippers, and corkscrews, or anything else that might arouse suspicion.

To avoid having your checked luggage chosen for hand inspection, don't cram bags full. The U.S. Transportation Security Administration suggests packing shoes on top and placing personal items you don't want touched in clear plastic bags.

CHECKING LUGGAGE

You're allowed to carry aboard one bag and one personal article, such as a purse or a laptop computer. Make sure what you carry on fits under your seat or in the overhead bin. Get to the gate early, so you can board as soon as possible, before the overhead bins fill up.

Baggage allowances vary by carrier, destination, and ticket class. On international flights you're usually allowed to check two bags weighing up to 70 pounds (32 kilograms) each, although a few airlines allow checked bags of up to 88 pounds (40 kilograms) in first class. Some international carriers don't allow more than 66 pounds (30 kilograms) per bag in business class and 44 pounds (20 kilograms) in economy. If you're flying to or through the United Kingdom, your luggage cannot exceed 70 pounds (32 kilograms) per bag. On domestic flights, the limit is usually 50 to 70 pounds (23 to 32 kilograms) per bag. In general, carry-on bags shouldn't exceed 40 pounds (18 kilograms). Most airlines won't accept bags that weigh more than 100 pounds (45 kilograms) on domestic or international flights. Expect to pay a fee for baggage that exceeds weight limits. Check baggage restrictions with your carrier before you pack.

Airline liability for baggage is limited to $2,500 per person on flights within the United States. On international flights it amounts to $9.07 per pound or $20 per kilogram for checked baggage (roughly

$640 per 70-pound bag), with a maximum of $634.90 per piece, and $400 per passenger for unchecked baggage. You can buy additional coverage at check-in for about $10 per $1,000 of coverage, but it often excludes a rather extensive list of items, shown on your airline ticket.

Before departure, itemize your bags' contents and their worth, and label the bags with your name, address, and phone number. (If you use your home address, cover it so potential thieves can't see it readily.) Include a label inside each bag and **pack a copy of your itinerary.** At check-in, make sure each bag is correctly tagged with the destination airport's three-letter code. Because some checked bags will be opened for hand inspection, the U.S. Transportation Security Administration recommends that you leave luggage unlocked or use the plastic locks offered at check-in. U.S. Transportation Security Administration Contact Center (TSA) screeners place an inspection notice inside searched bags, which are resealed with a special lock.

If your bag has been searched and contents are missing or damaged, file a claim with the TSA Consumer Response Center as soon as possible. If your bags arrive damaged or fail to arrive at all, file a written report with the airline before leaving the airport.

🡒 Complaints **TSA** ☎ 866/289-9673 ⊕ www.tsa.gov.

PASSPORTS & VISAS

When traveling internationally, carry your passport even if you don't need one. Not only is it the best form of ID, but it's also being required more and more. **Make two photocopies of the data page** (one for someone at home and another for you, carried separately from your passport). If you lose your passport, promptly call the nearest embassy or consulate and the local police.

U.S. passport applications for children under age 14 require consent from both parents or legal guardians; both parents must appear together to sign the application. If only one parent appears, he or she must submit a written statement from the other parent authorizing passport issuance

for the child. A parent with sole authority must present evidence of it when applying; acceptable documentation includes the child's certified birth certificate listing only the applying parent, a court order specifically permitting this parent's travel with the child, or a death certificate for the non-applying parent. Application forms and instructions are available on the Web site of the U.S. State Department's Bureau of Consular Affairs (⊕ http://travel.state.gov).

ENTERING DENMARK

Australian, British, Canadian, New Zealand, and U.S. citizens need only a valid passport to enter Denmark or any Scandinavian country for stays of up to three months.

PASSPORT OFFICES

The best time to apply for a passport or to renew is in fall and winter. Before any trip, check your passport's expiration date, and, if necessary, renew it as soon as possible.

🡒 Australian Citizens **Passports Australia** Australian Department of Foreign Affairs and Trade ☎ 131-232 ⊕ www.passports.gov.au.

🡒 Canadian Citizens **Passport Office** ⊠ To mail in applications: 70 Cremazie St., Gatineau, Québec J8Y 3P2 ☎ 800/567-6868 or 819/994-3500 ⊕ www.ppt.gc.ca.

🡒 New Zealand Citizens **New Zealand Passports Office** ☎ 0800/22-5050 or 04/474-8100 ⊕ www.passports.govt.nz.

🡒 U.K. Citizens **U.K. Passport Service** ☎ 0870/521-0410 ⊕ www.passport.gov.uk.

🡒 U.S. Citizens **National Passport Information Center** ☎ 877/487-2778, 888/874-7793 TDD/TTY ⊕ travel.state.gov.

SAFETY

Generally speaking, Denmark has a low crime rate and you should feel safe going out at night or to large gatherings (such as a parade). It's always a good idea to leave your valuables at your hotel, if possible in a room safe. You can leave a "Do not Disturb" sign on your door to give the impression that someone's in the room when you're out.

Don't wear a money belt or a waist pack, both of which peg you as a tourist. Distribute your cash and any valuables (including your credit cards and passport) be-tween a deep front pocket, an inside jacket or vest pocket, and a hidden money pouch. Do not reach for the money pouch once you're in public.

WOMEN IN DENMARK

Women are safe everywhere in Denmark; exercise the same caution here as you would at home. If you carry a purse, choose one with a zipper and a thick strap that you can drape across your body; ad-just the length so that the purse sits in front of you at or above hip level. (Don't wear a money belt or a waist pack.) Store only enough money in the purse to cover casual spending. Distribute the rest of your cash and any valuables between deep front pockets, inside jacket or vest pockets, and a concealed money pouch.

SENIOR-CITIZEN TRAVEL

Seniors over 60 are entitled to discount tickets (often as much as 50% off) on buses, trains, and ferries throughout Scandi-navia, as well as reductions on special City Cards. Eurail offers discounts on ScanRail and Eurail train passes (➪ Train Travel).

To qualify for age-related discounts, men-tion your senior-citizen status up front when booking hotel reservations (not when checking out) and before you're seated in restaurants (not when paying the bill). Be sure to have identification on hand. When renting a car, ask about pro-motional car-rental discounts, which can be cheaper than senior-citizen rates.

⚠ Educational Programs Elderhostel ⊠ 11 Ave. de Lafayette, Boston, MA 02111 ☎ 877/426-8056, 978/323-4141 international callers, 877/426-2167 TTY 🖷 877/426-2166 ⊕ www.elderhostel.org. **Interhostel** ⊠ University of New Hampshire, 6 Garrison Ave., Durham, NH 03824 ☎ 800/733-9753 or 603/862-1147 🖷 603/862-1113 ⊕ www.learn.unh.edu.

SPORTS & THE OUTDOORS

FISHING

Licenses are required for fishing along the coasts; requirements vary from one area to another for fishing in lakes, streams, and the ocean. Licenses cost about DKr 100 for a year, DKr 75 for a week, and DKr 25 for a day, and you can buy them at any post office. Remember—it is illegal to fish

within 1,650 feet of the mouth of a stream. Contact the Danish Tourist Board for more information.

⚠ Danish Tourist Board ⊠ Vesterbrog. 6D, Vesterbro, DK-1620 Copenhagen ☎ 33/11-14-15 🖷 33/93-14-16 ⊕ www.visitdenmark.dk.

GOLF

Danish golf courses can be a real chal-lenge, with plenty of water, roughs that live up to their name, and wind that is often a factor. Due to environmental con-trols, chemical fertilization is prohibited, so greens tend to be flatter with fewer breaks. Motorized riding carts are prohib-ited for general use, though most courses have one on hand for anyone with (docu-mented) ambulatory problems.

Danish golf courses are open to any player who is a member of a certified golf club or has a valid handicap card. When entering a clubhouse to pay a greens fee, you will be asked to present documentation of membership in a club or a card stating your handicap. This can present a problem for Americans, many of whom are unfa-miliar with this system and can produce no such evidence. The Danes are generally flexible when a golfer doesn't have a card, but it's wise to have some sort of docu-mentation handy just in case.

⚠ Dansk Golf Union ⊠ Brøndby Stadium 20, DK-2605 Brøndby ☎ 43/26-27-00 🖷 43/26-27-01 ⊕ www.dgu.org/danishgolffederation/.

STUDENTS IN DENMARK

Ungdomsinformationen provides informa-tion on visas, jobs, volunteer work, and studying in Denmark. You can find the English information by clicking on "New in Town" or "Find a Place to Live" in the left-hand column on the home page.

⚠ IDs & Services STA Travel ⊠ 10 Downing St., New York, NY 10014 ☎ 800/777-0112 24-hr service center, 212/627-3111 🖷 212/627-3387 ⊕ www.sta. com. **Travel Cuts** ⊠ 187 College St., Toronto, On-tario M5T 1P7, Canada ☎ 800/592-2887 in the U.S., 416/979-2406 or 866/246-9762 in Canada 🖷 416/979-8167 ⊕ www.travelcuts.com. **Ungdomsinfor-mationen** (Young Information) ⊠ Rådhusstræde 13, DK-1466, Copenhagen ☎ 33/73-06-50 🖷 33/73-06-49 ⊕ www.ui.dk.

TAXES

All hotel, restaurant, and departure taxes and V.A.T. (what the Danes call *moms*) are automatically included in prices.

VALUE-ADDED TAX

V.A.T. is 25%; non-EU citizens can obtain an 18% refund. The more than 1,500 shops that participate in the tax-free scheme have a white TAX FREE sticker on their windows. Purchases must be at least DKr 300 per store and must be sealed and unused in Denmark. At the shop you'll be asked to fill out a form and show your passport. The form can then be turned in at any airport or ferry customs desk, where you can choose a cash or charge-card credit. Keep all your receipts and tags; occasionally customs authorities do ask to see purchases, so pack them where they will be accessible.

When making a purchase, **ask for a V.A.T. refund form** and find out whether the merchant gives refunds—not all stores do, nor are they required to. Have the form stamped like any customs form by customs officials when you leave the country or, if you're visiting several European Union countries, when you leave the EU. Be ready to show customs officials what you've bought (pack purchases together, in your carry-on luggage); budget extra time for this. After you're through passport control, take the form to a refund-service counter for an on-the-spot refund (which is usually the quickest and easiest option), or mail it to the address on the form (or the envelope with it) after you arrive home.

A service processes refunds for most shops. You receive the total refund stated on the form. Global Refund is a Europe-wide service with 210,000 affiliated stores and more than 700 refund counters—located at major airports and border crossings. Its refund form is called a Tax Free Check. The service issues refunds in the form of cash, check, or credit-card adjustment. If you don't have time to wait at the refund counter, you can mail in the form to an office in Europe or Canada instead.

🗗 V.A.T. Refunds Denmark Global Refund ✉ Alléen 84, 1st fl., DK-2770 Kastrup 🕾 32/52-55-66

🖷 32/52-55-61. **Global Refund Canada** 🖚 Box 2020, Station Main, Brampton, Ontario L6T 3S3 🕾 800/993-4313 🖷 905/791-9078 ⊕ www. globalrefund.com.

TELEPHONES

Telephone exchanges throughout Denmark were changed over the past couple of years. If you hear a recorded message or three loud beeps, chances are the number you are trying to reach has been changed. Contact the main Danish operator, TDC, for current numbers.

Denmark, like most European countries, has a different cellular-phone switching system from the one used in North America. Newer phones can handle both technologies; check with the dealer where you purchased your phone to see if it can work on the European system. If all else fails, several companies rent cellular phones to tourists. Contact local tourist offices for details.

AREA & COUNTRY CODES

The country code for Denmark is 45. When dialing a Denmark number from abroad, drop the initial "0" from the local area code. The country code is 1 for the United States and Canada, 61 for Australia, 64 for New Zealand, and 44 for the United Kingdom.

DIRECTORY & OPERATOR ASSISTANCE

Most operators speak English. For national directory assistance, dial 118; for an international operator, dial 113; for a directory-assisted international call, dial 115. You can reach U.S. operators by dialing local access codes.

INTERNATIONAL CALLS

Dial 00, then the country code (1 for the United States and Canada, 44 for Great Britain), the area code, and the number. It's very expensive to call or fax from hotels, although the regional phone companies offer a discount after 7:30 PM. You can save a lot on the price of calls by purchasing a country-specific telephone card from any post office or one of the many kiosks and groceries in Copenhagen's Vesterbro and Nørrebro neighborhoods.

LOCAL CALLS

Phones accept 1-, 2-, 5-, 10-, and 20-kroner coins. Pick up the receiver, dial the number, always including the area code, and wait until the party answers; then deposit the coins. You have roughly a minute per krone; on some phones you can make another call on the same payment if your time has not run out. When it does, you will hear a beep and your call will be disconnected unless you deposit another coin. Coin-operated phones are becoming increasingly rare; it is cheaper and less frustrating to buy a local phone card from a kiosk.

Dial the eight-digit number for calls anywhere within the country. For calls to the Faroe Islands (298) and Greenland (299), dial 00, then the three-digit code, then the five-digit number.

LONG-DISTANCE SERVICES

AT&T, MCI, and Sprint access codes make calling long-distance relatively convenient, but you may find the local access number blocked in many hotel rooms. First ask the hotel operator to connect you. If the hotel operator balks, ask for an international operator, or dial the international operator yourself. One way to improve your odds of getting connected to your long-distance carrier is to travel with more than one company's calling card (a hotel may block Sprint, for example, but not MCI). If all else fails, call from a pay phone. If you are traveling for a longer period of time, consider renting a cell-phone from a local company.

⊿ Access Codes AT&T USADirect ☎ 800/10010 ⊕ www.travel.att.com. **World Phone** ☎ 800/10022 ⊕ www.mci.com. **Sprint Global One** ☎ 800/10877 ⊕ www.sprint.com.

TIME

Denmark is one hour ahead of Greenwich Mean Time (GMT) and six hours ahead of Eastern Standard Time (EST). All of Europe goes over to Daylight Savings Time from March to October, and during this time Denmark is two hours ahead of GMT (though still one hour ahead of London).

TIPPING

It has long been held that the egalitarian Danes do not expect to be tipped. This is

often the case, but most people do tip and those who receive tips appreciate them. Service is included in hotel bills. Many restaurants frequented by tourists have started adding a gratuity to bills, although you should check your bill to see if a service charge has already been included. If not, a token tip at bars or restaurants is the general rule of thumb.

The same holds true for taxis—if a bill comes to DKr 58, most people will give the driver DKr 60. If the driver is extremely friendly or helpful, tip more at your own discretion. Hotel porters expect about DKr 5 per bag.

TOURS & PACKAGES

Because everything is prearranged on a prepackaged tour or independent vacation, you spend less time planning—and often get it all at a good price.

For information on excursions and tours, call the Danish Tourist Board, Copenhagen Excursions, or Auto–Paaske.

⊿ Auto-Paaske ⊠ Yderlandsvej 2-8, Amager, DK-2300 Copenhagen ☎ 32/66-00-00 ⊟ 32/66-00-25 ⊕ www.auto-paaske.dk. **Copenhagen Excursions** ⊠ Rådhuspl. 57, Downtown, DK-1550 Copenhagen ☎ 32/54-06-06 ⊟ 32/57-49-05 ⊕ www.cex.dk. **Danish Tourist Board** ⊠ Vesterbrog. 6D, Vesterbro, DK-1620 Copenhagen ☎ 33/11-14-15 ⊟ 33/93-14-16 ⊕ www.visitdenmark.dk.

BIKE TOURS

Copenhagen-based BikeDenmark combines the flexibility of individual tours with the security of an organized outing. Choose from seven preplanned 5- to 10-day tours, which include bikes, maps, two fine meals per day, hotel accommodations, and hotel-to-hotel baggage transfers. BikeDenmark tours can be booked directly by fax, via their Web site, or through any travel agency below. Many U.S. tour companies can arrange booking. Try Borton Oversees, Nordique Tours Norvista, ScanAm World Tours, or Gerhard's Bicycle Odysseys.

Bike and Sea also leads biking tours through southern Jutland, Funen, and southern Zealand.

⊿ Bike and Sea ⊠ Svendborgvej 83-85, DK-5260 Odense ☎ 66/13-13-37 ⊟ 66/13-13-38 ⊕ www.

bikeandsea-denmark.com. **BikeDenmark** ✉ Olaf Poulsens Allé 1A, DK-3480 Fredensborg ☎ 48/48-58-00 🖶 48/48-59-00 ⊕ www.bikedenmark.com. **Borton Overseas** ✉ 5412 Lyndale Ave. S, Minneapolis, MN 55419 ☎ 800/843-0602 or 612/822-4640 🖶 612/822-4755 ⊕ www.bortonoverseas.com. **Gerhard's Bicycle Odysseys** ⬠ Box 757, Portland, OR 97207 ☎ 800/966-2402 🖶 503/223-5901 ⊕ www.since1974.com. **Nordique Tours Norvista** ☎ 800/995-7997 or 310/645-7527 🖶 310/645-1071 ⊕ www.nordiquetours.com. **ScanAm World Tours** ✉ 108 N. Main St., Cranbury, NJ 08512 ☎ 800/545-2204 (toll-free) 🖶 609/655-1622 ⊕ www.scandinaviantravel.com.

BOOKING WITH AN AGENT

Travel agents are excellent resources. But it's a good idea to collect brochures from several agencies, as some agents' suggestions may be influenced by relationships with tour and package firms that reward them for volume sales. If you have a special interest, find an agent with expertise in that area. The American Society of Travel Agents (ASTA) has a database of specialists worldwide; you can log on to the group's Web site to find one near you.

Make sure your travel agent knows the accommodations and other services of the place being recommended. Ask about the hotel's location, room size, beds, and whether it has a pool, room service, or programs for children, if you care about these. Has your agent been there in person or sent others whom you can contact?

Do some homework on your own, too: local tourism boards can provide information about lesser-known and small-niche operators, some of which may sell only direct.

BUYER BEWARE

Each year consumers are stranded or lose their money when tour operators—even large ones with excellent reputations—go out of business. So check out the operator. Ask several travel agents about its reputation, and try to **book with a company that has a consumer-protection program.** (Look for information in the company's brochure.) In the United States, members of the United States Tour Operators Association are required to set aside funds (up to $1 million) to help eligible customers cover payments and travel arrangements in the event that the company defaults. It's also a good idea to choose a company that participates in the American Society of Travel Agents' Tour Operator Program; ASTA will act as mediator in any disputes between you and your tour operator.

Remember that the more your package or tour includes, the better you can predict the ultimate cost of your vacation. Make sure you know exactly what is covered, and beware of hidden costs. Are taxes, tips, and transfers included? Entertainment and excursions? These can add up.

🚩 **Tour-Operator Recommendations American Society of Travel Agents** (⇨ Travel Agencies). **CrossSphere–The Global Association for Packaged Travel** ✉ 546 E. Main St., Lexington, KY 40508 ☎ 800/682-8886 or 859/226-4444 🖶 859/226-4414 ⊕ www.CrossSphere.com. **United States Tour Operators Association (USTOA)** ✉ 275 Madison Ave., Suite 2014, New York, NY 10016 ☎ 212/599-6599 🖶 212/599-6744 ⊕ www.ustoa.com.

TRAIN TRAVEL

Trains within Europe are well connected to Denmark, with Copenhagen serving as the main hub; however, it's often not much cheaper than flying, especially if you make your arrangements from the United States. A ScanRail Pass offers discounts on train, ferry, and car transportation in Denmark, Finland, Sweden, and Norway. The Eurail-Pass, purchased only in the United States, is accepted by the Danish State Railways and on some ferries operated by DSB.

DSB and a few private companies cover the country with a dense network of services, supplemented by buses in remote areas. Hourly intercity trains connect the main towns in Jutland and Funen with Copenhagen and Zealand, using high-speed diesels, called IC-3s, on the most important stretches. All these trains make 1-hour crossings of the Great Belt Bridge. You can reserve seats (for an extra DKr 15) on intercity trains, and you *must* have a reservation if you plan to cross the Great Belt. Buy tickets at stations. From London, the transit takes 18 hours, including ferry. Call the British Rail European Travel Center or Wasteels for information.

CUTTING COSTS

To save money, **look into rail passes.** But be aware that if you don't plan to cover many miles you may come out ahead by buying individual tickets. The ScanRail Pass, which affords unlimited train travel throughout Denmark, Finland, Norway, and Sweden and restricted ferry passage in and beyond Scandinavia, comes in various denominations. It is much better to buy the ScanRail Pass before you leave home, as you will have more flexibility to use it. You can order five days of travel within 60 days ($291); 10 days within 60 days ($390); or 21 days consecutive use ($453). All prices given are for second-class travel. In Denmark you will still be able to reserve a seat for DKr 20 with your pass, and you will be given the option of a no-smoking or smoking car.

A ScanRail Pass will also allow you free or discounted travel on selected ferries, boats, and buses. Most ferries offer 50% discount (e.g. Frederikshavn-Goteborg on the Stena Line). There is a 25% discount on railway museums (there is a large one in Odense, Funen, and a few very small ones in other areas) in Denmark, and a 50% discount on the private railway lines Frederikshavn-Skagen (Skagensbanan) and Hjorring-Hirtshals (Hjorring Privatbaner). You can also receive a discounted price on the following hotel chains: Best Western, Sokos Hotels, Choice Hotels, and VIP Backpackers Resorts.

With a ScanRail 'n Drive Pass, you get any five days of unlimited train travel, along with two days car rental with unlimited mileage in Denmark, Finland, Norway, and/or Sweden; you have two months to complete your travel. Train passage is second class. The car rental is chosen from three car categories with manual transmission. Local tax is included with the rental, and the same bonuses apply as above on ferries. You can purchase extra travel days of Avis car rental for Denmark, Finland, Norway, and Sweden and the third and fourth person sharing the car need only purchase a ScanRail Pass. For two adults traveling, the price ranges from $678 to $738.

In the United States, call Rail Europe, Nordic Saga Tours, ScanAm World Tours, Passage Tours, or DER Travel Services for rail passes. In Canada, contact Rail Europe. You can also buy the ScanRail Pass at the train stations in most major cities, including Copenhagen, Odense, and Århus, but you will not have as much of a time frame in which to use the pass. The ScanRail Pass and Interail and Eurail passes are also valid on all DSB trains.

Call Arriva for train travel in central and northern Jutland, or the DSB Travel Office for the rest of the country.

🚆 Train Information **Arriva** ☎ 72/13-96-00 ⊕ www.arriva.dk. **DSB Travel Office** ☎ 70/13-14-15 ⊕ www.dsb.dk.

🚆 Rail Passes **DER Travel Services** ✉ 9501 W. Devon Ave., Rosemont, IL 60018 ☎ 800/782-2424 🖷 888/712-5727 ⊕ www.der.com. **Nordic Saga Tours** ✉ 303 5th Ave. S, Suite 109, Edmonds, WA 98020 ☎ 800/840-6449 or 425/673-4800 🖷 425/673-2600 ⊕ www.nordicsaga.com. **Passage Tours** ✉ 239 Commercial Blvd., Fort Lauderdale, FL 33308 ☎ 954/776-7188 🖷 954/776-7070 ⊕ www.passagetours.com. **Rail Europe** ☎ 888/382-7245 in the U.S., 800/361-7245 in Canada ⊕ www.raileurope.com in the U.S., www.raileurope.ca in Canada. **ScanAm World Tours** ✉ 108 N. Main St., Cranbury, NJ 08512 ☎ 800/545-2204 🖷 609/655-1622 ⊕ www.scandinaviantravel.com. **Wasteels** ✉ Skoubog. 6, Downtown, DK-1158 Copenhagen ☎ 33/14-46-33 🖷 33/14-08-65 ⊕ www.wasteels.dk.

TRAVEL AGENCIES

A good travel agent puts your needs first. Look for an agency that has been in business at least five years, emphasizes customer service, and has someone on staff who specializes in your destination. In addition, **make sure the agency belongs to a professional trade organization.** The American Society of Travel Agents (ASTA) has more than 10,000 members in some 140 countries, enforces a strict code of ethics, and will step in to mediate agent-client disputes involving ASTA members. ASTA also maintains a directory of agents on its Web site; ASTA's TravelSense.org, a trip planning and travel advice site, can also help to locate a travel agent who caters to your needs. (If a travel agency is also acting as your tour operator, *see* Buyer Beware *in* Tours & Packages.) 🖬 Local Agent Referrals **American Society of Travel Agents (ASTA)** ✉ 1101 King St., Suite 200, Alexandria, VA 22314 ☎ 800/965-2782 24-hr hotline, 703/739-2782 🖶 703/684-8319 🌐 www. astanet.com and www.travelsense.org. **Association of British Travel Agents** ✉ 68-71 Newman St., London W1T 3AH ☎ 020/7637-2444 🖶 020/7637-0713 🌐 www.abta.com. **Association of Canadian Travel Agencies** ✉ 130 Albert St., Suite 1705, Ottawa, Ontario K1P 5G4 ☎ 613/237-3657 🖶 613/237-7052 🌐 www.acta.ca.**Australian Federation of Travel Agents** ✉ Level 3, 309 Pitt St., Sydney, NSW 2000 ☎ 02/9264-3299 or 1300/363-416 🖶 02/9264-1085 🌐 www.afta.com.au. **Travel Agents' Association of New Zealand** ✉ Level 5, Tourism and Travel House, 79 Boulcott St., Box 1888, Wellington 6001 ☎ 04/499-0104 🖶 04/499-0786 🌐 www. taanz.org.nz.

VISITOR INFORMATION

Learn more about foreign destinations by checking government-issued travel advisories and country information. For a broader picture, consider information from more than one country.

🖬 Tourist Information **Danish Tourist Board** ✉ 655 3rd Ave., New York, NY 10017 ☎ 212/885-9700 🖶 212/885-9726 ✉ 55 Sloane St., London SW1X 9SY ☎ 44/20-7259-5959 🖶 44/20-7259-5955 ✉ Level 4, 81 York St., Sydney NSW 2000 ☎ 61/2-9262-5832 🖶 61/2-9290-1981 🌐 www.visitdenmark.com. **Danmarks Turistråd (Danish Tourist Board)** ✉ Vesterbrog. 6D, Vesterbro, DK-1620 Copenhagen ☎ 33/11-14-15 🖶 33/93-14-16 🌐 www.visitdenmark.com.

🖬 Government Advisories **Australian Department of Foreign Affairs and Trade** ☎ 300/139-281 travel advisories, 02/6261-1299 Consular Travel Advice 🌐 www.smartraveller.gov.au or www.dfat.gov.au. **Consular Affairs Bureau of Canada** ☎ 800/267-6788 or 613/944-6788 🌐 www.voyage.gc.ca. **New Zealand Ministry of Foreign Affairs and Trade** ☎ 04/439-8000 🌐 www.mft.govt.nz. **U.K. Foreign and Commonwealth Office** ✉ Travel Advice Unit, Consular Directorate, Old Admiralty Bldg., London SW1A 2PA ☎ 0870/606-0290 or 020/7008-1500 🌐 www.fco.gov.uk/travel. **U.S. Department of State** ✉ Bureau of Consular Affairs, Overseas Citizens Services Office, 2201 C St. NW, Washington, DC 20520 ☎ 202/647-5225, 888/407-4747 or 317/472-2328 for interactive hotline 🌐 www.travel.state.gov.

WEB SITES

Do check out the World Wide Web when planning your trip. You'll find everything from weather forecasts to virtual tours of famous cities. Be sure to visit Fodors.com (🌐 www.fodors.com), a complete travel-planning site. You can research prices and book plane tickets, hotel rooms, rental cars, vacation packages, and more. In addition, you can post your pressing questions in the Travel Talk section. Other planning tools include a currency converter and weather reports, and there are loads of links to travel resources.

Www.denmark.dk is literally one-stop shopping for everything you need to know about Denmark. **Www.visitdenmark.com** is the official tourism Web site. The Royal Library at Copenhagen's Web site, **www. kb.dk/index-en.htm,** offers information, services, and a catalog. The Embassy of Denmark in Washington, D.C., has a site, **www.ambwashington.um.dk/en,** that contains much useful information.

Copenhagen

WORD OF MOUTH

"I'll always love Copenhagen. Wander up and down the Strøget. Eat dinner at one of the many alfresco restaurants on Greyfriars Square. Watch the changing of the guard at Amalienborg at noon. Have a beer (best draft beer in the world) at '90 Vin Stue on Gammel Kongevej."
—Snoopy

"Tivoli Gardens are only semi-impressive by day, but at night, all lit up, it's a magical place, with some of the world's best people-watching."
—Annam

Updated by
Bruce Bishop

COPENHAGEN—KØBENHAVN IN DANISH—has no glittering skylines, few killer views, and only a handful of meager skyscrapers. Bicycles glide alongside manageable traffic at a pace that's utterly human. The early-morning air in the pedestrian streets of the city's core, Strøget, is redolent of freshly baked bread and soap-scrubbed storefronts. If there's such a thing as a cozy city, this is it.

Extremely livable and relatively calm, Copenhagen is not a microcosm of Denmark, but rather a cosmopolitan city with an identity of its own. Denmark's political, cultural, and financial capital is inhabited by 1.5 million Danes, a fifth of the national population, as well as a growing immigrant community. Filled with museums, restaurants, cafés, and lively nightlife, the city has its greatest resource in its spirited inhabitants. The imaginative, unconventional, and affable Copenhageners exude an egalitarian philosophy that embraces nearly all lifestyles and leanings.

The town was a fishing colony until 1157, when Valdemar the Great gave it to Bishop Absalon, who built a castle on what is now Christiansborg. It grew as a center on the Baltic trade route and became known as *købmændenes havn* (merchants' harbor) and eventually København. In the 15th century it became the royal residence and the capital of Norway and Sweden. A hundred years later, Christian IV, a Renaissance king obsessed with fine architecture, began a building boom that crowned the city with towers and castles, many of which still stand. They are almost all that remain of the city's 800-year history; much of Copenhagen was destroyed by two major fires in the 18th century and by British bombing during the Napoleonic Wars.

Despite a tumultuous history, Copenhagen survives as the liveliest Scandinavian capital. With its backdrop of copper towers and crooked rooftops, the venerable city is amused by playful street musicians and performers, soothed by one of the highest standards of living in the world, and spangled by the thousand lights and gardens of Tivoli.

EXPLORING COPENHAGEN

The sites in Copenhagen rarely jump out at you; the city's elegant spires and tangle of cobbled one-way streets are best sought out on foot at an unhurried pace. Excellent bus and train systems can come to the rescue of weary legs. The city is not divided into single-purpose districts; people work, play, shop, and live throughout the central core of this multilayered, densely populated capital.

Be it sea or canal, water surrounds Copenhagen. A network of bridges and drawbridges connects the two main islands—Zealand and Amager—on which Copenhagen is built. The seafaring atmosphere is indelible, especially around Nyhavn and Christianshavn.

Some Copenhagen sights, especially churches, keep short hours, particularly in fall and winter. It's a good idea to call directly or check with the tourist offices to confirm opening times.

When you arrive in the city, get settled in your hotel, turn in for a good night's sleep, and get yourself ready for some serious walking. Copenhagen maps out perfectly for the pedestrian, with nearly all the main attractions less than a half-hour's walk from Christiansborg Slot, at the center of downtown. If you're in town for an extended visit or would rather save your legs, the subway, bus, and suburban S-train networks can take you wherever you want to go.

If you have 3 days

Begin your first day at Rådhus Pladsen (City Hall Square) and follow Strøget, a pedestrian-only avenue, toward Nyhavn. Leave Strøget briefly at Amagertorv to visit the parliament building, Christiansborg; then, return to Strøget and make your way to the waterfront, all the while training an occasional glance at the shop windows in case anything catches your eye. Nyhavn is a good place to rest and refuel. You could take this opportunity to sample a classic Danish lunch of smørrebrød washed down with beer and *snaps* (schnapps). After lunch, head up to the royal palace of Amalienborg and take some time to explore the Bredgade area and find your way back to your hotel. If the weather is nice, the evening can be spent in Tivoli, but have your dinner outside the park to avoid the exorbitant prices. Early on the second day, take a boat excursion to see the city and its famed *Den Lille Havfrue (The Little Mermaid)* statue from the harbor. If you would prefer to get off and take pictures at the statue, make sure to take a DFDS Seaways sightseeing boat. In the afternoon, cross the inner harbor to the neighborhood of Christianshavn for a stroll along its canals toward Vor Frelsers Kirken (Church of Our Savior), where you can have a great aerial view of Copenhagen from the unique spire. This route leads you past the alternative compound of Christiania—settled by hippies in the 1970s—and beyond to the exclusive neighborhood of Holmen. The third day of your stay ought to be spent exploring the outlying Vesterbro neighborhood, with its cafés and shops. For art-lovers, the Ny Carlsberg Glyptotek would make a good several-hour detour on the way down Vesterbrogade.

If you have 7 days

Spend the first three days of your week as outlined above. The fourth and fifth days of your itinerary should be used to visit a few more of Copenhagen's fine museums. Among the best remaining are Rosenborg Slot and the Dansk Design Center, neither of which should be missed. A morning visit to Rosenborg Slot can be followed by an afternoon tour of the botanical gardens and a dinner in Nørrebro. Alternatively, you could head north from the castle and while away the afternoon along the paths and moats of Churchill Park, grabbing your evening meal in Østerbro. The final two days should be spent on day trips outside of the city proper. A day in Charlottenlund should begin with the astounding French impressionism collection at the Ordrupgaard, which can be followed with a snack at the adjacent café and a few hours at the town's pleasant beach, which is considerably less crowded during the week. Use the final day to skip town again for the verdant Deer Park in Klampenborg, or the seaside town of Dragør.

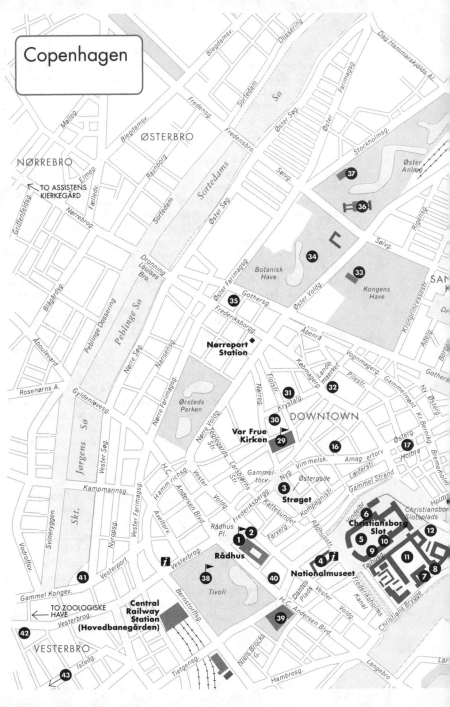

Copenhagen

NØRREBRO

ØSTERBRO

TO ASSISTENS
KIERKEGÅRD

Botanisk
Have

Kongens
Have

Nørreport
Station

Ørsteds
Parken

DOWNTOWN

Vor Frue
Kirken

Rådhus
Pl.

Rådhus

Strøget

Christiansborg
Slot

Nationalmuseet

Tivoli

TO ZOOLOGISKE
HAVE

Central
Railway
Station
(Hovedbanegården)

VESTERBRO

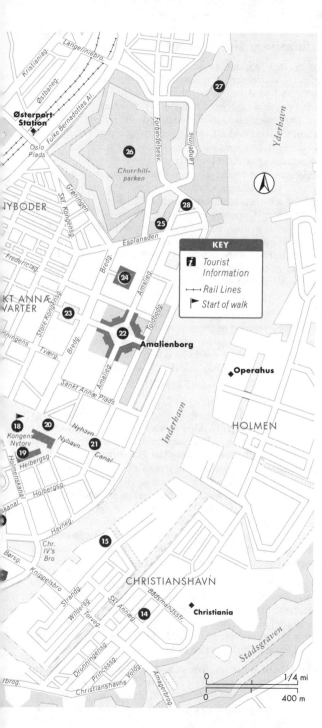

Rådhus Pladsen, Christiansborg Slot & Strøget

In 1728 and again in 1795, fires broke out in central Copenhagen with devastating effect. Disaster struck again in 1807, when the British fleet, under the command of Admiral Gambier, unleashed a heavy bombardment on the city and destroyed many of its oldest and most beautiful buildings. The attack also inflicted hundreds of civilian casualties. These events still shape modern Copenhagen, which was rebuilt with wide, curved-corner streets—making it easier for fire trucks to turn—and large, rectangular apartment buildings centered on courtyards. Arguably the liveliest area of the city, central Copenhagen is packed with shops, restaurants, businesses, and apartment buildings, as well as the crowning architectural achievements of Christian IV—all of it overflowing with Danes and visitors. Copenhagen's central spine consists of the five consecutive pedestrian strands known as Strøget and the surrounding tangle of roads and courtyards—less than a mile square in total. Across the capital's main harbor is the smaller, 17th-century Christianshavn. In the early 1600s this area was mostly a series of shallows between land, which were eventually dammed. Today Christianshavn's colorful boats and postcard maritime character make it one of the toniest parts of town.

a good walk

The city's heart is the Rådhus Pladsen, home to the baroque-style **Rådhus ❶** ⌐ and its clock tower. On the east side of the square is the landmark **Lurblæserne ❷**. Off the square's northeastern corner is Frederiksberggade, the first of the five pedestrian streets making up **Strøget ❸**, Copenhagen's shopping district. Walk northeast past the cafés and trendy boutiques to the double square of Gammeltorv and Nytorv.

Down Rådhusstræde toward Frederiksholms Kanal, the **Nationalmuseet ❹** contains an amazing collection of Viking artifacts. Cross Frederiksholms Kanal to Christiansborg Slotsplads, a small atoll divided by the canal and dominated by the burly **Christiansborg Slot ❺**. North of the castle is **Thorvaldsens Museum ❻**, devoted to the works of one of Denmark's most important sculptors, Bertel Thorvaldsen. On the south end of Downtown is the three-story Romanesque **Kongelige Bibliotek ❼**, edged by carefully tended gardens and tree-lined avenues. To the south, on the harbor side of the royal library, is its glass-and-granite annex, nicknamed the "Black Diamond." The newest addition to the library complex is the **Dansk Jødisk Museum ❽**. Back on the south face of Christiansborg are the **Teatermuseet ❾** and the **Kongelige Stald ❿**.

On the street that bears its name is the **Tøjhusmuseet ⓫**, and a few steps away are the architecturally marvelous **Børsen ⓬** and the **Holmens Kirke ⓭**. To the southeast is **Christianshavn**, connected to downtown by the drawbridge Knippelsbro. Farther north, the former Holmen shipyard houses major institutions, several departments of Københavns Universitet, and the new Opera House, which opened in January 2005.

From nearly anywhere in the area you can see the green-and-gold spire of **Vor Frelsers Kirken ⓮**. Northwest of the church, the **Dansk Arkitektur Center ⓯** occupies a hulking old warehouse on Strandgade. Back across the Knippels Torvegade Bridge, about 1½ km (less than a mile) down

Børgsgade through Højbroplads, is Amagertorv, one of Strøget's five streets. Farther west down the street is the 18th-century **Helligaandskirken ⑯**. On Strøget's Østergade, the massive spire of **Nikolaj Kirken ⑰** looks many sizes too large for the tiny cobblestone streets below.

TIMING The walk itself takes about 2 hours. Typically, Christiansborg Slot and its ruins and the Nationalmuseet both take at least 1½ hours to see— even more for Viking fans. The hundreds of shops along Strøget are enticing, so plan extra shopping and café time—at least as much as your wallet can spare. Note that many attractions on this walk are closed Sunday or Monday, and some have odd hours; always call ahead or check with the tourist information office.

What to See

⑫ Børsen (Stock Exchange). This masterpiece of fantasy and architecture is the oldest stock exchange in Europe. The Børsen was built between 1619 and 1640, with the majority of the construction in the 1620s. Christian IV commissioned the building in large part because he wanted to make Denmark the economic superpower and crossroads of Europe. Rumor has it that when it was being built he was the one who twisted the dragons' tails on the spire that tops the building. When it was first opened, it was used as a sort of medieval mall, filled with shopping stalls. Though parts of the Børsen still operate as a stock exchange, the bulk of the building houses the Chamber of Commerce, and therefore it's open only to accredited members and brokers. ⊠ *Christiansborg Slotspl., Downtown.*

off the
beaten
path

★ **CHRISTIANIA** – If you are nostalgic for 1960s counterculture, head to this anarchists' commune on Christianshavn. Founded in 1971, when students occupied army barracks, it is now a peaceful community of nonconformists who run a number of businesses, including a bike shop, bakery, rock-music club, and communal bathhouse. Wall cartoons preach drugs and peace, but the inhabitants are less fond of cameras—picture-taking is forbidden. ⊠ *Prinsesseg. and Bådsmandsstr., Christianshavn* ☎ *32/57–60–05 guided tours* ⊕ *www.christiania.org/folderus.*

❺
Fodor'sChoice
★ **Christiansborg Slot** (Christiansborg Castle). Surrounded by canals on three sides, the massive granite castle is where the queen officially receives guests. From 1441 until the fire of 1795, it was used as the royal residence. Even though the first two castles on the site were burned, Christiansborg remains an impressive baroque compound, even by European standards. Free tours of the **Folketinget** (Parliament House; ☎ 33/37–55–00 ⊕ www.folketinget.dk) are given Monday through Saturday from June to mid-August, as well as on Sunday from July to mid-August; tours run Sunday to Friday from mid-August through September, and on weekdays from October through April. English-language groups begin at 2. At the **Kongelige Repræsantationlokaler** (Royal Reception Chambers; ☎ 33/92–64–92), you're asked to don slippers to protect the floors. Admission is DKr 60; entry is via guided tour only. Tours are given daily May through September, and Tuesday, Thursday, and weekends from October through April; English-language tours are at 11, 1,

CloseUp
COUNTERCULTURAL CHRISTIANIA

A SMALL COMMUNITY in the middle of Copenhagen, occupying an area no bigger than a hundred acres, is the true heart and soul of the 1960s counterculture revolution. Christiania, originally designed as an anarchist's commune, has been a safe haven from the vagaries of modern city life for more than thirty years. Christiania was built on the foundations of self-government, communal living, and freedom. Without automobile traffic and street lights, Christiania begets an idyllic charm. Certainly other places in the world resemble Christiania in spirit—the Haight-Ashbury district in San Francisco comes to mind—but none can match Christiania's salt-of-the-earth feel. Today, the village stands as a utopian experiment.

A friend and I were met with a questioning glance when we asked our Danish taxi driver to take us to Christiania. The area, we would soon learn, is viscerally divisive among the Danish population, who consider it either a project in communal cooperation or a national eyesore. It's been recognized by the government of Denmark as a "free zone," which means that the village governs itself. As we passed through the village gates, a sign overhead clued us into the culture we were about to dive into: "You are now leaving the E.U."

On the outside, Christiania might seem like a rundown Jamaican shantytown, but the warmth of Christianians more than makes up for their lack of comfortable housing. Greenery overhangs ledges and runs down walls, in stark contrast to the ubiquitous graffiti art, created (legally) by village residents. There are no street lights, no cars—nothing that would keep the village from being a creative, free-thinking haven. This means that there are also no hard drugs (marijuana is allowed), violence, or weapons.

Once inside Christiania, we noticed a high number of atypical restaurants. An outdoor fast-food joint in the center of the village, for example, served consistently engaging Thai food. We also discovered tons of bars and clubs along the main drag, Prinsessegade. Our favorite was Woodstock. They serve premium Danish lagers for a reasonable sum and stay open until the last paying customer leaves. Across from Woodstock is Musikloppen, an infamous music club within Christiania known for attracting popular Danish rock bands (such as Kashmir) as well as the occasional international act (like The Fugees). The staff behind the bar may seem contemptuous to outsiders at first, but they're warm and welcoming to foreigners who have an open mind.

As we made our way around Christiania, we noticed a certain slogan everywhere: "Bevar Christiania," or "Save Christiania." The slogan has become a common saying among Christianians, nearly replacing the standard goodbye and hello in Danish because of the current political debate surrounding the village. Although Christiania is an autonomous community within Copenhagen, some people are looking to close the village down because residents don't own their houses, and, as such, are seen as squatters. A strong, outside police presence is now in the village—one that many Christianians consider harassment. Only time will tell if the villagers' self-reliant way of life will continue as it has for decades, or disappear as a footnote in Danish history.

–Nima Adl

and 3. The **Højesteret** (Supreme Court), on the site of the city's first fortress, was built by Bishop Absalon in 1167. The guards at the entrance are knowledgeable and friendly; call them first to double-check the court's complicated opening hours.

While the castle was being rebuilt around 1900, the Nationalmuseet excavated the **ruins** (☏ 33/92–64–92) beneath it. The resulting dark, subterranean maze contains fascinating models and architectural relics. The ruins are open October through April, daily 10–4, and admission is DKr 25.

Wander around **Højbro Plads** and the delightful row of houses that borders the northern edge of Slotsholmen. The quays here were long ago Copenhagen's fish market, but today most fresh fish is transported directly from boats to the city's fish shops and supermarkets. However, one lone fisherwoman still hawks fresh fish, marinated herring, and eel in the early morning. She is the last fishmonger you'll see carrying on the tradition. ✉ *Prins Jørgens Gård 1, Downtown.*

Christianshavn. Cobbled avenues, antique street lamps, and Left Bank charm make up one of the oldest neighborhoods in the city. Even the old system of earthworks—the best preserved of Copenhagen's original fortification walls—still exists. In the 17th century, Christian IV offered what were patches of partially flooded land for free, and with additional tax benefits; in return, takers would have to fill them in and construct sturdy buildings for trade, commerce, housing for the shipbuilding workers, and defense against sea attacks. Gentrified today, the area harbors restaurants, cafés, and shops, and its ramparts are edged with green areas and walking paths, making it the perfect neighborhood for an afternoon or evening amble. The central square, Christianshavn Torv, is where all activity emanates from, and Torvegade, a bustling shopping street, is the main thoroughfare. For a pleasant break, relax at one of the cafés along Wilders Canal, which streams through the heart of town.

⓯ Dansk Arkitektur Center. The Danish Architecture Center occupies an old wharf-side warehouse built in 1880. The hulking structure fell into a state of disrepair after lying fallow for many years, but was rescued, renovated, and reopened in 1986. The center hosts rotating exhibitions that cover trends and trendsetters in Danish architecture and architectural design. ✉ *Strandg. 27B, Christianshavn* ☏ *32/57–19–30* ⊕ *www.dac. dk* ✉ *DKr 40; exhibitions vary* ⊙ *Weekdays 10–5.*

❽ Dansk Jødisk Museum (Danish Jewish Museum). In a wing of the Royal Library, this national center of Jewish culture, art, and history opened in June 2004. Objects of both secular and religious interest are on display, including paintings, prints, jewelry, scrapbooks, films, and much more. The site was designed by Daniel Libeskind, the architect behind the winning design proposal for the World Trade Center memorial in New York City. The museum also gives extensive coverage to the Danish resistance movement, whose work during World War II helped bring nearly all of Denmark's 7,000 Jews to safety in Sweden. The museum is the first minority museum in the country. ✉ *Proviantpassegen. 6, Down-*

town ☎ *33/11–22–18* ⊕ *www.jewmus.dk* 🎫 *DKr 40* ⊙ *June–Aug.,*
Tues.–Sun. 10–5; Sept.–May., Tues.–Fri. 1–4, weekends 11–5.

⑯ Helligaandskirken (Church of the Holy Ghost). This 18th-century church
was founded by an abbey of the Holy Ghost and is still one of the city's
oldest places of worship. Its choir contains a font by the sculptor Thorvaldsen, and more modern art is found in the large exhibition room—
once a hospital—that faces Strøget. ✉ *Niels Hemmingsensg. 5,*
Amagertorv section, Downtown ☎ *33/18–16–45* ⊕ *www.*
helligaandskirken.dk 🎫 *Free* ⊙ *Weekdays 9–1, Sat. 10–noon.*

> **off the beaten path**

HOLMEN – Previously isolated from central Copenhagen, this former
navy base just north of Christianshavn produced ships and
ammunition until the 1980s. It was formally opened as the site of the
1995 United Nations Summit on Human Development and played an
important role as a cultural area during Copenhagen's 1996 reign as
the Cultural Capital of Europe. Today, among its several cultural
venues is the city's biggest performance space, the Torpedo Hall,
where torpedoes were actually assembled. You'll also find the Danish
Art Academy's Architecture School, the National Theater School, the
Rhythmic Music Conservatory, and the Danish Film School, all of
which host special activities. The most famous new resident is, of
course, the new Opera House, that opened in 2005 at a cost of DKr
2.5 billion.

⑬ Holmens Kirke (Islet's Church). Two of the country's most revered naval
heroes are buried here: Niels Juel crushed the Swedish fleet at Køge in
1677, and Peder Tordenskjold defeated Charles XII of Sweden during
the Great Northern War in the early 18th century. ✉ *Holmenskanal,*
Christianshavn ☎ *33/11–37–40* ⊕ *www.holmenskirke.dk* 🎫 *Free*
⊙ *Weekdays 9–2, Sat. 9–noon, Sun. during services.*

> **need a break?**

Øieblikket Espresso Bar m.m (✉ Søren Kierkegaards Pl. 1,
Downtown ☎ 33/47–49–50) operates out of a prime corner on the
ground floor of the Royal Library's Black Diamond. The "m.m" in
the name means "and more." It's named after a literary journal to
which philosopher Søren Kierkegaard once contributed—and you,
too, may be inspired to wax poetic as you gaze out over the harbor
and bask in the sunlight streaming through the soaring glass walls. In
summer the café sets up outdoor tables. When summer days turn
nippy you can stay snug indoors, while enjoying the illusion of being
outside, thanks to the natural light that floods in at all angles. The
simple fare includes croissants, brownies, and sandwiches made on
fluffy round buns.

❼ Kongelige Bibliotek (Royal Library). The Royal Library houses the country's largest collection of books, newspapers, and manuscripts. Among
the more than 2 million volumes are accounts of Viking journeys to
America and Greenland and original manuscripts by Hans Christian
Andersen and Karen Blixen (Isak Dinesen). If you happen to be in the

area, ramble around the statue of philosopher Søren Kierkegaard (1813–55), the formal gardens, and tree-lined avenues surrounding the building. The library's massive glass-and-granite annex, called the Black Diamond, looms between the main building and the waterfront. The Black Diamond hosts temporary historical exhibits that often feature books, manuscripts, and artifacts culled from the library's extensive holdings. The **National Museum of Photography,** also housed in the Black Diamond, contains a far-reaching collection of more than 25,000 Danish and international photographs, from which temporary exhibits display selections. ⊠ *Søren Kierkegaards Pl. 1, Downtown* ☎ *33/ 47–47–47* ⊕ *www.kb.dk* ⌨ *Library free, temporary exhibits DKr 30* ⊙ *Library and museum Mon.–Sat. 10–7.*

❿ **Kongelige Stald** (Royal Stables). Between 9 and noon, time seems to stand still while riders, elegantly clad in breeches and jackets, exercise the horses. The vehicles, including coaches and carriages, and harnesses on display have been used by the Danish monarchy from 1778 to the present. ⊠ *Christiansborg Ridebane 12, Downtown* ☎ *33/40–10–10* ⌨ *DKr 20* ⊙ *May–Sept., Fri.–Sun. 2–4; Oct.–Apr., weekends 2–4.*

❷ **Lurblæserne** (Lur Blower Column). Topped by two Vikings blowing an ancient trumpet called a *lur,* this column displays a good deal of artistic license—the lur dates from the Bronze Age, 1500 BC, whereas the Vikings lived a mere 1,000 years ago. City tours often start at this important landmark, which was erected in 1914. ⊠ *East side of Rådhus Pl., Downtown.*

★ ☾ ❹ **Nationalmuseet** (National Museum). An 18th-century royal residence, peaked by massive overhead windows, has contained—since the 1930s— what is regarded as one of the best national museums in Europe. Extensive permanent exhibits chronicle Danish cultural history from prehistoric to modern times—included is one of the largest collections of Stone Age tools in the world—and Egyptian, Greek, and Roman antiquities are on display. The children's museum, with replicas of period clothing and all sorts of touchable items, transforms history into something to which children under age 12 can relate. ⊠ *Ny Vesterg. 10, Downtown* ☎ *33/13–44–11* ⊕ *www.natmus.dk* ⌨ *DKr 50, free Wed.* ⊙ *Tues.–Sun. 10–5.*

⓱ **Nikolaj Kirken** (Nicholas Church). Though the green spire of the imposing church—named for the patron saint of seafarers—appears as old as the surrounding medieval streets, it is actually relatively young. The current building was finished in 1914; the previous structure, which dated from the 13th century, was destroyed in the 1795 fire. Today the church is a contemporary art gallery and exhibition center that often shows experimental work. ⊠ *Nikolaj Pl. 10, Downtown* ☎ *33/93–16–26* ⊕ *www. nikolaj-ccac.dk* ⌨ *DKr 20, free Wed.* ⊙ *Daily noon—5.*

need a break? | **Café Nikolaj** (⊠ Nikolajpl., Downtown ☎ 33/93–16–26), inside Nikolaj Kirken, is a reliable, inexpensive café with good pastries and light meals. It's open noon to 3 for lunch and until 5 for cakes and drinks. From June through August, you can eat on the open terrace.

▶ **❶ Rådhus** (City Hall). Completed in 1905, the mock-Renaissance building dominates **Rådhus Pladsen** (City Hall Square), the hub of Copenhagen's commercial district. Architect Martin Nyrop's creation was popular from the start, perhaps because he envisioned that it should give "gaiety to everyday life and spontaneous pleasure to all . . ." A statue of Copenhagen's 12th-century founder, Bishop Absalon, sits atop the main entrance.

Besides being an important ceremonial meeting place for Danish VIPs, the intricately decorated Rådhus contains the first **World Clock**. The multidial, superaccurate astronomical timepiece has a 570,000-year calendar and took inventor Jens Olsen 27 years to complete before it was put into action in 1955. If you're feeling energetic, take a guided tour up the 350-foot bell tower for the panoramic, but not particularly inspiring, view.

The modern glass-and-gray-steel **bus terminal** flanking the square's northwest side has French granite floors, pear-tree-wood shelving, and underground marble bathrooms. The $2.8 million creation proved so architecturally contentious—more for its placement than for its design—that there was serious discussion of moving it.

Look up to see one of the city's most charming bronze sculptures, created by the Danish artist E. Utzon Frank in 1936. Diagonally across Rådhus Pladsen, atop a corner office building, are a **neon thermometer** and a **gilded barometer**. On sunny days there's a golden sculpture of a girl on a bicycle; come rain, a girl with an umbrella appears. ✉ *Rådhus Pl., Downtown* ☎ *33/66–25–82* 🖭 *Tower tours DKr 20* ☉ *Rådhus weekdays 8–5. Tours Oct.–May, Mon.–Sat. at noon; June–Sept., weekdays at 10, noon, and 2, Sat. at noon.*

need a break? **Vandkunsten** (✉ Rådhusstr. 17, Downtown ☎ 33/13–90–40) is a mom-and-pop joint that makes great Italian-inspired sandwiches and salads, and they offer free coffee while you wait. The shop is tiny, but the efficient service keeps customers moving. There is only one table inside and it's usually surrounded by customers; so long as the weather is nice, get something to go and seek out a sunny spot for munching.

★ **❸ Strøget.** Though it is referred to by one name, the city's pedestrian spine, pronounced *Stroy-et*, is actually a series of five streets: Frederiksberggade, Nygade, Vimmelskaftet, Amagertorv, and Østergade. By mid-morning, particularly on Saturday, it is congested with people, baby strollers, and street performers. Past the swank and trendy, and sometimes flashy and trashy, boutiques of **Frederiksberggade** is the double square of **Gammeltorv** (Old Square) and **Nytorv** (New Square), in summer often crowded with street vendors selling cheap jewelry.

In 1728 and again in 1795, much of Strøget was heavily damaged by fire. When rebuilding, the city fathers straightened and widened the streets. You can still see buildings from this reconstruction period, as well as a few that survived the fires.

In addition to shopping, you can enjoy Strøget for strolling, as hundreds do. Outside the posh fur and porcelain shops and bustling cafés and restaurants, the sidewalks have a festive street-fair atmosphere.

⑨ Teatermuseet (Theater Museum). After you brush up on theater and ballet history, wander around the boxes, stage, and dressing rooms of the **Royal Court Theater** of 1767, which King Christian VII had built as the first court theater in Scandinavia. Tours can be arranged. ⊠ *Christiansborg Ridebane 10/18, Downtown* ⊕ *33/11–51–76* ⊕ *www. teatermuseet.dk* ⊠ *DKr 30* ⊙ *Tues.–Thurs. 11–3, weekends 1–4.*

⑥ Thorvaldsens Museum. The 19th-century artist Bertel Thorvaldsen (1770–1844) is buried at the center of this museum in a simple, ivy-covered tomb. Strongly influenced by the statues and reliefs of classical antiquity, he is recognized as one of the world's greatest neoclassical artists, having completed commissions all over Europe. The museum, once a coach house for Christiansborg, now houses Thorvaldsen's interpretations of classical and mythological figures, and an extensive collection of paintings and drawings by other artists that Thorvaldsen assembled while living—for most of his life—in Rome. The outside frieze by Jørgen Sonne depicts the sculptor's triumphant return to Copenhagen after years abroad. ⊠ *Bertel Thorvaldsen Pl. 2, Downtown* ☎ *33/32–15–32* ⊕ *www.thorvaldsensmuseum.dk* ⊠ *DKr 20, free Wed.* ⊙ *Tues.–Sun. 10–5. Guided tours in English Sun. at 3.*

⑪ Tøjhusmuseet (Royal Danish Arsenal Museum). This Renaissance structure—built by King Christian IV and one of central Copenhagen's oldest—contains impressive displays of uniforms, weapons, and armor in a 600-foot-long arched hall. ⊠ *Tøjhusg. 3, Downtown* ☎ *33/11–60–37* ⊕ *www.thm.dk* ⊠ *DKr 40* ⊙ *Aug.–June, Tues.–Sun. noon–4; July, daily 10–4.*

⑭ Vor Frelsers Kirken (Church of Our Savior). The green-and-gold spire of this baroque church has dominated the Christianshavn area since it was completed in 1752. Local legend has it that the staircase encircling it was built curling the wrong way around, and that when its architect, Laurids de Thurah, reached the top and realized what he'd done, he jumped. In this case, however, legend is erroneous: de Thurah died in his own bed in 1759. ⊠ *Skt. Annæg. 29, Christianshavn* ☎ *32/57–27–98* ⊕ *www.vorfrelserskirke.dk* ⊙ *Apr.–Aug., daily 11–4:30; Sept.–Mar., daily 11–3:30. Tower closed Nov.–Mar. and in inclement weather.*

Around Amalienborg & Points North

The Sankt Annæ Kvarter district of the city was dubbed New Copenhagen when King Christian IV began to expand the city northeastward in the 17th century, building Sankt Annæ Fort (now the Churchillparken and Kastellet) in the process. The district takes its name from the religious order of St. Anne, which valiantly staffed a 16th-century syphilis ward in the area.

North of Kongens Nytorv the city becomes a fidgety grid of parks and wider boulevards pointing northwest across the canal toward upscale

Østerbro—wreathed by manors commissioned by wealthy merchants and blue bloods. In the mid-1700s King Frederik V donated parcels of this land to anyone who agreed to build from the work of architect Niels Eigtved, who also designed the Kongelige Theater. The jewel of this crown remains Amalienborg and its rococo mansions.

a good walk

At the end of Strøget, **Kongens Nytorv** ⓲ ☛ is flanked on its south side by the **Kongelige Teater** ⓳ and backed by **Charlottenborg** ⓴, which contains the Danish Academy of Fine Art (call to see if an exhibition has opened the castle to the public). The street leading southeast from Kongens Nytorv is **Nyhavn** ㉑, a onetime sailors' haunt and now a popular waterfront hub. From the south end of the harbor (and the north end of Havnegade) high-speed craft leave for Malmö, Sweden; farther north, Kvæsthusbroen—at the end of Sankt Annæ Plads—is the quay for boats to Oslo, Norway, and Bornholm, Denmark; farther north still, just before the perch of *The Little Mermaid,* ships depart for Swinoujscie, Poland.

West of the harbor front is the grand square called Sankt Annæ Plads. Perpendicular to the oblong square is Amaliegade, its wooden colonnade bordering the cobbled square of **Amalienborg** ㉒, the royal residence with a pleasant garden on its harbor side. Steps west from the square is Bredgade, where the baroque **Marmorkirken** ㉓ flaunts its Norwegian marble structure. Farther north off Bredgade is the rococo **Kunstindustrimuseet** ㉔. Continuing north on Bredgade (you can also take the more colorful, café-lined Store Kongensgade, just west), turn right onto Esplanaden and you'll see the enormously informative **Frihedsmuseet** ㉕. At the Churchillparken's entrance stands the English church, St. Albans. In the park's center, the **Kastellet** ㉖ serves as a reminder of the city's grim military history. At its eastern perimeter is Langelinie, a waterfront promenade with a view of Denmark's best-known pinup, *Den Lille Havfrue* ㉗. Wending your way back toward Esplanaden and the town center, you'll pass the **Gefion Springvandet** ㉘.

TIMING   This walk amid parks, gardens, canals, and building exteriors should take a full day. If the weather is nice, linger in the parks, especially the Kastellet and Amalienhaven, and plan on a long lunch at Nyhavn. The Kunstindustrimuseet merits about an hour, more if you plan on perusing the design books in the museum's well-stocked library. The Frihedsmuseet may require more time: its evocative portrait of Danish life during World War II intrigues even the most history-weary teens. Avoid taking this tour Monday, when some sites are closed.

What to See

㉒ **Amalienborg** (Amalia's Castle). The four identical rococo buildings occupying this square have housed the royals since 1784. The Christian VIII palace across from the queen's residence houses the **Amalienborg Museum,** which displays the second part of the Royal Collection (the first is at Rosenborg Slot) and chronicles royal lifestyles between 1863 and 1947. Here you can view the study of King Christian IX (1818–1906) and the drawing room of his wife, Queen Louise. Rooms are packed with family gifts and regal baubles ranging from tacky knickknacks to Fabergé treasures, including a nephrite-and-ruby table clock, and a small costume collection.

THE DANISH ROYALS

HE EQUITABLE DANES *may believe that excessive pride is best kept hidden, but ask about their Queen and this philosophy promptly flies out the window. The passion for Queen Margrethe II is infectious, and before long you may find yourself waving the Dannebrog flag along with the rest of them when the Queen passes through. Graceful and gregarious, Queen Margrethe II is the embodiment of the new Danish crown, a monarchy that is steeped in history yet decidedly modern in its outlook.*

Denmark's royal lineage has its roots in the 10th-century Kingdom of Gorm the Old. His son, Harald Bluetooth, established the royal headquarters in Zealand, where it remains to this day. Copenhagen's stately Amalienborg Slot has been the official royal residence since 1784. From here Queen Margrethe reigns in a true Danish style marked by sociability, not stuffiness. Renowned for her informal charm, the Queen has fostered an open, familial relationship between the royal house and the Danish public. Queen Margrethe's nurturing role has evolved naturally in a country of Denmark's petite size and population. Though she lives in Copenhagen, the Queen is far from Zealand-bound.

Margrethe wasn't always destined to be queen. When she was born in 1940, the law of succession was limited to sons, and it wasn't until 1953 that the law was ratified to include female accession of the throne. She was groomed to become queen, and on her 18th birthday stepped into her position as heir apparent to the crown. She studied archaeology and political science both at home and abroad, at the Universities of Copenhagen, Århus, Cambridge, and the Sorbonne. In 1967 Margrethe

married Prince Henrik, born a count near Cahors, France.

Today's modern monarchy is perhaps best exemplified by what the Queen does when she takes off her crown. An accomplished artist and illustrator, the Queen designed the costumes for an acclaimed television production of Hans Christian Andersen's The Shepherdess and the Chimney Sweep. She also illustrated an edition of J. R. R. Tolkien's The Lord of the Rings. Her paintings have been exhibited in galleries, where they command top prices, all of which she donates to charity.

If there's anyone in the royal circle who has captured the public's hearts like Queen Margrethe once did, it's Hong Kong–born Princess Alexandra, who married Prince Joachim in 1995, but divorced him in 2004. The Princess not only cuts a gracious figure in her gown and crown, but has also endeared herself forever to the Danes, and to the Queen Mother, by learning to speak flawless Danish and—here's the topper—with hardly a trace of an accent. The birth of two sons, Nikolai and Felix, has not diminished her popularity. Although divorced, the couple is friendly and can be seen together at some charitable functions.

Crown Prince Frederik (born in 1968), the future king, married Australian Mary Donaldson in 2004 at Copenhagen Cathedral. 180 million people worldwide watched the event. At this writing, they were expecting their first child in October 2005.

In the square's center is a magnificent equestrian statue of King Frederik V by the French sculptor Jacques François Joseph Saly. It reputedly cost as much as all the buildings combined. Every day at noon, the Royal Guard and band march from Rosenborg Slot through the city for the changing of the guard. At noon on Queen Margrethe's birthday, April 16, crowds of Danes gather to cheer their monarch, who stands and waves from her balcony. On Amalienborg's harbor side are the trees, gardens, and fountains of **Amalienhaven.** ✉ *Christian VIII's Palace–Amalienborg Pl., Sankt Annæ Kvarter* ☎ *33/12–21–86* ✆ *DKr 75* ⊙ *May–Oct., daily 10–4; Nov.–Apr., Tues.–Sun. 11–4. Guided tours in English July–Sept., weekends at 1* PM.

㉑ Charlottenborg (Charlotte's Castle). This Dutch baroque–style castle was built by Frederik III's half brother in 1670. Since 1754 the garden-flanked property has housed the faculty and students of the Danish Academy of Fine Art. It is open only during exhibits, which occur year-round. ✉ *Nyhavn 2, Downtown* ☎ *33/13–40–22* ⊕ *www. charlottenborg-art.dk* ✆ *DKr 30* ⊙ *During exhibitions, daily 10–5 (Wed. until 7).*

The Danish Museum of Art & Design. Key design figures such as Poul Henningsen, Kaare Klint, and Arne Jacobsen are prominenetly featured at this museum dedicated to all things design. Permanent exhibits include 20th-century Danish decorative art and industrial design, Chinese ceramics, 18th-century French and German porcelain industries, and English and French furniture. The museum first opened its doors to the public in 1895. ✉ *Bredgade 68, 1206 Kobenhavn* ☎ *33/18–56–56* ⊕ *www.kunstindustrimuseet.dk* ✆ *Dkr 40* ⊙ *Tues.–Fri. 10–4, Sat.–Sun. 12–4. Closed Mon.*

㉗ Den Lille Havfrue (*The Little Mermaid*). On the Langelinie promenade, this somewhat overhyped 1913 statue commemorates Hans Christian Andersen's lovelorn creation, and is the subject of hundreds of travel posters. Donated to the city by Carl Jacobsen, the son of the founder of Carlsberg Breweries, the innocent waif has also been the subject of some cruel practical jokes, including decapitation and the loss of an arm, but she is currently in one piece. Especially on a sunny Sunday, the Langelinie promenade is thronged with Danes and visitors making their pilgrimage to see the statue. On this occasion, you may want to read the original Hans Christian Andersen tale; it's a heart-wrenching story that's a far cry from the Disney animated movie. ✉ *Langelinie promenade, Østerbro.*

㉑ Det Kongelige Teater (The Royal Danish Theater). The stoic, pillared, and gallery-front theater is the country's preeminent venue for music, opera, ballet, and theater. Nearly all theater works performed are in Danish, while operas are in their original language with Danish over-titles on a screen above the stage. The Royal Danish Ballet performs on the older stage in the main building; its repertoire ranges from classical to modern works.

The current building was opened in 1874, though the annex, known as **Stærekassen** (Nesting Box) was not inaugurated until 1931. The Nesting Box got its name due to an obscure likeness to a birdhouse. Statues of Danish poet Adam Oehlenschläger and author Ludvig Holberg—whose works remain the core of Danish theater—flank the facade. Born in Bergen, Norway, in 1684, Holberg came to Denmark as a student and stayed. Often compared to Molière, he wrote 32 of his comedies in a "poetic frenzy" between 1722 and 1728, and legend has it that he complained of interminable headaches the entire time. He published the works himself, made an enormous fortune, and invested in real estate. In the mid-'90s an annex designed by Norwegian architect Sverre Fehn was planned for construction on the eastern side of the theater, but it has yet to open. The theater closes for the summer months. ⊠ *Tordenskjoldsg. 3, Downtown* ☎ *33/69–69–33, 33/69–69–69 for tickets* ⊕ *www.kgl-teater.dk* ⊠ *Guided tours DKr 75* ⊙ *Guided tours Sun. at 11; no tours May 27–Aug. 5.*

㉕ **Frihedsmuseet** (Resistance Museum). Evocative, sometimes moving displays commemorate the heroic Danish resistance movement, which saved 7,000 Jews from the Nazis by hiding and then smuggling them to Sweden. The homemade tank outside was used to spread the news of the Nazi surrender after World War II. ⊠ *Churchillparken, Sankt Annæ Kvarter* ☎ *33/13–77–14* ⊕ *www.frihedsmuseet.dk* ⊠ *DKr 40, free Wed.* ⊙ *May–mid-Sept., Tues.–Sat. 10–4, Sun. and holidays 10–5; mid-Sept.–Apr., Tues.–Sat. 10–3, Sun. and holidays 10–4.*

㉘ **Gefion Springvandet** (Gefion Fountain). Not far from *The Little Mermaid* yet another dramatic myth is illustrated. The goddess Gefion was promised as much of Sweden as she could plough in a night. The story goes that she changed her sons to oxen and used them to portion off what is now the island of Zealand. ⊠ *East of Frihedsmuseet, Sankt Annæ Kvarter.*

㉖ **Kastellet** (Citadel). At Churchill Park's entrance stands the spired Anglican (or Episcopal) church **St. Albans.** From there, walk north on the main path to reach the Citadel. The structure's smooth, peaceful walking paths, marina, and greenery belie its fierce past as a city fortification. Built in the aftermath of the Swedish siege of the city on February 10, 1659, the double moats were among the improvements made to the city's defense. The Citadel served as the city's main fortress into the 18th century; in a grim reversal during World War II, the Germans used it as headquarters during their occupation. ⊠ *Center of Churchill Park, Sankt Annæ Kvarter* ⊠ *Free* ⊙ *Daily 6 AM–dusk.*

⌐ ⑱ **Kongens Nytorv** (King's New Square). A mounted statue of Christian V dominates the square. Crafted in 1688 by the French sculptor Lamoureux, the subject is conspicuously depicted as a Roman emperor. Every year, at the end of June, graduating high school students arrive in horse-drawn carriages and dance beneath the furrowed brow of the sober statue. ⊠ *Between Gothersg., Holmenskanal, and Tordenskjoldsg., Downtown.*

need a break? Dozens of restaurants and cafés line Nyhavn. **Cap Horn** (⊠ Nyhavn 21, Downtown ☎ 33/12–85–04) is among the best, with moderately priced and completely organic Danish treats served in a cozy, art-filled dining room that resembles a ship's galley. Try the fried plaice swimming in a sea of parsley butter with boiled potatoes. In summertime try to grab a sidewalk table, the perfect place to enjoy an overstuffed focaccia sandwich and a Carlsberg.

㉔ Kunstindustrimuseet (Museum of Decorative Art). Originally built in the 18th century as a royal hospital, the fine rococo museum houses a large selection of European and Asian crafts. Also on display are ceramics, silverware, tapestries, and special exhibitions that often focus on contemporary design. The museum's excellent library is stocked with design books and magazines. A small café also operates here. ⊠ *Bredg. 68, Sankt Annæ Kvarter* 🕾 *33/18–56–56* ⊕ *www.kunstindustrimuseet. dk* 🖾 *DKr 40; additional fee for some special exhibits* ☉ *Permanent collection Tues.–Sun. noon–4, Wed. noon–6; special exhibits Tues.–Fri. 10–4 (Wed. 10–6), weekends noon–4.*

㉓ Marmorkirken (Marble Church). Officially the Frederikskirke, this ponderous baroque sanctuary of precious Norwegian marble was begun in 1749 and remained unfinished from 1770 to 1874 due to budget constraints. It was finally completed and consecrated in 1894. Around the exterior are 16 statues of various religious leaders from Moses to Luther, and below them stand sculptures of outstanding Danish ministers and bishops. The hardy can scale 273 steps to the outdoor balcony. From here you can walk past the exotic gilded onion domes of the **Russiske Ortodoks Kirke** (Russian Orthodox Church), just to the north of the Marmorkirken. ⊠ *Frederiksg. 4, off Bredg., Sankt Annæ Kvarter* 🕾 *33/12–01–44* ⊕ *www.marmorkirken.dk* 🖾 *Church free, tower DKr 20* ☉ *Mon., Tues., and Thurs. 10–5; Wed. 10–6; weekends noon–5. Guided tours mid-June–Aug., daily 1–3; Sept.–mid-June, weekends 1–3.*

★ **㉑ Nyhavn** (New Harbor). This harbor-front neighborhood was built 300 years ago to attract traffic and commerce to the city center. Until 1970 the area was a favorite haunt of sailors. Though restaurants, boutiques, and antiques stores now outnumber tattoo parlors, many old buildings have been well preserved and have retained the harbor's authentic 18th-century maritime character; you can even see a fleet of old-time sailing ships from the quay. Hans Christian Andersen lived at various times in the Nyhavn houses at numbers 18, 20, and 67.

Northwest toward Nørrebro

By the 1880s, many of the buildings that now line Nørrebro were being hastily thrown up as housing for area laborers. Many of these flats—typically decorated with a row of pedimented windows and a portal entrance—have been renovated through a massive urban-renewal program. But to this day, many fall flat of typical modern amenities. Due to the cheaper rents, an influx of young, hip inhabitants have begun to call this neighborhood home. On the Nørrebrogade and Sankt Hans Torv of today you'll discover a fair number of cafés, restaurants, clubs, and shops.

a good walk

Take the train from Østerport Station, off Oslo Plads, to Nørreport Station on Nørre Voldgade and walk down Fiolstræde to **Vor Frue Kirken** ㉙ ▶. The church's very tall copper spire and four shorter ones crown the area. Backtrack north on Fiolstræde, to the main building of **Københavns Universitet** ㉚; on the corner of Krystalgade is the **Københavns Synagoge** ㉛. Fiolstræde ends at the Nørreport train station. Perpendicular to Nørre Voldgade is Frederiksberggade, which leads northwest to the neighborhood of Nørrebro; to the southeast after the Kultorvet, or Coal Square, Frederiksberggade turns into the pedestrian street Købmagergade. From anywhere in the area, you can see the stout **Rundetårn** ㉜: the round tower stands as one of Copenhagen's most beloved landmarks, with an observatory open on autumn and winter evenings. North from the Rundetårn on Landemærket, Gothersgade gives way to **Rosenborg Slot** ㉝, its Dutch Renaissance design standing out against the vivid green of the well-tended Kongens Have. For a heavier dose of plants and living things, head across Øster Voldgade to the 25-acre **Botanisk Have** ㉞. South of the garden is the **Arbejdermuseet** ㉟, which profiles the lives of workers from the late 1800s to the present.

Leave the garden's north exit to reach the **Statens Museum for Kunst** ㊱, notable for exceptional Matisse works. An adjacent building houses **Den Hirschsprungske Samling** ㊲, with 19th-century Danish art on display. Nearby, on the east side of Øster Voldgade, is **Nyboder,** a neighborhood full of tidy homes built by Christian IV for the city's sailors.

TIMING   All of the sites on this tour are relatively close together and can be seen in roughly half a day. Note that some sites close Monday or Tuesday; call ahead. The tour can be easily combined with the one that follows—just head back to Nørreport Station and catch a train to Hovedbanegården.

What to See

㉟ **Arbejdermuseet** (Workers' Museum). The vastly underrated museum chronicles the working class from 1870 to the present, with evocative life-size "day-in-the-life-of" exhibits, including reconstructions of a city street and tram and an original apartment once belonging to a brewery worker, his wife, and eight children. Changing exhibits focusing on Danish and international social issues are often excellent. The museum also has a 19th-century-style restaurant serving old-fashioned Danish specialties and a '50s-style coffee shop. ⊠ *Rømersg. 22, Downtown* ☎ *33/ 93-25-75* ⊕ *www.arbejdermuseet.dk* ⊠ *DKr 50* ☉ *Daily 10–4.*

off the beaten path

★ **ASSISTENS KIRKEGÅRD** (Assistens Cemetery) – This peaceful, leafy cemetery in the heart of Nørrebro is the final resting place of numerous great Danes, including Søren Kierkegaard (whose last name means "church garden," or "cemetery"), Hans Christian Andersen, and physicist Niels Bohr. In summer the cemetery takes on a cheerful, city-park air as picnicking families, young couples, and sunbathers relax on the sloping lawns amid the dear departed. ⊠ *Kapelvej 2, Nørrebro* ☎ *35/37–19–17* ⊕ *www.assistens.dk* ⊠ *Free* ☉ *May–Aug., daily 8–8; Sept., Oct., Mar., and Apr., daily 8–6; Nov.–Feb., daily 8–4.*

At the bar-café-restaurant combo **Barstarten** (⊠ Kapelvej 1, Nørrebro ☎ 35/24–11–00 ⊕ www.barstarten.dk) you can get three squares, snacks, and a dizzying array of beverages. The kitchen whips up simple French-Italian country cooking and a new menu appears every two weeks. A favorite is Barstarten's Menu, a three-course affair with a wine list to accompany the food. DJs liven up the scene late on weekend nights with a soul-and-funk repertoire.

🥣 **Botanisk Have** (Botanical Garden). Trees, flowers, ponds, sculptures, and a spectacular 19th-century Palmehuset (Palm House) of tropical and subtropical plants blanket the garden's 25-plus acres. There's also an observatory and a geological museum. Take time to explore the gardens and watch the pensioners feed the birds. Some have been coming here so long that the birds actually alight on their fingers. ⊠ *Gothersg. 128, Sankt Annæ Kvarter* ☎ *35/32–22–40* ⊕ *www.botanic-garden.ku.dk* 🎫 *Free* ⊙ *May–Sept., daily 8:30–6; Oct.–Apr., Tues.–Sun. 8:30–4.*

🥣 **Den Hirschsprungske Samling** (The Hirschsprung Collection). This museum showcases paintings from the country's Golden Age—Denmark's mid-19th-century school of naturalism—as well as a collection of paintings by the late-19th-century artists of the Skagen School. Their luminous works capture the play of light and water so characteristic of the Danish countryside. ⊠ *Stockholmsg. 20, Østerbro* ☎ *35/42–03–36* ⊕ *www.hirschsprung.dk* 🎫 *DKr 35, free Wed.* ⊙ *Mon. and Wed.–Sun. 11–4.*

🥣 **Københavns Synagoge** (Copenhagen Synagogue). The contemporary architect Gustav Friedrich Hetsch borrowed from the Doric and Egyptian styles in creating this arklike synagogue. ⊠ *Krystalg. 12, Downtown* ☎ *33/12–88–88* ⊙ *Daily services 4:15.*

🥣 **Københavns Universitet** (Copenhagen University). The main building of Denmark's leading institution for higher learning was constructed in the 19th century on the site of a medieval bishops' palace. The university was founded nearby in 1479. ⊠ *Nørreg. 10, Downtown* ☎ *35/32–26–26* ⊕ *www.ku.dk.*

Near Copenhagen University is **Sømods Bolcher** (⊠ Nørreg. 24 or 36, Downtown ☎ 33/12–60–46), a Danish confectioner that has been on the scene since the late 19th century. Children and candy-lovers relish seeing the hard candy pulled and cut by hand.

Nyboder. Tour the neat, mustard-color enclave of Nyboder, a perfectly laid-out compound of flat, long, former sailors' homes built by Christian IV. Like Nyhavn, the area was seedy and boisterous at the beginning of the 1970s, but today has become one of Copenhagen's more fashionable neighborhoods. At **Nyboder Mindestuer** (⊠ Skt. Paulsg. 24, Christianshavn ☎ 33/32–10–05 🎫 DKr 10) you can view an exhibition of everyday life in Nyboder from its inception in 1631 to the present day. The people at this exhibition center also arrange guided tours of the neighborhood. ⊠ *West of Store Kongensg. and east of Rigensg., Sankt Annæ Kvarter.*

③③ Rosenborg Slot (Rosenborg Castle). This Dutch Renaissance castle con-
Fodor's Choice tains ballrooms, halls, and reception chambers, but for all of its grandeur,
★ there's an intimacy that makes you think the king might return any minute.
Thousands of objects are displayed, including beer glasses, gilded clocks,
golden swords, family portraits, a pearl-studded saddle, and gem-encrusted
tables; an adjacent treasury contains the royal jewels. The castle's setting is equally welcoming: it's in the middle of the **Kongens Have** (King's
Garden), amid lawns, park benches, and shady walking paths.

King Christian IV built Rosenborg Castle as a summer residence but loved
it so much that he ended up living and dying here. In 1849, when the
absolute monarchy was abolished, all the royal castles became state property, except for Rosenborg, which is still passed down from monarch
to monarch. Once a year, during the fall holiday, the castle stays open
until midnight, and visitors are invited to explore its darkened interior
with bicycle lights. ⊠ *Øster Voldg. 4A, Sankt Annæ Kvarter* ☎ *33/
15–32–86* 💷 *DKr 65* ☉ *Nov.–Apr., Tues.–Sun. 11–2; May and Sept.,
daily 10–4; June–Aug., daily 10–5; Oct., daily 11–3.*

★ **③② Rundetårn** (Round Tower). Instead of climbing the stout Round Tower's
stairs, visitors scale a smooth, 600-foot spiral ramp on which—legend
has it—Peter the Great of Russia rode a horse alongside his wife, Catherine, who took a carriage. From its top, you enjoy a panoramic view of
the twisted streets and crooked roofs of Copenhagen. The unusual
building was constructed as an observatory in 1642 by Christian IV and
is still maintained as the oldest such structure in Europe.

The art gallery has changing exhibits, and occasional concerts are held
within its massive stone walls. An observatory and telescope are open
to the public evenings mid-October through March, and an astronomer
is on hand to answer questions. ⊠ *Købmagerg. 52A, Downtown* ☎ *33/
73–03–73* ⊕ *www.rundetaarn.dk* 💷 *DKr 20* ☉ *Sept.–May, Mon.–Sat.
10–5, Sun. noon–5; June–Aug., Mon.–Sat. 10–8, Sun. noon–8. Observatory mid-Oct.–Mar., Tues. and Wed. 7 PM–10 PM.*

③⑥ Statens Museum for Kunst (National Art Gallery). Old-master paintings—
including works by Rubens, Rembrandt, Titian, El Greco, and Frago-
nard—as well as a comprehensive array of antique and 20th-century
Danish art make up the gallery collection. Also notable is the modern
art, which includes pieces by a very small but select group of artists, including Henri Matisse, Edvard Munch, Henri Laurens, Emil Nolde, and
Georges Braque. The space also contains a children's museum, an amphitheater, a documentation center and study room, a bookstore, and
a restaurant. A sculpture garden filled with classical, modern, and whimsical pieces flanks the building. ⊠ *Sølvg. 48–50, Sankt Annæ Kvarter*
☎ *33/74–84–94* ⊕ *www.smk.dk* 💷 *DKr 50, free Wed.* ☉ *Tues. and
Thurs.–Sun. 10–5, Wed. 10–8.*

⌐ **②⑨ Vor Frue Kirken** (Church of Our Lady). The site of this cathedral has drawn
worshippers since the 13th century, when Bishop Absalon built a chapel
here. Today's church is actually a reconstruction: the original church
was destroyed during the Napoleonic Wars. Five towers top the neoclassical structure. Inside you can see Thorvaldsen's marble sculptures

depicting Christ and the 12 Apostles, and Moses and David cast in bronze. ✉ *Nørreg. 8, Frue Pl., Downtown* ☎ *33/37–65–40* ⊕ *www.domkirken. dk* ✐ *Free* ☉ *Daily 8–5.*

In & Around Vesterbrogade

To the southwest of the city are the vibrant working-class and immigrant neighborhoods of Vesterbro, where you'll find a good selection of inexpensive ethnic restaurants and shops. Like the area around Nørrebro, the buildings date from the late 1800s and were constructed for workers. From Vesterbro, Vesterbrogade leads farther west to the neighborhood of Frederiksberg. Originally a farming area that supplied the royal households with fresh produce, Frederiksberg is now lined with residences of the well-heeled and home to the zoo and a vibrant theater district.

a good walk

Begin your tour from Copenhagen's main station, Hovedbanegården. When you exit on Vesterbrogade, take a right and you can see the city's best-known attraction, **Tivoli** ❸ ▶. Just southeast of the gardens, on Hans Christian Andersens Boulevard, the neoclassical **Ny Carlsberg Glyptotek** ❸ contains one of the most impressive collections of antiquities and sculpture in northern Europe. Just north on Hans Christian Andersens Boulevard, across the street from Tivoli's eastern side, is the sleek **Dansk Design Center** ❹, with innovative temporary exhibits that showcase Danish and international design. To the west of the main station and tucked between Skt. Jørgens Sø (St. Jørgens Lake) and the main arteries of Vestersøgade and Gammel Kongevej is the **IMAX Tycho Brahe Planetarium** ❹.

Vesterbro, which resembles New York's Lower East Side for its bohemian vibe and ethnically diverse population, is along Vesterbrogade near Tivoli. Running parallel to the south is **Istedgade,** Copenhagen's halfhearted red-light district.

Farther west on Vesterbrogade is **Københavns Bymuseum** ❹, its entrance flanked by a miniature model of medieval Copenhagen. Beer enthusiasts can head south on Enghavevej and take a right on Ny Carlsbergvej to see the **Carlsberg Bryggeri** ❹. The visitor center, nearby on Gamle Carlsbergvej, has exhibits on the brewing process and Carlsberg's rise to fame.

TIMING These sights can be seen in half a day, and could be combined easily with a walk around Nørrebro. Tivoli offers charms throughout the day; visit in the late afternoon, and stay until midnight, when colored lights and fireworks (on Wednesday and weekend nights) illuminate the park. Be sure to call ahead, since some places may be closed Monday or Tuesday.

What to See

❹ **Carlsberg Bryggeri** (Carlsberg Brewery). As you approach the world-famous Carlsberg Brewery, the unmistakable smell of fermenting hops greets you, a pungent reminder that this is beer territory. (Indeed, near the brewery is the appealing little neighborhood of Humleby; "humle" means "hops.") Four giant Bornholm-granite elephants guard the brewery's main

CARLSBERG BREWERIES: ALE & ARTY

CARLSBERG. A BEER BY ANY OTHER NAME does not bring to mind the sculptures of Giacometti, archaeological undertakings in Rome, or the music of Miles Davis. In Denmark, however, the company behind the world-famous beer supports almost everything that is a part of Danish culture. Call it the ale of art: perhaps the most altruistic beer in the world.

Carlsberg Breweries, which since 1970 has included the United Breweries/ Tuborg, is owned by the Carlsberg Foundation. The umbrella organization annually pumps about DKr 125 million ($15.6 million) into Danish science, arts, and humanities—programs that touch nearly every aspect of Danish life. Under its own distinct statutes, the New Carlsberg Foundation, a branch of the mother foundation, kicks in DKr 40 million ($4.9 million) to the visual arts every year. While there is a strong tradition of corporate-backed foundations in Denmark, and many companies offer support to the arts and sciences, Carlsberg's scope and commitment to the culture of a single country is unique in the world.

Since its establishment in 1902, the New Carlsberg Foundation has helped build and support the Ny Carlsberg Glyptotek and its collection of antiquities. This Copenhagen museum boasts one of the world's finest collections of Etruscan art, and Europe's finest collection of Roman portraits. The museum's permanent collection contains French sculpture, including works by Rodin and Degas, impressionist and postimpressionist paintings by Manet, Cézanne, and Gauguin, and a Danish collection. Many Danish curators attribute the nation's grand state of the arts largely to the New Carlsberg Foundation. According to one, losing its sponsorship would "be a disaster." But what kind of beer company pours the bulk of its profits into art? Herein lies what makes Carlsberg so unusual. The brewery does not own the foundation: the foundation owns a 51% majority stake in the brewery.

While the New Carlsberg Foundation technically handles endowments for the visual arts, the larger Carlsberg Foundation, which supports the sciences and humanities, overlaps into the area of fine art. Among the wide range of projects they have funded: major archaeological excavations in the Roman Forum, studies of the ancient mosaics of the St. George Rotunda in Thessaloniki, Greece, and the complete and continued support of the Frederiksborg Museum north of Copenhagen. A royal residence that burned in 1859 was rebuilt and established as a museum of Danish history by J. C. Jacobsen; it now serves as the nation's portrait museum.

Between the larger foundation and the brewery itself are several smaller foundations, which further support music, industry, and society in general. The Carlsberg Brewery is also the owner of many businesses that deal in the decorative arts, including Holmegaard glass, Royal Copenhagen, and Georg Jensen, all of which exist under the umbrella company Royal Scandinavia. Of course, Carlsberg's associate concern, Tivoli Gardens, is considered by many a work of art in and of itself. Carlsberg also helps to fund annual events such as the Copenhagen Jazz Festival and the Roskilde Rock Festival, as well as concerts and performances by international artists. Clearly, there is more to these noble suds than meets the lips.

entrance on Ny Carlsbergvej. Nearby, on Gamle Carslbergvej, is the visitor center, in an old Carlsberg brewery. Colorful displays take you step by step through the brewing process. You can also walk through the draft-horse stalls; at the end of your visit, you're rewarded with a few minutes to quaff a complimentary beer. The free **Carlsberg Museum** (✉ Valby Langgade 1, Vesterbro ☎ 33/21–01–12), open weekdays 10 to 3, offers a further look into the saga of the Carlsberg family, and how it managed to catapult Carlsberg from a local name into one of the most famous beers in the world. ✉ *Gamle Carlsbergvej 11, Vesterbro* ☎ *33/27–13–14* ⊕ *www.carlsberg.com* ▱ *Free* ☉ *Tues.–Sun. 10–4.*

④⓪ Dansk Design Center (Danish Design Center). This sleek, glass-panel structure looms in sharp contrast to the old-world ambience of Tivoli just across the street. More of a design showroom than a museum, the center's highlights are the innovative temporary exhibits on the main floor. Past exhibits have included "75 years of Bang & Olufsen," which covered the famed Danish audio-system company, and "Tooltoy," a playful, interactive exhibit of toys over the last century. One-third of the temporary exhibits showcase Danish design; the rest focus on international design. The semipermanent collection on the ground floor (renewed every other year) often includes samples from the greats, including chairs by Arne Jacobsen, several artichoke PH lamps (designed by Poul Henningsen), and Bang & Olufsen radios and stereos. Note how the radios they made in the '50s look more modern than many of the radios today. The center's shop carries a wide range of Danish design items and selected pieces from the temporary exhibits. You can enjoy light meals in the atrium café, sitting amid the current exhibits. ✉ *H. C. Andersens Blvd. 27, Downtown* ☎ *33/69–33–69* ⊕ *www.ddc.dk* ▱ *DKr 40* ☉ *Mon., Tues., Thurs., and Fri. 10–5; Wed. 10–9; weekends 11–4.*

④① IMAX Tycho Brahe Planetarium. This modern, cylindrical planetarium, which appears to be sliced at an angle, features astronomy exhibits. It is Denmark's most advanced center for popularizing astronomy and space research and promoting knowledge of natural science. The **IMAX Theater** takes you on visual odysseys as varied as journeys through space and sea, the stages of the Rolling Stones, or Kuwaiti fires from the first Persian Gulf War. These films are not recommended for children under age seven. ✉ *Gammel Kongevej 10, Vesterbro* ☎ *33/12–12–24* ⊕ *www.tycho.dk/in_english* ▱ *DKr 90* ☉ *Thurs.–Tues. 10:30–8:30, Wed. 9:30–8:30.*

Istedgade. In what passes for a red-light district in Copenhagen, mom-and-pop kiosks and ethnic restaurants stand side by side with porn shops and shady outfits aiming to satisfy all proclivities. Istedgade, like neighboring Vesterbrogade, has diversified over the past several years, drawing artists and students. Thanks to the city's urban-renewal projects, cafés and businesses are also moving in, mostly on the southwest end of Istedgade, around Enghave Plads (Enghave Square). Mama Lustra, at No. 96–98, is a laid-back café with comfy armchairs and a mixed crowd of students and older artsy types. Though Istedgade is relatively safe, you may want to avoid the area near Central Station late at night. ✉ *South of and parallel to Vesterbrogade, running southwest from Central Station, Vesterbro.*

㊷ Københavns Bymuseum (Copenhagen City Museum). For a surprisingly evocative collection detailing Copenhagen's history, head to this 17th-century building in the heart of Vesterbro. A meticulously maintained model of 16th-century Copenhagen is kept outdoors from May through September; inside there is also a memorial room for philosopher Søren Kierkegaard, the father of existentialism. ⊠ *Vesterbrog. 59, Vesterbro* ☎ *33/21–07–72* ⊕ *www.kbhbymuseum.dk* ✉ *DKr 20, free Fri.* ⊙ *May–Sept., Wed.–Mon. 10–4; Oct.–Apr., Wed.–Mon. 1–4.*

㊴ Ny Carlsberg Glyptotek (New Carlsberg Museum). Among Copenhagen's
Fodor'sChoice   most important museums—thanks to its exquisite antiquities and Gau-
★   guins and Rodins—the neoclassical New Carlsberg Museum was donated in 1888 by Carl Jacobsen, son of the founder of the Carlsberg Brewery. Surrounding its lush indoor garden, a series of nooks and chambers houses works by Degas and other impressionists, plus an extensive assemblage of Egyptian, Greek, Roman, and French sculpture, not to mention Europe's finest collection of Roman portraits and the best collection of Etruscan art outside Italy. A modern wing, designed as a three-story treasure chest by the acclaimed Danish architect Henning Larsen, houses an impressive pre-impressionist collection that includes works from the Barbizon school; impressionist paintings, including works by Monet, Alfred Sisley, and Pissarro; and a postimpressionist section, with 50 Gauguin paintings plus 12 of his very rare sculptures. Note that extensive rebuilding of this museum will continue during 2006. Some exhibits remain open. Access to the museum until June 28, 2006, will be via the temporary entrance at Tietgensgadc 25. ⊠ *Dantes Pl. 7, Vesterbro* ☎ *33/41–81–41* ⊕ *www.glyptoteket.dk* ✉ *DKr 40, free Wed. and Sun.* ⊙ *Tues.–Sun. 10–4.*

㊳ Tivoli. Copenhagen's best-known attraction, conveniently next to its
Fodor'sChoice   main train station, attracts an astounding number of visitors: 4 million
★   people from mid-April to mid-September. Tivoli is more sophisticated than a mere amusement park: among its attractions are a pantomime theater, an open-air stage, 38 restaurants (some of them very elegant), and frequent concerts, which cover the spectrum from classical to rock to jazz. Fantastic flower exhibits color the lush gardens and float on the swan-filled ponds.

The park was established in the 1840s, when Danish architect George Carstensen persuaded a worried King Christian VIII to let him build an amusement park on the edge of the city's fortifications, rationalizing that "when people amuse themselves, they forget politics." On Wednesday and weekend nights, elaborate fireworks are set off, and every day the Tivoli Guard, a youth version of the Queen's Royal Guard, performs. Try to see Tivoli at least once by night, when 100,000 colored lanterns illuminate the Chinese pagoda and the main fountain. Call to double-check prices, which vary throughout the year and often include family discounts at various times during the day. Tivoli is also open from late November to Christmas. ⊠ *Vesterbrog. 3, Vesterbro* ☎ *33/15–10–01* ⊕ *www.tivoli.dk* ✉ *Grounds DKr 68, ride pass DKr 195* ⊙ *Mid-Apr.–mid-Sept., Sun.–Wed. 11–11, Thurs. 11 AM–midnight, Fri. 11 AM–1 AM, Sat. 11 AM–midnight; late Nov.–Dec. 23, Sun.–Wed. 11–9, Fri. and Sat. 11–10.*

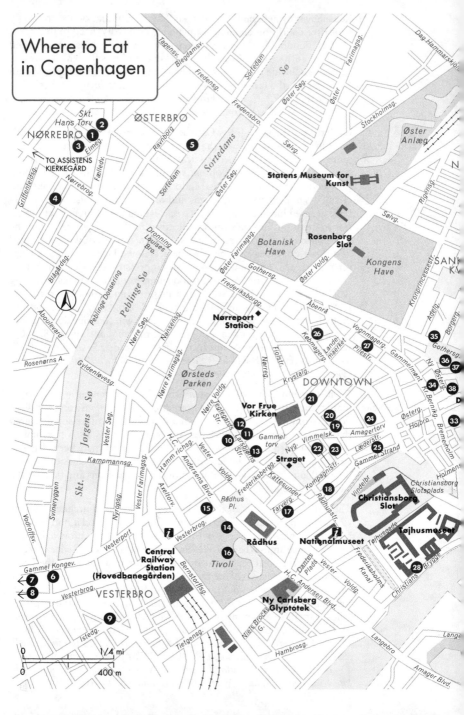

Where to Eat in Copenhagen

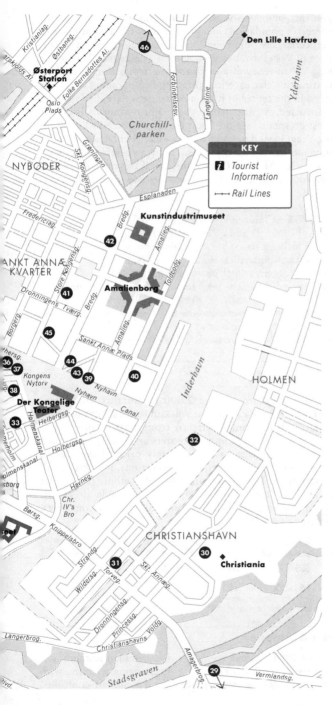

Vesterbro. Students, union workers, and immigrants (who account for 15% of Vesterbro's population) inhabit this area. It's a great place to find ethnic groceries, discount shops, and cheap international restaurants. The face of Vesterbro, however, has been gentrified. Due to the city's ongoing urban-renewal and clean-up efforts, the spruced-up Vesterbro is attracting chic eateries, stores, and clubs, along with their arty customers. In the center of it all, a new café square, Halmtorvet, has been constructed. An area where you might not normally go has become a must-go spot to see the latest trends. Nightclubs like headline-grabbing Vega, Ideal Bar, and Byens Lys-Cafe PH have opened, as have the restaurants Carlton and Apropos. The area's best clothing shops, such as Hubsch, Don Ya Doll, Gurlie Hurly, and Designer Zoo are at the western end of Istedgade. ⊠ *At southwestern end of Vesterbrogade, Vesterbro.*

off the beaten path

ZOOLOGISK HAVE – Children love the Zoological Gardens, which are home to 3,300 animals and 264 species. The small petting zoo and playground includes cows, horses, rabbits, goats, and hens. The indoor rain forest has butterflies, sloths, alligators, and other tropical creatures. Sea lions, lions, and elephants are fed in the early afternoon. Be warned: on sunny weekends, the line to enter runs far down Roskildevej; get here early. ⊠ *Roskildevej 32, Frederiksberg* ☎ *70/20–02–00* ⊕ *www.zoo.dk* ⊠ *DKr 95* ☉ *June–Aug., daily 9–6; Sept. and Oct., daily 9–5; Apr. and May, weekdays 9–5, weekends 9–6; Nov.–Feb., daily 9–4; Mar. weekdays 9–4, weekends 9–5.*

WHERE TO EAT

In Copenhagen, with its more than 2,000 restaurants, traditional Danish fare spans all price categories: you can order a light lunch of traditional smørrebrød, munch alfresco from a street-side *pølser* (sausage) cart, or dine out on Limfjord oysters and local plaice. Even the most upscale restaurants have moderately priced fixed menus. Though few Danish restaurants require reservations, it's best to call ahead to avoid a wait. The city's more affordable ethnic restaurants are concentrated in Vesterbro, Nørrebro, and the side streets off Strøget. And for less-expensive, savory noshes in stylish surroundings, consider lingering at a café.

WHAT IT COSTS In Danish kroner				
$$$$	**$$$**	**$$**	**$**	**¢**
AT DINNER over 200	151–200	121–150	90–120	under 90

Prices are for a main course at dinner.

Christianhavn, Holmen & Amager

★ **$$$$** ✕ **Era Ora.** Since 1983 this has been the premier Italian restaurant in the city, if not the country. It's known for its changing set menu with many courses that do not use cream or butter, and its climate-controlled wine cellar containing 90,000 bottles of solely Italian vintages. Burnt-umber walls and black, chocolate brown, and white accents predominate in the Ole Tønnesen-designed dining room; yellow and green roses on the tables contrast well with black suede banquettes and crisp white linens. Founder Elvio Milleri and co-owner Alessandro Jacoponi attentively greet each table and explain the various courses and the wine pairings to be offered. You'll be served between 9 and 17 (small) courses, depending on your appetite and time commitment—there is no à la carte menu. The tiny seafood antipasti, including octopus with homemade pasta and a touch of mascarpone cheese, fares well opposite a later main course of St. Peter fish; it's light and delicate in a fresh tomato sauce. The green-apple sorbet, served in between two courses, is presented in a block of ice, showing an attention to detail not found elsewhere. This is a full, special night out; prepare to spend at least four hours dining leisurely. ⊠ *Overgaden neden Vandet 33-B, Christianshavn* ☎ *32/54–06–93* ⊕ *www.era-ora.dk* ⚖ *Reservations essential* ☰ *AE, DC, MC, V* ☽ *Closed Sun.*

$$$$
Fodor'sChoice
★

✕ **noma.** Located in an old waterfront warehouse relatively close to the new Opera House, this property has won raves and accolades since its opening day. Chef Rene Reszip and his innovative team marry the best Nordic ingredients (wild berries, mushrooms, local vegetables and herbs) with musk ox, game, Jutland marsh lamb, and Faroe Islands scallops. The seven-course tasting menu with complementary wines is a delight, and is served in an understated, minimalist-chic atmosphere on Royal Copenhagen china. An à la carte menu is also available. The marinated and fried pork tenderloin with parsnip and lingonberry sauce is a stand-out, as is the dessert of homemade hazelnut-and-vanilla ice cream with raisins marinated in aquavit. Service is knowledgable and attentive. This is one of the very few new Danish restaurants making gourmets everywhere take note of an inventive, quintessentially north-Atlantic inspired cuisine. ⊠ *Strandgade. 93, Christianshavn* ☎ *32/96–32–97* ⊕ *www.noma.dk* ⚖ *Reservations essential* ☰ *AE, DC, MC, V* ☽ *Closed Sun. No lunch Sat.*

$$–$$$

✕ **Spiseloppen.** Round out your visit to the Free State of Christiania with a meal at Spiseloppen, a 160-seat warehouse restaurant that was a military storage facility and an army canteen in its former life. Upon entering Christiania, wind your way past shaggy dogs, their shaggy owners, graffiti murals, and wafts of patchouli. (There are few street signs, so just ask; Spiseloppen is the neighborhood's best-known restaurant.) From the outside, this run-down warehouse with splintered windows may seem a bit forbidding, but inside it's a different story. Climb up rickety stairs to the second floor and you're rewarded with a loft-size dining room with low, wood-beam ceilings and candles flickering on the tables. The menu highlights are fresh and inventive vegetarian and fish dishes, which might include artichokes stuffed with eggplant or portobello mushrooms served with squash, mango, and papaya. One floor down is Loppen, a club that hosts midweek jazz sessions and DJ dance nights on the weekends. Some contend that this place doesn't have the deals it once had, but you're still in the heart of happy hippiedom. ⊠ *Bådsmandsstr. 43, Christianshavn* ☎ *32/57–95–58* ☰ *MC, V* ☽ *Closed Mon. No lunch.*

$-$$$ ✕ **Krunch.** The motto here is "gastronomy within ecology." Krunch serves natural, organic foods from reliable sources and attempts to integrate an environmentally friendly spirit into every facet of the experience. Within these guiding principles, the objective of the owners is to create authentic French-bistro atmosphere and cuisine. The four-course menu changes seasonally; it typically consists of a choice of a fish, meat, or vegetarian main course and an assortment of side dishes. Krunch is also a fine spot for kids. ⊠ *Øresundsvej 14, Amager* ☎ *32/84–50–50* ⊕ *www.krunch.dk* ☰ *MC, V* ⊘ *Closed Mon.*

Downtown

★ **$$$$** ✕ **Kommandanten.** Fancifully decorated by master florist Tage Andersen with brushed-iron-and-copper furniture, down pillows, and foliage-flanked lights, this is among the city's most exclusive dinner spots, attracting well-heeled businesspeople and local celebrities. The adventuresome international fare might include dishes such as rabbit with bouillon-cooked lentils, herbs, and bacon, and marinated salmon with oysters and parsley. Jackets are recommended. ⊠ *Ny Adelg. 7, Downtown* ☎ *33/12–09–90* ⊕ *www.kommandanten.dk* ☰ *AE, DC, MC, V* ⊘ *Closed Sun.*

★ **$$$$** ✕ **Kong Hans Kælder.** Five centuries ago this was a Nordic vineyard—now it's one of Scandinavia's finest restaurants. Chef Thomas Rode Andersen's French-Danish-Asian–inspired dishes employ the freshest local ingredients and are served in a medieval subterranean space with whitewashed walls and vaulted ceilings. Try the foie gras with raspberry-vinegar sauce or the warm oysters in vichyssoise with smoked cheese and lemon. ⊠ *Vingårdstr. 6, Downtown* ☎ *33/11–68–68* ⊕ *www.konghans. dk* ☰ *AE, D, MC, V* ⊘ *Closed Sun. No lunch.*

$$$$ ✕ **Krogs.** This elegant canal-front restaurant has developed a loyal clientele—both foreign and local—for its old-fashioned atmosphere and its innovative fish dishes. Pale-green walls are simply adorned with paintings of old Copenhagen. The menu includes such specialties as pan-grilled lobster flavored with vanilla oil, and monkfish fillets in a beurre-blanc sauce flavored with arugula and tomato. Jackets are recommended. Krogs is also open for lunch until 4 PM. ⊠ *Gammel Strand 38, Downtown* ☎ *33/15–89–15* ⚲ *Reservations essential* ☰ *AE, DC, MC, V* ⊘ *Closed Sun.*

$$$$ ✕ **The Paul.** From a glass of Bollinger champagne as an aperitif to the **Fodor'sChoice** very last course at dinner (a rhubarb tart with tea ice cream on caramel), ★ dining at The Paul is a highlight of a visit to Copenhagen. Located in the middle of Tivoli, and only open during the park's season (mid-May to mid-September), this exquisite dining room in a glass-encircled pavilion seems to be favored by everyone in the entertainment world, and it witnesses unannounced visits from members of the Danish royal family. A great deal of the restaurant's success comes from the inventiveness and pure enthusiasm of chef/co-owner Paul Cunningham, originally from England and now a happy Danish transplant and a celebrity chef in the country. He takes traditional Danish cuisine and combines influences from other regions; for example, succulent sea bass might be served with Spanish olives and almonds in oil and paired with a crisp Spanish Riesling. The seven-course prix-fixe menu is lovingly prepared from an open kitchen overlooking a chef's table, and service is flawless, with the right amount of explanation regarding courses and wine pairings. Giant white candles and American Beauty roses are everywhere, even in the washrooms—where you'll also find disposable toothbrushes and toothpaste. Three course lunches start at DKr 450. ⊠ *Tivoli, Verserbrogade 3.* ☎ *33/75–07–75* ⊕ *www.thepaul.dk* ⚄ *Reservations essential* ☰ *AE, DC, MC, V* ⊗ *Closed mid-Sept.–mid-May.*

$$$$ ✕ **Restaurant D'Angleterre.** Formerly named "Wiinblad," the signature restaurant of the elegant Hotel D'Angleterre was refurbished in 2005 and is now concentrating on modern French cuisine. Starters such as giant crab with avocado and mint oil blend well with fallow deer with rhubarb gravy and morels as a main course. ⊠ *D'Angleterre, Kongens Nytorv 34, Downtown* ☎ *33/37–06–19* ⊕ *www.remmen.dk* ☰ *AE, DC, MC, V.*

★ $$$$ ✕ **Tyvenkokkenhanskoneoghendeselsker.** If you've seen Peter Greenaway's dark and brilliant film *The Cook, the Thief, His Wife, and Her Lover* (with its macabre feast scenes), you may wonder what lies in store at this half-timber town-house restaurant with the same name. It's worth finding out. The same daring humor that inspired the unusual name is exhibited in the innovative seven-course menu, which changes every few weeks. You might be served baked cod in an aromatic coffee sauce or warm rooster simmered in spices and served with horseradish sauce. Desserts include pineapple with mint tortellini. Sit upstairs for a view of the cheery, orange- and yellow-walled old houses that lean against each other just across the narrow street. ⊠ *Magstr. 16, Downtown* ☎ *33/16–12–92* ⊕ *www.tyven.dk* ⚄ *Reservations essential* ☰ *DC, MC, V* ⊗ *Closed Sun. No lunch.*

$$$$ ✕ **Wallmans Salonger.** Forget Vegas, and skip Paris: some of Scandinavia's brightest young talents sing and dance their way through this outstanding revue, located in the city's old circus building (it's practically across the street from the main entrance of Tivoli). The performers are also your waiters, and somehow find time to serve a four-course meal in between Cirque du Soleil–style acrobatics, singing, costume-changes, and choreography. You'll undoubtedly have a good time. The food, which includes standard meat and fish options, is pretty good for dinner theater, but don't expect gastromonic excellence. Reservations are recommended. ⊠ *Cirkusbygningen Jernbaneg. 8, Downtown* ☎ *70/27–74–74* ☰ *MC, V* ⊗ *Closed Sun.–Tues.*

$$$–$$$$ ✕ **L'Alsace.** Set in the cobbled courtyard of Pistolstræde and hung with paintings by Danish surrealist Wilhelm Freddie, this restaurant is peaceful and quiet, and has attracted such diverse diners as Queen Margrethe, Elton John, and the late Pope John Paul II. The hand-drawn menu lists oysters from Brittany, terrine de foie gras, and *choucrôute à la Strasbourgeoise* (a hearty mélange of cold cabbage, homemade sausage, and pork). Try the superb fresh-fruit tarts and cakes for dessert, and ask to sit in the patio overlooking the courtyard. ⊠ *Ny Østerg. 9, Downtown* ☎ *33/14–57–43* ⊕ *www.alsace.dk* ☰ *AE, DC, MC, V* ⊗ *Closed Sun.*

$–$$$$ ✕ **Café Ketchup.** You have a choice at this informal, upbeat eatery: for light meals (at light prices), try the lively front café, where you can settle into a red-and-white wicker chair next to the large picture windows and watch the world go by on chic Pilestræde. Try the spring rolls with smoked salmon and cod, flavored with ginger and coriander. The café also serves a tasty brunch (yogurt with muesli, toast with turkey, mozzarella, and bacon, and black currant–fig marmalade) from 10 to 1. For more-substantial fare, venture into the restaurant decorated with old French Perrier ads and lighted with white candles. Starters include a potato-and-wasabi soup served with a spicy crab cake, and bruschetta topped with a mango salsa. Main dishes range from halibut stuffed with crab-meat and herbs to marinated duck breast served with sun-dried tomatoes and fennel salad sprinkled with pine nuts. By night the place turns into a lively bar and club. There is also a Café Ketchup in Tivoli, with a large terrace and a similar menu. ⊠ *Pilestr. 19, Downtown* 🖀 *33/ 32–30–30* ⊕ *www.cafeketchup.dk* ▤ *DC, MC, V* ☾ *Closed Sun.*

$$$ ✕ **Søren K.** Occupying a bright corner of the Royal Library's modern Black Diamond extension, this cool-tone restaurant, with clean lines, blond-wood furnishings, and recessed ceiling lights, serves bold French-Scandinavian concoctions using no cream, butter, or stock. The result is a menu of flavorful dishes that please the palate without weighing you down. A popular selection is the five-course menu entitled "a couple of hours in the company of fish," which has featured items such as tuna in soy and sesame sauce or mussels drizzled with lemon and thyme. Vegetarian dishes include tofu marinated with red wine and topped with roasted sesame seeds, radishes, and passion fruit. For waterfront views, choose one of the many tables that sit flush up against the Black Diamond's looming glass walls. In summer, you can enjoy your meal on the outside terrace. ⊠ *Søren Kierkegaards Pl. 1 (inside the Black Diamond), Downtown* 🖀 *33/47–49–49* ⊕ *www.sorenk.dk* ▤ *DC, MC, V* ☾ *Closed Sun.*

$$$ ✕ **Sult.** Norwegian author Knut Hamsun's novel *Sult* now shares its moniker with this restaurant on the premises of the Danish Film Institute. The cuisine is Mediterranean, with strong North African and Asian influences. Try the mussels with carrots in a cream sauce or roast guinea fowl with sweet potatoes. The wine list is impressive. ⊠ *Vognmagerg. 8B, Downtown* 🖀 *33/74–34–17* ⊕ *www.sult.dk* ▤ *MC, V* ☾ *Closed Mon.*

$$–$$$ ✕ **El Mesón.** Smoothly worn wooden tables, earthen crockery, and dim lighting characterize the dining room of this Spanish restaurant. The knowledgeable waitstaff serves generous portions of beef spiced with spearmint, lamb with honey sauce, and paella Valenciano—a mixture of rice, chicken, ham, shrimp, lobster, squid, green beans, and peas—for two. ⊠ *Hauser Pl. 12 (behind Kultorvet), Downtown* 🖀 *33/ 11–91–31* ▤ *AE, DC, MC, V* ☾ *Closed Sun. No lunch.*

★ **$$–$$$** ✕ **Reinwalds.** The comfortable black teak chairs with blue upholstery signal the beginning of a series of delightful encounters with comfort and fine food in a pleasant, modern setting. The tables spread out at sufficient intervals to prevent intrusions of privacy or conversation overlap with neighboring diners. The informative waitstaff ensure that service is far above the norm—they're adept at complementing selected dishes with a fine wine. The three- to five-course menus change monthly, according to the season's harvest. You might find offerings like creamy curry soup with rooster and quail eggs or baked sea bream with almond pesto. ⊠ *Farveg. 15, Downtown* 📞 *33/91–82–80* ⊕ *www.reinwalds. dk* 🖹 *AE, DC, MC, V* ⊗ *Closed Sun.*

$–$$$ ✕ **Peder Oxe.** On a 17th-century square, this lively, countrified bistro has rustic tables and 15th-century Portuguese tiles. All entrées—among them grilled steaks, fish, and the best fancy burgers in town—come with an excellent self-service salad bar. Damask-covered tables are set with heavy cutlery and opened bottles of hearty Pyrénées wine. A clever call-light for the waitress is above each table. In spring, when the high northern sun is shining but the warmth still has not kicked in, you won't do badly sitting outside in the Gråbrødretorv (Gray Friars' Square) sipping drinks while wrapped in blankets left thoughtfully for patrons in wicker chairs. ⊠ *Gråbrødretorv 11, Downtown* 📞 *33/11–00–77* ⊕ *www.pederoxe.dk* 🖹 *DC, MC, V.*

$–$$ ✕ **Flyvefisken.** Silvery stenciled fish swim along blue-and-yellow walls in this Thai eatery. Spicy dishes include chicken with cashew nuts and herring shark in basil sauce. It's always a busy spot, with media and PR types hanging around, enjoying wet and dry noodles and all manner of typical Thai fare. ⊠ *Larsbjørnsstr. 18, Downtown* 📞 *33/14–95–15* 🖹 *DC, MC, V* ⊗ *Closed Sun. No lunch.*

$–$$ ✕ **Københavner Caféen.** You know you're in for a real Danish meal when you can smell the vinegary *rød kål* (red cabbage, a Danish staple) upon entering. Dimly lighted and warm, with a dark-wood and burgundy color scheme, this local favorite just oozes with *hygge* (coziness). Old photographs of Danish royalty line the walls, and a 1798 street lamp stands alongside the inviting bar. Choose from a wide range of smørrebrød selections and also a formidable lineup of down-home Danish dishes such as *frikkedeller* (pork meatballs) and butter-fried salmon with boiled potatoes. In summer the kitchen offers a traditional Danish Christmas meal "so that everyone can experience Denmark's Christmas traditions." The meal includes roast pork with red cabbage and the much-loved *ris à l'amande* (rice pudding) for dessert. Hidden inside is an almond, and whoever finds it receives a small present. These summer Christmas meals have become so popular that they are generally offered only to tour groups, but it's worth asking when you reserve. ⊠ *Badstuestr. 10, Downtown* 📞 *33/32–80–81* ⚱ *Reservations essential* 🖹 *MC, V.*

$–$$
Fodor'sChoice
★ ✕ **Riz Raz.** This Middle Eastern restaurant hops with young locals, families, couples, and anyone who appreciates good value and spicy fare. The inexpensive all-you-can-eat buffet is heaped with lentils, tomatoes, potatoes, olives, hummus, warm pita bread, yogurt and cucumbers, pickled vegetables, and bean salads. Don't be put off by the hordes—just join them, either in the restaurant's endless labyrinth of dining rooms or in the jam-packed summertime patio. The main location is on Kompagnistræde, between Christiansborg Slot and Strøget; there's a second branch behind Vor Frue Kirken. ⊠ *Riz Raz Bla, Kompagnistr. 20, Vesterbro* 📞 *33/15–05–75* ⊠ *Store Kannikestr. 19, Downtown* 📞 *33/32–33–45* ⊕ *www.rizraz.dk* 🖹 *DC, MC, V.*

$–$$ ✕ **Victor.** Excellent people-watching and good bistro fare are the calling cards at this French-style corner café. It's best during weekend lunches, when young and old gather for such specialties as rib roast, home-made pâté, and smoked salmon and cheese platters. Come here for one of the best brunches in town. Be warned however that the formal restaurant in the back of the space is quite expensive—order from the front café side for a less expensive meal. ⊠ *Ny Østerg. 8, Downtown* ☎ *33/ 13–36–13* ⊕ *www.cafevictor.dk* ☱ *AE, DC, MC, V.*

¢–$$ ✗ **Husmanns Vinstue.** If you're looking for old-world Denmark, this is it. Founded in 1888, this warmly lighted basement restaurant is housed in a former stable dating from 1727, which accounts for the low ceilings. Beer mugs dangle above the bar, dark-green lamps shed light onto the heavy wooden tables, and black-and-white photographs of Copenhagen hang on the walls. Until 1981 women were allowed to enter only if accompanied by a male, a rule established by one of the restaurant's female owners. Even Walt Disney and the Danish royal family have tucked into the hearty Danish smørrebrød. While other Danish lunch spots may serve salads and lighter cuisine, here you can feast on all types of herring (fried, curried, marinated, and spiced), smoked eel with scrambled eggs, beef tartare with egg yolk, homemade sausage, and roast beef with potato salad, all served on your choice of rye or white bread. ⊠ *Lars-bjørnsstr. 2, Downtown* ☎ *33/11–58–86* ⊕ *www.husmannvinstue.dk* ⚞ *Reservations essential* ☱ *AE, DC, MC, V* ☻ *No dinner.*

¢–$$ ✗ **Pasta Basta.** This bright, casual eatery just off the Strøget is always crammed with happy diners. Pasta Basta has all the ingredients for its well-deserved success: an all-you-can-eat fresh pasta and salad bar for a refreshingly low price (DKr 79). The cheerful staff navigates a dining area marked by orange walls, an innovative mural, and glass-top tables painted in green and blue swirls. Main courses on the changing menu may include pasta with prawns, spinach, and chili peppers, or smoked salmon served with pasta in a creamy sauce of scallops, spinach, and herbs. Pasta Basta is one of the city's only restaurants (barring fast-food and shawarma joints) that serves food until 3 AM (and until 5 AM on Friday and Saturday). During these early-morning hours the restaurant is popular with dancers and musicians from the Royal Theater and other venues, who come in to relax and dine after their evening performances. ⊠ *Valkendorfsg. 22, Downtown* ☎ *33/ 11–21–31* ☱ *DC, MC, V.*

$ ✗ **Atlas Bar.** The health-food café Atlas Bar in the basement of restaurant Flyvefisken serves excellent food to a steady stream of students and hipsters. The snug eatery serves Oriental-inspired and fusion dishes, such as Manila chicken (chicken breasts in a tomato sauce with garlic, ginger, and chili) and medallions of venison. Atlas is also a favorite of vegetarians for its tempting menu of healthful, tasty dishes. ⊠ *Larsbjørnsstr. 18, Downtown* ☎ *33/15–03–52* ☱ *DC, MC, V* ☻ *Closed Sun.*

¢ ✗ **La Galette.** Tucked into a bright little courtyard, this cheery creperie serves an array of savory crepes, including the Asterix, stuffed with ratatouille, egg, and chives, and the Quimper, with spinach, egg, bacon, and cheese. The luscious lineup of sweet crepes includes everything from banana and chocolate to flambéed caramel apples. ⊠ *Larsbjørnsstr. 9, Downtown* ☎ *33/32–37–90* ☱ *MC, V* ☻ *No lunch Sun.*

Nørrebro

$$-$$$$ ✕ **Nørrebro Bryghus.** This microbrewery opened in September 2003 and has been an instant hit in this former metal factory. It's owned by Anders Kissemeyer, the former master brewer of the Carlsberg Brewery—a position he held for 16 years. The Brewery has 160 seats in a two-story restaurant, and offers a courtyard beer garden in summer. Lunches include tasty salads, sandwiches, and burgers; in the evening you can order three to four courses starting from DKr 298. ✉ *Ryesgade 3 Nørrebro* ☎ *35/30–05–30* ⊕ *www.noerrebrobryghus.dk* ⊟ *MC, V.*

$ ✕ **Pussy Galore's Flying Circus.** Done up with a few Arne Jacobsen Swan chairs, naive wall paintings, and tables smashed up against each other, this trendy gathering place frequented by both young families and black-clad poseurs is supposed to be as kitschy as its name. While the mix of decor is retro and does a good job of setting a '60s stage, the regulars who come here make it feel more like a low-key neighborhood bar. There's surprisingly down-to-earth and affordable fare, with eggs and bacon and other brunch items along with hefty burgers and wok-fried delectables. Chairs and tables move outdoors (with parasol heaters) at the first hint of spring. ✉ *Skt. Hans Torv 30, Nørrebro* ☎ *35/24–53–00* ⊕ *www.pussy-galore.dk* ⊟ *DC, MC, V.*

$ ✕ **Sebastopol.** Students and locals crowd this laid-back eatery for brunch and on weekend evenings, but it's a good choice if you want to get off the beaten tourist path. The menu is varied with lots of salads, warm sandwiches, and burgers—and just about the most American-style brunch in the city. When it's warm (or close to it), tables are set outside on the square, where there's great people-watching. ✉ *Skt. Hans Torv 32, Nørrebro* ☎ *35/36–30–02* ⚖ *Reservations not accepted* ⊟ *AE, DC, MC, V.*

$ ✕ **Laundromat Café.** Here's a way to not only wash your clothes (in a sound-proofed room), but also enjoy breakfast, lunch, or dinner, or have a coffee or one of a big selection of beers. Best of all is the library containing 4,000 used books. The cafe serves salads, burgers, steaks, pastas, fish soups, and homemade desserts. ✉ *Elmgade 14, Nørrebro* ☎ *35/35–26–72* ⊟ *MC, V.*

¢ ✕ **Tibet.** Although they've replaced the traditional yak meat and milk dishes with beef and organic cows' milk, this restaurant comes really close to making authentic Tibetan fare. National favorites *momo* (steamed dumplings with vegetable or meat filling) and *thentuk* (rice noodles with lamb or beef) share the menu with a selection of dishes from the Szechuan province of China. ✉ *Blagårds Plads 10, Nørrebro* ☎ *35/36–85–05* ⊟ *No credit cards* ⊗ *Closed Mon.*

Sankt Annæ Kvarter & Østerbro

★ $$$$ ✕ **Godt.** The name says it all: this elegant little two-story restaurant with cool gray walls, silvery curtain partitions, and tulips in clear-glass bottles is *godt* (good). Actually, it's very, very good—so good that Godt has become the buzz of the town. The superb French-Danish menu showcases Chef Colin Rice's commitment to fresh ingredients and seasonal produce, which he buys every morning. Rice prepares a daily set menu, and you can choose to have three, four, or five courses. Dishes may include a black-bean and crab soup or a fillet of venison drizzled with truffle sauce. ☒ *Gothersg. 38, Sankt Annæ Kvarter* ☎ *33/15–21–22* ⚖ *Reservations essential* ▭ *DC, MC, V* ⊘ *Closed Sun. and Mon. No lunch.*

$$$ ✗ **Els.** When it opened in 1853, the intimate Els was the place to be seen before the theater, and the painted Muses on the walls still watch diners rush to make an eight o'clock curtain. Antique wooden columns complement the period furniture, including tables inlaid with Royal Copenhagen tile work. The nouvelle French four-course menu changes every two weeks, always incorporating game, fish, and market produce. Legend has it that Hans Christian Andersen used to come here for a hot meal, and he actually dedicated a poem to this place. Jackets are recommended. ☒ *Store Strandstr. 3, Sankt Annæ Kvarter* ☎ *33/14–13–41* ⊕ *www.restaurant-els.dk* ⚖ *Reservations essential* ▭ *AE, DC, MC, V* ⊘ *No lunch Sun.*

★ **$$$** ✗ **Le Sommelier.** The grande dame of Copenhagen's French restaurants is appropriately named. The cellar boasts more than 800 varieties of wine, and you can order many of them by the glass. Exquisite French dishes are complemented by an elegant interior of pale yellow walls, rough-hewn wooden floors, brass chandeliers, and hanging copper pots. Dishes include guinea fowl in a foie-gras sauce or lamb shank and crispy sweet-breads with parsley and garlic. While waiting for your table, you can sidle up to the burnished dark-wood and brass bar and begin sampling the wine. ☒ *Bredg. 63–65, Sankt Annæ Kvarter* ☎ *33/11–45–15* ⊕ *www.lesommelier.dk* ▭ *AE, DC, MC, V.*

$$$ ✗ **Zeleste.** This restaurant specializes in an inventive and refreshing strain of fusion cuisine. Outfitted with a short but well-worn bar, a covered and heated atrium, and—upstairs—a U-shape dining room, it serves as a soothing respite to Nyhavn's canal-front party. Although the food is usually excellent, if you're ravenous, ask specifically about portions—otherwise, you could end up with some tiny slivers of fried foie gras or a few tortellini. For lunch, the famished will do well with either the focaccia sandwich or the lobster salad served with toast and an excellent roux dressing; if the latter is not at your table within five minutes, you get a free glass of champagne. There is outdoor seating in summer. ☒ *Store Strandstr. 6, Sankt Annæ Kvarter* ☎ *33/16–06–06* ⊕ *www.zeleste.dk* ⚖ *Reservations essential* ▭ *DC, MC, V.*

$$–$$$ ✗ **Le Saint Jacques.** The tiny dining room here barely accommodates a dozen tables, but whenever the sun shines, diners spill out from its icon-filled spaces to occupy tables facing busy Østerbrogade. The chef and owners come from some of the finest restaurants in town, but claim they started this place to slow down the pace and enjoy the company of their customers. The fare changes according to what is available at the market, but expect fabulous culinary combinations—smoked salmon with crushed eggplant, Canadian scallops with leeks and salmon roe in a beurre blanc sauce, sole with basil sauce and reduced balsamic glaze, and a savory *poussin* (young, small chicken) with sweetbreads scooped into phyllo pastry atop a bed of polenta and lentils. ☒ *Skt. Jakobs Pl. 1, Øster-bro* ☎ *35/42–77–07* ⊕ *www.danielletz.com* ⚖ *Reservations essential* ▭ *DC, MC, V.*

$$–$$$ ✗ **Nyhavns Færgekro.** Locals pack into this waterfront café every day at lunchtime, when the staff unveils a buffet with 10 kinds of herring. An unsavory sailors' bar when Nyhavn was the city's port, the butter-yellow building retains a rustic charm. Waiters duck under rough wood beams when they deliver your choice of the delicious dinner specials, which might be salmon with dill sauce or steak with shaved truffles. In summer, sit outside and order an aquavit, the local spirit that tastes like caraway seeds. ✉ *Nyhavn 5, Sankt Annæ Kvarter* ☎ *33/15–15–88* ⊕ *www.nyhavnsfaergekro.dk* ▤ *DC, MC, V.*

$$ ✗ **Ida Davidsen.** Five generations old, this world-renowned lunch spot is **FodorśChoice** synonymous with smørrebrød, and the reputation has brought crowds. ★ The often-packed dining area is dimly lighted, with worn wooden tables and news clippings of famous visitors on the walls. Creative sandwiches include the H. C. Andersen, with liver pâté, bacon, and tomatoes. The terrific smoked duck is smoked by Ida's husband, Adam, and served alongside a horseradish-spiked cabbage salad. ✉ *Store Kongensg. 70, Sankt Annæ Kvarter* ☎ *33/91–36–55* ⊕ *www.idadavidsen.dk* ⊿ *Reservations essential* ▤ *AE, DC, MC, V* ☾ *Closed weekends and July. No dinner.*

$$ ✗ **Told & Snaps.** This authentic Danish smørrebrød restaurant adheres **FodorśChoice** to tradition by offering a long list of Danish delights, and the fare is some- ★ what cheaper than the city's benchmark smørrebrød restaurant Ida Davidsen. The butter-fried sole with rémoulade is a treat, as is the steak tartare. Wine is of course an option, but as this is true Danish cuisine, why not beer and *snaps* (Danish grain alcohol)? ✉ *Toldbodg. 2, Sankt Annæ Kvarter* ☎ *33/93–83–85* ⊕ *www.toldogsnaps.dk* ▤ *No credit cards* ☾ *Closed Sun. No dinner.*

$ ✗ **Lai Hoo.** Denmark's Princess Alexandra, a native of Hong Kong, is known to be a fan of this Chinese restaurant near the city's main square. Although the restaurant has a big take-out business, if you choose to dine in you can call for a reservation. The lunch specialty is an inspired variety of steamed dumplings (dim sum), and the best bet at dinner is the fixed menu—try the salt-baked prawns in pepper or the luscious lemon duck. ✉ *Store Kongensg. 18, Sankt Annæ Kvarter* ☎ *33/93–93–19* ▤ *MC, V* ☾ *No lunch Mon.–Wed.*

Vesterbro & Frederiksberg

$$$$ ✗ **Formel B.** The name stands for "basic formula," but this French-Danish fusion restaurant is anything but basic. Kirk, a third-generation chef, is fanatical about freshness, and this comes through in every dish. Dishes might include mussel soup flavored with wood sorrel; smoked salmon with dill seeds, spinach, and bacon; or panfried chicken with parsley root and horseradish, accompanied by all its parts—the liver, the heart, the craw, and the red comb—served on an array of small plates. Dessert is a work of art: a collection of individual delicacies is arranged on a large, white eye-shape platter and drizzled with a passion-fruit glaze and pine nuts. Kirk prepares a six-course menu (DKr 600; wine pairings are an additional DKr 600) daily, depending on what seasonal ingredients are available. There is no à la carte menu. ✉ *Vesterbrog. 182, Frederiksberg* ☎ *33/25–10–66* ⊕ *www.formel-b.dk* ⊿ *Reservations essential* ▤ *AE, DC, MC, V* ☾ *Closed Sun. No lunch.*

$$$–$$$$ ✕ **Cofoco.** The name is an acronym for Copenhagen Food Consulting, and its reasonable prices for a three-course meal (DKr 225) in very fashionable surroundings have made it an instant hit in the city. Beautiful chandeliers cast soft light over earth-tone walls and linens. Lamb and fish dishes dominate the menu, and appetizers may include foie gras, crab salad with asparagus, or spinach salad with ricotta. You can reserve a table online, but make sure you do it that way or by phone, as the restaurant fills up frequently on weekends. ⊠ *Abel Cathrines Gade. 7 Vesterbro* ☎ *33/13–60–60* ⊕ *www.cofoco.dk/kontakt.asp* ⚖ *Reservations essential* ⊟ *DC, MC, V* ⊙ *Closed Sun.*

$–$$$ ✕ **Copenhagen Corner.** Diners here feast on superb views of the Rådhus Pladsen and terrific smørrebrød, which compensate for the uneven pace of the harried but hardworking staff and some of the less appealing dishes on the menu. Specialties include fried veal with bouillon gravy and fried potatoes; entrecôte in garlic and bordelaise sauce with creamed potatoes; and a herring plate with three types of spiced, marinated herring and boiled potatoes. Although the restaurant seats 250, try to call ahead for a reservation. ⊠ *Vesterbrog. 1, Vesterbro* ☎ *33/91–45–45* ⊕ *www.remmen.dk* ⊟ *AE, DC, MC, V.*

$–$$ ✕ **Delicatessen.** Happily defying labels, this casual diner-café-bar is done up in Dansk design—silver-gray bucket seats and a stainless-steel-top bar—and serves hearty brunches and global cuisine by day and cocktails and DJ-spun dance tunes by night. Linger over scrambled eggs with bacon and a steaming cup of coffee (served from 11 AM), or tuck into the international cuisine of the month, which runs from North African to Thai to Italian. The menu might include pad thai; lamb curry with basmati rice, mint, and yogurt; or roast pork with thyme and zucchini. A trip to the bathroom is good for grins: on your way you pass by two fun-house mirrors; look to one side, and you're squat and fat. Look to the other, and you're slender and tall. ⊠ *Vesterbrog. 120, Vesterbro* ☎ *33/22–16–33* ⊕ *www.delicatessen.dk* ⊟ *V.*

¢–$$ ✕ **Yan's Wok.** The former chef of Lai Hoo mans the wok here, serving Hong Kong–style cuisine, as well as peppery dishes from Szechuan province. The theater menu is a great deal and runs from 4 to 6, while a slightly higher-priced card is offered during dinner hours. Regardless of the hour, you can be sure of getting tasty meals at bargain prices. ⊠ *Bagerstr. 9, Vesterbro* ☎ *33/23–73–33* ⊟ *DC, MC, V* ⊙ *Closed Mon. No lunch.*

WHERE TO STAY

Copenhagen is well served by a wide range of hotels, overall among Europe's most expensive. The hotels around the somewhat run-down red-light district of Istedgade—which looks more dangerous than it is—are the least expensive. Copenhagen is a compact, eminently walkable city, and most of the hotels are in or near the city center, usually within walking distance of most of the major sights and thoroughfares.

Breakfast is almost always included in the room rate, except in some of the pricier American-run hotel chains. Rooms have bath or shower unless otherwise noted. Note that in Copenhagen, as in the rest of Denmark, half (to three-fourths) of the rooms usually have showers only (while the rest have showers and bathtubs), so make sure to state your preference when booking.

	$$$$	$$$	$$	$	¢
WHAT IT COSTS In Danish Kroner					
FOR 2 PEOPLE	over 1,700	1,400–1,700	1,000–1,400	700–1,000	under 700

Prices are for two people in a standard double room, including service charge and tax.

Amager & Kastrup

$$$$ ▣ **Hilton Copenhagen Airport.** This calm oasis immediately takes the stigma away from common airport hotels that seem to be only brief stopgaps for weary travelers. Four 12-story buildings surround a bright atrium. Half of the rooms have views of the city's skyline; the other half look out onto Terminal 3 of the airport. Executive floors 11 and 12 have special amenities and offer complimentary access to a club room. Rooms have broad windows and are decorated in a modern Scandinavian style with indigenous woods from sustainable forests; the bathrooms are spacious. Befitting its location, arrival/departure terminals are in the lobby, and the airport's main terminal is just across the street. Although there is a train station in the airport, a Metro station is also due to open at the hotel's entrance in 2007, which will spare travelers expensive taxi rides downtown. ⊠ *Ellehammersvej 20, Copenhagen Airport, DK–2770 Kastrup* ☎ *32/50–15–01* ⊟ *32/52–85–28* ⊕ *www.hilton.dk* ⇴ *375 rooms, 7 suites* ♿ *3 restaurants, indoor pool, gym, sauna, bar, meeting rooms, some pets allowed, no-smoking rooms* ☰ *AE, DC, MC, V.*

$$$$ ▣ **Radisson SAS Scandinavia.** South across the Stadsgraven from Christianshavn, this is one of northern Europe's largest hotels, and Copenhagen's token skyscraper. An immense lobby, with cool, recessed lighting and streamlined furniture, gives access to the city's only casino. Guest rooms are large and somewhat institutional but offer every modern convenience, making this a good choice if you prefer familiar comforts over character. The hotel's Dining Room restaurant, overlooking Copenhagen's copper towers and skyline, is a fine site for a leisurely lunch, while the dinner menu tempts guests with a changing list of six main courses concocted from fresh seasonal ingredients. The restaurant is closed Sunday. ⊠ *Amager Blvd. 70, Amager, DK–2300* ☎ *33/96–50–00* ⊟ *33/96–55–00* ⊕ *www.radissonsas. com* ⇴ *542 rooms, 43 suites* ♿ *4 restaurants, cable TV, indoor pool, Internet room, meeting rooms* ☰ *AE, DC, MC, V.*

¢ ▣ **Amager Danhostel.** This simple lodging is 4½ km (3 mi) outside town, close to the airport. The hostel is spread over nine interconnected, single-story buildings. The student backpackers and frugal families who stay here have access to the communal kitchen or can buy breakfast and dinner from the restaurant. There are a few rooms with two beds and private baths for a slightly higher price. Before 5 PM on weekdays, take Bus 46 from the main station directly to the hostel. After 5, from Rådhus Pladsen or the main station, take Bus 250 to Sundbyvesterplads, and

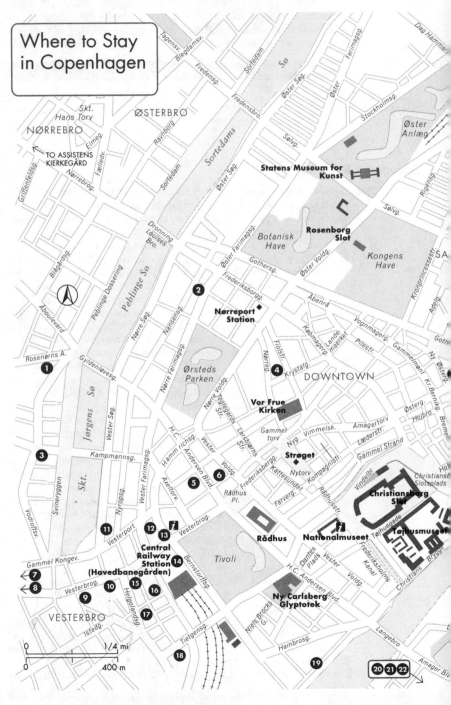

Where to Stay in Copenhagen

NØRREBRO

Skt. Hans Torv

ØSTERBRO

TO ASSISTENS KIERKEGÅRD

Statens Museum for Kunst

Øster Anlæg

Rosenborg Slot

Botanisk Have

Kongens Have

Dronning Louises Bro.

Peblinge Sø

2

Nørreport Station

Ørsteds Parken

4

DOWNTOWN

Vor Frue Kirken

Rosenørns A.

1

Jørgens Sø

Skt.

3

Gammel torv

Strøget

5 **6**

Nytorv

Christiansborg Slot

Rådhus Pl.

11 **12** **13** **i**

Christiansborg Slot

Nationalmuseet **i**

Tøjhusmuseet

Central Railway Station (Hovedbanegården) **14**

Rådhus

7

8

Tivoli

10 **15** **16**

9

VESTERBRO

17

Ny Carlsberg Glyptotek

0   1/4 mi

0   400 m

18

19

20 **21** **22**

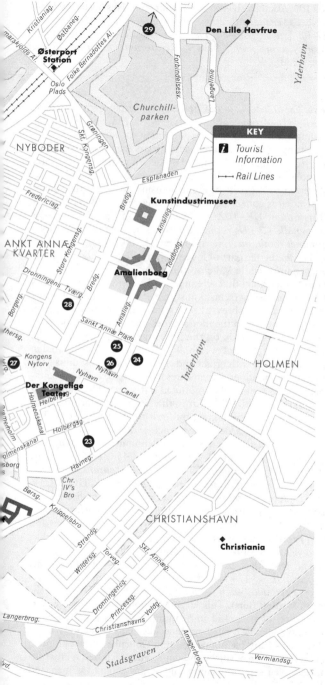

change to Bus 100. Ask the driver to signal your stop. This hostel is wheelchair-accessible. ☒ *Vejlands Allé 200, Amager, DK–2300* ☏ *32/52–29–08* 🖷 *32/52–27–08* ⊕ *www.copenhagenyouthhostel.dk* ⇆ *64 rooms with 2 beds, 80 family rooms with 5 beds* ♿ *Restaurant, laundry facilities, Internet room* ▤ *MC, V.*

Downtown

$$$$ 🏨 **D'Angleterre.** The grande dame of Copenhagen welcomes royalty, politi-
Fodor'sChoice cians, and rock stars—from Margaret Thatcher to Madonna—in pala-
★ tial surroundings: an imposing New Georgian facade leads into an English-style sitting room. Standard guest rooms are furnished in pastels, with overstuffed chairs and a mix of modern and antique furniture. The spit-and-polish staff accommodates every wish. The elegant Restaurant D'Angleterre serves excellent French cuisine. In winter the square in front of the hotel is converted into a skating rink. ☒ *Kongens Nytorv 34, Downtown, DK–1021* ☏ *33/12–00–95* 🖷 *33/12–11–18* ⊕ *www.remmen.dk* ⇆ *118 rooms, 19 suites* ♿ *Restaurant, indoor pool, bar, Internet room, meeting rooms* ▤ *AE, DC, MC, V.*

$$$$ 🏨 **Skt. Petri.** For the better part of a century, a beloved budget department store nicknamed Dalle Valle occupied this site. It has been supplanted by this luxury hotel that screams trendy, designer style, and it's a big hit with interior designers, fashionistas, and (presumably) followers of home-improvement TV shows. From a talking elevator telling you how fabulous the place is, to the model types manning the front desk, you know you're in for a walk on the pretentious side. That said, the individual rooms, designed by Per Arnoldi, are functional, decorated in a spare, modern aesthetic, with bright and cheery colors. Most units have a terrace or balcony. The larger corner suites have two terraces with stainless-steel furniture, as well as wall-mounted flat-screen TVs, dining tables and desks, and Arnoldi's Pop Art in the bedroom, which may not be to everyone's taste. The breakfast buffet is the best in the city. The hotel envelops an atrium garden and terrace and is, overall, pure (albeit expensive) comfort for the new-ish millennium. ☒ *Krystalg. 22, Downtown, DK–1172* ☏ *33/45–91–00* 🖷 *33/45–91–10* ⊕ *www. hotelsktpetri.com* ⇆ *241 rooms, 27 suites* ♿ *Restaurant, café, bar, meeting rooms, no-smoking rooms, parking (free)* ▤ *AE, DC, MC, V.*

$$$–$$$$ 🏨 **Strand.** You can't stay closer to the harbor than here: just a five-minute walk from Nyhavn, this pleasant hotel is housed in a waterfront warehouse dating from 1869. The cozy lobby has brown leather couches and old maritime pictures on the walls. The rooms are small but comfortable, with blue-and-yellow bedspreads and sparkling bathrooms. ☒ *Havneg. 37, Downtown, DK–1058* ☏ *33/48–99–00* 🖷 *33/48–99–01* ⊕ *www. copenhagenstrand.dk* ⇆ *174 rooms, 2 suites* ♿ *Restaurant, bar, meeting rooms, some pets allowed, no-smoking rooms* ▤ *AE, DC, MC, V.*

$$–$$$$ 🏨 **Copenhagen Marriott Hotel.** This large Marriott on the city's waterfront (and the first of its brand in Scandinavia), has great views of Christianshavn, and it's a well-oiled machine, like many well-known chain hotels. Sadly, it lacks any feeling of being in Copenhagen, let alone in Denmark. It has superior business and conference facilities, a great fitness room, and even separate sauna and steam rooms for men and women, but vacationers might prefer to spend time at a hotel that has more local flavor, ambience, and character. Guest rooms are very comfortable and of a good size, but breakfast is not included in the rate. The restaurant and bar (Terraneo) advertise Mediterranean cuisine. ✉ *Kalvebod Brygge. 5, DK–1560* ☎ *88/33–99–00* 🖷 *88/33–12–99* ⊕ *www.marriott.com/cphdk* 🖘 *378 rooms, 17 suites* ⚭ *Restaurant, bar, health club, gift shop, meeting rooms, parking (fee), some pets allowed, no-smoking rooms* 🖃 *AE, DC, MC, V.*

$$$ ⛫ **Ascot.** This downtown hotel, popular with European businesspeople and group tours, was formerly a public bathhouse designed in 1902 and built by Martin Nyrop, the same architect who did Copenhagen Town Hall. All that remains of the hotel's former incarnation are the black granite columns in the lobby, and wall reliefs of bathing women and men. There are a variety of rooms, apartments, and suites, some much better located than others; ask for a street, rather than a courtyard, view. Rooms aren't terribly fancy, but they're clean and comfortable. The breakfast buffet in the turn-of-the-20th-century dining room is ample and nourishing. One big benefit of the Ascot is that it's less than a five-minute walk to Tivoli. The staff is friendly and efficient. ✉ *Studiestr. 61, Downtown, DK–1554* ☎ *33/12–60–00* 🖷 *33/14–60–40* ⊕ *www.ascothotel. dk* 🖘 *171 rooms, 4 suites* ⚭ *Cable TV, bar, meeting room, parking (fee), some pets allowed* 🖃 *AE, DC, MC, V.*

$$ ⛫ **Ibsens Hotel.** This winsome, family-owned hotel near Nørreport Station has cozy, immaculate rooms and a lovely courtyard. The friendly staff is particularly attentive and goes out of its way to help. The attention to detail is evident in the hotel's decor—each floor has its own theme. The Scandinavian floor showcases cool and modern local designs, while the Bohemian floor is filled with antique furnishings. The breakfast room is a lovely place to start your morning. ✉ *Vendersg. 23, Downtown, DK–1363* ☎ *33/13–19–13* 🖷 *33/13–19–16* ⊕ *www. ibsenshotel.dk* 🖘 *118 rooms, 3 suites* ⚭ *Restaurant, bar, some pets allowed, no-smoking rooms* 🖃 *AE, DC, MC, V.*

Sankt Annæ Kvarter & North

$$$$ ⛫ **Clarion Neptun.** This elegant central hotel was bought years ago with the intention of making it the bohemian gathering place of Copenhagen, but these days it is more practical than artsy and welcomes business guests, tourists, and even large tour groups. The lobby and lounge are light, with classical furnishings and pale tones, and guest rooms have a tasteful modern decor. Many rooms face an interior covered courtyard. Next door is the hotel's Restaurant Gendarmen, run by a group of young restaurateurs who have created a dinner menu on the concept of old-meets-new, marrying traditional Danish dishes (roast pork or cod) with nouveau touches, such as a light truffle or blueberry sauce. The traditional lunch menu consists of good old Danish fare, like smørrebrød. ✉ *Skt. Annæ Pl. 18–20, Sankt Annæ Kvarter, DK–1250* ☎ *33/ 96–20–00* 🖷 *33/96–20–66* ⊕ *www.choicehotels.dk* 🖘 *133 rooms* ⚭ *Restaurant, bar, babysitting, meeting rooms, free parking, some pets allowed* 🖃 *AE, DC, MC, V.*

★ **$$$$** ▦ **Nyhavn 71.** In a 200-year-old warehouse, this quiet, soothing hotel is a good choice for privacy-seekers. It overlooks the old ships of Nyhavn, and its interiors have been preserved with their original thick plaster walls and exposed brick. The rooms are tiny but cozy, with warm woolen spreads, dark woods, soft leather furniture, and crisscrossing timbers. ✉ *Nyhavn 71, Sankt Annæ Kvarter, DK–1051* ☎ *33/43–62–00* 🖷 *33/43–62–01* ⊕ *www.71nyhavnhotelcopenhagen.dk* ➷ *150 rooms, 3 suites* ♻ *Restaurant, bar, meeting rooms, free parking, some pets allowed, no-smoking rooms* ▤ *AE, DC, MC, V.*

$$$$ ▦ **Phoenix.** This luxury hotel has automatic glass doors, crystal chandeliers, and gilt touches everywhere. Originally built in the 1680s, the hotel was then torn down and rebuilt into a plush, Victorian-style hotel in 1847, rising from its rubble just like the mythical Phoenix rose from its ashes, and thus its name. The suites and business-class rooms are adorned with faux antiques and 18-karat-gold-plated bathroom fixtures; the standard rooms are very small, measuring barely 9 feet by 15 feet. It's so convenient to city-center attractions that the hotel gets a fair amount of street noise; light sleepers should ask for rooms above the second floor. Downstairs is Murdoch's Books & Ale, a snug pub done up in mahogany and brass, with antique Danish tomes lining its bookshelves. The pub serves smørrebrød and light meals, including a green salad topped with chicken marinated in balsamic vinegar and a ham-and-onion quiche. It's closed Sunday. ✉ *Bredg. 37, Sankt Annæ Kvarter, DK–1260* ☎ *33/ 95–95–00* 🖷 *33/33–98–33* ⊕ *www.phoenixcopenhagen.dk* ➷ *206 rooms, 7 suites* ♻ *Restaurant, bar, meeting rooms, parking (fee), some pets allowed, no-smoking rooms* ▤ *AE, DC, MC, V.*

★ **$$$** ▦ **Admiral.** A five-minute stroll from Nyhavn, overlooking old Copenhagen and Amalienborg, the monolithic Admiral was once a grain warehouse dating from 1787, but now provides travelers with no-nonsense accommodations. It's one of the less-expensive top hotels, cutting frills and prices. Massive stone walls are broken by rows of tiny windows; guest rooms are spare, with jutting beams and modern prints. ✉ *Toldbodg. 24–28, Sankt Annæ Kvarter, DK–1253* ☎ *33/74–14–14* 🖷 *33/ 74–14–16* ⊕ *www.admiralhotel.dk* ➷ *314 rooms, 52 suites* ♻ *Restaurant, bar, nightclub, meeting room, free parking, some pets allowed, no-smoking rooms* ▤ *AE, DC, V.*

$$ ▦ **Skovshoved.** This delightful, art-filled inn is 8 km (5 mi) north of town, near a few old fishing cottages beside the yacht harbor. Licensed since 1660, it has retained its provincial charm. Larger rooms overlook the sea, smaller ones rim the courtyard; all have both modern and antique furnishings. The best way to get here is to take Bus 6 from Rådhus Pladsen or the S-train to Charlottenlund and walk 10 minutes from the station. ✉ *Strandvejen 267, DK–2920 Charlottenlund* ☎ *39/64–00–28* 🖷 *39/64–06–72* ⊕ *www.skovshovedhotel.dk* ➷ *23 rooms, 3 suites* ♻ *Restaurant, billiards, bar, meeting rooms* ▤ *AE, DC, MC, V.*

FodorśChoice
★

Vesterbro & Frederiksberg

$$$$ ▦ **Radisson SAS Royal.** Towering over the heart of town, this high-rise hotel was originally designed by Arne Jacobsen in 1960. Recently the owners spent several years—and plenty of kroner—in re-embracing its

FodorśChoice
★

Jacobsen look, and the result is a paean to the legendary designer. The graceful lobby has blue and white Jacobsen Swan and Egg chairs that are arranged in circles and illuminated by the ceiling's recessed lights. The soothing hotel rooms are paneled in light maple and outfitted with Jacobsen chairs and lamps. Even the heavy door handles, functionally designed to fill the palm, were created by Jacobsen. The most famous room is 606, which looks just like it did in 1960, with all the original furnishings, including a nifty desktop that opens to reveal a lighted makeup mirror. Many of the rooms boast views over Tivoli and the city center's copper-top buildings. The top-floor restaurant, Alberto K, serves top-notch Scandinavian-Italian cuisine. You don't have to be a hotel guest to bask in Jacobsen's aura. For the price of a cocktail you can hang out in the elegant hotel bar, sitting on—and amid—Jacobsen designs. ⊠ *Hammerichsg. 1, Vesterbro, DK–1611* ☎ *33/42–60–00* 🖷 *33/42–61–00* ⊕ *www.radissonsas.com* ⤳ *260 rooms, 6 suites* ⚐ *Restaurant, room service, gym, bar, Internet room, meeting rooms, parking (fee), some pets allowed, no-smoking rooms* ▭ *AE, DC, MC, V.*

$$$$ ▥ **Scandic Copenhagen.** Rising over Copenhagen's lakes, alongside the cylindrical IMAX Tycho Brahe Planetarium, is this modern high-rise hotel. The comfortable rooms, done up in cool tones and blond-wood furnishings, have splendid views. One side of the hotel overlooks the peaceful lakes, and the other side the bustling heart of Copenhagen, including Tivoli. The higher up you go, the better the view, so inquire about a room on the 17th floor, which is the highest floor that still has standard doubles; it's suites-only on the 18th. ⊠ *Vester Søg. 6, Vesterbro, DK–1601* ☎ *33/14–35–35* 🖷 *33/32–12–23* ⊕ *www.scandic-hotels.com/copenhagen* ⤳ *480 rooms, 6 suites* ⚐ *Restaurant, room service, gym, sauna, bar, concierge, meeting rooms, parking (fee), some pets allowed, no-smoking rooms* ▭ *AE, DC, MC, V.*

$$$–$$$$ ▥ **First Hotel Vesterbro.** Looming over Vesterbrogade—and just a five-minute walk from Tivoli—this four-star deluxe hotel is Denmark's third largest. The sun-drenched lobby, with floor-to-ceiling windows, has white pillars, blond-wood tables, and gray Dansk design armchairs. The rooms have pale yellow walls, cherrywood furnishings, and contemporary lithographs. Female travelers may want try out the "First Lady" rooms, which include adjustable mirrors and makeup remover in the bathrooms, fluffy bathrobes, an electric kettle, and women's magazines. The hotel's highlight is its magnificent brick-wall atrium awash in sunlight and hanging plants, and outfitted with marble tables and rounded wicker chairs; the ample complimentary breakfast buffet is served here. Complimentary access is offered to a full-service fitness center nearby. ⊠ *Vesterbrog. 23–29, Vesterbro, DK–1620* ☎ *33/78–80–00* 🖷 *33/78–80–80* ⊕ *www.firsthotels.com* ⤳ *403 rooms, 1 suite* ⚐ *Restaurant, gym, bar, meeting rooms, parking (fee), some pets allowed, no-smoking rooms* ▭ *AE, DC, MC, V.*

$$$–$$$$ ▥ **Grand Hotel.** In operation since the turn of the 20th century, the Grand Hotel went through a soft refurbishment (new carpets, linens, lighting, pictures) of its lobby and all of its guest rooms in the spring of 2005. An Italian restaurant serves good fare, and there's also a café on-site. The old-style lobby is presided over by a crystal chandelier, and this hotel has definite old-world charm. Some guest rooms have tiny (albeit newly painted) bathrooms, so inquire about this when booking, if you want a more spacious bathroom. ⊠ *Vesterbrog. 9, Vesterbro, DK–1620* ☎ *33/27–69–00* 🖷 *33/27–69–01* ⊕ *www.grandhotelcopenhagen.dk* ⇔ *161 rooms, 2 suites* ⚘ *Restaurant, room service, bar, concierge, meeting rooms, parking (fee), no-smoking rooms* ▤ *AE, DC, MC, V.*

$$–$$$$ 🖹 **Sofitel Copenhagen Plaza.** With its convenient location and plush homey atmosphere, this hotel has attracted the likes of Tina Turner and Keith Richards. Close to Tivoli and the main station, the building puts its best foot forward with a stately lobby and the adjacent Plaza Restaurant, which serves haute French-Italian cuisine. The older rooms are scattered with antiques; newer ones are furnished in a more modern style. The Library Bar is an elegantly cozy and atmospheric place for a drink, but the prices can be staggeringly high. ⊠ *Bernstorffsg. 4, Vesterbro, DK–1577* ☎ *33/14–92–62* 🖷 *33/93–93–62* ⊕ *www.sofitel.dk* ⇔ *87 rooms, 6 suites* ⚘ *Restaurant, room service, bar, concierge, meeting rooms, parking (fee), some pets allowed, no-smoking rooms* ▤ *AE, DC, MC, V.*

$$$ 🖹 **DGI Byen.** "An unusual meeting place" is how the DGI Byen presents itself, and it's a thoroughly apt description. This state-of-the-art recreation and sports center, just behind Central Station, boasts a bowling alley, climbing wall, shooting range, swimming pool, spa, and 104-room hotel. The hotel rooms are an exquisite blend of Danish design. Dark blue furnishings and blond-wood floors are softly illuminated by cylindrical lamps. Short poems by the much-loved Danish philosopher Piet Hein grace the cool gray walls. Though most rooms have doubly insulated windows, you can sometimes hear the distant rumble of trains entering the station. The last train passes by at around 12:30 AM, so ask for a quiet room if you're a light sleeper. The pool is free to hotel guests; nonguests pay DKr 46. You can pamper yourself with a range of soothing treatments at the full-service spa, but it costs extra. Ask about the substantially lower weekend rates. ⊠ *Tietgensg. 65, Vesterbro, DK–1704* ☎ *33/29–80–00* 🖷 *33/29–80–80* ⊕ *www.dgi-byen.dk* ⇔ *104 rooms* ⚘ *Restaurant, café, pool, sauna, spa, bowling, meeting rooms, parking (fee), no-smoking rooms* ▤ *AE, DC, MC, V.*

$$–$$$ 🖹 **Guldsmeden.** This family hotel, in a 19th-century Vesterbro building, has rooms decorated and restored in French-colonial style with wood paneling, stucco, and high ceilings. The amenities of the rooms differ; they may have four-poster beds, bathtubs, fireplaces, or furnished balconies. Every room has original art on the walls and hand-picked teak furniture. The owner has a similar, very comfortable property in Århus, with the same name. ⊠ *Vesterbrog. 66, Vesterbro, DK–1620* ☎ *33/22–15–00* 🖷 *33/22–15–55* ⊕ *www.hotelguldsmeden.dk* ⇔ *64 rooms, some without bath; 4 suites* ⚘ *Café, some pets allowed* ▤ *AE, D, MC, V.*

$–$$ 🖹 **Saga.** This is one of the newer, refurbished hotels in the vicinity of Central Station. Some rooms have just a sink, while others have full bathrooms. Breakfast is included in the price, and the hotel is good for families. ⊠ *Colbjørnsensg. 18–20, Vesterbro, DK–1652* ☎ *33/24–49–44*

🚈 *33/24–60–33* ⊕ *www.sagahotel.dk* ↯ *79 rooms, 31 with bath* ♿ *Some pets allowed* ☰ *AE, DC, MC, V* ⦿ *BP.*

$ 📺 **Triton.** Despite seedy surroundings, this streamlined hotel attracts a cosmopolitan clientele thanks to a central location in Vesterbro. The large rooms, in blond-wood and warm tones, all include modern bathroom fixtures. The buffet breakfast is exceptionally generous and the staff friendly. There are also family suites with a bedroom and a sitting area with a sofa bed. ✉ *Helgolandsg. 7–11, Vesterbro, DK–1653* 📠 *33/ 31–32–66* 🚈 *33/31–69–70* ⊕ *www.ibishotel.dk* ↯ *123 rooms* ♿ *Bar, some pets allowed* ☰ *AE, DC, MC, V.*

¢–$ 📺 **Crown.** Tucked into a small brick courtyard just off busy Vesterbrogade, this simple hotel has small but comfortable rooms with pale-yellow walls and light-green curtains. Some rooms overlook Vesterbrogade and the rest face the interior courtyard. The rooftop breakfast room floods with sunlight in summer and offers pleasant bird's-eye views of the Vesterbro neighborhood. ✉ *Vesterbrog. 41, Vesterbro, DK–1620* 📠 *33/21–21–66* 🚈 *33/21–00–66* ⊕ *www.ibishotel.dk* ↯ *80 rooms* ♿ *Bar, meeting rooms, some pets allowed, no-smoking rooms* ☰ *AE, DC, MC, V.*

¢–$ 📺 **Sct. Thomas.** Two friends from rural Denmark, Torgut and Rene, run this small and intimate hotel, which is a good value for the money. Among its pluses are its location—a short walk from the center of town in Fredericksberg's theater district—and its new beds (part of 2005 refurbishments). There aren't tons of facilities, but there are bicycle rentals, a sitting room with Internet access, and an included breakfast. Check out the hotel's Web site for a video showing the exterior and interiors of the building. ✉ *Frederiksberg Allé, Vesterbro, DK–1621* 📠 *33/21–64–64* 🚈 *33/ 25–64–60* ⊕ *www.hotelsctthomas.dk* ↯ *42 rooms, 26 with bath* ♿ *Internet room, free parking, no-smoking rooms* ☰ *V.*

¢ 📺 **Cab–Inn Scandinavia.** This bright hotel is just west of the lakes and Vesterport Station. Its impeccably maintained rooms are very small, but designed with efficiency to include ample showers, fold-away and bunk beds, and even electric kettles. The hotel is popular with business travelers in winter and kroner-pinching backpackers and families in summer. Its sister hotel, the Cab–Inn Copenhagen Express, is just around the corner at Danasvej 32-34, and there is yet another Cab–Inn right behind Tivoli at Mitchellsgade 14. ✉ *Vodroffsvej. 55, Fredericksberg, DK–1900* 📠 *35/36–11–11 Cab–Inn Scandinavia, 33/21–04–00 Cab–Inn Copenhagen Express, 33/46–16–16 Cab–Inn Mitchellsgade* ⊕ *www. cabinn.dk* ↯ *201 rooms* ♿ *Bar, meeting rooms, parking (fee)* ☰ *AE, DC, MC, V.*

¢ 📺 **Euroglobe.** This is a no-frills spot for the traveler who's looking for a comfortable bed with a roof overhead. Rooms are minimal, and guests share two common bathrooms on each floor. There's a little kitchen area on each floor where coffee, tea, or soups can be prepared. With breakfast included, this spot is a fine choice for the frugal. ✉ *Niels Ebbesensvej 20, Frederiksberg, DK–1911* 📠 *33/79–79–54* ⊕ *www. euroglobe.dk* ↯ *47 rooms without bath* ♿ *Some pets allowed* ☰ *No credit cards.*

NIGHTLIFE & THE ARTS

Nightlife

Most nightlife is concentrated in the area in and around Strøget, though there are student and "leftist" cafés and bars in Nørrebro and more upscale spots in Østerbro. Vesterbro, whose main drags are Vesterbrogade and Istedgade, has become quite the nightlife neighborhood, with several new bars and cafés. Many restaurants, cafés, bars, and clubs stay open after midnight, a few until 5 AM. Copenhagen used to be famous for jazz, but unfortunately that has changed, with many of the best clubs closing down. However, you can find nightspots catering to almost all musical tastes, from ballroom music to house, rap, and techno, in trendy clubs sound tracked by local DJs. The area around Nikolaj Kirken has the highest concentration of trendy discos and dance spots. Copenhagen's club scene can be fickle—new venues crop up regularly, often replacing last year's red-hot favorites. Call ahead or check out *Copenhagen This Week* (⊕ www.ctw.dk) for current listings. The stylish, biannual magazine *Scandinavian Living* (⊕ www.cphliving.dk) includes informative listings on the latest bars, restaurants, and shops. It also features articles on Danish culture, food, and architecture and is available at stores, hotels, and the tourist office.

Bars & Lounges

Copenhagen is peppered with hip restaurants that get even hipper in the evening, when they morph into lively nightspots. **Bang & Jensen** (✉ Istedg. 130, Vesterbro ☎ 33/25–53–18 ⊕ www.bangogjensen.dk), in the way-too-cool Vesterbro neighborhood, is a regular café during the day. From 9 PM until 2 AM, however, it turns into a cocktail bar jamming with loud music and a disco ambience. The **D'Angleterre Hotel** (✉ Kongens Nytorv 34, Downtown ☎ 33/37–06–64) is home to a tiny English-style bar that's just the place to soak up the posh hotel's ambience without forking over the kroner to stay here. When the hotel restaurant closes at 10 PM, bar guests can sit at tables by windows looking out on Copenhagen's most beautiful square, Kongens Nytorv. Moreover, after a peaceful drink or two, you will be within walking distance of a slew of other, more raucous nighttime spots. It stays open until 1 AM nightly. **Delicatessen** (✉ Vesterbrog. 120, Vesterbro ☎ 33/22–16–33 ⊕ www.delicatessen.dk) serves international cuisine by day, but after 11 PM Thursday through Saturday, it's time for cocktails and dancing to DJ-spun house, hip-hop, and rock. **Café Ketchup** (✉ Pilestr. 19, Downtown ☎ 33/32–30–30), just off the Strøget, draws an informal—though not un-savvy—crowd that gabs and grooves to the sounds of funk, house, hip-hop, and African music. It gets cooking after 11 PM on weekends, once cocktails start replacing coffee. **Charlie's Bar** (✉ Pilestr. 33, Downtown ☎ 33/32–22–89) insists that there are other beers in Copenhagen besides the omnipresent Carlsberg and Tuborg, and serves more than 46 draft and bottled beers to prove it. You can sample a handful of Danish microbreweries or Hoegaarden beer from Belgium. Indeed, there's no better place to enjoy such diversity than at this bar, which calls itself "proudly independent, independently proud" because it doesn't kowtow to the two big Danish brands. The dark room with low ceilings, owned by a transplanted Scotsman, is refreshingly unpretentious, with a laid-back crowd of regulars, both locals and expats.

Hviids Vinstue (✉ Kongens Nytorv 19, Downtown ☎ 33/15–10–64 ⊕ www.hvlidsvinstue.dk) dates from the 1730s and attracts all kinds, young and old, singles and couples, for a glass of wine or cognac. The **Library** (✉ Bernstorffsg. 4, Vesterbro ☎ 33/14–92–62), in the Plaza, is an elegant spot for a quiet but pricey drink. **"90"** ("halvfems" in Danish; ✉ Gammel Kongevej 90, Frederiksberg ☎ 33/31–84–90), which goes only by its street number, is the only watering hole that many Copenhagen old-timers trust for a "real beer." Unfortunately, it can take up to 15 minutes for the harried bartender to pull your draft pint. The small, atmospheric bar with dark orange walls and heavy wooden tables is the second home to a cast of crusty Copenhagen characters and outspoken barflies. At lunch, do as the locals do and buy smørrebrød from around the corner, and then bring it into the bar where you can settle in at one of the tables and enjoy your meal with one of the famous drafts. (There's a DKr 5 charge just to sit at the table.) **Peder Oxe's basement** (✉ Gråbrødretorv 11, Downtown ☎ 33/11–11–93) is casual and young, though nearly impossible to squeeze into on weekends.

The **Vega** (✉ Enghavevej 40, Vesterbro ☎ 33/25–80–12 ⊕ www.vega. dk) complex has become one of Copenhagen's premier clubs, as it has attracted everyone from Björk to Robbie Williams to Kylie Minogue, and internationally renowned DJs, such as Fat Boy Slim. Located in trendy Vesterbro in a 1950s trade-union building, Vega is divided into four rooms: Big Vega (Store Vega), the concert and dance club venue with a capacity of 1,500; Little Vega (Lille Vega), very popular on Friday and Saturday nights with up to 500 partygoers; the Ideal Bar; and the two-room Vega Lounge, a more intimate setting on the top floor of the building.

Cafés
Café life appeared in Copenhagen in the 1970s and quickly became a compulsory part of its urban existence. The cheapest sit-down eateries in town (a cappuccino and sandwich often cost less than DKr 60), cafés are lively and relaxed at night. The crowd is usually an interesting mix. Once run-down and neglected, the up-and-coming Istedgade strip is beginning to sprout cheery cafés and restaurants.

Bjørg's (✉ Vester Voldg. 19, Downtown ☎ 33/14–53–20) has a zinc bar, red seating, and lots of large windows. Guests slouch over huge burgers, club sandwiches, and excellent coffees. **Dan Turrell** (✉ Store Regneg. 3-5, Downtown ☎ 33/14–10–47), an old café, has become terribly chic lately, partly due to its good food and candlelight. At the fashionable **Europa** (✉ Amagertorv 1, Downtown ☎ 33/14–28–89), people-watching and coffee naturally go together. **Krasnapolsky** (✉ Vesterg. 10, Downtown ☎ 33/32–88–00) packs a young, hip, and painfully well-dressed audience at night, while a more mixed group populates its confines on placid afternoons.

Mama Lustra (✉ Istedg. 96, Vesterbro ☎ 33/25–26–11) looks like it could be a corner of your grandma's attic, with mismatched chairs, old wooden tables, and brass candleholders. Sink into a stuffed chair and sip a coffee or glass of Spanish wine while gazing out over busy Istedgade. The place also serves a simple but tasty brunch with cured ham, Italian sausages, and scrambled eggs, and an assortment of sandwiches including a vegetarian favorite—sun-dried tomatoes, pesto, and arugula. On Sunday, it hosts storytelling and spoken-word sessions. **Norden** (✉ Østerg. 61, Downtown ☎ 33/11–77–91) resides at the intersection of Købmagergade and Strøget. Substantial portions make up for minimal table space at this art nouveau–style café. **Rust** (✉ Guldbergsg. 8, Nørrebro ☎ 35/24–52–00) is a constantly crowded all-in-one rock club–restaurant–café on Nørrebro's main square, Skt. Hans Torv. Hearty, fresh dishes are served inside, while grill food is served on the terrace. **Sebastopol** (✉ Skt. Hans Torv 32, Nørrebro ☎ 35/36–30–02) teems with gussied-up locals in the evening and serves an ample weekend brunch. **Sommersko** (✉ Kronprinsensg. 6, Downtown ☎ 33/14–81–89) is the granddaddy of Copenhagen cafés, with a surprisingly varied menu (try the delicious french fries with pesto or the wok specialties) and an eclectic crowd. **Victor** (✉ Ny Østerg. 8, Downtown ☎ 33/13–36–13) is all brass and dark wood, just right for a light lunch.

Casino

The **Casino Copenhagen** (✉ Amager Blvd. 70, Amager ☎ 33/96–59–65 ⊕ www.casinocopenhagen.dk), at the SAS Scandinavia Hotel, has American and French roulette, blackjack, baccarat, and slot machines. Admission is DKr 80 (you must be 18 years old and show a photo ID), and a dress code (jackets required; no athletic clothing or jeans) is enforced. Outerwear must be left at the wardrobe, for a fee. The dealers and croupiers are not shy about reminding winners that a tip of a certain percentage is customary, even after hitting just one number on the roulette wheel. The casino is open daily 2 PM to 4 AM.

Discos, Dancing & Live Music

Most discos open at 11 PM, charging covers of about DKr 50–DKr 100 and selling drinks at steep prices. **Absalon** (✉ Frederiksbergg. 38, Downtown ☎ 33/16–16–98 ⊕ www.club-absalon.dk), popular with nearly everyone, has lively live music on the ground floor and a disco above. **Club Mambo** (✉ Vester Voldg. 85, Downtown ☎ 33/11–97–66 ⊕ www.salsaclub.dk) is the United Nations of discos, with an international crowd dancing to salsa and other Latin rhythms. **Columbus** (✉ Nørrebrog. 22, Nørrebro ☎ 35/37–00–51) is a lively salsa club where the activity gets hot as a chili pepper on a good night. Excellent salsa lessons are available to the uninitiated and out-of-practice. **Level CPH** (✉ Skinderg. 45, Downtown ☎ 33/13–26–25) pulsates to '80s dance tunes and features a roomy dance floor and a reconstructed airport lounge–like area, outfitted with real airplane seats. **Luft Kastellet** (✉ Strandg. 100-B, Christianshavn ☎ 70/26–26–24) fosters a beachlike atmosphere with its indoor-outdoor layout and harborside location. Guests often dance barefoot on the sand-covered floors to modern jazz, funk, or lounge-inspired chill-out tunes. **Nasa** (✉ Gothersg. 8F, Boltens Gård, Sankt Annæ

Kvarter 🕾 33/93–74–15 ⊕ www.nasa.dk) has an exclusive "members only" policy, which has earned it legendary status among Copenhagen's nightclubs. The choosy doorman screens the throngs outside based on his impression of their looks, clothes, and attitude. Luckily, rumor has it that Nasa is relaxing its door policy. Once inside, you get to hobnob in cool, white interiors with the city's chic and moneyed set and local celebrities (Prince Frederik occasionally drops by). Underneath Nasa are two other clubs, Club Bahia and Blue Buddha, with a more casual vibe and much more lax door policies.

Park Café (✉ Østerbrog. 79, Østerbro 🕾 35/42–62–48) offers an old-world café with live music downstairs, a disco upstairs, and a movie theater just next door. **Den Røde Pimpernel** (✉ Bernstorffsg. 3, Vesterbro 🕾 33/ 75–07–60) draws an adult audience for dancing to live orchestras, trios, and old-time music. The very popular English-style **Rosie McGees** (✉ Vesterbrog. 2A, Vesterbro 🕾 33/33–31–11 ⊕ www.rosiemcgees. dk) pub serves American and Mexican eats and encourages dancing, with DJs performing regularly, and the odd drag show thrown in for good measure. **Sofiekælderen** (✉ Overgaden oven Vandet 32, Christianshavn 🕾 32/57–27–87 ⊕ www.sofiekaelderen.dk) is a veteran of the Copenhagen night scene and serves as a frequent hangout for local musicians. Live music plays on Thursday, a DJ spins on Friday, and live jazz on Saturday afternoons gives way to piano-bar tunes in the evening. The kitchen serves simple fare to accompany cocktails. **Stereo Bar** (✉ Linnésg. 16A, Downtown 🕾 33/13–61–13 ⊕ www.stereobar.dk) has lava lamps and '70s furnishings; plays house, soul, and funk music on Friday and Saturday; and draws an eclectic crowd, from design students to writers, providing your best chance for an interesting conversation in Copenhagen's club scene. The **Søpavillionen** (✉ Gyldenløvsg. 24, Vesterbro 🕾 33/15–12–24 ⊕ www.soepavillonen.dk) invariably inspires first-time visitors to ask, "what *is* that building?" The ornate white wooden structure next to Copenhagen's lakes was built in 1894. The pavilion hosts seminars and private events on weekdays and functions as a dance club until 5 AM on weekends, featuring live music and DJs. **Woodstock** (✉ Vesterg. 12, Downtown 🕾 33/11–20–71) is among the city's most enduring clubs. A mixed audience grooves to music from the '50s to the '80s.

Gay Bars & Establishments

Given Denmark's longtime liberal attitudes toward homosexuality, it's not surprising that Copenhagen has a thriving and varied gay nightlife scene. In August, Copenhagen celebrates "Mermaid Pride," its boisterous annual gay-pride parade. For more information, call or visit the **Landsforeningen for Bøsser og Lesbiske** (Gay and Lesbian Association; ✉ Teglgårdstr. 13, Boks 1023, Downtown, DK–1007 🕾 33/13–19–48 ⊕ www.lbl.dk), which has a library and more than 45 years of experience. Check out the free paper *Panbladet* (www.panbladet.dk), or the gay guides *Gayguide* (www.gayguide.dk) and *Copenhagen Gay Life* (www.copenhagen-gay-life.dk) for listings of nightlife events and clubs, and other topical information of special interest to the gay individual.

HOTELS **Carsten's Guest House** (✉ Christians Brygge. 28, 5th fl., Vesterbro ☎ 33/14–91–07 ⊕ www.carstenguesthouse.dk) is a popular guesthouse which offers rooms (DKr 420–DKr 550), a bed in the youth hostel (DKr 165), or a holiday apartment (DKr 850–DKr 1,250) in the middle of town. Breakfast is an extra DKr 65. **Hotel Windsor** (✉ Fredericksborrgg. 30, Downtown ☎ 33/11–08–30 🖶 33/11–63–87 ⊕ www.hotelwindsor.dk) is a gay-friendly hotel that doubles as a great diner for breakfast.

BARS **Amigo Bar** (✉ Schønbergsg. 4, Downtown ☎ 33/21–49–15) really gets going after midnight with campy karaoke songs and lots of customers anxious to party. It's popular with men of all ages. For a show-tune showdown, head for the piano bar at **Café Intime** (✉ Allég. 25, Frederiksberg ☎ 38/34–19–58 ⊕ www.cafeintime.dk), where you can sip cocktails. It's easy to meet people at **Can Can** (✉ Mikkel Bryggersg. 11, Downtown ☎ 33/11–50–10), a small place with a friendly bartender and a mostly male clientele.

The small **Central Hjørnet** (✉ Kattesundet 18, Downtown ☎ 33/11–85–49 ⊕ www.centralhjornet.dk) has been around for about 60 years. The dark, casual **Cosy Bar** (✉ Studiestr. 24, Downtown ☎ 33/12–74–27 ⊕ www.cosybar.dk) is the place to go in the wee hours (it usually stays open until 8 AM). **Heaven Café** (✉ Kompagnistr. 18, Downtown ☎ 33/15–19–00 ⊕ www.heaven-copenhagen.dk) is the latest addition to the gay café scene, serving light meals to a casual crowd of locals and foreigners. Meals in the upstairs restaurant are fairly priced and attract a steady clientele. **Jeppes Club** (✉ Allég. 25, Frederiksberg ☎ 38/87–32–48) is patronized mainly by gay women and is open on the first and last Friday of every month. **Masken Bar & Café** (✉ Studiestr. 33, Downtown ☎ 33/91–09–37 ⊕ www.maskenbar.dk) is a relaxed bar welcoming both men and women. **Men's Bar** (✉ Teglgårdstr. 3, Downtown ☎ 33/12–73–03) is men-only with a leather-and-rubber dress code. **Jailhouse Event Bar& Restaurant** (✉ Studiestræde. 12, Downtown ☎ 33/15–22–55 ⊕ www.jailhousecph.dk) isn't as odd a place as the name sounds, even if it is decorated like a city jail. Waiters are in varied police uniforms, and overall, it's a fun, convivial atmosphere attracting men in a wide range of age groups. **Oscar Café & Bar** (✉ Rådhus Pl. 77, Downtown ☎ 33/12–09–99) is a relaxed spot for a drink or a cup of coffee, and a good place to chat with locals. **PAN Club** (✉ Knabrostr. 3, off Strøget, Downtown ☎ 33/11–37–84 ⊕ www.pan-cph.dk) packs men and women into its five levels and two dance areas; there's a total of six bars. It's considered to be one of Europe's biggest gay dance clubs.

Jazz Clubs

Hard times have thinned Copenhagen's once-thriving jazz scene. Most of the clubs still open headline local talents, but European and international artists also perform, especially in July, when the Copenhagen Jazz Festival spills over into the clubs. Many jazz clubs host Sunday-afternoon sessions that draw spirited crowds of Danes. **Copenhagen Jazzhouse** (✉ Niels Hemmingsensg. 10, Downtown ☎ 33/15–26–00 ⊕ www.jazzhouse.dk) attracts European and some international names to its chic, modern, barlike interior. **Drop Inn** (✉ Kompagnistr. 34, Downtown ☎ 33/11–24–04) draws a capacity crowd for its popular Sunday-afternoon jazz sessions. The bar was designed with the audience in mind. The stage faces an informal semicircle of chairs and booths so there isn't a bad seat in the house. The eclectic decor includes wrought-iron, wreath-shape candelabras, iron statues of winged bacchanalian figures, and an M. C. Escher–style ceiling fresco. **Jazzhuset Vognporten** (✉ Rådhusstr. 13, Downtown ☎ 33/15–63–53 ⊕ www.swinging-copenhagen.dk), with exposed concrete walls decorated with local art, showcases traditional New Orleans–style jazz acts on Friday and Saturday. (It's closed Sunday.) During the day it functions as a café, in whose sunlit back room you can enjoy coffee, beer, and light sandwiches. An adjoining theater features everything from Shakespeare to experimental plays. **La Fontaine** (✉ Kompagnistr. 11, Downtown ☎ 33/11–60–98) is Copenhagen's quintessential jazz dive, with sagging curtains, impenetrable smoke, and hep cats. This is a must for jazz lovers.

Rock Clubs

Copenhagen has a good selection of rock clubs, most of which cost less than DKr 50. Almost all are filled with young, fashionable crowds. Clubs tend to open and go out of business with some frequency, but you can get free entertainment newspapers and flyers advertising gigs at almost any café.

Lades Kælder (✉ Kattesundet 6, Downtown ☎ 33/14–00–67 ⊕ www.lades.dk), a local hangout just off Strøget, hosts bands that play good old-fashioned rock and roll. **Loppen** (✉ Bådsmandsstr. 43, Christianshavn ☎ 32/57–84–22 ⊕ www.loppen.dk), in Christiania, is a medium-size concert venue featuring some of the bigger names in Danish music (pop, rock, urban, and jazz) and budding artists from abroad. Cover charges can range from DKr 60 to DKr 80. The **Pumpehuset** (✉ Studiestr. 52, Downtown ☎ 33/93–19–60 ⊕ www.pumpehuset.dk) is the place for soul and rock, and gets some big names. Ticket prices can be steep. **Rust** (✉ Guldbergsg. 8, Nørrebro ☎ 35/24–52–00 ⊕ www.rust.dk) is a smaller club, mainly featuring rock, pop, and urban acts. Live music is available only on Thursday. **Stengade 30** (✉ Steng. 18, Nørrebro ☎ 35/39–09–20 ⊕ www.stengade30.dk), named for an address right down the street from the actual club, is a smallish rock venue doubling as a bar that remains open through the night. **Vega** (✉ Enghavevej 40, Vesterbro ☎ 32/25–70–11 ⊕ www.vega.dk) has evening rock bands, after which the dance club plays house and techno, dragging action into the wee hours.

The Arts

The most complete English calendar of events is listed in the tourist magazine *Copenhagen This Week* (www.ctw.dk), and includes musical and theatrical events as well as films and exhibitions. Copenhagen's main theater and concert season runs from September through May, and tickets can be obtained either directly from theaters and concert halls or from ticket agencies. **Billetnet** (☎ 38/48–11–22 ⊕ www.billetnet.dk), a box-office service available at all post offices, has tickets for most major events. The main phone line is often busy; for information go in person to any post office. There's one on Købmagergade, just off Strøget. Same-day purchases at the box office at **Tivoli** (✉ Vesterbrog. 3, Downtown ☎ 33/15–10–12) are half price if you pick them up after noon; the half-price tickets are for shows all over town, but the ticket center also has full-price tickets for the park's own performances. The box office is open weekdays 11 to 5.

Film

Films open in Copenhagen a few months to a year after their U.S. premieres. There are about 60 cinemas in the greater Copenhagen area. The Danes are avid viewers, willing to pay DKr 70 per ticket, wait in lines for premieres, and read subtitles. Call the theater for reservations, and pick up tickets (with assigned seat numbers) an hour before the movie. Most theaters have a café. **Cinemateket** (⊠ Gothersg. 55, Downtown ☎ 33/74–34–12 ⊕ www.dfi.dk), in the Danish Film Institute building, runs art films—often a series with a theme—and houses an excellent gift shop and café. **Grand Teatret** (⊠ Mikkel Bryggersg. 8, Downtown ☎ 33/15–16–11 ⊕ www.grandteatret.dk) shows new foreign and art films, and is next door to its sister café. **Vester Vov Vov** (⊠ Absalonsg. 5, Vesterbro ☎ 33/24–42–00 ⊕ www.vestervovvov.dk) is an alternative venue for art-house and second-run films.

Opera, Ballet, Theater & Music

Concert and festival information is available from the **Dansk Musik Information Center** (DMIC; ⊠ Gråbrødre Torv 16, Downtown ☎ 33/11–20–66 ⊕ www.mic.dk).

The **Opera Copenhagen** (Operahurst) (⊠ Ekvipagemestervej 10, Dock Island, Holmen ☎ 33/69–69–33 ⊕ www.operahus.dk) is the long-awaited home of the Royal Danish Opera on the southern side of the harbor on Dock Island, Holmen. It opened in January 2005, only three years after construction began. It was funded virtually by one individual, Denmark's wealthiest man, Mærsk McKinney-møller, who bankrolled the project. He chose Henning Larsen, one of Denmark's best architects, to plan and design the Opera House, and its unique location allows it to be seen throughout the entire inner harbor. You approach the Opera House via water taxi or water bus. The interior of the theater hall is being called the "conch." Depending on the orchestra's pit size, the hall contains between 1,400 and 1,700 seats. The building features many roof terraces and a cafeteria with a view over Holmen and Øresundsbroen. In response to its splendid new space, the Royal Danish Opera plans to increase its repertoire in 2006/07 to seven or eight new productions per season. The ticket office opens 90 minutes before performances, and standing-room-only tickets are available from the Royal Theater Tickets Office on Tordenskjoldsgade the same day after 1 PM. Tickets can also be purchased through Billetnet (above).

Det Kongelige Teater (The Royal Theater; ⊠ Kongens Nytorv, Downtown ⅅ Box 2185, 1017 Kobenhavn K ☎ 33/69–69–33 ⊕ www.kgl-teater.dk), where the season runs October to May, is home to the Royal Danish Ballet, one of the premier companies in the world. Plays are exclusively in Danish. For information and reservations, call the theater. Beginning at the end of July, you can order tickets for the next season by writing to the theater.

DENMARK'S CINEMA VERITÉ

CAUTION: WATCHING contemporary Danish films may induce dizziness and nausea and provoke a mild depression (or, if you prefer, a newfound understanding of the human capacity for evil). Whatever your take, it's the type of cinema that's hard to take sitting down, even with a tub of buttered popcorn in your lap. Denmark's bad boy of film is Lars von Trier, who has been called "bold, angry, and defiant" by one critic, and "ineptitude coupled with arrogance" by another. His best-known films include Dancer in the Dark (2000) starring the Icelandic singer Björk, Breaking the Waves (1996) with actress Emily Watson, and Europa (1991) for which von Trier won the Palm d'Or prize at Cannes. His latest movie, Dogville (2003), starred Nicole Kidman, Lauren Bacall, and James Caan.

Von Trier is also the founder of Dogma 95, a union of Danish filmmakers who took a collective "Vow of Chastity" in 1995 to eschew modern (read: Hollywood) filmmaking methods and get back to the basics—handheld cameras instead of tripods, and no artificial lighting, special effects, or dubbed-in musical scores. The result, both in content and in camera angles, has been moving—some would say stomach-churning—to say the least. A hyggelig (cozy) evening turns hellish in the 1998 film The Celebration, directed by Dogma 95 cofounder Thomas Vinterberg. Something in this disturbing tale clicked with worldwide audiences, because the film won the Special Jury prize at Cannes and screened in both the mainstream and art house circuits to great acclaim. The tagline could well have been lifted straight from Shakespeare's Hamlet, that "something is rotten in the state of Denmark." What starts out as a refined, candlelit celebration for the father's 60th

birthday soon degenerates into accusations and innuendo. Vinterberg shot the entire film with handheld cameras and used minimal extra lighting. The effect for the moviegoer is one of sitting right there at the dinner table, amid the tearful allegations and finger-pointing. That the audience is both participant and voyeur is, of course, exactly what Vinterberg intended.

Von Trier, Vinterberg, and their cronies hark from a rich cinematic tradition. Danish film blossomed in the 1930s with a spate of successful comedies and probing documentaries. The German occupation of Denmark from 1940 to 1945 proved to be a blessing in disguise for Danish cinema. All films from Allied countries were banned, giving rise to a proliferation of homegrown films. It was during the Occupation that Carl Theodor Dreyer, considered to be one of Denmark's most daring and brilliant filmmakers, solidified his already acclaimed filmic reputation with the making of Day of Wrath, an allegorical protest against the German invasion. Denmark's best-known contribution to the contemporary international film scene is director Bille August, who made a name for himself in the 1980s with a series of acclaimed films including, in 1987, Pelle the Conqueror, based on the novel by Danish author Martin Andersen Nexø.

Like any well-paced thriller, a surprise finale awaits: Von Trier is working on what he calls a "filmic monument"—tentatively titled Dimension—which he films a tiny part of each year. It's due for release in 2025 and, judging from his previous films, you won't want to miss it when it comes to a theater near you.

If you are in search of experimental opera then **Den Anden Opera** (✉ Kronprinsensg. 7, Downtown ☎ 33/32–38–30 ⊕ www.denandenopera. dk) is worth a visit. **Dansescenen** (✉ Øster Fælled Torv 34, Østerbro ☎ 34/ 35–83–00 ⊕ www.dansescenen.dk) hosts various modern and experimental dance performances, some of which are put together by their choreographer-in-residence. **Kanonhallen** (✉ Øster Fælled Torv 37, Østerbro ☎ 35/43–20–21 ⊕ www.kanonhallen.net) runs a modern dance troupe in the city. **Nyt Dansk Danseteater** (✉ Guldbergsg. 29A, Nørrebro ☎ 35/ 39–87–87 ⊕ www.nddt.dk) has a modern dance company but not a performance space; Copenhagen performances are held at other venues.

Tivoli Concert Hall (✉ Tietgensg. 20, Downtown ☎ 33/15–10–12) offers more than 150 concerts each summer, presenting a host of Danish and foreign soloists, conductors, and orchestras.

London Toast Theatre (✉ Kochsvej 18, Frederiksberg ☎ 33/22–86–86 ⊕ www.londontoast.dk) hosts English-language theater productions. **Københavns Internationale Teater (KIT)** (Copenhagen International Theatre; ✉ Vesterg. 5, 3rd fl., Downtown ☎ 33/15–15–64 ⊕ www.kit.dk) offers an interesting lineup of entertainment for all ages between June and August. Under the title "Summerscene," KIT presents international contemporary theater, dance, inventive circus-style shows, and myriad other performances.

SPORTS & THE OUTDOORS

Beaches

North of Copenhagen along the old beach road, **Strandvejen** is a string of lovely old seaside towns and beaches. **Bellevue Beach** (✉ Across street from Klampenborg Station, Klampenborg) is packed with locals and has cafés, kiosks, and surfboard rentals. **Charlottenlund Fort** (Bus 6 from Rådhus Pl.) is a bit more private, but you have to pay (about DKr 20) to swim off the pier. The beaches along the tony town of **Vedbæk**, 18 km (11 mi) north of Copenhagen, are not very crowded as they are not as close to Copenhagen or as easily accessible by public transportation.

Closest to the city, the route along **Amager Strandvej** to and from the airport is a 12-km (7½-mi) stretch of beaches and wooded areas. Helgoland beach, on the north end of this strand, has bathhouses and a long dock and requires a token entrance fee.

Biking

Bike rentals are available throughout the city, and most roads have bike lanes. You might also be lucky and find an advertisement-flanked "city bike," parked at busy points around the city including Kongens Nytorv and the Nørreport train station. Deposit DKr 20 and pedal away; your money is returned when you return the bike. The city bikes are out and about from May to September. The Copenhagen Right Now tourist information office has city bike maps with suggested bike routes including a route of the city's ramparts or of the Copenhagen harbor. Follow all traffic signs and signals; bicycle lights and reflectors must be used at night. The **Danish Cyclist Federation** (✉ Rømersg. 5, Downtown ☎ 33/32–31–21 ⊕ www.dcf.dk) has information about biking in the city. **Copenhagen Right Now** (✉ Vesterbrog. 4A, Downtown ☎ 70/22–24–42 ⊕ www.visitcopenhagen.com) can provide information about bike-rental companies and routes throughout the city.

Canoeing

About 15 km (10 mi) north of Copenhagen, especially in the Lyngby area, several calm lakes and rivers are perfect for canoeing: the Mølleå (Mølle River) and the Bagsværd, Lyngby, and Furesø (Bagsværd, Lyngby, and Fur lakes). Hourly and daily rentals and package canoe tours are available throughout the region.

Golf

Although almost all courses in Denmark are run by private clubs, anybody who is a member of a club approved by a recognized authority—such as USPGA or R & A—can play. You will generally be asked to present a handicap card, something many American golfers do not carry around with them. It might be a good idea to have some proof of membership with you when you go to sign in. Otherwise, you will need to convince the staff you are indeed a golfer. It would be wise to call beforehand to find out if and when it is possible to play. Most golf-course staffs are accommodating, especially for visitors. At this writing, there were only three pay-and-play courses within a 30-km (20-mi) radius of Copenhagen, and they tend to be crowded. They also follow varying restrictions that tend to be as strict as those of private clubs. Most courses have handicap limits, normally around 28, for prospective players. Clubs, bags, and handcarts can be rented at virtually all courses, but motorized carts are a rarity. With few exceptions, carts may not be used without a letter from a doctor stating it is necessary. Some clubs do not accept reservations; call for details.

Copenhagen Golf Center (✉ Golfsvinget 16–20, Vallenbæk ☎ 43/64–92–93 ⊕ www.cgc.dk) is one of the publicly accessible courses close to the city center. The 18-hole course is rather flat but challenging; there is a variety of practice facilities, including a driving range. **Copenhagen Indoor Golf Center** (✉ Refshalevej 177-B, Holmen ☎ 32/66–11–00 ⊕ www.cigc.dk) is a newly expanded indoor practice center in what was once the huge B & W shipbuilding plant. Pros are on hand to give lessons at the driving and chipping ranges or the practice green. The 18-hole course at **Københavns Golf Klub** (✉ Dyrehaven 2, Lyngby ☎ 39/63–04–83) is said to be Scandinavia's oldest. It is located on the former royal hunting grounds, which are now a public park, so golfers must yield to people out strolling and to the herds of wild deer who live in the park. Greens fees are about DKr 280; check local rules about obstructions. One of Denmark's best courses, a frequent host of international tournaments, is the 18-hole **Rungsted Golf Klub** (✉ Vestre Stationsvej 16, Rungsted Kyst ☎ 45/86–34–44 ⊕ www.rungstedgolfklub.dk). A 30 handicap for all players is required on weekdays; on weekends and holidays the required handicap is 24 for men and a 29 for women. In 2003 **Simons Golf Club** (⊠ Nybovej 5, Kvistgård ☎ 49/19–14–78 ⊕ www.simonsgolf.dk) became the first course in Denmark to host European Tour competition. One of the finest in the country, the course was made even more challenging for the professionals who played there. There are fine practice facilities; call to check about the handicap requirement. A hotel, the Nyborgaard Hotel, is located next to the first green of the golf course.

Horseback Riding

You can ride at the Dyrehavebakken (Deer Forest Hills) at **Fortunens Ponyudlejning** (⊠ Ved Fortunen 33, Lyngby ☎ 45/87–60–58). A one-hour session (English saddle), in which both experienced and inexperienced riders go out with a guide, costs about DKr 100.

Axel Mattssons Rideskole (⊠ Bellevuevej. 10-12, Klampenborg ☎ 39/64–08–22) is another facility for riding and lessons. It's open weekdays 7 AM–9 PM and weekends 7 AM–5 PM.

Running

The 6-km (4-mi) loop around the three lakes just west of city center—Skt. Jørgens, Peblinge, and Sortedams—is a runner's nirvana. There are also paths at the Rosenborg Have; the Frederiksberg Garden (near Frederiksberg Station, corner of Frederiksberg Allé and Pile Allé); and the Dyrehaven, north of the city near Klampenborg.

Soccer

Danish soccer fans call themselves Rooligans, which loosely translates as well-behaved fans, as opposed to hooligans. These Rooligans idolize the national team's soccer players as superstars. When the rivalry is most intense (especially against Sweden and Norway), fans don face paint, wear head-to-toe red and white, incessantly wave the Dannebrog (Danish flag), and have a good time whether or not they win. The biggest stadium in town for national and international games is **Parken** (⊠ Øster Allé 50, Østerbro ☎ 35/43–31–31). **Billetnet** (☎ 70/15–65–65) sells tickets for all matches. Prices are about DKr 140 for slightly obstructed views at local matches, DKr 220–DKr 320 for unobstructed; international matches are more expensive.

Swimming

Swimming is very popular here, and the pools (all of which are indoor) are crowded but well maintained. Separate bath tickets can also be purchased. Admission to local pools (DKr 20–DKr 50) includes a locker key, but you have to bring your own towel. Most pools are 25 meters long. The **DGI Byen Swim Center** (⊠ Tietgensg. 65, Vesterbro ☎ 33/29–80–00 ⊕ www.dgi-byen.dk) contains a massive oval pool with 100-meter lanes and a nifty platform in the middle that can be raised for parties and conferences. The swim center also has a children's pool and a "mountain pool," with a climbing wall, wet trampoline, and several diving boards. Admission to the swim center is DKr 50. During the popular monthly "spa night," candles are placed around the pool; dinner and wine are served on the raised pool platform; and massages and other spa services are offered. The beautiful **Frederiksberg Svømmehal** (Fredericksberg Swimming Baths; ⊠ Helgesvej 29, Frederiksberg ☎ 38/14–04–00) maintains its old art deco decor of sculptures and decorative tiles. It's open weekdays 7 AM–9 PM and weekends 9 AM–3 PM. The 50-meter **Lyngby Svømmehal** (⊠ Lundtoftevej 53, Lyngby ☎ 45/97–39–60) has a separate diving pool. In the modern concrete **Vesterbro Svømmehal** (⊠ Angelg. 4, Vesterbro ☎ 33/22–05–00), many enjoy swimming next to the large glass windows.

SHOPPING

A showcase for world-famous Danish design and craftsmanship, Copenhagen seems to have been designed with shoppers in mind. The best buys are such luxury items as crystal, porcelain, silver, and furs. Look for offers and sales (*tilbud* or *udsalg* in Danish) and check antiques and secondhand shops for classics at cut-rate prices. Although prices are inflated by a hefty 25% Value-Added Tax (Danes call it MOMS), non–European Union citizens can receive about an 18% refund. For more details and a list of all tax-free shops, ask at the tourist office for a copy of the *Tax-Free Shopping Guide.*

The **Information Center for Danish Crafts and Design** (⊠ Amagertorv 1, Downtown ☎ 33/12–61–62 ⊕ www.danishcrafts.dk) provides helpful information on the city's galleries, shops, and workshops specializing in Danish crafts and design, from jewelry to ceramics to wooden toys to furniture. Its Web site has listings and reviews of the city's best crafts shops.

Shopping Districts & Malls

The pedestrian-only **Strøget** and adjacent Købmagergade are *the* shopping streets, but wander down the smaller streets for lower-priced, offbeat stores. The most exclusive shops are at the end of Strøget, around Kongens Nytorv, and on Ny Adelgade, Grønnegade, and Pistolstræde. **Kronprinsensgade** has become the in-vogue fashion strip, where a number of young Danish clothing designers have opened boutiques. **Bredgade,** just off Kongens Nytorv, is lined with elegant antiques and silver shops, furniture stores, and auction houses. A very popular mall in the city is the gleaming **Fisketorvet Shopping Center** (☎ 33/36–64–00), built in what was Copenhagen's old fish market. It's near the canal, south of the city center, within walking distance of Dybbølsbro Station and the Marriott Hotel. It includes 100 shops, from chain clothing stores (Mang, Hennes & Mauritz) and shoe shops (including the ubiquitous Ecco) to a smattering of jewelry, watch, and stereo retailers, such as Swatch and Bang & Olufsen. Fast-food outlets abound, and there are 10 cinemas. **Field's** (⊠ Next to the Ørestad Metro Station (or E20 Frakørsel, exit 19) ⊕ www.fields.dk) is the mall of interest for many Danes (and shopping-crazed Swedes) right now. It's near the Copenhagen Airport and has 130 stores and a full floor devoted to food, entertainment, and leisure pursuits. It's open weekdays 10–8 and Saturday 9–5.

Department Stores

Hennes & Mauritz (✉ Amagertorv 21–24, Downtown ☎ 33/73–70–90), H & M for short, the Swedish chain, has stores all over town. They offer reasonably priced clothing and accessories for men, women, and children; best of all are the to-die-for baby clothes. **Illum** (✉ Østerg. 52, Downtown ☎ 33/14–40–02), not to be confused with Illums Bolighus, is well stocked, with a lovely rooftop café and excellent basement grocery. **Magasin** (✉ Kongens Nytorv 13, Downtown ☎ 33/11–44–33 ⊕ www. magasin.dk), Scandinavia's largest department store, also has a top-quality basement marketplace.

Specialty Stores

Antiques

For silver, porcelain, and crystal, the well-stocked shops on **Bredgade** are upscale and expensive. **Danborg Gold and Silver** (✉ Holbergsg. 17, Downtown ☎ 33/32–93–94) is one of the best places for estate jewelry and silver flatware. **Dansk Møbelkunst** (✉ Bredg. 32, Sankt Annæ Kvarter ☎ 33/32–38–37 ⊕ www.dmk.dk) is spacious and elegant, and home to one of the city's largest collections of vintage Danish furniture. Some of the pieces are by Arne Jacobsen, Kaare Klimt, and Finn Juhl, whose lustrous, rosewood furnishings are some of the finest examples of Danish design. **H. Danielsens** (✉ Læderstr. 11, Downtown ☎ 33/13–02–74) is a good bet for silver, Christmas plates, and porcelain. **Kaabers Antikvariat** (✉ Skinderg. 34, Downtown ☎ 33/15–41–77) is an emporium for old and rare books, prints, and maps. The dozens of **Ravnsborggade** (✉ Nørrebro ☎ 35/37–88–89 ⊕ www.ravnsborggade.dk) stores carry traditional pine, oak, and mahogany furniture, and smaller items such as lamps and tableware. Some of them sell tax-free items and can arrange shipping. **Royal Copenhagen** (✉ Amagertorv 6, Downtown ☎ 33/13–71–81 ⊕ www.royalcopenhagen.com), along Strøget, carries old and new china, porcelain patterns, and figurines, as well as seconds.

Audio Equipment

For high-tech design and acoustics, **Bang & Olufsen** (✉ Østerg. 3, Downtown ☎ 33/15–04–22 ⊕ www.bang-olufsen.dk) is so renowned that its products are in the permanent design collection of New York's Museum of Modern Art. (Check prices at home first to make sure you are getting a deal.)

Clothing

It used to be that Danish clothing design took a back seat to the famous Dansk-designed furniture and silver, but increasingly that's no longer the case. If you're on the prowl for the newest Danish threads, you'll find a burgeoning number of cooperatives and designer-owned stores around town, particularly along Kronprinsensgade, near the Strøget.

Artium (✉ Vesterbrog. 1, Vesterbro ☎ 33/12–34–88) offers an array of colorful, Scandinavian-designed sweaters and clothes alongside useful and artful household gifts. **Bruuns Bazaar** (✉ Kronprinsensg. 8, Downtown ☎ 33/32–19–99 ⊕ www.bruunsbazaar.com) has its items hanging in the closet of almost every stylish Dane. Here you can buy the Bruuns label—inspired designs with a classic, clean-cut Danish look—and other high-end names, including Gucci. **ICCompanys** (✉ Raffinaderivej 10., Downtown ☎ 32/66–77–88 ⊕ www.inwear.dk) carries a trendy, youthful style, typified by the Danish Matinique label. **Mett–Mari** (✉ Vesterg. 11, Downtown ☎ 33/15–87–25) is among the most inventive handmade women's clothing shops. **Munthe plus Simonsen** (✉ Grønneg. 10, Downtown ☎ 33/32–03–12 ⊕ www.muntheplissimon.com/05/) sells innovative and playful—and pricey—Danish designs. **Petitgas Herrehatte** (✉ Købmagerg. 5, Downtown ☎ 33/13–62–70) is a venerable shop for old-fashioned men's hats. The **Sweater Market** (✉ Frederiksbergg. 15, Downtown ☎ 33/15–27–73) specializes in thick, traditional, patterned, and solid Scandinavian sweaters.

Crystal & Porcelain

Minus the VAT, such Danish classics as Holmegaards crystal and Royal Copenhagen porcelain are usually less expensive than they are back home. Signed art glass is always more expensive, but be on the lookout for seconds as well as secondhand and unsigned pieces. **Bodum Hus** (✉ Østerg. 10, on Strøget, Downtown ☎ 33/36–40–80 ⊕ www.bodum.com) shows off a wide variety of reasonably priced Danish-designed functional, and especially kitchen-oriented, accoutrements; the milk foamers are indispensable for cappuccino lovers. **Royal Copenhagen** (✉ Amagertorv 6, Downtown ☎ 33/13–71–81 ⊕ www.royalcopenhagen.dk) has firsts and seconds of its famous porcelain ware. The **Royal Copenhagen Factory** (✉ Søndre Fasanvej 9, Frederiksberg ☎ 38/34–10–04 ⊕ www.royalcopenhagen.com) offers a look at the goods at their source. The factory runs tours through its facilities on weekdays from 10 to 4. Holmegaards Glass can also be purchased at the Royal Copenhagen store on Amagertorv. Alternatively, you can travel to their dedicated factory **Holmegaards Glasværker** (✉ Glasværkvej 45, Holme-Olstrup ☎ 55/54–50–00), 97 km (60 mi) south of Copenhagen near the town of Næstved. **Rosenthal Studio-Haus** (✉ Frederiksbergg. 21, on Strøget, Downtown ☎ 33/14–21–01 ⊕ www.rosenthal.dk) offers the lead-crystal wildlife reliefs of Mats Johansson as well as the very modern functional and decorative works of many other Italian and Scandinavian artisans.

Fur

Denmark, the world's biggest producer of ranched minks, is the place to go for quality furs. Furs are ranked into four grades: Saga Royal (the best), Saga, Quality 1, and Quality 2. **Birger Christensen** (✉ Østerg. 38, Downtown ☎ 33/11–55–55), purveyor to the royal family and Copenhagen's finest furrier, deals only in Saga Royal quality. The store presents a new collection yearly from its in-house design team. Expect to spend about 20% less than in the United States for same-quality furs ($5,000–$10,000 for mink, $3,000 for a fur-lined coat), but as always, it pays to do your homework before you leave home. Birger Christensen is also among the preeminent fashion houses in town, carrying labels like Donna Karan, Chanel, Prada, Kenzo, Jil Sander, and Yves Saint Laurent. **A. C. Bang** (✉ Lyngby Hovedg. 55, Lyngby ☎ 45/88–00–54) carries less expensive furs than Birger Christensen, but has an old-world, old-money aura and very high quality.

Furniture & Design

Illums Bolighus (⊠ Amagertorv 10, Downtown ☎ 33/14–19–41) is part gallery, part department store, showing off cutting-edge Danish and international design—art glass, porcelain, silverware, carpets, and loads of grown-up toys. **Lysberg, Hansen & Therp** (⊠ Bredg. 75, Sankt Annæ Kvarter ☎ 33/14–47–87 ⊕ www.lysberg.dk), one of the most prestigious interior-design firms in Denmark, has sumptuous showrooms done up in traditional and modern styles. **Paustian** (⊠ Kalkbrænderiløbskaj 2, Østerbro ☎ 39/16–65–65 ⊕ www.paustian.dk) offers you the chance to peruse elegant contemporary furniture and accessories in a building designed by Dane Jørn Utzon, the architect of the Sydney Opera House. You can also have a gourmet lunch at the Restaurant Paustian (it's open only for lunch). **Tage Andersen** (⊠ Ny Adelg. 12, Downtown ☎ 33/93–09–13) has a fantasy-infused floral gallery-like shop filled with one-of-a-kind gifts and arrangements; browsers (who generally don't purchase the expensive items) are charged a DKr 45 admission.

Silver

Check the silver standard of a piece by its stamp. Three towers and "925S" (which means 925 parts out of 1,000) mark sterling. Two towers are used for silver plate. The "826S" stamp (also denoting sterling, but less pure) was used until the 1920s. Even with shipping charges, you can expect to save 50% versus American prices when buying Danish silver (especially used) at the source. **Georg Jensen** (⊠ Amagertorv 4, Downtown ☎ 33/11–40–80 ⊕ www.georgjensen.com) is one of the most recognized names in international silver, and his elegant, austere shop is aglitter with sterling. Jensen has its own museum next door. **Danish Silver** (⊠ Bredg. 22, Sankt Annæ Kvarter ☎ 33/11–52–52), owned by longtime Jensen collector Gregory Pepin, houses a remarkable collection of classic Jensen designs from holloware and place settings to art deco jewelry. Pepin, an American who has lived in Denmark for over a decade, is a font of information on Danish silver design, so if you're in the market, it's well worth a visit. **Ira Hartogsohn** (⊠ Palæg. 8, Sankt Annæ Kvarter ☎ 33/15–53–98) carries all sorts of silver knickknacks and settings. **Sølvkælderen** (⊠ Kompagnistr. 1, Downtown ☎ 33/13–36–34) is the city's largest (and brightest) silver store, carrying an endless selection of tea services, place settings, and jewelry.

Street Markets

Check with the tourist office or the tourist magazine *Copenhagen This Week* (⊕ www.ctw.dk) for flea markets. Bargaining is expected. When the weather gets warm, it's time for outdoor flea markets in Denmark and the adventure of finding treasure among a vast amount of goods. Throughout summer and into autumn, there are six major flea markets every weekend. Two of the sites are right downtown. Along the walls of the cemetery **Assistens Kirkegård** (⊠ Nørrebro), where Hans Christian Andersen and Søren Kierkegaard are buried, there is a flea market on Saturday with vendors who carry cutlery, dishes, clothes, books, and

THE RISE OF DANISH DESIGN

WHAT DO THE SWAN, the Egg, and the Ant have in common? All are chairs designed by the legendary Danish designer Arne Jacobsen. His furniture designs, along with those of numerous other Danes from Hans J. Wegner to Finn Juhl, have made their way into living rooms, offices, and museums around the world.

The timeless allure of Danish design, which had its heyday in the 1950s, has ensured its enduring success. Lego is as popular now—even amid the modern computer mania—as when it was first designed back in the '50s. Bang & Olufsen radios from the late 1940s look positively futuristic alongside their blocky counterparts from the same era. And Danish furniture, from Jacobsen's stylishly simple chairs to Wegner's rounded, organic furniture are still displayed in design showrooms across the globe as the picture of modernity.

Whereas plenty of '50s designs have made a comeback for their kitsch value, Danish furniture never went out of style. The reason lies in its roots. Danish furniture designs are grounded in early-19th-century classicism, characterized by simple lines and a deliberate lack of decoration. This led many Danish designers to later embrace functionalism, which became the cornerstone of Danish design. Faced with this rapidly growing design movement, socialist Denmark did what it does best, and initiated various government aid programs to support new designers. In 1924 the Royal Academy of Fine Arts founded its furniture design school, appointing renowned designer and architect Kaare Klimt as one of its first lecturers.

The rallying cry behind Danish designs in the 1940s and '50s continued to be "form follows function." Danish designers elevated the concept of functionalism to a new level, basing their designs wholly on the human body, and all its infinite needs and variations. "A chair is only finished when someone sits in it," said Wegner, summing up the era's design ethic with his signature simplicity. A cabinet maker by trade, Wegner is credited with creating the chair (called, appropriately enough, "The Chair") that first introduced Danish design to an international audience. In 1950 the American magazine Interiors featured on its cover Wegner's Round Chair (as it was originally titled), naming it the world's most beautiful chair. Kennedy and Nixon each sat in one of these Wegner chairs during their televised presidential debates, resulting in more American commissions than Wegner and his round-the-clock factory workers could handle. Denmark became the darling of the international design world, a position that it's held onto ever since.

The use of organic materials is a natural offshoot of functionalism, and Danish designers were early masters in employing wood—from rich mahogany to pale beech—in their designs. "The feeling for materials is universal," says Wegner. "Love of wood is something that all of mankind has in common."

For all the international success of Danish furniture, it's the Danes themselves who are its greatest fans. Settle into the well-appointed living room of many a Dane, and chances are that you're sitting on a Wegner chair at a table designed by Finn Juhl; a Poul Henningsen lamp might be lighting up the room, and you will likely be slicing your Danish meatballs with Jacobsen-designed cutlery.

various other wares. At **Gammel Strand** on Friday and Saturday, the "market" is more of an outdoor antiques shop; you might find porcelain and crystal figurines, silver, or even, on occasion, furniture. **Kongens Nytorv** hosts a Saturday flea market in the shadow of the Royal Theater; the pickings are not so regal, but if you arrive early enough, you might nab a piece of jewelry or some Danish porcelain. **Israel Plads** (⊠ Near Nørreport Station, Downtown) has a Saturday flea market from May through October, open 8–2. More than 100 professional dealers vend classic Danish porcelain, silver, jewelry, and crystal, plus books, prints, postcards, and more. The side street **Ravnsborggade** (⊠ Nørrebro ⊕ www.ravnsborggade.dk) is dotted with antiques shops that move their wares outdoors on Sunday.

SIDE TRIPS FROM COPENHAGEN

Experimentarium

8 km (5 mi) north of Copenhagen.

☺ In the beachside town of Hellerup is the **Experimentarium,** where more than 300 exhibitions are clustered in various "Discovery Islands," each exploring a different facet of science, technology, and natural phenomena. A dozen body- and hands-on exhibits allow you to take skeleton-revealing bike rides, measure your lung capacity, stir up magnetic goop, play ball on a jet stream, and gyrate to gyroscopes. Once a bottling plant for the Tuborg Brewery, this center organizes one or two special exhibits a year; past installations have included interactive exhibits of the brain and tongue-wagging, life-size dinosaurs. Take Bus 6 or 650S from Rådhus Pladsen or the S-train to Hellerup; transfer to Bus 21 or 650S. Alternatively, take the S-train to Svanemøllen Station, then walk north for 10 minutes. ⊠ *Tuborg Havnevej 7, Hellerup* ☏ *39/27–33–33* ⊕ *www. experimentarium.dk* ⊠ *DKr 115* ☉ *Mon. and Wed.–Fri. 9:30–5, Tues. 9:30–9, weekends and holidays 11–5.*

Charlottenlund

10 km (6 mi) north of Copenhagen (take Bus 6 from Rådhus Pladsen or S-train to Charlottenlund Station).

Just north of Copenhagen is the leafy, affluent coastal suburb of Charlottenlund, with a small, appealing beach that gets predictably crowded on sunny weekends. A little farther north is Charlottenlund Slot (Charlottenlund Palace), a graceful mansion that has housed various Danish royals since the 17th century. Today, it houses only offices and is not open to the public. The surrounding peaceful palace gardens, however, are open to all, and Copenhageners enjoy coming up here for weekend ambles and picnics.

☺ A favorite with families is the nearby **Danmarks Akvarium** (Danmarks Aquarium), a sizable, well-designed aquarium near the palace with all the usual aquatic suspects, from gliding sharks to brightly colored tropical fish to snapping crocodiles. ⊠ *Kavalergården 1, Charlottenlund*

🕾 *39/62–32–83* ⊕ *www.akvarium.dk* 🖃 *DKr 75* ◔ *Nov.–Jan., daily 10–4; Feb.–Apr., daily 10–5; May–Aug., daily 10–6; Sept. and Oct., daily 10–5.*

Fodor's Choice
★ While in Charlottenlund, don't miss the remarkable **Ordrupgaard,** one of the largest museum collections of French impressionism in Europe outside France. Most of the great 19th-century French artists are represented, including Manet, Monet, Matisse, Cézanne, Renoir, Degas, Gauguin, Alfred Sisley, Delacroix, and Pissarro. Particularly noteworthy is Delacroix's 1838 painting of George Sand. The original painting depicted Sand listening to her lover Chopin play the piano. For unknown reasons, the painting was divided, and the half portraying Chopin now hangs in the Louvre. The Ordrupgaard also has a superb collection of Danish Golden Age painters, from Christen Købke to Vilhelm Hammershøj, who has been called "the Danish Edward Hopper" because of the deft use of light and space in his haunting, solitary paintings. Perhaps best of all is that much of the magnificent collection is displayed, refreshingly, in a non-museum-like setting. The paintings hang on the walls of what was once the home of museum founder and art collector Wilhelm Hansen. The lovely interior of this graceful manor house dating from 1918 has been left just as it was when Hansen and his wife Henny lived here. The white-and-gold ceiling has intricate flower moldings, and the gleaming dark-wood tables are set with Royal Copenhagen Flora Danica porcelain. Interspersed among the paintings are windows that provide glimpses of the surrounding lush, park-size grounds of beech trees, sloping lawns, a rose garden, and an orchard. ✉ *Vilvordevej 110, Charlottenlund* 🕾 *39/64–11–83* ⊕ *www.ordrupgaard.dk* 🖃 *DKr 65* ◔ *Tues., Thurs., and Fri. 1–5; Wed. 10–8; weekends 11–5.*

need a break? Before or after your visit to the Ordrupgaard museum, wind down next door at the soothing **Ordrupgaard Café** (✉ Vilvordevej 110, Charlottenlund 🕾 39/63–00–33 ⊕ www.cafeordrupgaard.dk), housed in the former stable of the manor house–turned–museum. Large picture windows overlook the wooded grounds, and museum posters of French and Danish artists line the café's whitewashed walls. Sink into one of the rustic cane chairs and enjoy the daily changing menu of light Danish–French dishes, such as the smoked salmon drizzled with lime sauce or a fluffy ham quiche served with fresh greens. For an afternoon snack, try a pastry along with a pot of coffee that you can refill as often as you wish. On Sunday from noon to 2 it serves a hearty brunch of eggs, bacon, smoked ham, and rye bread. The café is open Tuesday–Sunday, noon–5. Credit cards are not accepted.

Dragør

★ *22 km (14 mi) southeast of Copenhagen (take Bus 30 or 33 from Rådhus Pladsen).*

On the island of Amager, less than a half hour from Copenhagen, the quaint fishing town of Dragør (pronounced *drah*-wer) feels far away in distance and time. The town is set apart from the rest of the area around Copenhagen because it was settled by Dutch farmers in the 16th century. King Christian II ordered the community to provide fresh produce and flowers for the royal court. Today neat rows of terra-cotta–roof houses trimmed with wandering ivy, roses, and the occasional waddling goose characterize the still meticulously maintained community. If there's one color that characterizes Dragør, it's the lovely pale yellow (called Dragør gul, or Dragør yellow) of its houses. According to local legend, the former town hall's chimney was built with a twist so that meetings couldn't be overheard.

As you're wandering around Dragør, notice that many of the older houses have an angled mirror contraption attached to their street-level windows. This *gade spejl* (street mirror), unique to Scandinavia, was—and perhaps still is—used by the occupants of the house to "spy" on the street activity. Usually positioned at seat-level, this is where the curious (often the older ladies of town) could pull up a chair and observe all the comings and goings of the neighborhood from the warmth and privacy of their own homes. You can see these street mirrors all across Denmark's small towns and sometimes in the older neighborhoods of the bigger cities.

The **Dragør Museum,** in one of the oldest houses in town, sits near the water on Dragør's colorful little harbor. The collection includes furniture from old skipper houses, costumes, drawings, and model ships. The museum shop has a good range of books on Dragør's history. ⊠ *Havnepl., Dragør* ☎ *32/53–41–06* ⊕ *www.dragoermuseum.dk* ⊠ *DKr 20* ☉ *May–Sept., Tues.–Sun. noon–4.*

A ticket to the Dragør Museum also affords entrance to the **Mølsted Museum,** which displays paintings by the famous local artist Christian Mølsted, whose colorful canvases capture the maritime ambience of Dragør and its rich natural surroundings. ⊠ *Dr. Dichs Pl. 1, Dragør* ☎ *32/53–41–06* ⊕ *www.dragoermuseum.dk* ⊠ *DKr 20* ☉ *May–Aug., weekends noon–4.*

You can swing by the **Amagermuseet** in the nearby village of Store Magleby, 2 km (1 mi) west of Dragør. The museum is housed in two thatch-roof, whitewashed vintage farmhouses, which were once the home of the Dutch farmers and their families who settled here in the 16th century. The farmhouses are done up in period interiors, with original furnishings and displays of traditional Dutch costumes. Round out your visit with an outdoor stroll past grazing dairy cows and through well-tended vegetable gardens flourishing with the same vegetables that the settlers grew. ⊠ *Hovedg. 4 and 12, Dragør* ☎ *32/53–93–07* ⊕ *www. amagermuseet.dk* ⊠ *DKr 30* ☉ *May–Sept., Tues.–Sun. noon–4; Oct.–Apr., Wed. and Sun. noon–4.*

Where to Stay & Eat

$$$ ✕ **Restaurant Beghuset.** This handsome restaurant with rustic stone floors and green-and-gold painted doors is named Beghuset (Pitch House), because this is where Dragør's fishermen used to boil the pitch that waterproofed their wooden ships. The creative Danish cuisine includes fried pigeon with mushrooms, grapes, and potatoes drizzled with a thyme-and-balsamic-vinegar dressing. The front-room café was once an old dry-foods store, hence all the old wooden shelves and drawers behind the bar. Here you can order simple (and inexpensive) dishes such as a beef patty with onions and baked potatoes, and wash them down with a cold beer. ⊠ *Strandg. 14, Dragør* ☎ *32/53–01–36* ⊕ *www.beghuset.dk* ⊟ *AE, DC, MC, V* ☉ *Closed Mon.*

$–$$$ ✕ **Dragør Strandhotel.** Dragør's harborside centerpiece is this spacious, sunny restaurant and café, its exterior awash in a cool yellow like so many of the buildings in town. The Strandhotel started life as an inn, nearly 700 years ago, making it one of Denmark's oldest inns. Danish royalty used to stay here in the 1500s, after going swan hunting nearby, and in the 1800s Søren Kierkegaard was a regular guest. Though it has kept the "hotel" in its name, today it is only a restaurant. Owned and run by the Helgstrand family for the past 25 years, the Strandhotel has retained its former charms—vintage wooden cupboards and colored ceramics—with views of Dragør's small, bustling harbor. The menu is, disappointingly, tourist-driven (with items such as Mexi-burgers and Caesar salads), but the restaurant also serves Danish fare, including frikkadeller with potato salad; fillet of sole with rémoulade; and cod with red beets, mustard sauce, and chopped boiled egg. ⊠ *Strandlinien 9, Dragør* ☎ *32/52–00–75* ⊕ *www.dragoerstrandhotel.dk* ⊟ *DC, MC, V* ☉ *Closed mid-Oct.–mid-Mar.*

$ ⊞ **Dragør Badehotel.** Built in 1907 as a seaside hotel for vacationing Copenhageners, this plain, comfortable hotel is still geared to the summer crowds, yet manages to maintain its wonderfully low prices (you'd easily pay twice the price in Copenhagen). The basic rooms have dark-green carpets and simple furniture; half the rooms include little terraces that face toward the water, so make sure to ask for one when booking. The bathrooms are small and basic, with a shower only (no bathtubs). Breakfast, which is included in the price, is served on the outside terrace in summer. ⊠ *Drogdensvej 43, DK–2791 Dragør* ☎ *32/53–05–00* ⊟ *32/53–04–99* ⊕ *www.badehotellet.dk* ⊠ *34 rooms* ⚭ *Restaurant, bar, meeting room, some pets allowed* ⊟ *AE, DC, MC, V.*

Klampenborg, Bakken & Dyrehaven

15 km (9 mi) north of Copenhagen (take Bus 6 from Rådhus Pladsen or S-train to Klampenborg Station).

As you follow the coast north of Copenhagen, you'll come upon the wealthy enclave of Klampenborg, whose residents are lucky enough to have the pleasant **Bellevue Beach** nearby. In summer this luck may seem double-edged, when scores of city-weary sun-seekers pile out at the Klampenborg S-train station and head for the sand. The Danes have a perfect word for this: they call Bellevue a *fluepapir* (flypaper) beach. Still and all, Bellevue is an appealing seaside spot to soak up some rays, especially considering that it's just a 20-minute train ride from Copenhagen.

Klampenborg is no stranger to crowds. Just a few kilometers inland, within the peaceful Dyrehaven, is **Bakken**, the world's oldest amusement park—and one of Denmark's most popular attractions. If Tivoli is champagne in a fluted glass, then Bakken is a pint of beer. Bakken's crowd is working-class Danes, and lunch is hot dogs and cotton candy. Of course Tivoli, with its trimmed hedges, dazzling firework displays, and evening concerts is still Copenhagen's reigning queen, but unpretentious Bakken makes no claims to the throne; instead, it is unabashedly about having a good time—being silly in the bumper cars, screaming at the top of your lungs on the rides, and eating food that's bad for you. There's something comfortable and nostalgic about Bakken's vaguely dilapidated state. Bakken has more than 100 rides, from quaint, rickety roller coasters (refreshingly free of that Disney gloss) to newer, faster rides to little-kid favorites such as Kaffekoppen, the Danish version of twirling teacups, where you sit in traditional Royal Copenhagen–style blue-and-white coffee cups. Bakken opens the last weekend in March, with a festive ride by motorcyclists across Copenhagen to Bakken. It closes in late August, because this is when the Dyrehaven park animals begin to mate, and during their raging hormonal stage the animals can be dangerous around children. ⊠ *Dyrehavevej 62, inside Dyrehaven, Klampenborg, (take S-train to Klampenborg Station)* ☎ *39/63–73–00* ⊕ *www.bakken.dk* 🖃 *Free, DKr 239 for a day pass to all rides in peak season (June 27–Aug. 7)* ◔ *Late Mar.–late Aug., daily 2 PM–midnight.*

★ Bakken sits within the verdant, 2,500-acre **Dyrehaven** (Deer Park), where herds of wild deer roam freely. Once the favored hunting grounds of Danish royals, today Dyrehaven has become a cherished weekend oasis for Copenhageners. Hiking and biking trails traverse the park, and lush fields beckon to nature-seekers and families with picnic hampers. The deer are everywhere; in the less-trafficked regions of the park you may find yourself surrounded by an entire herd of deer delicately stepping through the fields. The park's centerpiece is the copper-top, 17th-century **Eremitagen,** formerly a royal hunting lodge. It is closed to the public. Today, the Royal Hunting Society gathers here for annual lunches and celebrations, most famously on the first Sunday in November, when the society hosts a popular (and televised) steeplechase event in the park. The wet and muddy finale takes place near the Eremitagen when the riders attempt to make it across a small lake. Dyrehaven is a haven for hikers and bikers, but you can also go in for the royal treatment and enjoy it from the high seat of a horse-drawn carriage. The carriages gather at the park entrance near the Klampenborg S-train station. The cost is around DKr 40 for 15 minutes, DKr 60 to Bakken, DKr 250 to the Eremitagen, and DKr 400 for an hour. ⊠ *Park entrance is near Klampenborg S-train station, Klampenborg* ☎ *39/63–39–00.*

Where to Eat

★ **$$$–$$$$** ✗ **Strandmøllekroen.** The 200-year-old beachfront inn is filled with antiques and hunting trophies. The best views are of the Øresund from the back dining room. Elegantly served seafood and steaks are the mainstays, and for a bit of everything try the seafood platter, with lobster, crab claws, and Greenland shrimp. ⊠ *Strandvejen 808, Klampenborg* ☎ *39/63–01–04* ⊕ *www.strandmoellekroen.dk* 🖃 *AE, DC, MC, V.*

Frilandsmuseet

16 km (10 mi) northwest of Copenhagen.

North of Copenhagen is Lyngby, its main draw the Frilandsmuseet, an open-air museum. About 50 farmhouses and cottages representing various periods of Danish history have been painstakingly dismantled, moved here, reconstructed, and filled with period furniture and tools. Trees and gardens surround the museum; bring lunch and plan to spend the day. To get here, take the S-train to the Sorgenfri station, then walk right and follow the signs. ⊠ *Kongevejen, Lyngby* ☎ *33/13–44–41* ⊕ *www.frilandsmuseet.dk* ▧ *DKr 50, free Wed.* ☉ *Easter–Sept., Tues.–Sun. 10–5.*

Museet for Moderne Kunst (Arken)

20 km (12 mi) southwest of Copenhagen (take the S-train in the direction of either Hundige, Solrød Strand, or Køge to Ishøj Station, then pick up Bus 128 to the museum).

Architect Søren Robert Lund was just 25 when awarded the commission for this forward-looking museum, which he designed in metal and white concrete set against the flat coast southwest of Copenhagen. The museum, also known as the Arken, opened in March 1996 to great acclaim, both for its architecture and its collection. Unfortunately, for a couple of years following its opening it was plagued with a string of stranger-than-fiction occurrences, including a director with an allegedly bogus résumé. The situation has greatly improved, and today the museum's massive sculpture room exhibits both modern Danish and international art, as well as experimental works. Dance, theater, film, and multimedia exhibits are additional attractions. ⊠ *Skovvej 100, Ishøj* ☎ *43/54–02–22* ⊕ *www.arken.dk* ▧ *DKr 60* ☉ *Tues.–Sun. 10–5, Wed. 10–9.*

COPENHAGEN A TO Z

ADDRESSES

Copenhagen began as Havnen (the harbor), with the seat of local government near what is now Gammeltorv, just off the main pedestrian thoroughfare Strøget. Much of what is now the northeastern section of the downtown area was once under water. The harbor was dotted with islands. Through the centuries, various kings filled in the shallow waters and joined the islands to the mainland of Zealand. During those years, the ramparts of the city were constructed and a system of moats and other water defenses were created. Most maps of the city still reveal the general plan of older defense measures.

Copenhagen grew up within and, eventually, beyond these fortified ramparts. Many of the main neighborhood districts are named after what were once the few points of entry to the city. What can confuse some visitors is that the districts are named after points on the compass, but do not lie in that direction in relation to the city center. For instance,

Vesterport means "western bridge" (the bridge was the western entry to Copenhagen), while the district lies southwest of downtown.

Nowadays downtown Copenhagen (indicated by a KBH K in mailing addresses) is concentrated around Strøget, in an area containing lots of stores, cafés, restaurants, office buildings, and galleries, with residential properties on the upper floors. Just over a decade ago the center of town (including its northeastern subdistrict Sankt Annæ Kvarter) was the absolute center of all shopping, dining, and nightlife activity. It still is thriving, but some of the action has moved to neighboring districts.

A couple of centuries ago the districts of Vesterbro (KBH V), Nørrebro (KBH N), and Østerbro (KBH Ø) were once the outskirts of Copenhagen, named after the ports for entering the city. In the past decade nightlife and shops have moved into these districts to make them much sought-after spots to live and play. Halmtorv in Vesterbro was once a haunt for street walkers and other urchins, but has become an "in" and increasingly gentrified neighborhood in recent years. The area of Nørrebro closest to downtown was once the working-class area of the city, but now contains some of the hottest property in town after cafés and shops sprouted in the area. Østerbro was mostly a bourgeois bastion, but has turned into a center for young families with lots of opportunity for shopping and recreation.

The man-made island of Christianshavn (KBH K) was filled and raised between Copenhagen and Amager island by King Christian IV to bolster the city's defense installations. Many of the military fortifications can still be seen, such as the Holmen naval base, which has become a thriving spot for creative offices, nightlife, and new residential growth. To the south Amager Island (KBH S) is a main focus of development and expansion plans for the Copenhagen metropolitan region.

Regular mail addressed to Copenhagen should include the street name and number, postal code of the region, and a letter after Copenhagen to signify the neighborhood. For example, Wonderful Copenhagen's office is at Gammel Kongevej 1, DK-1610, Copenhagen V, Denmark. The "V" after Copenhagen stands for Vesterbro neighborhood, and DK-1610 is the country's zip or postal code.

AIR TRAVEL TO & FROM COPENHAGEN
For information, *see* Air Travel *in* Smart Travel Tips A to Z.

AIRPORTS & TRANSFERS
Copenhagen Airport, 10 km (6 mi) southeast of downtown in Kastrup, is the gateway to Scandinavia and the rest of Europe.
🏢 **Copenhagen International Airport** ☎ 32/31-32-31 ⊕ www.cph.dk.

TRANSFERS   Although the 10-km (6-mi) drive from the airport to downtown is quick and easy, public transportation is excellent and much cheaper than taking a taxi. The airport's sleek subterranean train system takes about 13 minutes to zip passengers into Copenhagen's main train station. Buy a ticket (DKr 25.50) upstairs in the airport train station at Terminal 3; a free airport bus connects the international terminal with the domestic terminal. Three trains an hour leave for Copenhagen, while a fourth travels to Roskilde. Trains also travel from the airport directly to Malmö, Sweden (DKr 60), via the Øresund Bridge, leaving every 20 minutes and taking 35 minutes in transit. Trains run on weekdays from 5 AM to midnight, on Saturday from 6 AM to midnight, and on Sunday from 6 AM to 11 PM.

SAS coach buses leave the international arrivals terminal every 15 minutes from 5:45 AM to 9:45 PM, cost DKr 50, and take 25 minutes to reach Copenhagen's main train station on Vesterbrogade. Another SAS coach from Christiansborg, on Slotsholmsgade, to the airport runs every 15 minutes between 8:30 AM and noon, and every half hour from noon to 6 PM. HT city buses depart from the international arrivals terminal every 15 minutes from 4:30 AM (Sunday 5:30 AM) to 11:45 PM, but take a long, circuitous route. Take Bus 250S for the Rådhus Pladsen and transfer. One-way tickets cost about DKr 22.50.

The 20-minute taxi ride downtown costs around DKr 170, though slightly more after 4 PM and weekends. Lines form at the international arrivals terminal. In the unlikely event there is no taxi available, there are several taxi companies you can call including Københavns Taxa.
🚖 Taxis **Københavns Taxa** ☎ 35/35-35-35.

BIKE TRAVEL
Bikes are delightfully well suited to Copenhagen's flat terrain and are popular among Danes as well as visitors. Bike rental costs DKr 75–DKr 300 a day, with a deposit of DKr 500–DKr 1,000. You may also be lucky enough to find a free city bike chained up at bike racks in various spots throughout the city, including Nørreport and Nyhavn. Insert a DKr 20 coin, which will be returned to you when you return the bike.
🚲 Bike Rentals **Københavns Cykler** ✉ Central Station, Reventlowsg. 11, Vesterbro ☎ 33/33-86-13 ⊕ www.rentabike.dk. **Østerport Cykler** ✉ Oslo Plads 9, Østerbro ☎ 33/33-85-13 ⊕ www.rentabike.dk. **Urania Cykler** ✉ Gammel Kongevej 1, Vesterbro ☎ 33/21-80-88 ⊕ www.urania.dk.

CAR RENTAL
All major international car-rental agencies are represented in Copenhagen; most are at Copenhagen Airport or near Vesterport Station. By Danish law, you must be 20 years of age or more to rent a vehicle, although the car rental company may require renters to be 25 years or older.
🚗 Avis ✉ Copenhagen Airport, Kastrup ☎ 32/51-22-99 or 32/51-20-99 ✉ Kampmannsg. 1, Vesterbro ☎ 70/24-77-07 ⊕ www.avis.dk. **Budget** ✉ Copenhagen Airport, Kastrup ☎ 32/52-39-00 ⊕ www.budget.com. **Europcar-Pitzner Auto** ✉ Copenhagen Airport, Kastrup ☎ 32/50-30-90 or 32/50-66-60 ✉ Gammel Kongevej 13A, Vesterbro ☎ 33/55-99-00 ⊕ www.europcar.comdk. **Hertz** ✉ Copenhagen Airport, Kastrup ☎ 32/50-93-00 or 32/50-30-40 ✉ Vester Farimagsg. 1, Vesterbro ☎ 33/17-90-00 ⊕ www.hertzdk.dk.

CAR TRAVEL
The E20 highway, via bridges, connects Fredericia (on Jutland) with Middelfart (on Funen), a distance of 16 km (10 mi), and goes on to Copenhagen, another 180 km (120 mi) east. Farther north, from Århus

(in Jutland) you can get direct auto-catamaran service to Kalundborg (on Zealand). From there, Route 23 leads to Roskilde, about 72 km (45 mi) east. Take Route 21 east and follow the signs to Copenhagen, another 40 km (25 mi). Make reservations for the ferry in advance through the Danish State Railways. Since the inauguration of the Øresund Bridge in 2000, Copenhagen is now linked to Malmö, Sweden. The trip takes about 30 minutes, and the steep bridge toll stands at DKr 220 per car at this writing, though prices are likely to decrease to encourage more use. All trips across the Øresund Bridge are paid in Sweden. If you are driving to Sweden, you pay the toll after you have crossed the bridge. If you are headed for Denmark, you pay the toll before you cross the bridge.

You can pay cash in the manned lanes. You may use the following currencies: DKr (Danish kroner), SEK (Swedish kroner), EUR (euro), NKr (Norwegian kroner), USD (US dollars), GBP (pounds sterling), and CHF (Swiss francs). Note that change is always in Danish kroner, no matter which currency you use to pay.

If you are planning on seeing the sites of central Copenhagen, a car is not convenient. Parking spaces are at a premium and, when available, are expensive. A maze of one-way streets, relatively aggressive drivers, and bicycle lanes make it even more complicated. If you are going to drive, choose a small car that's easy to parallel park, bring a lot of small change to feed the meters, and be very aware of the cyclists on your right-hand side: they always have the right-of-way. For emergencies, contact Falck.

🚗 **Auto Rescue/Falck** ☎ 70/10-20-30 ⊕ www.falck.dk. **Danish State Railways** (DSB) ✉ Hovedbanegården (main train station), Vesterbro ☎ 70/13-14-15.

EMERGENCIES

Denmark's general emergency number is ☎ 112. Emergency dentists, near Østerport Station, are available weekdays 8 PM–9:30 PM and weekends and holidays 10–noon. The only acceptable payment method is cash. Dr. Jesper Nygart, who speaks several languages and has an office behind the D'Angleterre Hotel, is listed as a Doctor on Call in *Copenhagen This Week*. For emergency doctors, look in the phone book under *læge*. After normal business hours, emergency doctors make house calls in the city center and accept cash only; night fees are a minimum of DKr 300–DKr 400. You can also contact the U.S., Canadian, or British embassies for information on English-speaking doctors.

🚑 **Doctors & Dentists** **Casualty Wards-Skadestuen** ✉ Italiensvej 1, Amager ☎ 32/34-32-34 ✉ Niels Andersens Vej 65, Hellerup ☎ 39/77-37-64 or 39/77-39-77. **Doctor Emergency Service** ☎ 70/13-00-41, 44/53-44-00 daily 4 PM–8 AM. **Dr. Jesper Nygart** ✉ Ny Østergade 10, Downtown ☎ 70/27-57-57. **Tandlægevagt** (Dental Emergency Service) ✉ Tandlægevagten. 14, Oslo Plads ☎ 35/38-02-51 ⊕ www.tandvagt.dk.
🚑 **Emergency Services** **Police, fire, and ambulance** ☎ 112.
🚑 **Hospitals** **Frederiksberg Hospital** ✉ Nordre Fasanvej 57, Frederiksberg ☎ 38/16-38-16. **Rigshospitalet** ✉ Blegdamsvej 9, Østerbro ☎ 35/45-35-45.
🚑 **24-Hour Pharmacies** **Sønderbro Apotek** ✉ Amangerbrog. 158, Amager ☎ 32/58-01-40 ⊕ www.apoteket.dk. **Steno Apotek** ✉ Vesterbrog. 6C, Vesterbro ☎ 33/14-82-66 ⊕ www.apoteket.dk.

ENGLISH-LANGUAGE MEDIA

BOOKS Boghallen, the bookstore of the Politiken publishing house, offers a good selection of English-language books. Arnold Busck has an excellent selection, and also textbooks, CDs, and comic books. Gad Boglader runs shops in various parts of the city, including one on Strøget and another in the new Royal Library, and offers a broad assortment of English-language volumes, fiction and nonfiction, along with other items of interest. Most of these stores have a large section devoted to Denmark and Danish literature. Another option for the bookworm would be to browse the many used-book shops that dot the city.

🚩 **Arnold Busck** ⊠ Kobmagerg. 49, Downtown ☎ 33/73-35-00 ⊕ www.arnoldbusck. dk. **Boghallen** ⊠ Rådhus Pl. 37, Downtown ☎ 33/47-25-60 ⊕ www.boghallen.dk. **Gad Boglader** ⊠ Vimmelskaftet 32, Downtown ☎ 33/15-05-58 ⊕ www.gad.dk.

NEWSPAPERS & *The Copenhagen Post* (www.cphpost.dk) is a weekly newspaper that
MAGAZINES covers Danish news in English. Particularly helpful is its insert, *In & Out*, with reviews and listings of restaurants, bars, nightclubs, concerts, theater, temporary exhibits, flea markets, and festivals in Copenhagen. Anyone planning on staying in Copenhagen for a long period should peruse the classified ads listing apartment-rental agencies and jobs for English-speakers. It's available at select bookstores, some hotels, and tourist offices. The biannual magazine *Scandinavian Living* (⊕ www. scandinavium.comau/scanliving.htm) includes articles on Scandinavian culture, food, and architecture and also lists the latest bars, restaurants, and shops. It's sold at the tourist office, as well as at some stores and hotels.

LODGING

LOCAL AGENTS In summer, reservations are recommended, but should you arrive without one, try the hotel booking desk at the Wonderful Copenhagen tourist information office. The desk offers same-day, last-minute prices (if available) for remaining rooms in hotels and private homes. A fee of DKr 50 is applied to each booking. You can also reserve private-home accommodations at Meet the Danes. The agency Hay4You has a selection of fully furnished apartments for rent to visitors staying in the city for a week or more. Young travelers looking for a room should head for Use It, the student and youth budget travel agency.

🚩 **Hay4You** ⊠ Vimmelskaftet 49, Downtown ☎ 33/33-08-05 🖷 33/32-08-04 ⊕ www. hay4you.dk. **Hotel booking desk** ⊠ Bernstorffsg. 1, Downtown ☎ 70/22-24-32 ⊕ www. visitcopenhagen.dk. **Meet the Danes** ⊠ Ravnsborgg. 2, 2nd fl., Nørrebro ☎ 33/46-46-46 🖷 33/46-46-47 ⊕ www.meetthedanes.dk. **Use It** ⊠ Rådhusstr. 13, Downtown ☎ 33/73-06-20 ⊕ www.useit.dk.

MONEY MATTERS

ATMS ATMs are located around town. Look for the red logos "Kontanten/ Dankort Automat." Here you can use Visa, Plus, MasterCard/Eurocard, Eurochequecard, and sometimes JCB cards to withdraw money. Machines are usually open 24 hours, but some are closed at night.

CURRENCY Almost all banks (including the Danske Bank at the airport) exchange
EXCHANGE money. Most hotels cash traveler's checks and exchange major foreign currencies, but they charge a substantial fee and give a lower rate. The

exception to the rule—if you travel with cash—are the several locations of Forex (including the main train station and close to Nørreport Station). For up to $500, Forex charges only DKr 20 for the entire transaction. Keep your receipt and it will even change any remaining kroner you may still have back to dollars or another currency for free. For traveler's checks, it charges DKr 10 per check. Den Danske Bank exchange is open during and after normal banking hours at the main railway station, daily June through August 7 AM–10 PM, and daily September through May, 7 AM–9 PM. American Express is open weekdays 9–5 and Saturday 9–noon. The Change Group—open April through October, daily 10–8, November through March, daily 10–6—has several locations in the city center. Tivoli also exchanges money; it is open May through September, daily noon–11 PM.

🚩 **American Express Corporate Travel** ✉ Nansensg. 19, Downtown ☎ 70/23–04–60 🌐 www.nymans.dk. The **Change Group** ✉ Vimmelskaftet 47, Downtown ☎ 33/93–04–18 ✉ Frederiksbergg. 5, Downtown ☎ 33/93–04–15 ✉ Østerg. 61, Østerbro ☎ 33/93–04–55 ✉ Vesterbrog. 9A, Vesterbro ☎ 33/24–04–47. **Den Danske Bank** ✉ Banegårdspl. (main train station), Vesterbro ☎ 33/12–04–11 ✉ Copenhagen Airport, Kastrup ☎ 32/46–02–80 🌐 www.danskebank.dk. **Forex** ✉ Hovedbanegården 22 (main train station), Vesterbro ☎ 33/11–22–20 ✉ Nørre Voldg. 90, Downtown ☎ 33/32–81–00 🌐 www.forex-valutaveksling.dk. **Tivoli** ✉ Vesterbrog. 3, Vesterbro ☎ 33/15–10–01 🌐 www.tivoli.dk.

TAXIS

The shiny computer-metered Mercedes and Volvo cabs are not cheap. The base charge is DKr 23, plus DKr 10 per kilometer (higher after 4 PM). A cab is available when it displays the sign FRI (free); one can be hailed or picked up in front of the main train station or at taxi stands, or by calling the numbers below. Outside the city center, always call for a cab, as your attempts to hail one will be in vain. Try Kobenhavns Taxa or Amager Øbro Taxi. A 40% surcharge applies if you order a cab at night or on the weekend.

🚩 **Amager Øbro Taxi** ☎ 32/52–31–11. **Kobenhavns Taxa** ☎ 35/35–35–35.

TOURS

The tourist office monitors all tours and has brochures and information. Most tours run through summer until September.

BIKE TOURS Basic bicycle tours of Copenhagen with City Safari run around 2½ hours and cover the main sights of the city, while there is a more comprehensive trip (4½ hours) with lunch included. The guides not only point out Copenhagen's main attractions and provide helpful information for travelers, but also give some insight into the daily routines of the Danes. Special theme tours are also available, such as a trip through historic Copenhagen, a tour to and around the Carlsberg brewery, a junket showing modern architecture, a route following the footsteps of Hans Christian Andersen, and an exciting Copenhagen-by-night trip. Prices range from DKr 150 to DKr 350 (lunch included).

If you would prefer that someone else do the peddling, an increasingly popular sightseeing method is provided by Quickshaw, one of the city's many cycle-taxi and -tour companies. Quickshaw bicycle chauffeurs can

accommodate two passengers and offer two best-of-Copenhagen sightseeing routes or allow you to dictate your own trip; they will even wait
out front while you visit museums or other points of interest. The cy-
clist-drivers are comfortable and adept as tour guides, narrating as they
pedal. The cycle-taxis in service are parked at 18 strategic sites in the
inner city.

🚲 **City Safari** ⊠ Dansk Arkitektur Center (Gammel Dok), Strandg. 27B, Christianshavn
☎ 33/23-94-90 ⊕ www.citysafari.dk. **Quickshaw** ⊠ Esplanaden 8D, Downtown
☎ 70/20-13-75.

BOAT TOURS   The Harbor and Canal Tour (1 hour) leaves from Gammel Strand and
the east side of Kongens Nytorv from May to mid-September. The City
and Harbor Tour (2½ hours) includes a short bus trip through town and
sails from the Fish Market on Holmens Canal through several more waterways, ending near Strøget. Contact Canal Tours or the tourist office
for times and rates. Just south of the embarkation point for the City and
Harbor Tour is the equally charming Netto Boats, which also offers hour-
long tours for about half the price of its competitors.

🚲 **Canal Tours** ☎ 32/96-30-00 ⊕ www.canal-tours.dk. **Netto Boats** ☎ 32/54-41-02
⊕ www.havnerundfart.dk.

BUS TOURS   The Grand Tour of Copenhagen (2½ hours) includes Tivoli, the New
Carlsberg Museum, Christiansborg Castle, the Stock Exchange, the
Danish Royal Theater, Nyhavn, Amalienborg Castle, Gefion Fountain,
Grundtvig Church, and Rosenborg Castle. The City Tour (1½ hours) is
more general, passing the New Carlsberg Museum, Christiansborg Castle, the Thorvaldsen Museum, the National Museum, the Stock Exchange,
the Danish Royal Theater, Rosenborg Castle, the National Art Gallery,
the Botanical Gardens, Amalienborg Castle, Gefion Fountain, and *The
Little Mermaid*. The Open Top Tours (about 1 hour), which are given
on London-style double-decker buses, include stops at Amalienborg, the
Stock Exchange, Christiansborg, *The Little Mermaid*, Louis Tussaud's
Wax Museum, the National Museum, the New Carlsberg Museum, Nyhavn, the Thorvaldsen Museum, and Tivoli. This tour gives attendees
the option to disembark and embark on a later bus. Only the Grand
Tour of Copenhagen, which covers the exteriors of the major sites, and
the Open Top Tour, which covers less ground but more quickly, operate year-round. It's always a good idea to call first to confirm availability.
Several other sightseeing tours leave from the Lur Blowers Column in
Rådhus Pladsen 57, late March through September. For tour information call Copenhagen Excursions or Open Top Tours.

🚲 **Copenhagen Excursions** ☎ 32/54-06-06 ⊕ www.cex.dk. **Open Top Tours** ☎ 32/
66-00-00 ⊕ www.sightseeing.dk.

WALKING TOURS   Due to its manageable size and meandering avenues, Copenhagen is a
great city for pedestrians. A number of companies offer walking tours
of parts of the city, some catering to Danes and others offering outings
in various languages. One of the best companies is Copenhagen Walking Tours, which schedules 10 different English-language guided tours.
In addition to tours related to culture and city history, the service offers a Copenhagen shopping primer and a tour of Jewish Copenhagen.
The outings begin at the Wonderful Copenhagen tourist information of-

fice on weekends—from June through August there are tours from Thursday through Sunday. In addition, there is also a special tour of Rosenborg Castle beginning in front of the palace at 11:30 on Tuesday.

Two-hour walking tours organized by Copenhagen Walks begin in front of the Wonderful Copenhagen office at 10:30 Monday through Saturday from May to September (call to confirm). There are three different routes: uptown on Monday and Thursday, crosstown on Tuesday and Friday, and downtown on Saturday. Richard Karpen, an American who has been living in Denmark for over a decade, leads the tours dressed as Hans Christian Andersen, offering information on both the interiors and exteriors of buildings and giving insight into the lifestyles, society, and politics of the Danes. His tour of Rosenborg Castle, including the treasury, meets at the castle at 1:30 Monday through Thursday from May to September. The Tourist Information Office is located on Vesterbrogade, across from Tivoli Gardens.

🚺 **Copenhagen Walking Tours** ☎ 40/81-12-17 ⊕ www.copenhagen-walkingtours.dk. **Copenhagen Walks** ☎ 32/84-74-35 ⊕ www.copenhagenwalks.com.

TRAIN TRAVEL
Copenhagen's Hovedbanegården (Central Station) is the hub of the DSB network and is connected to most major cities in Europe. Intercity trains leave every hour, usually on the hour, from 6 AM to 10 PM for principal towns in Funen and Jutland. To find out more, contact the DSB. You can make reservations at Central Station, at most other stations, and through travel agents.

🚺 **DSB Information** ☎ 70/13-14-15 ⊕ www.dsb.dk. **Hovedbanegården** ✉ Banegård-spl. 1, Downtown ☎ 33/14-17-01 ⊕ www.hovedbanen.dk.

TRANSPORTATION AROUND COPENHAGEN
Copenhagen is small, with most sights within 2½ square km (1 square mi) at its center. Wear comfortable shoes and explore downtown on foot. Or follow the example of the Danes and rent a bike. For those with aching feet, an efficient transit system is available.

The Copenhagen Card offers unlimited travel on buses, harbor buses, and Metro and suburban trains (S-trains), as well as admission to some 60 museums and sights throughout both metropolitan Copenhagen and Malmö, Sweden. They're valid for a limited time, though, and therefore only worthwhile if you're planning a nonstop, intense sightseeing tour. The Card also offers discounts on many other attractions and activities, including car rental and Scandlines' crossing of the Sound (Øresund) between Sweden and Denmark. An adult card also includes passage for two children up to 9 years old. The card costs DKr 199 (24 hours), DKr 429 (72 hours), and is DKr 129 and DKr 249 for children ages 10 to 15. It can be purchased at bus and train stations, tourist offices, and hotels, or from travel agents.

Trains and buses operate from 5 AM (Sunday 6 AM) to midnight. After that, night buses run every half hour from 1 AM to 4:30 AM from the main bus station at Rådhus Pladsen to most areas of the city and surroundings. Trains and buses operate on the same ticket system and divide Copenhagen and surrounding areas into three zones. Tickets are validated on a time basis: on the basic ticket, which costs about DKr 11 per hour, you can travel anywhere in the zone in which you started. A discount *klip kort* (clip card), good for 10 rides, costs DKr 85 and must be stamped in the automatic ticket machines on buses or at stations. (If you don't stamp your clip card, you can be fined up to DKr 500.) Get zone details for S-trains on the information line. The buses have a Danish information line with an automatic answering menu that is not very helpful, but try pressing the number 1 on your phone and wait for a human to pick up. The phone information line operates daily 7 AM–9:30 PM. You might do better by asking a bus driver or stopping by the HT Buses main office (open weekdays 9–7, Saturday 9–3) on the Rådhus Pladsen, where the helpful staff is organized and speaks enough English to adequately explain bus routes and schedules to tourists.

The HT harbor buses are ferries that travel up and down the canal, embarking from outside the Royal Library's Black Diamond, with stops at Knippelsbro, Nyhavn, and Holmen, and then back again, with lovely vistas along the way. The harbor buses run six times an hour, daily from 6 AM to 6:25 PM, and tickets cost around DKr 25. If you have a klip kort, you can use it for a trip on the harbor bus.

The Metro system runs regularly from 5 AM to 1 AM, and all night on weekends. Until the end of 2007 only two Metro lines are in operation linking the northern neighborhood of Vanløse to the beginning of southern Amager through the downtown area.

🔢 **Bus information** ☎ 36/13-14-15 ⊕ www.ht.dk. **Metro information** ☎ 33/11-17-00 ⊕ www.m.dk. **S-train information** ☎ 70/13-14-15 ⊕ www.rejseplan.dk.

TRAVEL AGENCIES

For student and budget travel, try Kilroy Travels Denmark. For charter packages, stick with Spies. Star Tour also handles packages.

🔢 **American Express Corporate Travel** ✉ Nansensg. 19, Downtown ☎ 70/23-04-60 ⊕ www.nymans.dk. **Carlson Wagonlit** ✉ Vester Farimagsg. 7, 2nd fl., Vesterbro ☎ 33/63-78-78 ⊕ www.cwt.dk. **DSB Travel Bureau** ✉ Hovedbanegården (main train station), Vesterbro ☎ 33/13-14-18 ⊕ www.dsb.dk/rejsebureau. **Kilroy Travels Denmark** ✉ Skinderg. 28, Downtown ☎ 70/15-40-15 ⊕ www.kilroytravels.dk. **Spies** ✉ Nyropsg. 41, Vesterbro ☎ 70/10-42-00 ⊕ www.spies.dk. **Star Tour** ✉ H. C. Andersens Blvd. 12, Vesterbro ☎ 70/11-10-50 ⊕ www.startour.dk.

VISITOR INFORMATION

The Wonderful Copenhagen tourist information office is open May through the first two weeks of September, daily 9–8; the rest of September through April, weekdays 9–4:30 and Saturday 9–1:30. Note that the tourist office hours vary slightly from year to year, so you may want to call ahead. Its well-maintained Web site includes extensive listings of sights and events. Youth information in Copenhagen is available from Use It. Listings and reviews of Copenhagen's museums (including temporary exhibits), sights, and shops are included on www.aok. dk. The Visit Denmark Web site has listings on hotels, restaurants, and sights in Copenhagen and around Denmark; AOK also has an excellent Web site on Copenhagen. For more information on the outlying fishing village of Dragør, visit the office or Web site of Dragør Tourist Information.

🔳 **AOK** ⊕ www.aok.dk. **Dragør Tourist Information** ✉ Havnepladsen 2, Dragør ☎ 32/53-41-06 ⊕ www.dragoer-information.dk. **Use It** ✉ Rådhusstr. 13, Downtown ☎ 33/73-06-20 ⊕ www.useit.dk. **Visit Denmark** ⊕ www.visitdenmark.com. **Wonderful Copenhagen** ✉ Vesterbrog. 4C, Vesterbro ☎ 70/22-24-42 ⊕ www.visitcopenhagen. com.

Zealand

WORD OF MOUTH

"Copenhagen's island, Zealand, has about everything you could want on a first trip to Denmark. The north shore has good beaches at Gilleleje & Hornbaek, plus Bellevue near Klampenborg just north of Copenhagen."

—Joe

Updated by
Bruce Bishop

THE GODDESS GEFION is said to have carved Zealand (Sjælland) from Sweden. If she did, she must have sliced the north deep with a fjord, while she chopped the south to pieces and left the sides bowing west. Though the coasts are deeply serrated, Gefion's myth is more dramatic than the flat, fertile land of rich meadows and beech stands.

Slightly larger than the state of Delaware, Zealand is the largest of the Danish islands. From Copenhagen, almost any point on it can be reached in an hour and a half, making it the most traveled portion of the country—and it is especially easy to explore thanks to the extensive road network. North of the capital, ritzy beach towns line up between Hellerup and Humlebæk. Helsingør's Kronborg, which Shakespeare immortalized in *Hamlet,* and Hillerød's stronghold of Frederiksborg, considered one of the most magnificent Renaissance castles in Europe, also lie to the north. To the west of Copenhagen is Roskilde, medieval Denmark's most important town, with an eclectic cathedral that served as northern Europe's spiritual center 1,000 years ago.

West and south, rural towns and farms edge up to seaside communities and fine white beaches, often surrounded by forests. Beaches with summer cottages, white dunes, and calm waters surround Gilleleje and the neighboring town of Hornbæk. The beach in Tisvildeleje is quieter and close to woods. Even more unspoiled are the Lilliputian islands around southern Zealand, virtually unchanged over the past century.

WHAT IT COSTS In Danish Kroner				
$$$$	**$$$**	**$$**	**$**	**¢**
RESTAURANTS over 180	141–180	121–140	90–120	under 90
HOTELS over 1,500	1,200–1,500	1,000–1,200	700–1,000	under 700

Restaurant prices are for a main course at dinner. Hotel prices are for two people in a standard double room, including service charge and tax.

Rungsted

❶ *21 km (13 mi) north of Copenhagen.*

Between Copenhagen and Helsingør is **Rungstedlund,** the elegant, airy former manor of Baroness Karen Blixen, who wrote *Out of Africa* and several accounts of aristocratic Danish life under the pen name Isak Dinesen. The manor house, where she lived as a child and to which she returned in 1931, is open as a museum and displays manuscripts, photographs, paintings, and memorabilia documenting her years in Africa and Denmark. Leave time to wander around the gardens. ⊠ *Rungsted Strandvej 111, Rungsted Kyst* ☎ *45/57–10–57 for combined train and admission tickets, 70/13–14–16 international, 70/13–14–15 domestic* 🖷 *45/57–10–58* ⊕ *www.karen-blixen.dk* 🖂 *DKr 40* ☉ *May–Sept., Tues.–Sun. 10–5; Oct.–Apr., Wed.–Fri. 1–4, weekends 11–4.*

Where to Eat

★ **$$$–$$$$** ✕ **Nokken.** The terrace, stretching from the base of the harbor to the waters of Øresund, provides a view of the sailboats returning to port

Most of Zealand can be explored on day trips from Copenhagen, which makes a nice hub. The exceptions are the northwestern beaches around the Sejerø Bugt (Sejerø Bay) and those south of Møn, all of which require at least a night's stay and a day's visit. If you have the time to take a more extended tour, the train and bus networks are extensive and can deliver you from point to point quite fluidly without routing you back through Copenhagen.

Numbers in the text correspond to numbers in the margin and on the Zealand & Its Islands map.

2

If you have

3 days

Rent a car or catch the train, and head up the east coast of Zealand toward 🚉 **Helsingør ❸** ⌐, stopping briefly in **Rungsted ❶** to see Isak Dinesen's home and in **Humlebæk ❷** to visit the beautiful Louisiana museum. If the weather is nice, have a sandwich on the beach. Make your way to Helsingør by evening and spend your first night there. Get up early the next morning and spend some time exploring Kronborg, Hamlet's castle, and continue up north towards **Hornbæk ❻**, **Gilleleje ❽**, or **Tisvildeleje ❾**, where you can spend the day swimming and lolling around on the beach. In the evening head for 🚉 **Hillerød ❺** and stroll around the city. The following day visit the beautiful Frederiksborg Slot and its baroque garden. From there, travel on to **Roskilde ⑬** to visit the impressive cathedral and the Viking Ship Museum. Return to Copenhagen in the evening.

If you have

7 days

Leave Copenhagen early in the morning, heading south toward **Møn ⑯** ⌐. Spend the day climbing the steep cliffs and visiting Liselund Slot. In the evening head for 🚉 **Ringsted ⑲**, where you can bed down after an exhausting day. In the morning take a stroll through Ringsted and then go to the village of Sorø for a beautiful walk. If Denmark's Viking history interests you, you can also spend the day in Trælleborg at the excavated site of a Viking encampment. Return to Ringsted to spend a second night there. On the third day drive northeast to **Lejre ⑭**, where you can visit the open-air museum or Ledreborg Slot. In the afternoon, move on to 🚉 **Roskilde ⑬** to see the sights and find lodging. On the fourth day leave in the morning for 🚉 **Hillerød ❺**, where you should base yourself for two days. Visit Frederiksborg Castle and continue to Fredensborg Castle for another impression of Danish royal digs. Take the sixth day to relax on one of the many beaches on the northern coast, spending the night in 🚉 **Hornbæk ❻** or camping on the beach at ⚠ **Dronningmølle ❼**. On the last day of your Zealand week, travel to **Helsingør ❸** to visit Kronborg and end the trip with a viewing of modern art at the Louisiana museum in **Humlebæk ❷**. Return to Copenhagen in the evening.

---

as well as a tranquil skyline in the evening. The elegant Italian-style interior pleasantly contradicts the classic French cuisine served. Seafood fresh from the sound is the main attraction but tournedos and other succulent meat dishes are also available. French reserves dominate the wine menu. ⊠ *Rungsted Havn 44, Rungsted Kyst* ☎ *45/57–13–14* ⊕ *www. nokken.dk* ▤ *AE, DC, MC, V.*

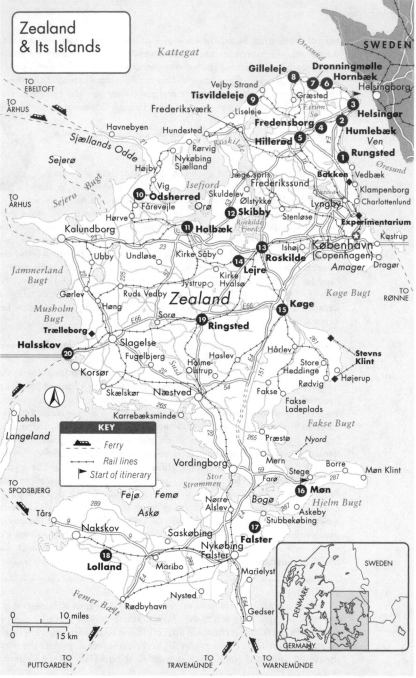

Zealand & Its Islands

Kattegat

SWEDEN

TO EBELTOFT

TO ÅRHUS

Gilleleje **8** Dronningmølle **7** Hornbæk **6**
Vejby Strand Helsingborg
Tisvildeleje **9** Græsted
Frederiksværk Liseleje *Esrum Sø* Helsingør **3**
Havnebyen Hundested Fredensborg **4** **2**
Sjællands Odde Rørvig Hillerød **5** Humlebæk
Sejerø Nykøbing Sjælland *Ven*
Højby Rungsted **1**
Vig *Isefjord* Jægerspris Frederikssund Bakken Vedbæk
TO ÅRHUS *Sejerø Bugt* Odsherred **10** Skuldelev Klampenborg
Hørve Fåreveile Orø Ølstykke Lyngby Charlottenlund
Kalundborg Skibby **12** Stenløse Experimentarium
Holbæk **11** *Roskilde Fjord* Kastrup
Ubby Undløse Kirke Såby Ishøj København **13** (Copenhagen)
Jammerland Bugt Lejre **14** Roskilde Amager Dragør
Gørlev Ruds Vedby Kirke Hvalsø
Musholm Bugt Høng Jystrup Zealand *Køge Bugt* TO RØNNE
Trælleborg Sorø Ringsted **19** Køge **15**
Halsskov Slagelse
Korsør **20** Fugelbjerg Haslev Hårlev Stevns Klint
Skælskør Holme-Olstrup Store Heddinge
Næstved Rødvig Højerup
Lohals Karrebæksminde Fakse
Langeland Fakse Ladeplads
Præstø *Fakse Bugt*
Vordingborg Nyord
TO SPODSBJERG Mern Stege Borre Møn Klint
Farø
Fejø Femø *Stor Strømmen* Bogø Møn **16**
Tårs Askø Nørre Alslev *Hjelm Bugt*
Nakskov Askeby Stubbekøbing
Saskøbing Falster **17**
Lolland **18** Nykøbing Falster
Maribo Marielyst
Femer Bælt Nysted
Rødbyhavn Gedser

KEY
 Ferry
 Rail lines
 Start of itinerary

0 ___ 10 miles
0 ___ 15 km

SWEDEN
DENMARK
GERMANY

TO PUTTGARDEN
TO TRAVEMÜNDE
TO WARNEMÜNDE

Humlebæk

② *10 km (6 mi) north of Rungsted, 31 km (19 mi) north of Copenhagen.*

Historically a fishing village, this elegant seaside town with a population of about 6,000 has of late become a suburb of both Copenhagen and Helsingør. In summer the town's many cottages fill with vacationers, and the gardens come alive with vibrant colors. The town takes its name from the plant *humle* (hops), which is abundant in the area.

Fodor'sChoice
★ ℭ
Humlebæk is home of the must-see **Louisiana**, a modern-art museum as famed for its stunning location and architecture as for its collection. Even if you can't tell a Monet from a Duchamp, you should make the 30-minute trip from Copenhagen to see its elegant rambling structure, surrounded by a large park. Housed in a pearly 19th-century villa surrounded by dramatic views of the Øresund waters, the permanent collection includes modern American paintings and Danish paintings from the COBRA (a trend in northern European painting that took its name from its active locations, Copenhagen, Brussels, and Amsterdam) and deconstructionism movements. Be sure to see the haunting collection of Giacomettis backdropped by picture windows overlooking the sound. The children's wing has pyramid-shape chalkboards, childproof computers, and weekend activities under the guidance of an artist or museum coordinator. To get here from the station, walk north about 10 minutes. ⊠ *Gammel Strandvej 13* ☎ *49/19–07–19* 🖷 *49/ 19–35–05* ⊕ *www.louisiana.dk* ⊠ *DKr 76* ⊘ *Thurs.–Tues. 10–5, Wed. 10–10.*

Helsingør

▶ ③ *14 km (8½ mi) north of Humlebæk, 45 km (28 mi) north of Copenhagen.*

Helsingør dates back to the early 13th century. It wasn't until the 1400s, when Erik of Pomerania established a tariff for all ships passing through the sound, that the town began to prosper. Perhaps Helsingør is best known as the home of Shakespeare's fictional Hamlet. Today more than 55,000 people populate the city.

Fodor'sChoice
★
At the northeastern tip of the island, Helsingør is the departure point for ferries to the Swedish town of Helsingborg, and it's the site of **Kronborg Slot** (Kronborg Castle), which was added to UNESCO's World Heritage List in 2000. William Shakespeare based *Hamlet* on Danish mythology's Amleth, and used this castle as the setting even though he had probably never seen it. Built in the late 16th century, it is 600 years younger than the Elsinore we imagine from the tragedy. It was built as a Renaissance tollbooth: from its cannon-studded bastions, forces collected Erik of Pomerania's much-hated Sound Dues, a tariff charged to all ships crossing the sliver of water between Denmark and Sweden. Coming through the entrance arch decorated in Flemish style, you'll see the castle lawn in front of an octagonal tower, the Trumpeters Tower, whose decoration stands out from the whole.

From the yard there is access to the royal chapel. Still true to its original Renaissance style from 1582, the chapel accommodates the royal throne, which has multicolor carved wood. Among the 27 rooms open to the public are two deserving of more attention: the so-called "lille sal" (small room) and the king's bedroom. In the "small room," on the second floor, hang seven tapestries made of silk and wool and created by the Flemish painter Hans Knieper between 1581 and 1586. What makes these tapestries exceptional is not merely their artistic quality but also their subject matter. They portray several Danish kings against backgrounds of stately buildings and luxuriant scenery, with German translations accompanying Danish verses describing their respective achievements. The ceiling of the king's bedroom is worth a couple of extra minutes. If you crane your neck, you can see four scenes of royal life painted by the Dutch artist Gerrit van Honthorst in 1630. Also well worth seeing are the 200-foot-long dining hall and the dungeons, where there is a brooding statue of Holger Danske (Ogier the Dane). According to legend, the Viking chief sleeps, but will awaken to defend Denmark when it is in danger. (The largest Danish resistance group during World War II called itself Holger Danske after its fearless forefather.) ⊠ *At the point on the harbor front* ☎ *49/21–30–78* ⊕ *www.ses.dk/ kronborgcastle* ⊡ *DKr 60* ⊙ *May–Sept., daily 10:30–5; Oct. and Apr., Tues.–Sun. 11–4; Nov.–Mar., Tues.–Sun. 11–3.*

Thanks to the hefty tolls collected by Erik of Pomerania, Helsingør prospered. Stroll past the carefully restored medieval merchants' and ferrymen's houses in the middle of town. On the corner of Stengade and Sankt Annæ gade near the harbor is **Sankt Olai Kirke** (St. Olaf's Church), the country's largest parish church and worth a peek for its elaborately carved wooden altar. ⊠ *Sankt Olai G. 51* ☎ *49/21–04–43 (9–noon)* ⊕ *www. helsingordomkirke.dk* ⊡ *Free* ⊙ *May–Sept., daily noon–3; Oct.–Apr., daily noon–2.*

Close to Sankt Olai Kirke is Sankt Marie Kirke with the 15th-century **Carmelite Kloster** (Carmelite Convent), one of the best-preserved examples of medieval architecture in Scandinavia. After the Reformation it was used as a hospital, and by 1630 it had become a poorhouse. ⊠ *Skt. Annæ G. 38* ☎ *49/21–17–74* ⊡ *DKr 10* ⊙ *Mid-May–mid-Sept., tour daily at 2; call ahead.*

If you want to know more about Helsingør, right next door to the Carmelite Kloster is the modest **By Museum** (Town Museum), which has exhibits of 19th-century handicrafts, dolls, and a model of the town. ⊠ *Skt. Annæ G. 36* ☎ *49/28–18–00* ⊡ *DKr 10* ⊙ *Weekdays noon–4.*

off the beaten path

MARIENLYST SLOT – One kilometer (½ mi) north of Helsingør is the Louis XVI–style Marienlyst Castle. Built in 1587, it provided King Frederik II with a garden, as well as a delicate change of scenery from the militant Kronborg. Today the castle has been renovated and the gardens replanted. Inside are paintings by north Zealand artists and a gallery with changing arts and crafts exhibitions. ⊠ *Marienlyst Allé* ☎ *49/28–37–91* ⊡ *49/21–20–06* ⊡ *DKr 25* ⊙ *Daily noon–4.*

Where to Stay & Eat

$$ ╳▣ **Hotel Hamlet.** A few minutes from the harbor, this overly renovated hotel has lost some of its charm but makes an attempt at character with raw timbers and deep-green walls. The rooms are furnished in rose schemes and dark wood, and all are comfortable, if nondescript. Downstairs, the Ophelia Restaurant serves traditional Danish seafood, steaks, and open-face sandwiches. ⊠ *Bramstr. 5, DK–3000* ☎ *49/21–05–91* 🖷 *49/ 26–01–30* 🖃 *36 rooms* ⌂ *Restaurant, bar, some pets allowed, no-smoking rooms* ☰ *AE, DC, MC, V.*

★ **$$$$** ▣ **Hotel & Casino Marienlyst.** The rooms in this hotel full of flashy neon lights, bolts of drapery, and glass are all plush and pastel and include plenty of conveniences. The hotel was completely refurbished in August 2002. Rooms on the sound side present a magnificent view of Kronborg Castle and the Swedish coastline, weather permitting—of course, these rooms with views are more expensive. The hotel offers live music on Friday and Saturday. ⊠ *Nordre Strandvej 2, DK–3000* ☎ *49/ 21–40–00* 🖷*49/21–49–00* ⊕*www.marienlyst.dk* 🖃*224 rooms, 17 suites* ⌂ *Restaurant, cafeteria, indoor pool, gym, bar, casino, nightclub, meeting rooms, some pets allowed, no-smoking rooms* ☰ *AE, DC, MC, V.*

¢ ▣ **Villa Moltke Vandrerhjem.** This youth hostel faces the sound and has a private beach. It is located 2 km (1 mi) from the city center, but is well served by both bus and train. Note that check-in is between 3 and 5 PM. Don't arrive unannounced, as you may not get a place to stay; it's best to reserve a room online. ⊠ *Nordre Strandvej 24, DK–3000* ☎*49/ 21–16–40* 🖷 *49/21–13–99* ⊕ *www.helsingorhostel.dk* 🖃 *180 beds* ⌂ *Cafeteria, fishing, badminton, Ping-Pong, soccer, library, laundry facilities* ☰ *MC, V.*

Sports & the Outdoors

GOLF   The **Helsingør Golf Klub** (⊠ Gamle Hellebækvej 73 ☎ 49/21–29–70 ⊕ www.helsingorgolf.dk) has 18 holes on a lush green course flanked by trees and, on clear days, views across the sound to Sweden. A weekday handicap of 36 for men and women, and a weekend handicap of 24 for men and 36 for women, is expected.

Nightlife & the Arts

In summer Kronborg Castle is the site of the **Hamlet Festival** (⊠ Havnepl. 1 ☎ 49/28–20–45 ⊕ www.hamletsommer.dk), during which internationally renowned theater companies offer outdoor performances of *Hamlet*. The schedule varies from year to year.

Fredensborg

❹ *15 km (9 mi) southwest of Helsingør, 33 km (20 mi) northwest of Copenhagen.*

Fredensborg means "town of peace," and it was here that the Great Nordic War peace treaty was concluded in 1722. The excellent Fredensborg Castle is a major draw, but the town also accommodates those who come to enjoy the great outdoors.

Commanding the town is the **Fredensborg Slot** (Castle of Peace), built by Frederik IV to commemorate the 1720 peace treaty with Sweden.

The castle, with a towering domed hall in the center, was originally inspired by French and Italian castles, but 18th-century reconstructions, concealing the original design, instead serve as a review of domestic architecture. The castle became a favorite of Frederik V, who lined the gardens with marble sculptures of ordinary people. It is now the summer residence of the royal family, and interiors are closed except in July. Queen Margrethe II resides in the castle some months every year, usually in the spring and autumn. When the Queen is present, the Royal Life Guards perform reveille at 8 AM and sound the tattoo (taps) at 10 PM. At noon there is the changing of the guard.

The stately **Slotshave** (castle garden), inspired by the French gardens of Versailles, is Denmark's largest historical garden and well worth a stroll. The garden is open to the public all year with the exception of *den reserverede have* (the reserved garden), which is used privately by the Danish Royal Family but open to the public in July. The reserved garden includes a flower garden, an herb garden, and the orangerie where Denmark's oldest myrtles, which date back to the 1750s, are preserved. ⊠ *Fredensborg* ☎ *33/40–31–87* ⊕ *www.ses.dk/1d70029* 🎫 *Castle DKr 40, reserved gardens DKr 40, combined ticket DKr 60* ☉ *Castle July, daily 1–5 (guided tours of Castle and Chapel every 15 mins); reserved gardens July, daily 9–5.*

off the beaten path

GRIBSKOV – On the opposite side of Lake Esrum from Fredensborg is Gribskov, the largest forest in Zealand (14,079 acres). This former royal hunting ground has kept its natural shape since the times of Valdemar II in the 13th century, except for the clearing works done after the hurricane of 1981. Gribskov is one of the few places in Denmark where visitors can have a sense of natural solitude while being immersed in a wooded cloak of mystery. Black woodpeckers, woodcocks, sandpipers, buzzards, goshawks, and deer can be seen among the oaks and flowering trees.

Where to Stay & Eat

$$
Fodor'sChoice
★

✕ **Skipperhuset.** On the grounds of the royal summer residence of Fredensborg Slot, this 18th-century former royal boathouse is on the shore of Lake Esrum. When weather permits, an alfresco meal as the sun sets across the lake is pure enchantment. The three-course menu changes every two weeks. Warm-smoked wild Baltic salmon served with spinach flash-fried in soy sauce and balsamic vinegar is a delightful favorite and a fabulous buy for the money. ⊠ *Skipperallé 6* ☎ *48/48–17–17* ⊕ *www. skipperhuset.dk* ▤ *MC, V* ☉ *Closed mid-Oct.–Easter.*

★ $$$$

✕▦ **Hotel Store Kro.** Built by King Frederik IV, this magnificent Renaissance annex to Fredensborg Castle is the archetypal stately inn. Inside are European antiques and paintings; outside, glass gazebos and classical statues overlook a lovely garden. The rooms are equally sumptuous, with delicately patterned wallpapers and antiques. The romantic restaurant, specializing in French fare, has a fireplace and grand piano. ⊠ *Slotsg. 6, DK–3480* ☎ *48/40–01–11* 🖷 *48/48–45–61* ⊕ *www.storekro.dk* 🛏 *49 rooms, 6 suites* ☿ *Restaurant, minibars, sauna, bar, meeting room* ▤ *AE, DC, MC, V.*

Piscataway Public Library

User name: PATEL,
HETALBEN V.

Title: Fodor's Denmark
Item ID: 39305001831286
Date charged: 10/3/2015,
13:51
Date due: 10/24/2015,23:
59

¢ ⊞ **Fredensborg Vandrerhjem.** This youth and family hostel offers a wide selection of sleeping arrangements. Both shared and private rooms (accommodating up to six people) are available. Breakfast can be ordered for DKr 45. The restaurant serves lunch and dinner for groups only; however, the kitchen is available to all guests. Private bedrooms with private bathrooms (shower only) are about DKr 460. Note that rooms come with all combinations of facilities from single rooms with sinks only to double rooms with private baths. ⊠ *Østrupvej 3, DK–3480* ☎ *48/ 48–03–15* 🖷 *48/48–16–56* ⊕ *www.fredensborghostel.dk* ⇕ *42 rooms (21 without bath)* ⚴ *Ping-Pong, playground* ⊟ *No credit cards.*

Sports & the Outdoors

Magnificent displays of hawks and eagles in flight can be seen at **Falkonergården.** Located 1 km (½ mi) northeast of Fredensborg, this former farm keeps alive the Danish tradition of hunting with hawks, a method used from the time of the Vikings until early in the 19th century. Falcons swooping at speeds approaching 300 kph (186 mph) can be witnessed in the hour-long shows. ⊠ *Davidsvænge 11* ☎ *48/48–25–83* ⊕ *www.falkonergaarden.dk* 🖷 *DKr 65* ⊙ *Showtimes: Apr. and May, Sun. at 2; June, Sept., and Oct., weekends at 2; July, Wed. at 10 and 5, Thurs. at 10, weekends at 5; Aug., Wed. and weekends at 5.*

The **Fredensborg Golf Club** (⊠ Skovsvinget 25 ☎ 48/47–56–59 ⊕ www. fgc.dk) has 18 holes surrounded by woodlands. Men are required to have a handicap of 38 on weekdays and 24 on weekends whereas women need a handicap of 43 and 30, respectively.

Hillerød

❺ *10 km (6 mi) southwest of Fredensborg, 40 km (25 mi) northwest of Copenhagen.*

Hillerød is the main town of Frederiksborg County and appropriately enough is at its center. The town, founded in the 15th century, has developed itself around the Frederiksborg Castle and nowadays is an important industrial area.

★ Hillerød's **Frederiksborg Slot** (Frederiksborg Castle) is probably Denmark's most beautiful royal residence. Acquired in 1560, the castle was rebuilt by King Frederik II, who gave his name to the building. That structure was eventually demolished by his son, king-cum-architect Christian IV, who rebuilt it as one of Scandinavia's most magnificent castles. With three wings and a lower portal entrance, the Dutch Renaissance building is enclosed by a moat, covers three islets, and is peaked with dozens of gables, spires, and turrets. The two-story marble gallery known as the **Great Hall,** with its audacious festooning of drapery, paintings, and reliefs, sits on top of the vaulted chapel where monarchs were crowned for more than 200 years. Devastated by a fire in 1859, the castle was reconstructed with the support of the Carlsberg Foundation and now includes the **Nationalhistoriske Museum** (National History Museum). Frederiksborg Slot has 69 rooms, all of them decorated as they were before the fire. Those works of art that had been destroyed were substituted by other private pieces from the Danish aristocracy. The castle has an admirable Renaissance chapel, **Slotskirke,** with abundant ornamentation. The three-aisle chapel has a wide gallery with large windows. Between them hang Denmark's most important coat of arms, the knights of the Elephant Order, and the Great Cross of Dannebrog. Look for the 17th-century aisle seats as well as the altarpiece and the pulpit made of mahogany with gold and silver panels. The carved organ, made in 1610 and restored in 1988, still proudly carries its original pipes and manual bellows. The lovely **Baroque Gardens,** rebuilt according to J. C. Krieger's layout from 1725, include a series of wide waterfalls that make the neatly trimmed park a lovely place for a stroll. In addition to the Web site listed below, ⊕ www.ses.dk/1d90029 has more information (in English) on the castle. ⊠ *Hillerød* ☎ *48/26–04–39* ⊕ *www.frederiksborgmuseet. dk* ⊠ *DKr 60; Baroque Gardens free* ☉ *Castle Apr.–Oct., daily 10–5; Nov.–Mar., daily 11–3. Baroque Gardens May–Aug., daily 10–9; Sept., Oct., Mar., and Apr., daily 10–7; Nov.–Feb., daily 10–4.*

off the beaten path

ESRUM KLOSTER – Fifteen kilometers (10 mi) north of Hillerød is the Cistercian monastery of Esrum. Originally built in the 1140s by Benedictine monks, the monastery was abandoned by this order and occupied by Cistercian monks in 1151. After the Lutheran reformation, the church was demolished and the building materials were used to erect the Castle of Kronborg in Helsingør. The oldest remains are from the late Middle Ages. ⊠ *Klosterg. 11, Esrum, DK–3230 Græsted* ☎ *48/36–04–00* ⊟ *48/39–80–16* ⊕ *www.esrum. dk/kloster* ⊠ *DKr 40* ☉ *May–mid-June and mid-Aug.–mid-Oct., Tues.–Sun. 10–4; mid-June–mid-Aug., Tues.–Sun. 10–5; mid-Oct.–Apr., Thurs.–Sun. 10–4.*

Where to Stay & Eat

$$$ ✕ **La Perla.** Simple but good Italian food is served in this beautiful old house in the very center of town. The decor is an interesting mix of Italian and Danish styles, a thoroughly modern twist on the Mediterranean. It opens daily at 11 AM. ⊠ *Torvet 1* ☎ *48/24–35–33* ⚑ *Reservations essential* ⊟ *AE, DC, MC, V.*

$$$ ✕ **Slotskroen.** Functioning as an inn since 1795, Slotskroen is one of the oldest buildings of this royal town. The restaurant has been completely renovated, but it maintains its antique flavor and stands out for its veal and ox dishes. It's a lunch restaurant, so it's only open from noon to 5. Along with an open-face sandwich buffet, it also offers a beautiful view of Castle Lake and Frederiksborg Castle. ⊠ *Slotsg. 67* ☎ *48/26–01–82* ⊕ *www.slokskroen.dk* ⊟ *AE, DC, MC, V* ☉ *No dinner.*

$–$$ ✕ **Spisestedet Leonora.** In the shadow of Frederiksborg Castle, this family restaurant bustles in what used to be the castle stables. Antique on the outside and bright orange on the inside with hanging prints and paintings of royalty and the castle, it is a popular stopover for castle visitors. The Danish menu ranges from quick open-face sandwiches to savory stews, soups, and steaks. ⊠ *Frederiksborgslot 5* ☎ *48/26–75–16* ⊕ *www. leonora.dk* ⊟ *DC, MC, V.*

$$ ▦ **Hotel Hillerød.** In a typically Scandinavian fashion, this hotel's decor is furnished with sensible Danish designs and luxurious lighting acces-

sories. The hotel's attentiveness extends to providing some rooms specifically for nonsmokers. Most rooms have kitchenettes and private terraces. Packages that include greens fees at a local golf course can be arranged. The entire hotel is accessible to wheelchair users. ✉ *Milnersvej 41, DK–3400* ☎ *48/24–08–00* 🖨 *48/24–08–74* ⊕ *www.hotelhillerod.dk* ➷ *74 rooms* ♿ *Restaurant, some kitchenettes, meeting room, some pets allowed, no-smoking rooms* ⊟ *AE, DC, MC, V.*

Hornbæk

❻ *27 km (17 mi) northeast of Hillerød, 47 km (29 mi) north of Copenhagen.*

Hornbæk is Denmark's answer to France's Riviera. Danish society's upper echelon maintains palatial summer homes here that line the streets closest to the water and are discreetly tucked away behind protective sand dunes. Regardless of your social standing, the bustling town offers lovely shopping opportunities and exciting nightlife year round. Summer brings the expansive beach alive with parties, volleyball tournaments, and more.

Where to Stay & Eat

★ **$$$$** ✗ **Novo Latino.** The elegant dining room is decorated in light, soft tones, but the terrace takes the cake with its outdoor fireplace. Inspired by classic Latin American cooking, Novo Latino modernizes the cuisine by adding its own touches. The chef here travels every autumn to the tropics to collect recipes and inspiration, which determine the menu for each coming year. For about DKr 500 the restaurant offers a six-course menu that keeps pace with seasonal products. This is the ideal place to try innovative dishes such as fish with chocolate sauce. A wide range of excellent wines from the New and Old Worlds is on hand at prices starting from DKr 300. ✉ *Nordre Strandvej 154, 5 km (3 mi) east of Hornbæk, Ålsgårde* ☎ *49/70–90–03* ⊟ *AE, DC, MC, V* ☉ *Closed Mon. and Oct.–Mar.*

★ **$$** ✗ **Hansen's Café.** This intimate restaurant, in a National Trust building constructed in 1783, is just a few steps from the harbor. The Danish art hanging from the timber walls provides a cozy ambience for a casual crowd that often lingers for drinks well after dinner. The daily menu is short but provides a taste of what's fresh—especially seafood. Try the lumpfish roe for a tasty local treat. Business hours vary so it's wise to call in advance. ✉ *Havnevej 19* ☎ *49/70–04–79* ⊕ *www.hansencafe.dk* ⊟ *DC, MC, V.*

$$$$ 🏠 **Havreholm Slot.** A few miles southwest of Hornbæk beach, this small former castle is surrounded by wooded grounds, which hide a couple of fair-sized ponds in their midst. The guesthouses' rooms and suites are decorated with Bang & Olufsen televisions and designer furniture; most open onto balconies or terraces. Rowboats are available for use on the ponds, as is fishing gear—just remember to get your fishing permit first. There are also tennis courts and a 9-hole par-3 golf course. The restaurant produces elaborate French cuisine at dinner and serves smørrebrød and Danish comfort food at lunch. ✉ *Klosterrisvej 4, Havreholm,*

DK–3100 📠 *49/75–86–00* 🖨 *49/75–80–23* ⊕ *www.havreholm.dk*
📲 *32 rooms, 3 suites* 🍴 *Restaurant, 9-hole golf course, indoor-outdoor pool, sauna, fishing, billiards, Ping-Pong, squash, meeting rooms* 🖃 *AE, DC, MC, V.*

$$$ 🖼 **Hotelpension Ewaldsgaarden.** This seaside pension is just a few blocks from the marina and the beach in a residential neighborhood just off one of the town's main (though quiet) streets. An informal family hotel, it is very casual, extremely well kept, and service is provided with commendable pride. In the restaurant the Danish food is not fancy, but it's authentic and exceptionally good. Breakfast is included. ✉ *Johannes Ewaldsvej 5, DK–3100* 📠 *49/70–00–82* 🖨 *49/70–00–82* ⊕ *www. ewaldsgaarden.dk* 📲 *12 rooms* 🍴 *Restaurant* 🖃 *No credit cards.*

¢ 🖼 **Hornbæk Bed & Breakfast.** Owned by an American-Danish couple, this country villa sits at the edge of the woods only 100 meters from the Danish Riviera. On fair days you can see the Swedish coastline out the window. The rooms are a decent size for the reasonable price, all no-smoking, and guests are allowed use of the kitchen. ✉ *Skovvej 15C, DK–3100* 📠 *49/76–19–10* 🖨 *49/76–19–11* ⊕ *www.hornbaekbandb.dk* 📲 *7 rooms without bath* 🍴 *Kitchen* 🖃 *No credit cards.*

Dronningmølle

❼ *10 km (6 mi) west of Hornbæk, 57 km (35 mi) north of Copenhagen.*

There's little more than a camping ground flanked by a very clean beach and a sculpture museum in Dronningmølle. The beauty of the area lies in the fact that it is largely undiscovered, so it's quite easy to find a spot on the sand away from the crowds.

★ In 1916 Rudolph Tegner (1873–1950) began to buy adjacent parcels of land to realize his dream of a museum and sculpture park dedicated to his own work. The centerpiece of the resultant **Rudolph Tegner Museum** is the 36-foot-high octagonal building in the center of which Tegner is buried. On display here are 191 of his sculptures in plaster, marble, and bronze; works in other media are represented including 12 paintings, many drafts, and several pieces of furniture he constructed. Tegner withstood the pressure toward conformity in Danish society during his era and his best works are both provocative and disquieting. ✉ *Museumsvej 19* 📠 *49/71–91–77* ⊕ *www.rudolphtegner.dk* 🎟 *DKr 25* ☉ *Mid-Apr.–May and Sept.–mid-Oct., Tues.–Sun. noon–5; June–Aug., Tues.–Sun. 9:30–5. Closed Mon.*

Where to Stay

¢ ⛺ **Dronningmølle Strandcamping.** Camp right on the sand and enjoy the best of the Danish Riviera without the crowds and high prices of other, better known coastal towns in north Zealand. The surrounding countryside is a nature conservation area and has trails and bicycle paths. Kitchen facilities are available. ✉ *Strandkrogen 2B, DK–3120* 📠 *49/ 71–92–90* 🖨 *49/71–98–93* ⊕ *www.dronningmolle.dk* 🎟 *DKr 185* 🍴 *Restaurant, cafeteria, miniature golf, sauna, shop, laundry facilities* 🖃 *No credit cards* ☉ *Closed mid-Sept.–mid-Apr.*

Gilleleje

❽ *3 km (2 mi) north of Dronningmølle, 58 km (36 mi) northwest of Copenhagen.*

At the northern tip of Zealand, Gilleleje was once a small fishing community. These days the population explodes every summer when northern Europeans take to its woods and fine, sandy beaches. It was a favorite getaway of philosopher Søren Kierkegaard, who wrote: "I often stood there and reflected over my past life. The force of the sea and the struggle of the elements made me realize how unimportant I was." The less existential can go for a swim and visit the philosopher's monument on a nearby hill. The old part of town, with its thatch-roof, colorfully painted houses, is good for a walk.

off the beaten path

NORDSJÆLLANDS SOMMERPARK – Situated 30 km (18 mi) west of Helsingør, this amusement park mixes water recreation with other attractions such as theater, concerts, and a mini zoo. The Sommerpark bus departs from the Gilleleje or Helsingør train station at 9:30 AM. ✉ *Kirkevej 33, Græsted* ☎ *48/71–41–41* 🖷 *48/71–66–05* ⊕ *www.sommerpark.dk* 💵 *DKr 50* ⊙ *Mid-June–mid-Aug., daily 10–8; mid-May–mid-June, daily 10–6.*

Tisvildeleje

❾ *28 km (17 mi) west of Gilleleje, 65 km (40 mi) northwest of Copenhagen.*

Tisvildeleje is one of the most popular beaches in north Zealand. There is more than 1 km (½ mi) of sandy beach backed by dunes and woods. The beaches are child-friendly and sandy. Overall, the natural surroundings here are exceptionally clean and charming, open and unspoiled.

Where to Stay & Eat

$ ✕🏠 **Havgården.** The refurbished old manor house offers comfortable lodging within a typical Danish building. Dinner, served from 6 PM, is primarily Danish—John Dory is the house specialty. The site also rents out vacation cottages, fully furnished with all the comforts of home. Payment with credit card is subject to a 6% surcharge. ✉ *Strandlyvej 1, DK–3210 Vejby Strand* ☎ *48/70–57–30* 🖷 *48/70–57–72* ⊕ *www.havgaarden.dk* 💤 *13 rooms* ♨ *Restaurant* ▤ *MC, V* ⊙ *Restaurant closed Sept.–May.*

¢   🏠 **Skt. Helene Vandrerhjem.** This holiday and conference complex is a 10-minute walk from the beach. The property has 28 chalets accommodating four to five people each; there are also 25 apartments and 40 single rooms, all with varying prices. The whole complex is ecofriendly, with a farm providing organic food on site. Guests are welcome to pitch in with the work. ✉ *Bygmarken 30, DK–3220* ☎ *48/70–98–50* 🖷 *48/70–98–97* ⊕ *www.helene.dk* 💤 *28 chalets, 25 apartments, 40 rooms* ♨ *Restaurant, cafeteria, miniature golf, tennis court, basketball, soccer, volleyball, laundry facilities.*

CloseUp
SUN, SAND & WAVES

FROM ANY POINT IN DENMARK you're never more than 50 kilometers (31 mi) away from the ocean, and for this reason the Danish people have developed a special fondness for their beaches. On Zealand there are plenty of calm, sandy strands, which are far gentler than their wilder and more abrasive— though more expansive—counterparts along the west coast of Jutland. The most pristine Zealand shorelines are on the northern edge of the island, where long stretches of lovely white sand are massaged by lapping waves. Though this is the preferred sunbathing spot for the Danish in-crowd, it's rarely a problem finding prime real estate on which to throw down your towel.

Generally speaking, the vast majority of the island's beaches across the island are of excellent quality and are easily accessible, making them great retreats for families with small children. Zealand's coastal playgrounds are defined by the people who frequent them, from the jet-set beaches of Hornbæk, where the babes and hunks strut their stuff, to the child-friendly sands of Tisvildeleje, where inner tubes and sand castles are the rule. During summer heat waves people even swim in Copenhagen's harbor.

You should be aware before you go that there are beaches where nudists, or naturists, as they say more commonly in Europe, put it all to the wind, and "nude beaches" are seldom designated as such. Indeed, by Danish law one can sunbathe or swim nude at a public beach so long as this does not bother anyone close by. Topless sunbathing is also common in Denmark, and one should take care to follow proper etiquette; avoid gawking and leave plenty of room between yourself and the bather in question. If you're fortunate enough to be of the "hot bod" variety, don't show off—the Danish rule is: "good body, low profile." And just so you know, it's not uncommon for beachgoers to change clothes on the beach as a matter of convenience.

Odsherred

🔟 45 km (28 mi) southwest of Gilleleje, 80 km (50 mi) northwest of Copenhagen (via Roskilde).

With steep cliffs, white-sand dunes, and acres of forests to admire, the Odsherred peninsula is a big draw to people who want to relax in beautiful surroundings. The long beaches have silky sand and offer plenty of opportunities to take a refreshing swim in Sejerø Bugt (Sejerø Bay). This hammer-shape peninsula, which curves around Sejerø Bugt, is dotted with hundreds of burial mounds. You can get here either by driving around the fjords to the south and through the town of Holbæk, or by driving to Hundested and catching the 25-minute ferry ride to Rørvig.

If you're a devotee of ecclesiastical art, make a pilgrimage to explore the frescoes of the Romanesque-Gothic-Renaissance **Højby Kirke** (Højby Church) in the town of Højby, near Nykøbing Sjælland. In the town of Fårevejle is the Gothic **Fårevejle Kirke**, with the Earl of Bothwell's chapel.

☾ Fewer than 5 km (3 mi) south of Nykøbing Sjælland, more than 500 animals of 85 different species can be seen at **Odsherreds Zoo Dyrepark.**

Children love the monkey house. Other inhabitants include raccoons, llamas, reptiles, exotic birds, and the unique black swan. On weekends children can ride ponies. ⊠ *Esterhøjvej 94–96, Asnæs* 🕾 *59/65–12–31* 🖴 *59/65–12–28* ⊕ *www.odsherreds-zoo.dk* 🖃 *DKr 65* ⊙ *Apr., Sept.–mid-Oct., daily 10–3:30; May, June, and Aug., daily 10–5; July, daily 10–6.*

Sjællands Odde (Zealand's Tongue), the tiny strip of land north of the Sejerø Bay, offers slightly marshy but secluded beach strands. Inside the bay, the beaches are once again smooth and blond. From here there is access to Århus and Ebeltoft in Jutland by ferry.

⑬ **Sommerland Sjælland,** Zealand's amusement park, caters to visitors of all ages. The dozens of activities include a roller coaster, an aqua park, and a small zoo with pony rides. Children under 10 especially enjoy *Miniland.* ⊠ *Gammel Nykøbingvej 169, Nykøbing Sjælland* 🕾 *59/31–21–00* ⊕ *www.sommerlandsj.dk* 🖃 *DKr 130* ⊙ *Mid-May–mid-June and mid-Aug.–Sept., weekends 10–6; mid-June–mid-Aug., daily 10–7.*

Where to Stay & Eat

¢–$$$ ✗ **Den Gyldne Hane.** Built at the beginning of the 19th century by a community of fishermen, Den Gyldne Hane is a family hotel best known for the fish dishes served in its restaurant. The view of the harbor overlooking the fishing boats makes for an enjoyable meal. ⊠ *Vestre Havnevej 34, DK–4583 Sjællands Odde* 🕾 *59/32–63–86* 🖴 *59/32–65–52* ⊕ *www.dengyldnehane.dk* ⊟ *DC, MC, V* ⊙ *Closed Dec.–Mar. No lunch.*

$$$ 🔛 **Dragsholm Slot.** Ideally located at Nekselø Bay, close to the forest and the beach, Dragsholm Castle, originally built in the 12th century, has been a home since the 18th century. Today the owners cultivate the land and raise their own livestock to provide wholesome ingredients for the restaurant on the premises. ⊠ *Dragsholm Allé 1, DK–4534 Hørve* 🕾 *59/65–33–00* 🖴 *59/65–30–33* ⊕ *www.dragsholm-slot.dk* ⬤ *28 rooms, 2 suites* ⟁ *Restaurant* ⊟ *AE, DC, MC, V.*

Holbæk

⑪ *83 km (51½ mi) southwest of Tisvildeleje (via Odsherred), 67 km (41½ mi) west of Copenhagen.*

Expanding out from the old fortress built in the 13th century by Valdemar II to defend Denmark against its attacking enemies, today Holbæk is an industrial and commercial town.

Situated close to the neo-Gothic Sankt Nicolai Kirke, the **Holbæk Museum** consists of three wooden buildings from the 17th century and another two from the 19th century. The museum collection showcases handicrafts, archaeological artifacts, and objects from the town's more recent history, such as household equipment from typical urban and rural houses of the 17th and 18th centuries. ⊠ *Klosterstr. 18* 🕾 *59/43–23–53* 🖴 *59/43–24–52* ⊕ *www.holbmus.dk* 🖃 *DKr 30* ⊙ *Tues.–Fri. 10–4, weekends noon–4.*

CHURCHES OF HOLBÆK FJORD – A 2-kilometer (1 mi) drive south of Holbæk down the A57 delivers you to **Tveje Merløse,** built in the 13th century and restored at the end of the 19th century. Luckily, you can still see the 13th-century frescoes here. Just 4 km (2½ mi) to the southwest stands the 12th-century **Søstrup Kirke,** with Byzantine-style frescoes. West along road 155 another 4 km (2½ mi) stands **Tuse Kirke,** a typical example of a rural church from the 13th century. Inside the church are Gothic frescoes from the 15th century. North on road A21 is the 12th-century **Hagested Kirke,** which has 13th-century frescoes.

Where to Stay & Eat

¢ ✕⌷ **Hotel Orø Kro.** On the tiny island of Orø, this hotel radiates tranquility with the blue of Isefjord on one side and green fields on the other. The restaurant stands out for its simple and tasty fish specialties. On a warm summer evening the inn's terrace is a delightful place to sit. The restaurant is closed on Monday. ⊠ *Byg. 57, Orø, DK–4300* ☎ *59/47–00–06* 🖷 *59/47–01–99* ⊕ *www.oroe.dk/kro* ☞ *21 rooms* ⑤ *Restaurant, some pets allowed* ⊟ *AE, MC, V.*

$$ ⌷ **Hotel Strandparken.** Beach and forest are the two views offered from the rooms of this hotel, which has a scenic location in the middle of a park just south of Holbæk Fjord. The pastel rooms are filled with flower prints and landscape paintings. Service is warm and attentive. ⊠ *Kalundborgvej 58, DK–4300* ☎ *59/43–06–16* 🖷 *59/43–32–76* ⊕ *www.hotelstrandparken.dk* ☞ *31 rooms* ⑤ *Restaurant, billiards, meeting room* ⊟ *AE, MC, V.*

Skibby

⑫ *26 km (16 mi) northeast of Holbæk, 65 km (40 mi) northwest of Copenhagen.*

Skibby is the main town of the little peninsula situated between Roskilde Fjord and Isefjord.

Four kilometers (2½ mi) east of Skibby is **Selsø Slot** (Selsø Castle), constructed in 1576 and reworked in 1734. The castle portrays life as it was for the aristocrats and their servants in the 1800s. The museum here displays original 17th-century interiors, as well as Renaissance furniture, weapons, clothes, domestic items, toys, and a collection of drawings. The altarpiece from 1605 and the pulpit from 1637 in the castle church exhibit Renaissance elements. ⊠ *Selsøvej 30A* ☎ *47/52–01–71* ⊕ *www.selsoe.dk* 🎟 *DKr 40* ☉ *May–mid-June and mid-Aug.–Oct., weekends 1–4; mid-June–mid-Aug., daily 11–4.*

off the beaten path

JÆGERSPRIS SLOT – At the north end of the peninsula stands this medieval castle. The baroque southern wing is from the 17th century, and the rest of the castle, save for the 15th-century northern wing, is from 1722–46. King Frederik VII maintained his residence here in the 19th century and the decor in the southern wing reflects this. The tomb of his wife, the Countess Danner, is in the castle's park. To the north extends Nordskoven, a forest of 100-year-old oaks. To see the castle you must join a guided tour—you can't just wander around on your own. Tours begin at the top of the hour and take 50 minutes. ⊠ *Slotsgården 15, Jægerspris* 🕾 *47/53–10–04* ⊕ *www.museer.fa.dk* 🖃 *DKr 35* ☉ *Apr.–Oct., Tues.–Sun. 11–4.*

Where to Stay & Eat

$$–$$$ ✕ **Sønderby Kro.** This typical countryside inn sits next to the village's duck pond and serves remarkably tasty veal dishes, curried herring, and shrimp. The restaurant is perhaps best known for its smørrebrød. ⊠*Sønderby Bro 2* 🕾*47/52–01–33* ⊕*www.sonderby-kro.dk* 🖃*No credit cards* ☉ *Closed Mon.*

$ 🖳 **Hotel Skuldelev Kro.** In the middle of the countryside, this inn has a peaceful environment in a beautiful location. Rooms are adequate even for families. Some rooms are available for nonsmokers. ⊠ *Østerg. 2B, DK–4050 Skuldelev* 🕾 *47/52–03–08* 🖴 *47/52–08–93* ⊕ *www.hotel-skuldelevkro.dk* 🗲 *32 rooms* ⚭ *Restaurant, pool, sauna, billiards, some pets allowed, no-smoking rooms* 🖃 *AE, DC, MC, V.*

Roskilde

⓭ *31 km (19 mi) southeast of Skibby, 36 km (22 mi) west of Copenhagen (on Rte. 156).*

Roskilde is Zealand's second-largest town and one of its oldest, having been founded in 998. The town is named for Roars Kilde, a Viking king. Today Roskilde has a bustling smelting and machinery industry and two prominent academic institutions, Roskilde University and the Danish Center for Energetic Research of Risø.

Fodor's Choice Roskilde was the royal residence in the 10th century and became the spir-
★ itual capital of Denmark and northern Europe in 1170, when Bishop Absalon built the **Domkirke** (cathedral) on the site of a church erected 200 years earlier by Harald Bluetooth, the Viking founder of the town. Overwhelming the center of town, the current structure took more than 300 years to complete, and thus provides a one-stop crash course in Danish architecture. Inside are an ornate Dutch altarpiece and the tombs—ranging from opulent to modest—of 38 Danish monarchs. Predictably, Christian IV is interred in a magnificent chapel with a massive painting of himself in combat and a bronze sculpture by Thorvaldsen. In modest contrast is the newest addition, the simple brick chapel of King Frederik IX, who died in 1972, outside the church. In November 2000 his wife Queen Ingrid joined him in his tomb at the foot of the cathedral. On the interior south wall above the entrance is a 16th-century clock depicting St. George charging a dragon, which hisses and howls, echoing throughout the church and causing Peter Døver, "the Deafener," to sound the hour. A squeamish Kirsten Kiemer, "the Chimer," shakes her head in fright but manages to strike the quarter-hours. Around the altar are the Kannikekoret, the wooden choir stalls carved in 1420. Each seat is topped with a panel depicting a Biblical scene. Behind the altarpiece is the alabaster and marble sarcophagus of Queen Margrethe I, who died in 1412. ⊠ *Domkirkestr. 10* 🕾 *46/35–16–24* ⊕ *www.roskildedomkirke.dk*

📧 *DKr 15* ⊗ *Apr.–Sept., weekdays 9–4:45, Sat. 9–noon, Sun. 12:30–4:45; Oct.–Mar., Tues.–Sat. 10–3:45, Sun. 12:30–3:45.*

Less than 1 km (½ mi) north of the cathedral, on the fjord, is the modern **Vikingeskibshallen** (Viking Ship Museum), containing five Viking ships sunk in the fjord 1,000 years ago. Submerged to block the passage of enemy ships, they were discovered in 1957. The painstaking recovery involved building a watertight dam and then draining the water from that section of the fjord. The splinters of wreckage were then preserved and reassembled. A deep-sea trader, warship, ferry, merchant ship, and fierce 92½-foot man-of-war attest to the Vikings' sophisticated and aesthetic boat-making skills. ⊠ *Vindeboder 12* 🖂 *46/30–02–00* ⊕ *www.vikingeskibsmuseet. dk* 📧 *May–Sept. DKr 75, Oct.–Apr. DKr 45* ⊗ *Daily 10–5.*

Where to Stay & Eat

$$$ ✕ **Svogerslev Kro.** Three kilometers (2 mi) west of Roskilde is the village of Svogerslev, a peaceful location for this traditional thatch-roof Danish inn. Exposed wooden beams make the interior a cozy place to tuck into the hearty Danish fare. The menu includes a vegetarian option as well as some international dishes such as Wiener schnitzel and steak. ⊠ *Hovedg. 45, Svogerslev* 🖂 *46/38–30–05* ⊕ *www.svogerslevkro. dk* 🖃 *AE, DC, MC, V.*

★ **$** ✕ **Club 42.** This popular Danish restaurant spills out onto the sidewalk in summer, while inside the roof opens over the dining room. The fare is typically Danish, including smørrebrød and spareribs, which are simply prepared and served with potato salad. ⊠ *Skomagerg. 42* 🖂 *46/ 35–03–11* 🖃 *MC, V.*

$$$$ 🏨 **Hotel Prindsen.** In downtown Roskilde, this 100-year-old hotel is popular with business guests for its convenient location. The elegant dark-wood lobby leads to the plain but homey and comfortable rooms. Downstairs, the restaurant and grill, Brasserie Prindsen, serves up a nice selection of seafood starters and meat and vegetarian main courses. ⊠ *Alg. 13, DK–4000* 🖂 *46/30–91–00* 🖃 *46/30–91–50* ⊕ *www.prindsen.dk* 🛏 *76 rooms, 3 suites* ᵭ *Restaurant, cafeteria, minibars, bar, meeting rooms, some pets allowed, no-smoking rooms* 🖃 *AE, DC, MC, V.*

¢ 🏨 **Roskilde Vandrerhjem.** This youth hostel, perfect for budget travelers, is on Roskilde Fjord, which is close to the town's green areas. Guests have use of the kitchen. ⊠ *Vindeboder 7, DK–4000* 🖂 *46/35–21–84* 🖃 *46/32–66–90* ⊕ *www.rova.dk* 🛏 *152 beds* ᵭ *Restaurant, laundry facilities* 🖃 *No credit cards.*

Nightlife & the Arts

For one weekend at the end of June, Roskilde holds one of Europe's biggest rock-music gatherings, the **Roskilde Festival** (⊕ www.roskilde-festival.dk). Some 75,000 people show up every year to enjoy the outdoor concerts.

When the town's youth are in the mood for live rock, they head to **Gimle** (⊠ Ringstedg. 30 🖂 46/35–12–13 ⊕ www.gimle.dk) on weekends. At **Bryggergården** (⊠ Alg. 15 🖂 46/35–01–03), or the Draft Horse, adults have a late supper and beer in cozy surroundings. During the summer, **Café Mulle Rudi** (⊠ Djalma Lunds Gård 7 🖂 46/37–03–25) is an arty spot with indoor and outdoor seating and live jazz.

VIKING VICTUALS

THE STOCK IMAGE of ruddy-cheeked Vikings feasting around a wooden table, tearing into oversized drumsticks with their bare hands and gulping down frothy mugs of mead may whiff of Hollywood epics, but it isn't so far off the mark. The Vikings were hearty eaters, loved their mead, and didn't use plates or utensils, except for the knives that they pulled from their sheaths, and occasionally wooden spoons. Legend has it that Skål!, the bottoms-up toast that is roared across Denmark dinner tables, came from the Vikings, who used to drink from skulls.

While the Vikings' primitive table manners likely raised a few eyebrows, the cuisine itself was exceptionally developed. For all their seafaring fame, Viking society was highly agricultural. They lived in communal farming settlements and harvested barley, oat, and wheat and a wide array of herbs and root vegetables, from rosemary and tarragon to parsnips and leeks. They also raised cattle, sheep, goats, pigs, ducks, and geese. They were avid hunters, roaming Denmark's wild countryside with their bows and arrows to hunt bear, wild boar, elk, and reindeer. Along the rich Scandinavian coastline they speared seals and whales and collected seabird eggs. The thick inland forest yielded nuts, berries, and wild plants. The Vikings flavored soups with nettles and forest onions, and for dessert they topped graham-flour pancakes with juicy bilberries. As for libations, they concocted everything from elderflower juice to the ever-popular honey-based mead.

The 300-year-long Viking era dates, appropriately enough, from its first raid on a small British island in the 8th century. It was, after all, the Viking's prowess at plundering and pillaging that brought them their well-deserved infamy. Wizard seamen and cunning conquerors, the Vikings swiftly plied the seas in their souped-up ships, rigged with massive sails and powered by muscled oarsmen. England became their favorite stomping grounds, but the rest of Europe was also prey. The Vikings penetrated the Frankish empire via its rivers, from the Elbe in Germany to the Seine in France, toppling Hamburg, Bordeaux, and Paris along the way. Conquering works up a fierce appetite, and the Vikings prepared their feasts with the same zeal with which they razed the countryside.

If art is the reflection of life—or, more accurately, what is important in life—then the celebration of food and drink were central to the Viking existence. Viking-era tapestries unfold with rollicking feast scenes, often in commemoration of battles won—and gold and silver confiscated.

For a taste of Viking life, try this at home: Wild Boar in Bilberry Sauce

1 kg wild boar meat

2 carrots

2 tablespoons honey

1 cup stock

butter

2 onions

fresh ginger

salt and pepper

In a frying pan, season the wild boar meat with salt and pepper and brown it in the butter and then place into a large pan. Peel and slice carrots and onions. Add carrots, onions, honey, ginger, and stock to the pan. Add a bit of salt and pepper. Cover and simmer over low heat for about one hour, or until meat reaches 75 degrees (Celsius).

Sports & the Outdoors

GOLF **Roskilde Golf Klub** (✉ Margrethehåbvej 116 ☎ 46/37–01–81 ⊕ www. roskildegolfklub.dk) has an 18-hole golf course with views of the twin-peak Roskilde Cathedral and the surrounding forest.

TOURS Boat excursions depart from the town's docks for dual-purpose (sightseeing and transportation) routes on Roskilde Fjord. The boats occasionally make stops at Frederikssund and Frederiksværk, but most passengers are there for a fun and scenic boat ride. Some refreshments can be purchased on board. **Saga Fjord** (☎ 46/75–64–60 ⊕ www. sagafjord.dk) operates more sightseeing-oriented trips.

Shopping

CRAFTS Between Roskilde and Holbæk is **Galleri Kirke Sonnerup** (✉ Englerupvej 62, Såby ☎ 46/49–26–70), with a good selection of pottery, glass, clothing, and woodwork produced by more than 50 Danish artists.

Lejre

⑭ *10 km (6 mi) west of Roskilde, 40 km (25 mi) west of Copenhagen.*

Archaeological digs unearthing the times of the Vikings show that Lejre has had a glorious past. During the 10th century the town reigned as the kingdom's most sacred place.

Fodor'sChoice The 50-acre **Lejre Forsøgscenter** (Lejre Archaeological Research Center) ★ ☺ compound contains a reconstructed village dating from the Iron Age and two 19th-century farmhouses. In summer a handful of hardy Danish families live here under the observation of researchers; they go about their daily routine—grinding grain, herding goats, eating with their hands, and wearing furs and skins—providing a clearer picture of ancient ways of life. In Bodalen (Fire Valley), children can try their own hand at such tasks as grinding corn, filing an ax, and sailing in a dugout canoe. ✉ Slangealleen 2 ☎ 46/48–08–78 ⊕ www.lejre-center.dk ☞ DKr 75 ☉ May–mid-June and mid-Aug.–mid-Sept., Tues.–Fri. 10–4, weekends 10–5; mid-June–mid-Aug., daily 10–5.

Ledreborg Slot is one of Denmark's finest examples of 18th-century building and landscape architecture. Built in 1742, Ledreborg Castle is now owned by the eighth generation of the Holstein-Ledreborg family. The main building contains a remarkable collection of paintings and furnishings from when it was first built. At the southern part there is an elaborate terraced garden in the 18th-century French style. ✉ Ledreborg Allé 2 ☎ 46/48–00–38 ⊕ www.ledreborgslot.dk ☞ DKr 75 ☉ May–mid-June and Sept., Sun. 11–5; mid-June–Aug., daily 11–5.

Køge

⑮ *20 km (13 mi) southeast of Lejre, 47 km (29 mi) southwest of Copenhagen.*

The well-preserved medieval town of Køge began its existence as a fishing village dependent on the herring trade. Køge is also known for the witch hunts that took place in the early 17th century. Today, with about

40,000 inhabitants, this satellite town of Copenhagen exists as a center of trade. It links to the big city by suburban train.

In the 17th century and later during the Napoleonic wars, Køge was witness to many naval battles. The Danish and Swedish fleets clashed repeatedly in order to gain control over the sound, which was the gateway to trade with the Baltic Sea.

Køge Museum is in a centrally located 17th-century merchant's house. On display are mementos and items belonging to Hans Christian Andersen, local costumes, and artifacts including an executioner's sword and a 13th-century stone font. The legend of the font is that it had to be removed from the town church after a crippled woman committed an unsavory act into it, hoping her bizarre behavior would cure her. Also on exhibit are 16th-century silver coins from a buried treasure containing more than 2,000 coins. The stash was found in the courtyard of Langkildes Gård. ✉ *Nørreg. 4* ☎ *56/63–42–42* ⊕ *www.dmol.dk* 🏷 *DKr 30* ☉ *June–Aug., daily 11–5; Sept.–May, Tues.–Fri. 1–5, Sat. 11–3, and Sun. 1–5.*

Kunstmuseet Køge Skitsesamling (Art Museum Køge Sketches Collection) has changing exhibitions and an extensive permanent collection of sketches, sculpture, and other modern Danish art. The museum features about 7,500 studies and models of paintings and sculptures created for public spaces throughout the country—it's the only museum of its kind in Denmark. Works on permanent loan from private individuals include the studies for *The Little Mermaid* by sculptor Edvard Eriksen. ✉ *Nørreg. 29* ☎ *56/67–60–20* ⊕ *www.dmol.dk* 🏷 *DKr 30* ☉ *Tues.–Sun. 10–5; Wed. 10–8.*

The old part of Køge is filled with 300 half-timber houses, all protected by the National Trust; it is a lovely area for a stroll. At the end of Kirkestræde is the 15th-century **Sankt Nicolai Kirke** (St. Nicholas Church). Once a lighthouse, its floor is now covered with more than 100 tombs of Køge VIPs. Carved angels line the church's walls, but most have had their noses struck off—a favorite pastime of drunken Swedish soldiers in the 1700s. ✉ *Kirkestr. 26* ☎ *56/65–13–59* 🏷 *Free* ☉ *Mid-June–Aug., weekdays 10–4, Sat. 10–noon; Sept.–mid-June, weekdays 10–noon. Tower tours mid-June–mid-Aug., weekdays every 30 mins. 10–1:30.*

off the beaten path

VALLØ SLOT – About 8 km (5 mi) south of Køge stands Vallø Slot, a large castle in Renaissance style from 1586. It was burnt down by a fire in 1893 and promptly rebuilt. The castle is surrounded by moats and reinforced with towers. Since 1737 noble families have used Vallø Slot for rest and relaxation. The gardens, the only part open to the public, are known for their roses and exotic plants. ✉ *Slotsg. 3, Vallø* ☎ *56/26–74–13* 🏷 *Free* ☉ *Daily 8–dusk.*

Where to Stay & Eat

$$$$ ✕ **Horizonten Restaurant.** For a great view, sit on the terrace overlooking the harbor. Horizonten's interior is modern and often decorated with exhibitions of local artists. The food here includes a mixture of Italian, French, Spanish, and Danish cuisine. Any of the grilled-fish dishes on the menu are a good option, but the seafood-and-fish platter is the highlight. Lunch is served only by prior reservation. ⊠ *Havnen 29A* ☎ *56/ 63–86–28* ⊕ *www.horizonten.dk* ⊟ *MC, V* ⊗ *Closed Mon.; Jan. and Feb., closed Sun.*

$$ ⊞ **Hotel Hvide Hus.** Built in 1966 and overlooking the Bay of Køge, the White House Hotel has fantastic views. The hotel is brightly decorated in a contemporary Danish style. ⊠ *Strandvejen 111, DK–4600* ☎ *56/ 65–36–90* ⊟ *56/66–33–14* ⊕ *www.hotelhvidehus.dk* ⊅ *127 rooms, 1 suite* ⚒ *Restaurant, cafeteria, sauna, bar, meeting room, some pets allowed, no-smoking rooms* ⊟ *AE, DC, MC, V.*

$ ⊞ **Hotel Vallø Slotskro.** Near Vallø Slot and surrounded by the castle's **FodorsChoice** beautifully landscaped grounds, this rural inn is a pleasant place to spend ★ a couple of days. The rooms are charming (some of them have beds with canopies), and the service is personable. ⊠ *Slotsg. 1, DK–4600* ☎ *56/ 26–70–20* ⊟ *56/26–70–71* ⊕ *www.valloeslotskro.dk* ⊅ *11 rooms, 7 with bath* ⚒ *Restaurant, bar, some pets allowed, no-smoking rooms* ⊟ *AE, DC, MC, V.*

Nightlife & the Arts
Even if the name suggests another thing, **Hugo's Vinkælder** (Hugo's Winecellar; ⊠ Brog. 19, courtyard ☎ 56/65–58–50 ⊕ www.hugos.dk) is an old beer pub, which was opened in 1968 on the ruins of a medieval monastery cellar. It is a favorite gathering spot for locals. There are beers from all over the world and sandwiches to go with them. On Saturday there is live jazz until midnight. It's closed Sunday.

off the beaten path Twenty-four kilometers (15 mi) south of Køge near Rødvig, the Stevns Klint chalk cliffs make a good stop. The 13th-century **Højerup Kirke** sits on the cliffs. Over time as the cliffs eroded, first the cemetery and then part of the church toppled into the sea. The church has now been restored and the cliffs below have been bolstered by masonry to prevent further damage. ⊠ *Højerup Byg., Stevns Klint, Store Heddinge* ☎ *56/50–36–88* ⊡ *DKr 15* ⊗ *Daily 11–5.*

Møn

▶ **⑯** *77 km (47 mi) south of Køge, 122 km (75 mi) south of Copenhagen.*

The island of Møn makes for a wonderful side trip from Copenhagen, especially in summer, and particularly if you like beaches, striking scenery, and orchids—the island has the greatest selection of the flower in all of Denmark. There's also plenty of woodland, ideal for hiking, picnics, and horseback riding. With fewer than 12,000 inhabitants, Møn has a slow, laid-back pace. North of Stege, the main town, is Ulvshale strand, one of the best beaches on the entire island, framed by forest growth with a network of nature trails and hiking tracks. Thanks to the coastal marshlands of Nyord, Møn also offers perfect opportunities for the amateur bird-watcher to pass a fascinating afternoon spotting some local and migratory birds from one of several bird-watching sites placed strategically around the area. You'll see holiday cottages in abundance here; they're very popular among Danes and other Europeans, who like to rent for a week or longer.

The whole island is pocked with nearly 100 Neolithic burial mounds, but it is most famous for its dramatic chalk cliffs, the northern **Møns Klint**, which is three times as large as Stevns Klint. Circled by a beech forest, the milky-white 75-million-year-old bluffs plunge 400 feet to a small, craggy beach—accessible by a path and more than 500 steps. Wear good walking shoes and take care: though a park ranger checks the area for loose rocks, the cliffs can crumble suddenly. Once here, Danish families usually hunt for fossils of cuttlefish, sea urchins, and other sea life. The cliffs are an important navigational marker for ships—an unusual landmark on south Zealand's otherwise flat topography.

Just inland from the northern section of the Møns Klint is **Liselund Slot**, a delightful 18th-century folly. Antoine de la Calmette, the island's sheriff and a royal chamberlain, took his inspiration from Marie-Antoinette's Hameau (Hamlet) at Versailles and built the small Liselund Castle in 1792 for his beloved wife. The thatch-roof palace—the only one of its kind in the world—has landscaping and gardens that were the opposite of the strict, symmetrically cut lines of the baroque garden of the day. A romantic garden of winding paths and hidden views also includes a Swiss house and a Norwegian cottage with elegant Pompeian interiors. In this lovely setting, Hans Christian Andersen wrote his fairy tale *The Tinder Box*. The palace has been open to the public since 1938, and if you walk behind it you'll find lakes with islands, making the spot ideal for a romantic picnic. This castle is not to be confused with a hotel of the same name. ⊠ *Langebjergvej 4, Borre* ☎ *55/ 81–21–78* 🖾 *DKr 20* ☉ *Tours (Danish and German only) May–Oct., Tues.–Fri. 10:30, 11, 1:30, and 2; weekends also 3 and 3:30.*

Møn's capital, **Stege** (population 2,000), received its town charter in 1268. A third of the island's 11,500 inhabitants live here. Stege began as a small fishing village and it expanded slowly around a castle erected in the 12th century. By the 15th century Stege was a commercial center for fishermen, peasants, and merchants. It was in this wealthy period that the town was encircled with moats and ramparts. The fortified town had three entranceways, each of them controlled by a gate tower. One of these gates, **Mølleporten**, raised around 1430, is still standing. You can enjoy a pleasant hour roaming around on Storegade, the main street, stopping for a bite to eat and drink at one of the many cafés and restaurants. Strolling along Søndersti and the ramparts will transport you to medieval times. Many of the plants which grow here are medicinal plants that date back to the Middle Ages.

The **Møns Museum** in Stege showcases antiques and local-history exhibitions and is well worth a stop. There are two areas to the museum: Empiregården, which displays typical living rooms from rural houses on Møn, and exhibitions with weaponry, photographs and amber; and Museumsgården, a 200-year-old farmstead. ⊠ *Storeg. 75, Stege* ☎ *55/ 81–40–67* ⊕ *www.aabne-samlinger.dk/moens* 🖾 *DKr 30* ☉ *May–Oct., daily 10–4.*

One of the island's medieval churches noted for its naive frescoes, **Fanefjord Kirke** may have been completed by a collaborative group of artisans. The whimsical paintings include scholastic and biblical doodlings. The church also maintains an original 13th-century aisle. The Fanefjord church is 12½ km (8 mi) southwest of Stege. Other churches in the area famed for their frescoes include the ones in Elmelunde and Keldby. Note that there are eight other churches in town usually open for a quick visit. ⊠ *Fanefjord Kirkevej 51, Askeby* ☎ *55/81–70–05* ☉ *Apr.–Sept., daily 7–4; Oct.–Mar., daily 8–4.*

Ten kilometers (6 mi) west of Stege is **Kong Asgers Høj** (King Asger's Hill), Denmark's biggest passage grave (a collection of upright stones supporting a horizontal stone slab to make a tomb) that dates from the early Stone Age. A 26-foot-long hall precedes the 32-foot grave chamber. During its history, the passage grave has periodically been used as a common grave for locals. You can pick up a brochure from the tourist office, detailing other ancient grave sites, including Klekkende Høj (Klekkende Mound), a double gallery grave from the Neolithic Age, and Grønsalen or Grønjæger's Mound, one of Denmark's largest and the largest on Møn (it's located at Fanefjord Church).

There are more than 42 artists practicing their crafts on Møn. A complete list of **galleries** is available at the tourist office, but expect to see painters, sculptors, potters, glass artists, goldsmiths, amber- and stonepolishers, and studios specializing in wickerwork and candle making. One excellent museum/gallery is **Smykkemuseet** (Museum for Jewelry; ⊠ Hjørnet 6, Damme, DK–4792 Askeby ☎ 55/81–76–08) in Store Damme, which is the only one of its kind in the country.

Where to Stay & Eat

Probably the most popular places to stay on the island are the 300 (more or less) holiday homes or cottages that the tourist office rents out on behalf of the owners. Bargains can be had, especially in the off-season, and all cottages have modern amenities. A holiday house on Møn is lovely in all seasons. The tourist office knows the cottages well and makes sure that they live up to their catalog description. This may be a viable alternative if you plan on staying on the island for a few days.

Other than the hotels listed below, the tourist office can also direct you to 21 bed-and-breakfasts, six campgrounds, two hostels, and six local homes that rent apartments.

$–$$ ✕▥ **Præstekilde Hotel.** On a small island close to the capital, this hotel has a splendid view of Stege Bay from the middle of the golf course. The service is efficient while maintaining the warmth of rural areas. The restaurant serves good French-inspired Danish food. The small, simply equipped rooms are decorated in light colors, giving a bright impression on sunny days. ⊠ *Klintevej 116, DK–4780 Keldby* ☎ *55/86–87–88* 🖶 *55/81–36–34* ⊕ *www.praestekilde.dk* ⇆ *46 rooms, 4 suites* ⌂ *Restaurant, minibars, 18-hole golf course, indoor pool, sauna, billiards, meeting rooms, some pets allowed, no-smoking rooms* ⊟ *AE, DC, MC, V.*

★ **$$$** ▥ **Liselund Ny Slot.** In a handsome, pale-yellow grand manor dating from 1887, this modern hotel on an isolated estate offers refined accommodations without being stodgy. The staircase and frescoed ceilings have been preserved and the rooms are fresh and simple, with wicker furnishings and pastel color schemes. Half the rooms overlook the forest and a pond filled with swans. The downstairs restaurant serves Danish cuisine. ⊠ *Langebjergvej 6, DK–4791 Borre* 🕾 *55/81–20–81* 🖶 *55/81–21–91* 🛏 *15 rooms* ♿ *Restaurant, meeting room* ▤ *AE, DC, MC, V.*

¢ 🖭 **Pension Bakkegården.** Between the view of the Baltic Sea and the Klinteskov forest, this small hotel farm offers the best qualities of the island. From here it is a simple and relaxing 20-minute stroll through the beech forest to see the cliffs of Møn. Partial board is available upon request. Six of the 12 rooms overlook the sea. If you're traveling with children, they will enjoy the cows, chickens, cats, and a dog. ⊠ *Busenevej 64, Busene, DK–4791 Borre* 🕾*55/81–93–01* 🖶*55/81–94–01* ⊕*www.bakkegaarden64. dk* 🛏 *12 rooms without bath* ♿ *Billiards* ▤ *No credit cards.*

Falster

🔞 *3 km (2 mi) south of Bogø; Nykøbing Falster is 49 km (30 mi) southeast of Stege, 134 km (83 mi) south of Copenhagen.*

Accessible by way of the striking Farø Bridge or the parallel Storstrømsbroen (Big Current Bridge) from Fredensborg, Falster is shaped like a tiny South America and has excellent blond beaches to rival those of its continental twin. Among the best are the southeastern Marienlyst and southernmost Gedser. Almost everywhere on the island are cafés, facilities, and water-sports rentals. Falster is also one of the country's major producers of sugar beets.

🐣 The **Middelaldercentret** (Center for the Middle Ages or Medieval Center), a reconstructed medieval village, invites school classes to dress up in period costumes and experience life in the late 14th century. Daytime visitors can participate in activities that change weekly—from cooking to medieval knife-making to animal herding—and on weekends folk dances and other cultural happenings. A whole marketplace is depicted here, as well as the rougher sides of life back then. There are trebuchet demonstrations (a weapon, or medieval siege engine, made either to batter masonry or to throw projectiles over walls), knight tournaments, archery, and yes, even fireball throwing and bonfires on Midsummer's Day. ⊠ *Ved Hamborgskoven 2, Nykøbing Falster* 🕾 *54/86–19–34* ⊕ *www.middelaldercentret.dk* 🛏 *DKr 80* ☉ *May–Sept., daily 10–4.*

Where to Stay & Eat

$$$–$$$$ ✕ **Czarens Hus.** This stylish old inn dates back more than 200 years, when it was a guesthouse and supply store for area farmers and merchants. Deep-green walls, gold trim, and chandeliers set the backdrop for antique furnishings. The specialty of the house is Continental European–Danish cuisine, which translates as creative beef and fish dishes, often served with cream sauces. Try the Zar Beuf (calf tenderloin in a mushroom-and-onion cream sauce). ⊠ *Langg. 2, Nykøbing Falster* 🕾 *54/85–28–29* ▤ *AE, DC, MC, V* ☉ *Closed Sun.*

$$–$$$ 🖭 **Hotel Falster.** This sleek and efficient hotel accommodates conference guests as well as vacationers with its comfortable yet businesslike de-

meanor. Rustic brick walls and Danish antiques mix with sleek Danish-design lamps and sculpture. Rooms are done in dark wood and modular furniture. ⊠ *Stubbekøbingvej 150, DK–4800 Nykøbing Falster* ☎ *54/85–93–93* 🖷 *54/82–21–99* ⊕ *www.hotel-falster.dk* ⟿ *68 rooms, 1 suite* ⌂ *Restaurant, gym, bar, meeting room, some pets allowed, no-smoking rooms* ⊟ *AE, DC, MC, V.*

Sports & the Outdoors

GOLF The 18-hole **Sydsjælland Golf Klub** (⊠ Præstø Landevej 39–Mogenstrup, DK–4700 Næstved ☎ 55/76–15–55) is more than 25 years old, and the park course is lined with a number of small lakes and streams. The highest accepted handicap is 36.

Lolland

🔞 *Sakskøbing is 19 km (12 mi) west of Nykøbing Falster and 138 km (85 mi) southwest of Copenhagen.*

The history of Lolland dates back more than 1,000 years, to a man named Saxe who sat at the mouth of the fjord and collected a toll. He later cleared the surrounding land and leased it. It became known as Saxtorp and eventually Sakskøbing, the island's capital. Though most people head straight for the beaches, the area (accessible by bridge from Nykøbing Falster) has a few sights, including a water tower with a smiling face and an excellent car museum near the central 13th-century Ålholm Slot (closed to the public). The **Ålholm Automobile Museum** is northern Europe's largest, with more than 200 vehicles. ⊠ *Ålholm Parkvej 17, Nysted* ☎ *54/87–19–11* ⊕ *www.aalholm.dk* 🎫 *DKr 75* ◉ *Mid-May–Aug., daily 10–5; Sept.–mid-Oct., weekends 10–4.*

⟳ The **Knuthenborg Safari Park**, 8 km (5 mi) west of Sakskøbing and also on Lolland, has a drive-through range where you can rubberneck at tigers, zebras, rhinoceroses, giraffes, and areas where you can mingle with and pet camels, goats, and ponies. Besides seeing 20 species of animals, children can marvel at Småland's to-scale relief map of southern Zealand or play on the jungle gym, minitrain, and other rides. ⊠ *Birketvej 1, Maribo, Bandholm* ☎ *54/78–80–89* ⊕ *www. knuthenborg.dk* 🎫 *DKr 110* ◉ *May, June, Aug., and Sept., daily 9–6; July, daily 9–8; Oct. 15–23, daily 9–6.*

Where to Stay

$$ 🏨 **Lalandia.** This massive water-park hotel has an indoor pool, beachside view, and lots of happy families. On the southern coast of Lolland, about 27 km (16 mi) southwest of Sakskøbing, the modern white apartments, with full kitchen and bath, accommodate up to eight people. There are three family-style restaurants—a steak house, Italian buffet, and pizzeria. The water park is free and open daily to guests from 10 to 8. ⊠ *Rødbyhavn, DK–4970 Rødby* ☎ *70/30–15–28* 🖷 *54/61–05–01* ⊕ *www.lalandia.dk* ⟿ *636 apartments* ⌂ *3 restaurants, 9-hole golf course, 5 tennis courts, indoor pool, health club, sauna, bar, playground, meeting room* ⊟ *AE, DC, MC, V.*

¢ 🏨 **Hotel Saxkjøbing.** Behind its yellow half-timber facade, this comfortable hotel is short on character and frills, but the rooms are bright, sunny, and modern, if very simply furnished. In the town center, the hotel is convenient to everything. Its family-style restaurant serves pizzas, steaks, and salads. ⊠ *Torvet 9, DK–4990 Sakskøbing* ☎ *54/70–40–39* 🖷 *54/ 70–53–50* ⊕ *www.hotel-saxkjobing.dk* ⇩ *24 rooms* ⚓ *Restaurant, billiards, bar, meeting room* ⊟ *AE, DC, MC.*

Ringsted

⑲ *95 km (59 mi) north of Sakskøbing (Lolland), 68 km (42 mi) south-west of Copenhagen (via Køge).*

During the Middle Ages Ringsted, built around a church and nearby 12th-century Benedictine abbey, became one of the most important Danish towns. The abbey was partially destroyed by a fire in the early 1900s. Nowadays Ringsted is known for being "the town in the middle," the traffic junction of Zealand.

⟳ The spirit of fairy tales is tangible at **Eventyrlandet** (Fantasy World), where, among over 1,000 animated mannequins, a life-size, animated model of Hans Christian Andersen tells his stories via a recorded tape playing in Danish, English, and German. Children enjoy Santa World and Cowboy Land while adults can discover the Adventure Gardens, where Moorish, Japanese, and Roman ornaments dot the well-preserved gardens. ⊠ *Eventyrvej 13, DK–4100* ☎ *57/61–19–30* ⊕ *www. fantasy-world.dk* 🎫 *DKr 75* ⊙ *June–Aug. and Oct.–Dec., daily 10–5.*

Sanct Bendts Kirke (St. Benedict's Church) is the only evidence left of the existence of the Benedictine monastery that thrived here in the 12th century. Inside, four Danish kings are buried, including Valdemar I, who died in 1182. ⊠ *Sct. Bendtsg. 3* ☎ *57/61–40–19* ⊙ *May–mid-Sept., daily 10–noon and 1–5; mid-Sept.–Apr., daily 1–3.*

off the beaten path

★ **SORØ** – Eighteen kilometers (11 mi) west of Ringsted is the town of Sorø, known for **Akademiet,** founded in 1623 by King Christian IV. The Academy was established in the abbey built by Bishop Absalon in 1142 and abandoned after the Lutheran reformation. The educational importance of the town increased thanks to the Danish writer Ludvig Holberg, who donated his whole inheritance to the academy on his death in 1754. The academy is on the banks of Sorø Sø (Lake Sorø) inside an extensive park. Not far from here is **Klosterkirke,** a Romanesque church built in the 12th century as a part of a Cistercian abbey. In this church are the remains of Bishop Absalon.

⟳ **BONBON-LAND** – Children adore this park in the tiny southern Zealand town of Holme-Olstrup between Rønnede and Næstved, 30 km (19 mi) south of Ringsted. Filled with rides and friendly costumed grown-ups, BonBon-Land is an old-fashioned playland, with a few eating and drinking establishments thrown in for adults. ⊠ *Gartnervej 2, DK–4684 Holme-Olstrup* ☎ *55/53–07–00* ⊕ *www. bonbonland.dk* 🎫 *DKr 150* ⊙ *Mid-May–mid-June and Aug., daily 9:30–5; mid-June–July, daily 9:30–8.*

Where to Stay

$$$-$$$$ ▣ **Skjoldenæseholm.** Any point of the island can be reached by car within an hour from this luxurious hotel in the very center of Zealand. Luxury prevails, from the Jacuzzis in the suites to the surrounding lush park and forest. Cottages for groups and families, one of them placed by the 15th hole in the nearby golf course, are available to rent. ⊠ *Skjoldenæsvej 106, DK–4174 Jystrup Midsjælland* ☎ *57/53–87–50* 🖨 *57/ 53–87–51* ⊕ *www.skj.dk* 🛏 *38 rooms, 5 suites* ⚭ *Restaurant, billiards, bar, meeting room* ⊟ *AE, DC, MC, V.*

Halsskov

⑳ *48 km (30 mi) west of Ringsted, 110 km (69 mi) southwest of Copenhagen.*

Europe's third-longest tunnel-bridge, Storebæltsbro—the entire fixed-link length of which is 18 km (11 mi)—links Halsskov, on west Zealand, to Nyborg, on east Funen. Rail traffic traverses the west bridge and tunnel while auto traffic passes on the east-and-west bridge.

The **Storebæltsbro og Naturcenter** (Great Belt Bridge Center), which details the tunnel-bridge construction process, includes videos and models and makes for an informative stop. There are activities for children and a café on-site. ⊠ *Storebæltsvej 88, Halsskov Odde, Korsør* ☎ *58/ 35–01–00* 🖼 *Free* ☉ *Mid-Apr.–mid-Oct., daily 10–5.*

> **off the beaten path**

TRÆLLEBORG – Viking enthusiasts will want to head 18 km (11 mi) northeast from Halsskov to Slagelse to see its excavated Viking encampment with a reconstructed army shelter. Harold Bluetooth's gigantic circular fortress from around AD 900 is the best-preserved castle of its kind, and together with the museum and the many activities offered in summer, Trelleborg is definitely worth a visit for the whole family. There are free guided tours in the summer, but they're offered in German and Danish only. ⊠ *Trælleborg Allé 4, Hejninge, Slagelse* ☎ *58/54–95–16* 🖼 *DKr 50* ☉ *Apr.–mid-Oct., Sat.–Thurs. 10–5.*

Zealand A to Z

AIRPORTS

Kastrup International Airport near Copenhagen is Zealand's only airport.
🛂 **Kastrup International Airport** ☎ 32/31-32-31 ⊕ www.cph.dk.

BIKE TRAVEL

Zealand's flat landscape allows for easy biking, and in summer touring this way can be a delightful experience. Most roads have cycle lanes, and tourist boards stock maps detailing local routes. For more biking information, call the Danish Cycling Association, the Danish Tourist Board, or the bicycle tour operator Bike Denmark.
🛂 **Bike Denmark** ⊠ Olaf Poulsens Allé 1A, DK–3480 Fredensborg ☎48/48-58-00 🖨48/ 48-59-00 ⊕ www.bikedenmark.com. **Danmarks Turistråd** (Danish Tourist Board)

✉ Vesterbrog. 6D, Vesterbro, DK-1620 Copenhagen ☎ 33/11-14-15 🖷 33/93-14-16 ⊕ www.visitdenmark.com. **Dansk Cyklist Forbund** (Danish Cyclist Federation) ✉ Rømersg. 7, Downtown, DK-1362 Copenhagen ☎ 33/32-31-21 🖷 33/32-76-83 ⊕ www.dcf.dk.

BOAT & FERRY TRAVEL

There are several DSB and Scandlines car ferries from Germany. They connect Kiel to Bagenkop, on the island of Langeland (from there, drive north to Spodsbjerg and take another ferry to Lolland, which is connected to Falster and Zealand by bridges); Puttgarden to Rødbyhavn on Lolland; and Travemünde and Warnemünde to Gedser on Falster. If you are driving from Sweden, take a car ferry from Hälsingborg to Helsingør. Molslinien runs routes between Jutland and Zealand, linking Kalundborg and Havnebyen to Århus, and Havnebyen to Ebeltoft.

The ScanRail Pass, for travel anywhere within Scandinavia (Denmark, Sweden, Norway, and Finland), and the Interail and EurailPasses are valid on some ferry crossings. Call the DSB Travel Office for information.

🚺 **DSB** ☎ 70/13-14-16 International, 70/13-14-15 domestic ⊕ www.dsb.dk. **Mols-Linien** 🖷 70/10-14-18 🖷 89/52-52-90 ⊕ www.molslinien.dk. **Scandinavian Seaways Ferries (DFDS)** ✉ Skt. Annæ Pl. 30, Sankt Annæ, DK-1295 Copenhagen ☎ 33/42-33-42 🖷 33/42-33-41 ⊕ www.dfds.com. **Scandlines** ☎ 33/15-15-15 🖷 35/29-02-01 ⊕ www. scandlines.dk.

BUS TRAVEL

The bus system is cumbersome and not as efficient as the train system; however, the sliver of northwestern peninsula known as Sjællands Odde can only be reached by bus. Trains leave from Holbæk to Højby, where you can bus to the tip of the point. Møn, Falster, and Halsskov are accessible by bus after the train drops you off at the closest station.

On the Web, go to ⊕ www.rejseplanen.dk for information on various transport possibilities, both train and bus connections, in all of Zealand.

CAR TRAVEL

Highways and country roads throughout Zealand are excellent, and traffic—even around Copenhagen—is manageable most of the time. As elsewhere in Denmark, take care to give right-of-way to the bikes driving to the right of the traffic. Zealand is connected to Funen, which is connected to Jutland, by the Storebæltsbroen, and it is connected to Malmö in Sweden by Øresund Bridge, which ends in Copenhagen. All trips across the Øresund Bridge are paid in Sweden. If you are driving to Sweden, you pay the toll after you have crossed the bridge. If you are headed for Denmark, you pay the toll before you cross the bridge.

BRIDGES 🚺 **Storebæltsbroen** ✉ Storebæltsvej 70, DK-4220 Korsør ☎ 70/15-10-15 🖷 58/30-30-80. **Øresundsbroen** ✉ Vester Søg. 10, Downtown, DK-1601 Copenhagen ☎ 33/41-60-00 🖷 33/93-52-04 ⊕ www.visitoresund. info/us.

EMERGENCIES

For police, fire, or ambulance assistance anywhere in Denmark, dial 112.

🏥 Major Hospitals **Helsingør Sygehus** ✉ Esrumvej 145, Helsingør ☎ 48/29-29-29. **Køge Amts Sygehus** ✉ Lykkebækvej 1, Køge ☎ 56/63-15-00. **Roskilde Amts Sygehus** ✉ Køgevej 7-13, Roskilde ☎ 46/32-32-00.

🏥 24-Hour Pharmacies **Hillerød** ✉ Slotsg. 26 ☎ 48/26-56-00 🖷 48/24-23-85. **Roskilde** ✉ Dom Apotek, Alg. 52 ☎ 46/32-32-77 🖷 46/32-88-22.

SPORTS & THE OUTDOORS

FISHING Zealand's lakes, rivers, and coastline teem with plaice, flounder, cod, and catfish. You can buy a fishing license for one day for DKr 25; for one week for DKr 75; or for one year for DKr 100. Along Zealand's coast it can be bought at any post office. Elsewhere, check with the local tourist office for license requirements. It is illegal to fish within 1,650 feet of the mouth of a stream.

TOURS

The turn-of-the-20th-century *Saga Fjord* gives tours of the waters of the Roskildefjord from April through September; meals are served on board. Schedules vary; call ahead for schedules and information. Another option is *Viking Ruten.*

Check with the local tourism boards for general sightseeing tours in the larger towns or for self-guided walking tours. Most tours of Zealand begin in Copenhagen. For information, call Copenhagen Excursions. The Afternoon Hamlet Tour (five hours) includes Frederiksborg Castle and the exterior of Fredensborg Palace and Kronborg Castle. The seven-hour Castle Tour of North Zealand visits Frederiksborg Castle and the outside of Fredensborg Palace, and stops at Kronborg Castle. The six-hour Roskilde Vikingland Tour includes the market and cathedral, Christian IV's Chapel, and the Viking Ship Museum.

🏛 Copenhagen Excursions ✉ Amager Strandvej 16, DK-2300 Copenhagen ☎ 32/54-06-06 🖷 32/57-49-05 ⊕ www.cex.dk. **Saga Fjord** ✉ Store Valbyvej 154, DK-4000 Roskilde ☎ 46/75-64-60 🖷 46/75-63-60 ⊕ www.sagafjord.dk.

TRAIN TRAVEL

Zealand's extensive rail network will get you where you need to go in much less time than the cumbersome bus system. Most train routes, whether international or domestic, are directed to and through Copenhagen. Routes to north and south Zealand almost always require a transfer at Copenhagen's main station. Every town in Zealand has a central train station, usually within walking distance of hotels and sights. The only part of the island not connected to the DSB network is the sliver of northwestern peninsula known as Sjællands Odde. For information, call the private railway company Arriva. Two vintage trains dating from the 1880s run from Helsingør and Hillerød to Gilleleje.

The Copenhagen Card, which includes train and bus transport as well as admission to some museums and sites, is valid within the HT bus and rail system, which extends north to Helsingør, west to Roskilde, and south to Køge. However, the Copenhagen Card is valid for a limited time, so it's only worthwhile if you're planning a nonstop, intense sightseeing tour.

𝟕 Arriva ☎ 70/27-74-82 ⊕ www.arrivatog.dk. **DSB** ☎ 70/13-14-16 international, 70/13-14-15 domestic ⊕ www.dsb.dk. **HT Bus** ⊠ Gammel Køge Landevej 3, DK-2500 Valby ☎ 36/13-14-15 🖴 36/13-18-97 ⊕ www.ht.dk. **Vintage trains** ☎ 48/30-00-30.

VISITOR INFORMATION
The Fiskeridirektoratet has information about fishing licenses and where to buy them.

𝟕 Danmarks Turistråd (Danish Tourist Board) ⊠ Vesterbrog. 6D, Vesterbro, DK-1620 Copenhagen ☎ 33/11-14-15. **Det grønne Sjælland** (Zealand Naturally) ⊕ www. sjaelland.com. **Fiskeridirektoratet (Danish Directory of Fisheries)** ⊠ Stormg. 2, Downtown, DK-1470 Copenhagen ☎ 33/96-30-00 🖴 33/96-39-03 ⊕ www.fd.dk. **Fredensborg Turistinformation** ⊠ Slotsg. 2, DK-3480 ☎48/48-21-00 🖴 48/48-04-65 ⊕ www.visitfredensborg.dk. **Frederiksdal Kanoudlejning** ⊠ Nybrovej 520, DK-2800 Lyngby ☎ 45/85-67-70 🖴 45/83-02-91. **Gilleleje Turistbureau** ⊠ Gilleleje Hovedg. 6F, DK-3250 Gilleleje ☎ 48/30-01-74 🖴 48/30-34-74 ⊕ www.gilleleje-turistbureau. dk. **Helsingør Turistbureau** ⊠ Havnepl. 3, DK-3000 ☎49/21-13-33 🖴 49/21-15-77 ⊕ www.visitfredensborg.dk. **Hillerød Turistbureau** ⊠ Slangerupg. 2, DK-3400 ☎ 48/ 24-26-26 🖴48/24-26-65 ⊕www.hillerodturist.dk. **Holbæk Turistbureau** ⊠Jernbanepl. 3, DK-4300 ☎ 59/43-11-31 🖴 59/44-27-44 ⊕ www.holbaek-info.dk. **Hornbæk Turistinformation** ⊠ Vestre Stejlebakke 2A, DK-3100 ☎49/70-47-47 🖴 49/70-41-42 ⊕ www.hornbaek.dk. **Køge Turistbureau** ⊠ Vesterg. 1, DK-4600 ☎ 56/67-60-01 🖴56/65-59-84 ⊕www.koegeturist.dk. **Nykøbing Falster Turistinformation** ⊠Østergåg. 7, DK-4800 ☎ 54/85-13-03 🖴 54/85-10-05 ⊕ www.tinf.dk. **Møn Turistbureau** ⊠ Storeg. 2, DK-4780 Stege ☎ 55/86-04-00 🖴 55/81-48-46 ⊕ www.visitmoen. com/english. **Næstved Turistbureau** ⊠ Det Gule Pakhus, Havnen 1, DK-4700 ☎ 55/ 72-11-22 🖴 55/72-16-67 ⊕ www.visitnaestved.com. **Odsherreds Turistbureau** ⊠ Svanestr. 9, DK-4500 Nykøbing Sjælland ☎ 59/91-08-88 🖴 59/93-00-24 ⊕ www. odsherred.com. **Midtsjælland Turistcenter** ⊠ Sct. Bendtsg. 6, DK-4100 Ringsted ☎57/62-66-00 🖴57/62-66-10 ⊕www.met-2000.dk. **Roskilde Festival** ⊠Havsteensvej 11, DK-4000 Roskilde ☎ 46/36-66-13 🖴 46/32-14-99 ⊕ www.roskilde-festival.dk. **Roskilde Turistbureau** ⊠ Gullandsstr. 15, DK-4000 ☎ 46/31-65-65 🖴 46/31-65-60 ⊕ www.destination-roskilde.dk. **Sakskøbing Turistbureau** ⊠ Torveg. 4, DK-4990 ☎ 54/70-56-30 🖴 54/70-53-90. **Slagelse Turistbureau** ⊠ Løveg. 7, DK-4200 ☎ 58/ 52-22-06 🖴 58/52-86-87 ⊕ www.vikingelandet.dk.

Funen & the Central Islands

WORD OF MOUTH

"In Odense, Hans Christian Andersen's house and museum are quite charming."

—sandra

"I wouldn't recommend [the Hans Christian Andersen Museum] unless you're a big fan or a child. The outdoor children's theatre in the garden next to a little pond is fairy-tale cute."

—Don

Updated by
Bruce Bishop

CHRISTENED THE GARDEN OF DENMARK by its most famous son, Hans Christian Andersen, Funen (Fyn) is the smaller of the country's two major islands. A patchwork of vegetable fields and flower gardens, the flat-as-a-board countryside is relieved by beech glades and swan ponds. Manor houses and castles pop up from the countryside like magnificent mirages. Some of northern Europe's best-preserved castles are here: the 12th-century Nyborg Slot, travel pinup Egeskov Slot, and the lavish Valdemars Slot. The fairy-tale cliché often attributed to Denmark springs from this provincial isle, where the only place with modern vigor or stress seems to be Odense, its capital. Trimmed with thatch-roof houses and green parks, the city makes the most of the Andersen legacy but surprises with a rich arts community at the Brandts Klædefabrik, a former textile factory turned museum compound.

Exploring Funen & the Central Islands

Towns in Funen are best explored by car. It's even quick and easy to reach the smaller islands of Langeland and Tåsinge—both are connected to Funen by bridges. Slightly more isolated is Ærø, where the town of Ærøskøbing, with its colorfully painted half-timber houses and winding streets, seems caught in a delightful time warp.

WHAT IT COSTS In kroner					
	$$$$	$$$	$$	$	¢
RESTAURANTS	over 180	141–180	121–140	90–120	under 90
HOTELS	over 1,500	1,200–1,500	1,000–1,200	700–1,000	under 700

Restaurant prices are for a main course at dinner. Hotel prices are for two people in a standard double room, including service charge and tax.

Timing

Wednesday and Saturday are market days in towns across Funen throughout the summer. Often held in the central square, these morning markets sell fresh produce, flowers, and cheeses. Castle concerts are held throughout the summer months at Egeskov, Nyborg, and Valdemars castles and the rarely opened Krengerup manor house near Assens.

Nyborg

▶ ❶ *136 km (85 mi) southwest of Copenhagen (including the bridge across the Great Belt), 30 km (19 mi) southeast of Odense.*

Like most visitors, you should begin your tour of Funen in Nyborg, a 13th-century town that was Denmark's capital during the Middle Ages. The city's major landmark, the moated 12th-century **Nyborg Slot** (Nyborg Castle), was the seat of the Danehof, the Danish parliament from 1200 to 1413. It was here that King Erik Klipping signed the country's first constitution, the Great Charter, in 1282. In addition to geometric wall murals and an armory collection, the castle houses changing art exhibits. ⊠ *Slotsg. 34* ☎ *65/31–02–07* ⊕ *www.museer-nyborg.dk* 🎫 *DKr 30; DKr 45 combined ticket with Nyborg Museum* ◎ *Mar.–May* *and Sept.–mid-Oct., weekdays 10–3; June and Aug., weekdays 10–4; July, weekdays 10–5.*

The **Nyborg Museum** occupies Mads Lerches Gård, a half-timber merchant's house from 1601, and provides an insight into 17th-century life. In addition to furnished period rooms, there's a small brewery. ⊠ *Slotspl. 11* ☎ *65/31–02–07* ⊕ *www.museer-nyborg.dk* ⊡ *DKr 30, DKr 45 combined ticket with Nyborg Slot* ☉ *Apr., May, and Sept., weekdays 10–3; June and Aug., weekdays 10–4; July, weekdays 10–5.*

Every Tuesday at 7 PM in July and August, look and listen for the **Nyborg Tappenstreg** (Nyborg Tattoo), a military march accompanied by music that winds through the streets in the center of town. This ceremony dates from the mid-17th century, when officers would march through the streets, rounding up all the soldiers from the bars and beer halls to return them to the barracks. The word "tattoo" has its roots in the old Dutch word "taptoo" (or "taptoe"), which means to close the tap of a barrel; the variant "taps" obviously claims the same etymology.

Where to Stay & Eat

$–$$$ ✕ **Central Cafeen.** In a 200-year-old town house in the center of town, this warm-tone restaurant with velvet seats has been open since 1854. To many a Nyborg native there's nowhere better in town for a Danish smørrebrød lunch or hearty dinner. Evidence of the customers' affection lines the walls and shelves, from old Carlsberg and Tuborg caps worn by the deliverymen to ancient shop scales—all gifts from happy diners after they retired or closed down their businesses. The menu includes roasted salmon with spinach and boiled potatoes, and fried pork with parsley sauce. Round out the meal with a plate of fresh Funen cheeses served with radishes and chives. In summer you can dine in the outdoor courtyard, surrounded by the neighborhood's yellow, half-timber houses. ⊠ *Nørreg. 6* ☎ *65/31–01–83* ▤ *AE, DC, MC, V* ☉ *Closed Sun. Oct.–June.*

$–$$$ ✕ **Danehofkroen.** Outside Nyborg Slot, this family-run restaurant does a brisk lunch business, serving traditional Danish meals to tourists who enjoy a view of the castle and its tree-lined moat. The menu is basic meat and potatoes, with such dishes as *flæskesteg* (sliced pork served with the crisp rind). ⊠ *Slotspl.* ☎ *65/31–02–02* ⊸ *Reservations essential* ▤ *V* ☉ *Closed Mon. and Oct.–May.*

$$$$ 🏨 **Hesselet.** A modern brick slab outside, this hotel is a refined Anglo-
Fodor'sChoice Asian sanctuary on the inside. Guest rooms have cushy, contemporary
★ furniture and Bang & Olufsen televisions; most have a splendid view of the Storebæltsbro suspension bridge. It has been known for its excellent cuisine since the 1970s, and new ownership in 2003 has not quelled the Hotel's stellar reputation. ⊠ *Christianslundsvej 119, DK–5800* ☎ *65/31–30–29* ⊟ *65/31–29–58* ⊕ *www.hesselet.dk* ⇝ *43 rooms, 4 suites* ⟿ *Restaurant, indoor pool, bar, meeting room* ▤ *AE, DC, MC, V.*

$$$ 🏨 **Nyborg Strand.** This large hotel complex, owned by the Best Western hotel chain, sprawls along the shoreline 1½ km (1 mi) east of Nyborg's city center. The Nyborg Strand caters to the conference crowd, with numerous meeting rooms and an antiseptic lobby that reverberates with the din of noisy groups. However, the seaside location can't

The hub of travel on the island of Funen is the city of Nyborg, though many head straight for Odense and its Hans Christian Andersen–related sights. Three fairy-tale castles grace the southern edges of Funen, and Det Fynske Øhav (The Fyn Archipelago), consisting of the small islands of Langeland, Tåsinge and Ærø, combines cultural heritage and natural beauty.

Numbers in the text correspond to numbers in the margin and on the Funen & the Central Islands map.

3

**If you have
3 days**

Starting in **Nyborg ❶** ⌐, seek out Nyborg Slot, the city's main attraction, and move on to **Ladby ❸** to see the *Ladbyskibet*, a preserved Viking ship. End your first day in ▦ **Kerteminde ❷** with a dinner and a stroll. In the morning travel to ▦ **Odense ❹** and spend the rest of the day brushing up on your fairy-tale knowledge and Hans Christian Andersen trivia, as well as visiting Brandts Klædefabrik, a vibrant artists' compound. On day three, make sure to swing by **Kværndrup ❽** and splendid Egeskov Slot before returning to Nyborg.

**If you have
5 days**

Spend your first day canvassing the sights of ▦ **Odense ❹** ⌐; by the end of the day you should have a good impression of H. C. Andersen's native town. Find your way southwest to **Assens ❺** the next morning to see the beautiful public garden there, and continue on toward ▦ **Svendborg ❼**, stopping in **Faaborg ❻** for dinner. Stay in ▦ **Tåsinge ❾** for two nights, using is as a base for day excursions to **Langeland ❿** and Valdemars Slot. On the fifth day route your northward trek through **Kværndrup ❽** and Egeskov Slot, ending your day in Nyborg.

---

be beat, and the summer rates, particularly for families, are surprisingly low, especially considering the hotel's lovely location. ✉ *Østerøvej 2, DK–5800* ☎ *65/31–31–31* 🖷 *65/31–37–01* ⊕ *www.nyborgstrand.dk* 🛏 *282 rooms, 2 suites* ⚭ *Restaurant, indoor pool, bar, meeting rooms, some pets allowed (fee)* 🗐 *AE, DC, MC, V.*

Nightlife & the Arts

★ Take on the Nyborg night at the popular **Café Anthon** (✉ Mellemg. 25 ☎ 65/31–16–64), a laid-back bar in the heart of town, with live jazz, blues, or rock on Friday and Saturday nights. The quirky decor includes an upright piano with a built-in aquarium and an old grandfather clock in the corner. The walls are hung with all sorts of instruments, from accordions to cellos to electric guitars, many of which were gifts from musicians who have played here.

Shopping

ANTIQUES Many of Funen's manor houses and castles now double as antiques emporiums. The largest is **Hindemae** (✉ Hindemaevej 86, Ullerslev ☎ 65/35–32–60 ⊕ www.hindemae.dk), which lies 12 km (7 mi) west of Nyborg. The site is only open to the public during auctions.

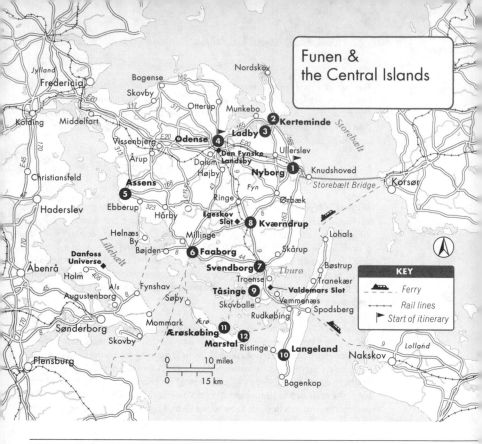

Kerteminde

2 *21 km (13 mi) north of Nyborg, 20 km (13 mi) northeast of Odense.*

Kerteminde is an important fishing village and popular summer resort. The pastel paints and red roofs of the town's houses contrast with the cool blues of the nearby Baltic, which supports recreational fishing, swimming, and other watersports in the summer. On Langegade, walk past the neat half-timber houses to Møllebakken and the **Johannes Larsen Museet,** dedicated to the work of the Danish painter (1867–1961). Across from a strawberry patch and a century-old windmill, the artist built a large country villa that has been perfectly preserved, right down to the teacups. In front is a sculpture of a woman done by Kai Nielsen. Local legend has it that one night, after a particularly wild party in Copenhagen, its legs were somehow broken off. An ambulance was called, and once it arrived, the enraged driver demanded that the artists pay a fine. A chagrined Larsen paid, and in return kept Nielsen's wounded sculpture. ⊠ *Møllebakken 14* ☎ *65/32–37–27* ⊕ *www.kert-mus.dk* ⊠ *DKr 60* ⊙ *June–Aug., daily 10–5; Mar.–May, Sept., and Oct., Tues.–Sun. 10–4; Nov.–Feb., Tues.–Sun. 11–4.*

Where to Stay & Eat

★ **$$$$** ✕ **Rudolf Mathis.** This busy harborside restaurant is topped by two chimneys, which are needed to ventilate the open grills where popular fish dishes are broiled. Favorites are catfish with butter, fennel, and Pernod sauce, and grilled turbot in green-pepper–and–lime sauce. ✉ *Dosseringen 13, 13 km (8 mi) northeast of Odense on Rte. 165* ☎ *65/32–32–33* ⊕ *www.rudolfmathis.dk* ⊟ *AE, DC, MC, V* ☉ *Closed Mon. and Jan. and Feb.*

$$$–$$$$ ✕ **Gittes Fiskehus.** Dine to the gentle sounds of lapping water at this friendly fish restaurant that extends out over Kerteminde's small canal amid colorful, bobbing fishing boats. Dishes include shrimp smothered in garlic, cream, rum, and Pernod, or the "Hemingway steak," a plate of blue marlin, the fish protagonist of *The Old Man and the Sea.* An additional dining room is housed inside a permanently moored boat that sits alongside the restaurant. Come summer, diners spill out onto the deck to enjoy their seafood in the sun. ✉ *Hindsholmvej 5* ☎ *65/32–12–38* ⊟ *MC, V* ☉ *Closed Sun.–Tues. No lunch Sept.–May.*

$ ✕▥ **Tornøes Hotel.** Steps from Kerteminde's harbor is this comfortable hotel with basic rooms, many of which have partial views of the waterfront. The handsome restaurant has pale yellow walls and matching tablecloths, and serves contemporary Danish fare, including a set "Kerteminde menu" of fried sole as well as crepes with ice cream and strawberries for dessert. Café Wenzel, a lively café-bar with light meals, has a pool table, and live music on the weekends. ✉ *Strandg. 2, DK–5300* ☎ *65/32–16–05* ⊟ *65/32–48–40* ⊕ *www.tornoeshotel.dk* ⇌ *28 rooms, 2 suites* ⌂ *Restaurant, bar, some pets allowed* ⊟ *AE, DC, MC, V.*

¢ ▥ **Danhostel Kerteminde Vandrehjem.** South of Kerteminde, this well-maintained hostel is surrounded by a peaceful patch of woodland and is just a few minutes' walk from the beach. Families flock here in summer, drawn by the low prices and a plethora of outdoor activities that awaits just beyond the front door, from hiking to biking to swimming. The rooms are outfitted in typical Danish hostel style, with sturdy wooden bunks and basic showers. An industrial-size kitchen and cafeteria—built to feed the large school groups that come through—serves breakfast. Sheets and towels also cost extra. If you pay by credit card, you'll have to pay a surcharge. ✉ *Skovvej 46, DK–5300 Kerteminde* ☎ *65/32–39–29* ⊟ *65/32–39–24* ⊕ *www.danhostel.dk* ⇌ *30 rooms with shower* ⊟ *MC, V.*

Shopping

CERAMICS   Just a few miles west of Kerteminde is **Bjørnholt Keramik** (✉ Risingevej 12, Munkebo ☎ 65/97–40–90), where you can watch ceramics being made.

off the beaten path

ROMSØ – The 250-acre, pristine island of Romsø, just a half-hour ferry ride from Kerteminde, attracts nature-lovers, hikers, and birdwatchers. A hardwood forest blankets half the island, making it something of a rarity among Denmark's islands, only a few of which have forests. More than 170 species of birds have been recorded here, and during their breeding season (March through June) part of the island is closed to visitors. Deer roam freely through the wooded areas, and hiking trails crisscross the island (bicycles are not allowed).

Romsø's population peaked at 50 after World War I, but after the lighthouse closed in 1973 the population dwindled to just a handful of residents. Bring all supplies that you might need, as there are no accommodations or food on the island. Camping is not permitted. A high-speed **passenger boat** (☎ 65/32–13–77 for reservations with Leif Hansen) connects Kerteminde with Romsø. The cost is around DKr 100 roundtrip. The boat operates only in the summer months, usually from June through August. Schedules change frequently, so call ahead or check with the tourist office.

Ladby

❸ *4 km (2½ mi) south of Kerteminde, 16 km (10 mi) east of Odense.*

The village of Ladby is best known as the home of the 1,100-year-old remains of the *Ladbyskibet.* This ship belonging to a Viking chieftain was buried along with the hunting dogs and horses he would need for Valhalla—the afterlife. Today you can see a massive hull-shaped indentation in the ground where the excavation took place. All the wooden parts of the ship disintegrated centuries ago, but exhibited at the site are the ship's anchor, and also the remains of the horses and hunting dogs. A replica of the ship (in real size) was in the works until the project stalled because of practical and financial difficulties; if and when it's completed, it will be shown alongside the burial site. ☒ *Vikingevej 123* ☎ *65/ 32–16–67* ⊕ *www.kert-mus.dk* ☒ *DKr 40* ☻ *June–Aug., daily 10–5; Mar.–May, Sept., and Oct., Tues.–Sun. 10–4; Nov.–Feb., Wed.–Sun. 11–3.*

Odense

▶ ❹ *20 km (12 mi) southwest of Ladby on Rte. 165, 144 km (90 mi) west of Copenhagen.*

It's no coincidence that Odense, the capital of Funen and third-largest city in Denmark, is reminiscent of a storybook village—much of its charm is built upon the legend of its most famous son, author Hans Christian Andersen. The town is named after another famous Scandinavian, Odin, the king of the Nordic gods. When you're in town, first see the flourishing Kongens Have (King's Garden) and 18th-century Odense Castle, now a government building. If you walk east on Østre Stationsvej to Thomas B. Thriges Gade and Hans Jensens Stræde, you'll come to ★ the **Hans Christian Andersen Hus** (H. C. Andersen House), which sits amid half-timber houses and cobbled streets. Inside, the storyteller's life is chronicled through his photographs, drawings, letters, and personal belongings. The library has Andersen's works in more than 100 languages, and you can listen to fairy tales on tape. ☒ *Bangs Boder 29* ☎ *65/ 51–46–01* ⊕ *www.odmus.dk* ☒ *DKr 50* ☻ *June–Aug., daily 9–6; Sept.–May, Tues.–Sun. 10–4.*

☺ The **Børnekulturehuset Fyrtøjet** (Children's Culture House, The Tinderbox) museum includes walk-through fairy-tale exhibits as well as studios where children can draw and write their own tales and plays and then dress up and perform them. ⊠ *Hans Jensen Str. 21* ☎ *66/14–44–11* ⊕ *www.fyrtoejet.com* ⊟ *DKr 60* ⊙ *Feb.–June, Tues.–Sun. 11–4; July, daily 10–5.*

The sleek **Carl Nielsen Museum** creates multimedia exhibits of the life and work of Denmark's most famous composer (1865–1931) and of his wife, the sculptor Anne Marie Carl-Nielsen (yes, that's the way she took his name). ⊠ *Claus Bergs G. 11* ☎ *65/51–46–01* ⊕ *www.odmus.dk* ⊟ *DKr 25* ⊙ *Jun.–Aug., Thurs. and Fri. 2–6, Sun. 12–4; Sept.–May, Thurs. and Fri. 4–6, Sun. 12–4.*

Møntergården, Odense's city museum, occupies four 17th-century row houses adjacent to a shady, cobbled courtyard. Exhibits range from medieval interiors to coverage of Denmark's Nazi occupation to an extensive and impressive collection of ancient coins from all over the world. ⊠ *Overg. 48–50* ☎ *65/51–46–01* ⊕ *www.odmus.dk* ⊟ *DKr 30* ⊙ *Tues.–Sun. 10–4.*

The stately **Skt. Knuds Kirke,** built from the 13th to the 15th century, is the only purely Gothic cathedral in Denmark. The intricate wooden altar covered with gold leaf was carved by German sculptor Claus Berg. Beneath the sepulchre are the bones of St. (King) Knud, killed during a farmers' uprising in 1086, and his brother. ⊠ *Toward the pedestrian zone of Skt. Knuds Kirkestræde, in front of Andersen Park.*

In the diminutive **Hans Christian Andersens Barndomshjem** (H. C. Andersen's Childhood Home), the young boy and his parents lived in three tiny rooms. The rooms are outfitted with rustic, period furnishings (chairs, lamps, a table) and little else, befitting a humble abode of the early 1800s. ⊠ *Munkemøllestr. 3–5* ☎ *66/13–13–72 Ext. 4601* ⊟ *DKr 10* ⊙ *June–Aug., daily 10–4; Sept.–May, Tues.–Sun. 11–3.*

Near the center of town is the elegant **Fyns Kunstmuseum** (Funen Art Museum), which displays a large and varied collection of Danish art from the 18th century to the present. Featured artists include Jens Juel, Vilhelm Hammershøj, P. S. Krøyer, and Robert Jacobsen. The museum's highlight is its comprehensive collection of Funen artists, from Johannes Larsen to Peter Hansen. ⊠ *Jernbaneg. 13* ☎ *66/13–13–72 Ext. 4601* ⊕ *www.odmus.dk* ⊟ *DKr 30* ⊙ *Tues.–Sun. 10–4.*

For something completely different, head just west of the center of town to the **Superbowl Odense,** an indoor entertainment center with bowling alleys, a restaurant, and a go-cart track. ⊠ *Grønøkken 3* ☎ *66/19–16–40.*

Odense River Cruises (☎ *65/95–79–96*) operates several boat trips on the Odense Å from Filosofgangen. You can catch a boat (May through mid-August, daily on the hour 10–5, returning 35 minutes later) downriver to the Fruens Bøge (Lady's Beech Forest) and then walk down Erik Bøghs Sti (Erik Bøgh's Footpath) to **Den Fynske Landsby** (the Funen Village). Among the country's largest open-air museums, it includes 25 farm buildings and workshops, a vicarage, a water mill, and a theater, which in summer stages adaptations of Andersen's tales. Afterward, cruise back to the town center or catch Bus 42, and walk down the boutique- and café-lined pedestrian street Vestergade (Kongensgade running perpendicular to the town hall), which in summer is abuzz with street performers, musicians, and brass bands. ☒ *Sejerskovvej 20* ☎ *65/51–46–01* ⊕ *www. odmus.dk* 🎫 *DKr 55* ⊙ *Mid-Apr.–May, Sept., and Oct., Tues.–Sun. 10–5; June–Aug., daily 10–7.*

Fodor's Choice   Occupying a former textile factory, the four-story artist compound
★   **Brandts Klædefabrik** houses the **Museet for Fotokunst** (Museum of Photographic Art), **Danmarks Grafiske Museum** (Danish Graphics Museum), **Dansk Presse Museum** (Danish Press Museum), and **Kunsthallen** (Art Gallery). National and international exhibits shown here vary widely, but the photography museum and the art gallery gravitate toward especially experimental work. The press museum chronicles the history of Denmark's printing trade, and houses lithography, bookbinding, and papermaking workshops. ☒ *Brandts Passage 37 and 43, north of the river and parallel to Kongensgade* ☎ *66/13–78–97* ⊕ *www.brandts.dk* 🎫 *Combined ticket DKr 50; photography museum DKr 25; graphics museum DKr 25; press museum DKr 25; art gallery DKr 30* ⊙ *July and Aug., daily 10–5; Sept.–June, Tues.–Sun. 10–5.*

Where to Eat

$$$$ ✕ **LPC** (La Petite Cuisine). This romantic little restaurant tucked in the Brandts Passage can accommodate about 40 diners. The southern French specialties change every day according to what can be purchased fresh at the market. Typical dishes include Asian-inspired marinated duck breast, grilled skewered salmon or catfish with vegetables, and white mocha parfait for dessert. Dishes can be combined in three- to five-course menus. ☒ *Brandts Passage 13* ☎ *66/14–11–00* ⊕ *www.lpc.dk* ◬ *Reservations essential* ⊟ *DC, MC, V.*

$$$–$$$$ ✕ **Marie Louise.** Overseen by the illustrious chef Michel Michaud (he now
Fodor's Choice   lives in Skagen), this is considered one of Funen's—if not Denmark's—
★   finest French restaurants. The elegant whitewashed dining room glitters with crystal and silver. The French-Danish menu typically offers such specialties as scalloped salmon with bordelaise sauce and grilled veal with lobster cream sauce. Business and holiday diners are sometimes treated to gratis extras—such as quail's-egg appetizers or after-dinner drinks. ☒ *Lottrups Gaard, Vesterg. 70–72* ☎ *66/17–92–95* ⊕ *www. restaurant-marielouise.dk* ⊟ *AE, DC, MC, V* ⊙ *Closed Sun. and Mon.*

$$$–$$$$ ✕ **Restaurant Under Lindetræet.** The snug corner restaurant, situated in the same cozy, cobblestoned neighborhood as the Hans Christian Andersen House, serves homestyle Danish fare, including grilled redfish with boiled potatoes. Copper pots and Andersen-style paper cutouts hang on the wall, alongside a portrait of the great man himself. Old-fashioned lamps shed light onto the tables, which are set with gold-rim plates. Burgundy velvet drapes divide parts of the dining room, making dining an intimate experience. ☒ *Ramsherred 2* ☎ *66/12–92–86* ◬ *Reservations essential* ⊟ *MC, V* ⊙ *Closed Sun. and Mon.*

$$–$$$$ ✕ **Klitgaard.** Named after its young owner-chef, Jacob Klitgaard, this chic, cool-tone restaurant serves a changing menu of innovative French-Italian fusion fare. The season drives the menu; market-fresh produce graces every dish, from the young Funen lamb with green asparagus to the lightly salted trout served with an herb mousse. Stuffed quail is seasoned with rosemary and accompanied by an endive salad; a fricassee

of scallops and asparagus is enveloped in a tangy lemon sauce. The fresh cuisine is complemented by a soothing decor of tan walls, hardwood floors, and cane furniture that glow softly under recessed lights. ⊠ *Gravene 4* ☎ *66/13–14–55* ⊕ *www.restaurantklitgaard.dk* ⌦ *Reservations essential* ⊟ *DC, MC, V* ☯ *Closed Sun. and Mon.*

$$$ ✕ **Carlslund.** Ask most any Odense local where to find the best *æggekage* in town, and he'll probably point you in this direction. Cholesterolwatchers, beware: æggekage is a rich dish consisting of a fluffy, cream-whipped, parsley-speckled omelet topped with either bacon strips or pork rinds. Dab on some mustard and scoop it up with hunks of rye bread. It's traditionally washed down with shots of aquavit. The place also serves an extensive Danish menu of fish and meat dishes. Dating from 1860, the cozy, low-ceiling restaurant sits in a wooded park on the outskirts of Odense. In summer Carlslund sets up an outdoor stage and hosts live jazz on the weekends, drawing hundreds. ⊠ *Fruens Bøge Skov 7* ☎ *66/91–11–25* ⊕ *www.restaurant-carlslund.dk* ⌦ *Reservations essential* ⊟ *DC, MC, V.*

$–$$$ ✕ **Den Gamle Kro.** Built within the courtyards of several 17th-century homes, this popular restaurant has walls of ancient stone topped by a sliding glass roof. The French-Danish menu includes fillet of sole stuffed with salmon mousse and Châteaubriand with garlic potatoes, but there's also inexpensive smørrebrød. ⊠ *Overg. 23* ☎ *66/12–14–33* ⊕ *www. den-gamle-kro.dk* ⊟ *DC, MC, V.*

$–$$$ ✕ **Franck A.** Overlooking the pedestrian street, this spacious, stylish café–restaurant–bar with exposed brick walls is Odense's answer to Copenhagen's trendy venues—minus the pretension. Hipsters and media types (it's a favorite with the folks from the local TV station) mingle over cocktails but, this being Odense, informality prevails. You're just as likely to sit next to families and older couples lingering over coffee. A rack of newspapers and Tintin comic books invites those who want to settle in for an afternoon read. Brunch is served all day; try the salmon–and–cherry-tomato omelet. The lunch and dinner menu of global cuisine runs the gamut from Thai chicken curry to hefty grilled burgers. Live music (usually Thursday through Saturday nights) draws a toe-tapping crowd until 3 AM; on Monday and Wednesday the place is open until 1 AM. On Thursday Franck A often hosts a popular '80s music night, with lively cover bands. ⊠ *Jernbaneg. 4* ☎ *66/12–27–57* ⊕ *www.francka.dk* ⊟ *MC, V.*

★ ¢–$ ✕ **Den Grimme Ælling.** The name of this chain restaurant means "the ugly duckling," but inside it's simply homey, with pine furnishings and a boisterous family ambience. It's extremely popular with tourists and locals alike, thanks to an all-you-can-eat buffet heaped with cold and warm dishes. ⊠ *Hans Jensens Str. 1* ☎ *65/91–70–30* ⊕ *www.grimme-aelling. dk* ⊟ *DC, MC.*

¢–$ ✕ **Målet.** A lively crowd calls this sports club its neighborhood bar. The schnitzel is served in a dozen creative ways from traditional schnitzel with sautéed potatoes and peas to Indian curry schnitzel with rice, chutney, and pineapple. After the steaming plates of food, watching and discussing soccer are the chief delights of the house. ⊠ *Jernbaneg. 17* ☎ *66/17–82–41* ⌦ *Reservations not accepted* ⊟ *No credit cards.*

Where to Stay

$$$ ⊞ **Clarion Hotel Plaza.** A five-minute walk from the train station, this stately hotel dates from 1915 and overlooks Odense's leafy central park, Kongens Have. An old-fashioned wooden elevator takes you up to the ample, comfortable rooms outfitted in traditional dark-wood furniture. Adjoining the pale-green lobby is the glass-walled Restaurant Rosenhaven, which serves contemporary Danish fare, including wild rabbit wrapped in cabbage and topped with honey and berry preserves, and lemon-accented fillet of sole served in a puff pastry with a tarragon and saffron aspic. ⊠ *Østre Stationsvej 24, DK–5000* ☎ *66/11–77–45* 🖨 *66/14–41–45* ⊕ *www.hotel-plaza.dk* 🖙 *61 rooms, 7 suites* ⟡ *Restaurant, gym, sauna, bar, meeting rooms* ▤ *AE, DC, MC, V.*

$$$ ⊞ **Radisson SAS–Hans Christian Andersen Hotel.** Around the corner from the Hans Christian Andersen House, this blocky brick conference hotel has a plant-filled lobby and ample rooms done up in warm shades of red and yellow. In fall and winter you have to battle your way through large conference groups to get to your room, but in summer it's half the normal price, and relatively quiet. ⊠ *Claus Bergs G. 7, DK–5000* ☎ *66/14–78–00 or 800/33–3333* 🖨 *66/14–78–90* ⊕ *www.radissonsas.com* 🖙 *145 rooms* ⟡ *Restaurant, gym, sauna, bar, casino* ▤ *AE, DC, MC, V.*

$–$$$ ⊞ **First Hotel Grand Odense.** More than a century old, with renovated fin-de-siècle charm, this imposing four-story, brick-front hotel greets guests with old-fashioned luxury. The original stone floors and chandeliers lead to a wide staircase and upstairs guest rooms that are modern with plush furnishings and sleek marble bathrooms. ⊠ *Jernabaneg. 18, DK–5000* ☎ *66/11–71–71* 🖨 *66/14–11–71* ⊕ *www.firsthotels.com* 🖙 *138 rooms, 3 suites* ⟡ *Restaurant, room service, sauna, bar, some pets allowed, no-smoking rooms* ▤ *AE, DC, MC, V.*

¢ ⊞ **Hotel Ydes.** This well-kept, bright, and colorful hotel is a good bet
Fodor'sChoice for students and budget-conscious travelers tired of barracks-type ac-
★ commodations. The well-maintained rooms are spotless and comfortable. ⊠ *Hans Tausens G. 11, DK–5000* ☎ *66/12–11–31* 🖨 *66/12–14–13* ⊕ *www.ydes.dk* 🖙 *25 rooms with bath* ⟡ *Café* ▤ *MC, V.*

Nightlife & the Arts

CAFÉS & BARS   Odense's central arcade is an entertainment mall, with bars, restaurants, and live music ranging from corny sing-alongs to hard rock. For a quiet evening, stop by **Café Biografen** (⊠ Brandts Passage ☎ 66/13–16–16) for an espresso, beer, or light snack, or settle in to see one of the films screened here. The **Air Pub** (⊠ Kongsg. 41 ☎ 66/14–66–08) is a Danish pub that caters to a thirty- and fortysomething crowd, with meals and a small dance floor. At the **Boogie Dance Café** (⊠ Nørreg. 21 ☎ 66/14–00–39), a laid-back crowd grooves to pop, disco, and '60s music. In the heart of town is **Franck A** (⊠ Jernbaneg. 4 ☎ 66/12–57–27), a spirited café-restaurant with arched windows overlooking the pedestrian street. Live music on the weekends—from pop to jazz—draws a stylish crowd, as does the popular '80s night on Thursday. The specialty at **Klos Ands** (⊠ Vineg. 76 ☎ 66/13–56–00) is malt whiskey.

CASINO   Funen's sole casino is in the slick glass atrium of the **SAS Hans Christian Andersen Hotel** (⊠ Claus Bergs G. 7, Odense ☎ 66/14–78–00), where you can play blackjack, roulette, and baccarat.

JAZZ CLUBS **Dexter's** (⊠ Vinderg. 65 ☏ 66/11–27–28) has all kinds of jazz—from Dixieland to fusion—Friday and Saturday nights. **Grøntorvet Café and Bar** (⊠ Sortebrødre Torv 9 ☏ 66/14–34–37) presents live jazz at 5 PM Thursday and 2 PM Saturday.

THEATER **Den Fynske Landsby** stages Hans Christian Andersen plays from mid-July to mid-August. In summer the young members of the **Hans Christian Andersen Parade** present a pastiche of the bard's fairy tales in a couple of different languages at Lotzes Have, an herb garden behind the Hans Christian Andersen Museum.

Sports & the Outdoors

GOLF There are two major golf attractions and another smaller course near Odense for golf enthusiasts. Although the island appears to be flat, subtle hills provide excellent, challenging terrain for the golfer. Courses are well-groomed, with a number of natural water hazards. Golf has become an extremely popular sport in Denmark, so it would be wise to call ahead of time to inquire about starting times and the dates of tournaments. It's also very easy to find someone to play with—just ask in the clubhouse. **Odense Eventyr Golfklub** (⊠ Falen 227 ☏ 66/65–20–15 ⊕ www.eventyrgolf.dk), 4 km (2½ mi) southwest of Odense, has three nine-hole courses, one of which is entirely composed of challenging par-3s. The **Odense Golf Klub** (⊠ Hestehaven 200 ☏ 65/95–90–00 ⊕ www.odensegolfklub.dk), 6 km (4 mi) southeast of Odense, has 27 holes on relatively flat ground with some woods. **Blommenlyst** (⊠ Vejruplundvej 20, Blommenlyst ☏ 65/96–71–20) is a pleasant nine-hole course with a driving range and putting greens 12 km (7 mi) west of Odense.

Shopping

Odense's compact city center is bustling with clothing, furniture, and shoe stores, and a Magasin department store. The main shopping strips are Vestergade and Kongensgade. Rosengårdcentret, one of Northern Europe's largest malls, is 5 km (3 mi) west of Odense. It has more than 125 shops and food outlets, including trendy clothing stores; jewelry, woodwork, and antiques shops; a multiplex cinema; and a post office.

Denmark is well known for its paper mobiles and cutouts, inspired, in part, by Hans Christian Andersen. Using a small pair of scissors and white paper, he would create cutouts to illustrate his fairy tales. Today replicas of Andersen's cutouts are sold at several Odense gift stores. Also popular are mobiles, often depicting Andersen-inspired themes like swans and mermaids. Uniquely Danish—and light on the suitcase—they make great gifts to take home.

Jam-packed with mobiles, cutouts, and Danish flags and dolls, **Klods Hans** (⊠ Hans Jensens Str. 34 ☏ 66/11–09–40) opened just after World War II to cater to all the American soldiers on leave who wanted to bring back Danish gifts. For fine replicas of Scandinavian Viking jewelry, head to **Museums Kopi Smykker** (⊠ Klareg. 3 ☏ 66/12–06–96). Each piece, in either sterling silver or gold, comes with a printed leaflet explaining its Viking origins. Among the offerings are silver bracelets of various weights, once used by the Vikings as currency; pendants of the Nordic god Odin, Odense's namesake; and a Viking "key to Valhalla." A modest selection of antiques is for sale at **Hønnerup Hovgård** (✉ Hovgårdsvej 6, Hønnerup ☎ 64/49–13–00); take Exit 55 to Route 161 toward Middelfart; follow the signs to Hønnerup.

Assens

⑤ *38 km (24 mi) southwest of Odense.*

★ Near the quiet town of Assens is one of the most extraordinary private gardens in Denmark: Tove Sylvest's sprawling **De 7 Haver** (The Seven Gardens). A privately owned botanical United Nations, the gardens represent the flora of seven European countries, including many plants rare to Denmark. ✉ *Å Strandvej 33, Ebberup* ☎ *64/74–12–85* ⊕ *www.visit-vestfyn.dk* 💳 *DKr 45* ⊙ *Apr.–Oct., daily 10–5.*

On the same street as Seven Gardens is the **Hviids Have**, a 1-acre Japanese garden complete with elegant ponds traversed by rough-plank walkways, as well as stone settings and modest amounts of greenery. ✉ *Å Strandvej 33, Ebberup* ☎ *64/74–11–02* ⊕ *www.visit-vestfyn.dk* 💳 *DKr 40* ⊙ *May–Oct., daily 10–6.*

⎧ off the ⎫
⎨ beaten ⎬
⎩ path ⎭

☾ **TERRARIET** – Children may appreciate this detour 18 km (11 mi) northeast to Funen's Terrarium, where they can examine all kinds of slippery and slithery creatures, including snakes, iguanas, alligators, and the nearly extinct blue frog. ✉ *Kirkehelle 5, Vissenbjerg* ☎ *64/47–18–50* ⊕ *www.reptil-zoo.dk* 💳 *DKr 57* ⊙ *June–Aug., daily 10–6; Sept.–May, daily 10–4.*

Faaborg

⑥ *30 km (18 mi) south of Odense (via Rte. 43).*

The beaches surrounding this lovely 13th-century town are invaded by sun-seeking Germans and Danes in summer. Four times a day you can hear the dulcet chiming of a carillon, the island's largest. In the town center is the controversial *Ymerbrønden* sculpture by Kai Nielsen, depicting a naked man drinking from an emaciated cow's udder while it licks a baby.

The 1725 **Den Gamle Gaard** (Old Merchant's House) chronicles the local history of Faaborg through furnished interiors and exhibits of glass and textiles. ✉ *Holkeg. 1* ☎ *63/61–20–00* ⊕ *www.fkm.nu* 💳 *DKr 30* ⊙ *Mid-May–Aug., daily 10:30–4:30; Apr.–mid-May, Sept., and Oct., weekends 11–3.*

The **Faaborg Museum for Fynsk Malerkunst** (Funen Painting Museum) has a good collection of turn-of-the-20th-century paintings and sculpture by the Funen Painters, a school of artists whose work captures the dusky light of the Scandinavian sun. ✉ *Grønneg. 75* ☎ *62/61–06–45* ⊕ *www.faaborgmuseum.dk* 💳 *DKr 40* ⊙ *Apr.–Oct., daily 10–4; Nov.–Mar., Tues.–Sun. 11–3.*

Where to Stay & Eat

$–$$$ ✕ **Vester Skerninge Kro.** Midway between Faaborg and Svendborg, this traditional inn is cluttered and comfortable. Pine tables are polished from years of serving hot stews and homemade *medister pølse* (mild grilled sausage) and æggekage. ⊠ *Krovej 9, Vester Skerninge* ☏ *62/24–10–04* ⊕ *www. vesterskerningekro.dk* ⊟ *AE, MC, V* ⊙ *Closed Tues. and Oct.–Mar.*

$$$$ ✕⊞ **Falsled Kro.** Once a smuggler's hideaway, the 500-year-old Falsled
Fodor'sChoice Kro is one of Denmark's most elegant inns, and a member of the Re-
★ lais & Chateaux group of hotels. A favorite among well-heeled Europeans, it has appointed its cottages sumptuously with European antiques and stone fireplaces. The restaurant combines French and Danish cuisines, using ingredients from markets in Lyon and its own garden. (The restaurant is closed Monday, except from May to October, when it is open for dinner.) ⊠ *Assensvej 513, DK–5642 Millinge, 13 km (8 mi) northwest of Faaborg on Millinge-Assens Hwy.* ☏ *62/68–11–11* ☐ *62/ 68–11–62* ⊕ *www.falsledkro.dk* ↻ *19 rooms, 8 suites* ♦ *Restaurant, cafeteria, bar, some pets allowed* ⊟ *AE, DC, MC, V.*

$$–$$$$ ✕⊞ **Steensgård Herregårdspension.** A long avenue of beeches leads to this 700-year-old moated manor house 7 km (4½ mi) northwest of Faaborg. The rooms are elegant, with antiques, four-poster beds, and yards of silk damask. The fine restaurant serves Danish classics crafted from the wild game from the manor's own reserve. ⊠ *Steensgård 4, DK–5642 Millinge* ☏ *62/61–94–90* ☐ *62/61–78–61* ⊕ *www. herregaardspension.dk* ↻ *15 rooms, 13 with bath* ♦ *Restaurant, tennis court, horseback riding* ⊟ *AE, DC, MC, V* ⊙ *Closed Feb.*

¢–$ ✕⊞ **Hotel Faaborg.** Rising over Faaborg's rustic main square, this small hotel is housed in a brick town house. The rooms are basic and simply furnished. The corner rooms overlook the central square. The Danish menu at the spacious restaurant includes baked cod smothered in a tomato ratatouille sauce with oregano, shallots, garlic, and anchovies. Veal is topped with honey-fried apple slices and served with seasonal vegetables. On weekdays it serves a decently priced lunch buffet, which includes herring, smoked salmon in a mustard sauce, and chicken salad. ⊠ *Torvet 13–15, DK–5600 Faaborg* ☏ *62/61–02–45* ☐ *62/61–08–45* ⊕ *www.hotelfaaborg.dk* ↻ *10 rooms with bath* ♦ *Restaurant, bar* ⊟ *AE, DC, MC, V.*

★ **$** ⊞ **Hotel Færgegaarden.** For well over 150 years this spot has been a favorite of budget-conscious tourists and traveling artists, with its traditional, dusty yellow and red facade. Newly refurbished, Færgegaarden offers elegantly modern rooms right on the medieval-era harbor front. ⊠ *Christian IXs Vej 31, DK–5600 Faaborg* ☏ *62/61–11–15* ☐ *62/ 61–11–95* ⊕ *www.hotelfg.dk* ↻ *24 rooms with bath* ♦ *Restaurant, some pets allowed* ⊟ *AE, DC, MC, V.*

Nightlife & the Arts

Near the waterfront is **Bar Heimdal** (⊠ Havneg. 12 ☏ 62/61–35–35), where Faaborg's fishermen crowd into booths and knock back cold ones after hauling in their nets. An inexpensive menu of simple Danish fare includes fillet of sole with tartar sauce and smoked ham with asparagus. In summer the sunny outdoor terrace draws a mixed crowd of tourists and locals. Just off Faaborg's main square is the homey **Oasen Bodega** (⊠ Strandg. 2 ☏ 62/61–13–15), frequented by regulars who enjoy lingering while imbibing the local brew. Most of the local residents sit by the wooden bar, and this can be a good place to strike up a conversation. **Tre Kroner** (⊠ Strandg. 1 ☎ 62/61–01–50) is a traditional watering hole with varied clientele and the enchantment of an inn from the turn of the 20th century. Perhaps Faaborg's most *hyggelig* hangout is the historic **Schankstube** (tap house; ⊠ Havneg. 12 ☎ 62/61–11–15), inside the harborside Hotel Færgegaarden. Housed in a former tap room, this small bar has worn wooden tables, yellow walls hung with richly colored paintings by Faaborg artists, and small windows with views of the harbor. The menu is traditional—*smørrebrød* and beer.

off the beaten path

LYØ, AVERNAKØ, AND BJØRNØ – A string of verdant little islands speckles the sea off Funen's southern coast. Three of these islands—Lyø, Avernakø, and Bjørnø—are easily accessible by ferry from Faaborg. Lyø, just 4 km (2½ mi) long, has a year-round population of 150 residents and a tangle of hiking and biking trails that lure Funen families in summer. In the center of the island sits Lyø village, a rustic assortment of half-timber houses and a church with a unique circular churchyard. Eight-km-long (5-mi-long) Avernakø is the hilliest and largest of the three islands, with several farmhouses, a pleasant little village, and a few meandering hiking trails. Bjørnø, 3 km (1½ mi) south of Faaborg, is the smallest island, both in population and size. What it lacks in human residents, however, it makes up with avian. A rich birdlife draws binocular-toting bird-watchers, particularly during the summer breeding season. If you wish to stay overnight on the islands, contact the Faaborg tourist office for information on local families who offer accommodation. The **Avernakø–Lyø ferry** (☎ 62/61–23–07 ⊕ www.oe-faergen.dk) travels five to seven times daily in summer from the Faaborg harbor. Travel time is about 30 minutes to Avernakø, and then another 30 minutes to Lyø, though the ferry sometimes arrives at Lyø first. The round-trip cost is about DKr 85. The **Bjørnø ferry** (☎ 20/29–80–50) departs from Faaborg three to five times daily; the trip takes 20 minutes, and costs about DKr 45.

Svendborg

❼ *25 km (15 mi) east of Faaborg (via Rte. 44 east), 44 km (28 mi) south of Odense.*

Svendborg is Funen's second-largest town, and one of the country's most important cruise harbors. It celebrates its eight-centuries-old maritime traditions every July, when old Danish wooden ships congregate in the harbor for the circular Funen *rundt*, or regatta. Play your cards right, and you might hitch aboard and shuttle between towns. Contact the tourist board or any agreeable captain. With many charter-boat options and good marinas, Svendborg is an excellent base from which to explore the hundreds of islands of the South Funen archipelago.

On Fruestræde near the market square at the center of town is the black-and-yellow **Anne Hvides Gård,** the oldest secular structure in Svendborg and one of the four branches of Svendborgs Omegns Museum (Svendborg County Museum). This evocative exhibit includes 18th- and

19th-century interiors and glass and silver collections. ⊠ *Fruestr. 3* ☎ *62/21–76–45* ⊕ *www.svendborgmuseum.dk* ⊠ *DKr 25* ☉ *Mid-June–Sept., Tues.–Sun. 10–5; Oct.–Dec., Wed.–Sun. 10–4.*

Bagergade (Baker's Street) is lined with some of Svendborg's oldest half-timber houses. At the corner of Grubbemøllevej and Svinget is the **Viebæl-tegård,** the headquarters of the Svendborg County Museum and a former poorhouse. You can wander through dining halls, washrooms, and the "tipsy clink," where, until 1974, inebriated citizens were left to sober up. ⊠ *Grubbemøllevej 13* ☎ *62/21–02–61* ⊕ *www.svendborgmuseum. dk* ⊠ *DKr 40* ☉ *June–Sept., Tues.–Sun. 10–5; Oct.–May, Tues.–Sun. 10–4.*

Changing contemporary-art exhibits are showcased at the two-story **SAK Kunstbygningen** (SAK Art Exhibitions), a skylit gallery-museum just to the west of the city center. The museum's highlight is the small collection of sculptures by Svendborg native Kai Nielsen. One of Denmark's most popular sculptors, Nielsen is best known for his sensual figures of women in languid repose and chubby angelic babies playing together. Nielsen's sculptures are displayed in a sun-drenched octagonal gallery with views over a leafy garden. His works are exhibited all over Denmark, most famously in Copenhagen's Ny Carlsberg Glyptotek. Here, his *Water Mother* fountain sculpture depicts a voluptuous woman reclining atop a lily pond, while a half-dozen plump, adorable babies crawl out of the water and over her curves, suckling at her breasts and dozing between her thighs. ⊠ *Vesterg. 27–31* ☎ *62/22–44–70* ⊠ *DKr 25* ☉ *Tues.–Sun. 11–4.*

need a break? In the heart of Svendborg, tucked behind the main street of Brogade, is a small, cobblestone courtyard surrounded by red half-timber houses. Dating from 1650, this charming square used to house Svendborg's general store. **Vintapperiet** (⊠ Brog. 37 ☎ 62/22–34–48), a snug, low-ceiling wine bar and shop, now occupies the square, and here you can taste your way—by the glass or by the bottle—through a range of top-notch French and Italian wines. Wine barrels line the entranceway; the small dining room, with less than a half dozen tables, overlooks the courtyard. They serve a light menu to complement the wines, including pâté and pungent cheese with hunks of bread and olives. It is open for lunch only, and closed on Sunday; in winter it's also closed on Monday.

Where to Stay & Eat

$$$ ✕ **Svendborgsund.** In a harborside building dating from 1682, this warm, maritime-theme restaurant serves traditional Danish cuisine, including pork tenderloin heaped with grilled onions and mushrooms and served with potatoes and pickled cucumbers. The extensive smørrebrød lunch menu includes marinated herring topped with egg yolk and fried fillet of plaice with shrimp, caviar, and asparagus. The summertime terrace is an inviting spot to soak up sun, beer, and the waterfront views. ⊠ *Havnepl. 5* ☎ *62/21–07–19* ⊕ *www.restaurantsvendborgsund.dk* ☰ *AE, DC, MC, V* ☉ *Closed Sun. Oct.–Mar.*

¢–$$ ✕ **Hotel Ærø.** A hodgepodge of ship parts and nautical doodads, this dimly lighted restaurant and inn looks like it's always been here. Brusque waitresses take orders from serious local trenchermen. The menu is staunchly old-fashioned, featuring *frikadeller* (fried meatballs), fried *rødspætte* (plaice) with hollandaise sauce, and dozens of smørrebrød options. ⊠ *Brog. 1, Ærøfærgen (at the Ærø ferry), DK–5700* 🕾 *62/21–07–60* 🏦 *63/20–30–51* ⊕ *www.hotel-aeroe.dk* 🖃 *DC, MC, V.*

★ $ 🏨 **Missionhotellet Stella Marris.** Southwest of Svendborg, this lovely seaside villa dates from 1904. An old-fashioned English-style drawing room, complete with piano, stuffed chairs, and an elegant chandelier, overlooks the villa's spacious gardens; follow a path through the greenery and you can dive right off the private pier into the sea. Each of the rooms has its own color scheme; one room has flowery wallpaper and white lace curtains, while another has a simple tan-and-rose decor. Bathrooms are basic and include a shower only. The hotel is part of Missionhotel, a Christian hotel chain in operation since the early 1900s. The Stella Marris is one of the few Missionhotels that still maintains an alcohol- and smoke-free environment. ⊠ *Kogtvedvænget 3, DK–5700* 🕾 *62/21–38–91* 🏦 *62/21–41–74* ⊕ *www.stellamaris.dk* 🔑 *25 rooms, 19 with bath* ⚴ *Dining room* 🖃 *AE, DC, MC, V.*

Nightlife & the Arts

BARS & LOUNGES   A diverse crowd congregates at **Banjen** (⊠ Klosterpl. 7 🕾 62/22–31–21) to hear live rock and blues. The popular blues shows, usually Friday and Saturday nights, attract all ages. Adjoining the bar is La Tumba nightclub, which throbs with dance music on the weekends. The beer flows freely at the cavernous pub **Børsen** (⊠ Gerritsg. 31 🕾 62/22–41–41), in a building dating from 1620. A young rowdy crowd of tourists and locals packs the place nightly. If this isn't your scene, skip the evening and stop by in the quieter early afternoon instead, when you can better enjoy your beer in the old-style pub atmosphere.

Chess (⊠ Vesterg. 7 🕾 62/22–17–16 ⊕ www.diskotek-chess.dk) is popular with a young crowd that comes for the live bands. **Crazy Daisy** (⊠ Frederiksg. 6 🕾 62/21–67–60 ⊕ www.svendborg.crazydaisy.dk) attracts a casual, over-21 crowd that dances to oldies and rock on Saturday night; a younger crowd pours in on Friday. The restaurant **Oranje** (⊠ Jessens Mole 🕾 62/22–82–92), an old sailing ship moored in the harbor, sometimes has live jazz in summer. Tucked back from the street, **Barbella Nightclub** (⊠ Vesterg. 10A 🕾 62/22–47–83) is a dimly lit bar with dark-rose walls and long wooden tables. A casual vibe and friendly staff draws a mixed-age crowd that mingles over cocktails, cheap bar grub (open-face sandwiches and meatballs), and live music in the evenings—jazz on Thursday; rock, pop, or classical on Friday and Saturday nights. On the first Sunday of the month the club has live jazz starting at around noon. (It's closed the other Sundays of the month.)

CAFÉS   In the heart of town is the spacious **Under Uret Café** (⊠ Gerritsg. 50 🕾 62/ 21–83–08), playfully decorated with oversize watches on the wall— "Under Uret" means "under watch." For prime people-watching, settle in at one of the outdoor tables. The café menu includes brunch, club sandwiches, burritos, and a range of salads, from Greek to Caesar. Come nightfall, there's live music ranging from soul to rock.

Shopping

Svendborg's **city center** is bustling with shops, particularly on Gerrits-gade and Møllergade, which are peppered with clothing stores, gift shops, and jewelers. For colorful, hand-blown glassworks head to **Glas Blæseriet** (⊠ Brog. 37A ☎ 62/22–83–73), which shares a half-timber court-yard in the center of town with the wine restaurant Vintapperiet. Glass-blower Bente Sonne's lovely nature-inspired creations—in pale greens, oranges, and blues—are decorated with seashells, starfish, lizards, fish, and lobsters. You can watch Sonne blowing glass weekdays 10–3:30. On Saturday the shop is open 10–3:30, with no glass-blowing demon-stration.

Kværndrup

❽ 15 km (9 mi) north of Svendborg, 28 km (18 mi) south of Odense.

Fodor'sChoice The moated Renaissance **Egeskov Slot**, one of the best-preserved island-★ castles in Europe, presides over this town. Peaked with copper spires and surrounded by Renaissance, baroque, English, and peasant gardens, the castle is still a private home, though visitors can see a few of the rooms, including the great hall, the hunting room, and the Riborg Room, where the daughter of the house was locked up from 1599 to 1604 after giving birth to a son out of wedlock. The castle also has an antique vehicle museum. (⊠ Kværndrup, 15 km/9 mi north of Svend-borg ☎ 62/27–10–16 ⊕ www.egeskov.com ⊠ Castle and museum DKr 145 ⊙ Castle May, June, Aug., and Sept., daily 10–5; July, daily 10–7; Museum June and Aug., daily 10–6; July, daily 10–8 (Wed. open until 11 PM); May and Sept., daily 10–5.

Tåsinge

❾ 3 km (2 mi) south of Svendborg (via the Svendborg Sound Bridge), 43 km (27 mi) south of Odense.

Tåsinge Island is known for its local 19th-century drama involving Elvira Madigan and her married Swedish lover, Sixten Sparre. The drama is featured in the 1967 Swedish film Elvira Madigan. Preferring heavenly union to earthly separation, they shot themselves and are now buried in the island's central Landet churchyard. Brides throw their bou-quets on the lovers' grave.

Fodor'sChoice Troense is Tåsinge's main town, and one of the country's best-pre-★ served maritime villages, with half-timber buildings and their hand-carved doors. South of town is **Valdemars Slot** (Valdemars Castle), dating from 1610, one of Denmark's oldest privately owned castles, now owned and run by Caroline Fleming and her husband. You can wander through al-most all of the sumptuously furnished rooms, libraries, and the candlelit church. There's also an X-rated 19th-century cigar box not to be missed. A yachting museum, with gleamingly restored yachts and skiffs, along with ship models and historical dioramas, explores Denmark's exten-sive yachting history. There are also toy and trophy museums within the castle. (⊠ Slotsalleen 100, Troense ☎ 62/22–61–06 ⊕ www.valdemarsslot.

dk ⊞ *DKr 110* ⊙ *May, June, and Aug., daily 10–5; July, daily 10–6; Sept., Tues.–Sun. 10–5.*

Where to Stay & Eat

$$$$ ✕ **Lodskroen.** This whitewashed, thatch-roof restaurant opened its doors in 1774 to serve as an inn for passing sailors. For the past 30 years it has been run by the husband-and-wife team of Hans and Kirsten Dahlgaard, who treat diners as if they were guests in their own home. In fact, diners are asked to not order more than two main dishes per table because, as a placard explains, "the cook, who is also the hostess, is always alone by the kitchen range and the food is never pre-prepared." The French-inspired Danish menu includes fillet of plaice stuffed with mushrooms, peppers, and herbs. For dessert, try the figs pickled in a sweet sherry and served with whipped cream. A surcharge is applied to credit cards. ⊠ *Troense Strandvej 80, Troense* ☎ *62/22–50–44* ⊟ *MC, V* ⊙ *Closed Mon.–Thurs. Feb., Nov., and Dec.; closed Jan. No lunch weekdays.*

¢–$$ ✕ **Bregninge Mølle.** If you've ever wondered what the inside of a windmill looks like, this is your chance to find out. Within the Bregninge windmill, built in 1805, circular stairs lead to this restaurant's three levels, each with 360-degree views of the surrounding sea and Tåsinge countryside. On a clear day you can see the southern tip of Jutland and the islands of Langeland and Thurø. The traditional Danish menu features *frikadeller* (fried meatballs) served with rice and peas, and æggekage. ⊠ *Kirkebakken 19, Bregninge* ☎ *62/22–52–55* ⊟ *MC, V* ⊙ *Closed mid-Oct.–Mar.*

FodorsChoice
★

$ ✕▥ **Hotel Troense.** Dating from 1908, this harborside hotel has bright, simply furnished rooms with fringed white bedcovers. One-third of the rooms look toward the harbor. The restaurant, with rose walls and a fireplace, serves a Danish menu with such dishes as salmon served with spinach topped with almonds. It also offers a couple of vegetarian dishes, including a pie stuffed with seasonal vegetables. The smørrebrød lunch menu includes open-face sandwiches of herring, salmon, eggs, liver pâté, or shrimp. The hotel often has discounted weekend deals that include breakfast and dinner. ⊠ *Strandg. 5, DK–5700 Troense* ☎ *62/22–54–12* ⊟ *62/22–78–12* ⊕ *www.hoteltroense.dk* ⇦ *30 rooms with bath* ⌂ *Restaurant, bar* ⊟ *AE, DC, MC, V.*

$ ✕▥ **Valdemars Slot.** The castle's guest rooms are not enormous, but they are nicely decorated in beige, ochre, light-green, and light-blue tones. Some have a view out to the north; others look out onto the adjacent yard and palace garden. Down below, a domed restaurant is ankle-deep in pink carpet and aglow with candlelight. Fresh French and German ingredients and wild game from the castle's reserve are the menu staples. Venison with cream sauce and duck breast *à l'orange* are typical of the French-inspired cuisine. A second eatery, Æblehaven, serves inexpensive sausages and upscale fast-food. ⊠ *Slotsalleen 100, DK–5700 Troense* ☎ *62/22–59–00* ⊟ *62/22–72–67* ⊕ *www.valdemarsslot.dk* ⇦ *8 rooms, 1 suite* ⌂ *2 restaurants* ⊟ *MC, V.*

¢ ▥ **Det Lille Hotel.** This red half-timber, thatch-roof family house–turned–small hotel has eight snug rooms (none with bath or shower) with pale green walls and flowery curtains. The well-tended back garden blooms brilliantly in summer. A breakfast of homemade bread and jam is included. You can rent a bike for around DKr 50 per day. Note that this is no-smoking hotel. ⊠ *Badstuen 15, DK–5700 Troense* ☏ *62/22–53–41* 🖷 *62/22–52–41* ⊕ *www.detlillehotel.dk* ↩ *8 rooms, 3 with bath* ♿ *Dining room* ▤ *MC, V* ⊘ *Closed Nov.–Mar.*

Shopping
For delicate hand-blown glass, visit **Glasmagerne** (⊠ Vemmenæsvej 10, Tåsinge ☏ 62/54–14–94).

Langeland

 16 km (10 mi) southeast of Troense, 64 km (40 mi) southwest of Odense.

Reached by a causeway bridge from Tåsinge, Langeland is the largest island of the southern archipelago, rich in relics, with smooth, tawny beaches. Bird-watching is excellent on the southern half of the island, where migratory flocks roost before setting off on their cross-Baltic journey. To the south are Ristinge and Bagenkop, two towns with good beaches; at Bagenkop you can catch the ferry to Kiel, Germany.

Sports & the Outdoors
FISHING Langeland has particularly rich waters for fishing, with cod, salmon, flounder, and gar. For package tours, boat rentals, or fishing equipment, contact **Ole Dehn** (⊠ Sønderg. 22, Tranekær ☏ 62/55–17–00).

Ærøskøbing

★ ⑪ *30 km (19 mi) south of Svendborg, 74 km (46 mi) south of Odense, plus a one-hour ferry ride, either from Svendborg or Langeland.*

The island of Ærø, where country roads wind through fertile fields, is aptly called the Jewel of the Archipelago. About 27 km (16 mi) southeast of Søby on the island's north coast, the storybook town of Ærøskøbing is the port for ferries from Svendborg. Established as a market town in the 13th century, it did not flourish until it became a sailing center during the 1700s. Today Ærøskøbing is a bewitching tangle of cobbled streets lined with immaculately preserved half-timber houses. Stop by the red 17th-century home at the corner of Vestergade and Smedegade, considered to be one of the town's finest examples of its provincial architecture. Ærøskøbing is a bastion of small-town Denmark: every morning the whistling postman, in a red jacket and black-and-gold cap, strides the streets and delivers the mail; the friendly mayor pedals home for lunch and waves to everyone on the way.

As you wander through town, you'll notice that many of the homes display a pair of ceramic dogs on their windowsills. Traditionally, these were used by sailors' wives to signal to outsiders—and, as rumor has it, potential suitors—the whereabouts of their husbands. When the dogs were facing in, it meant that the man of the house was home, and when the dogs were facing out, that he was gone. Ironically, these ceramic dogs were brought home, usually from the Orient, by the sailors themselves, who had received them as "gifts" from prostitutes they had been with.

The prostitutes gave these ceramic dogs as a cover-up, so that it appeared that they were selling souvenirs rather than sex.

Ferries provide the only access to Ærø. The ferry from Svendborg to Ærøskøbing takes 1 hour, 15 minutes. In addition, there's a one-hour ferry from Faaborg to Søby, a town on the northwest end of the island; and a shorter one from Rudkøbing—on the island of Langeland—to Marstal, on the eastern end of Ærø.

History is recorded in miniature at the **Flaske-Peters Samling** (Bottle-Ship Collection), thanks to a former ship's cook known as Peter Bottle, who painstakingly built nearly 2,000 bottle ships in his day. The combination of his life's work and the enthusiastic letters he received from fans and disciples around the world makes for a surprisingly moving collection. ⊠ *Smedeg. 22, Ærøskøbing* ☎ *62/52–29–51* ⌦ *DKr 25* ⊙ *May–Oct., daily 10–4; Nov.–Apr., Tues.–Fri. 1–3, weekends 10–noon.*

Ærø Museum houses numerous relics—including some from the Stone Age—culled from archaeological digs on the island. Also displayed are antique domestic furnishings from the homes of skippers on the island. Call ahead or check at the tourist office, because nonsummer hours can vary. ⊠ *Brog. 3–5, Ærøskøbing* ☎ *62/52–29–50* ⊕ *www.arremus.dk* ⌦ *DKr 20* ⊙ *May–mid-Oct., weekdays 10–4, weekends 11–3; mid-Oct.–Apr., weekdays 10–1.*

The two-story half-timber **Hammerichs Hus** (Hammerich's House) was once the home of sculptor Gunnar Hammerich. Today it features reconstructed period interiors of ancient Ærø homes, including antique maritime paintings, furniture, and porcelain pieces. ⊠ *Gyden 22, Ærøskøbing* ☎ *65/52–29–50* ⌦ *DKr 20* ⊙ *Mid-June–mid-Sept., weekdays noon–4.*

Where to Stay & Eat

★ ¢–$$ ✕ **Hos Grethe.** In the heart of town is this amiable restaurant, run by longtime local Grethe. The dining room, with low white ceilings and a black-and-white checkered floor, is nicknamed the *kongelogen* (the royal box) because of the royal portraits, past and present, that line the walls. Grethe is famous for her steaks, thick-cut and juicy, which come with large salads. In summer the outside terrace and beer garden overflow with day-trippers from the mainland. ⊠ *Vesterg. 39* ☎ *62/52–21–43* ▤ *MC, V* ⊙ *Closed Oct.–May. No lunch Apr.–mid-June and mid-Aug.–Sept.*

¢–$ ✕⛨ **Det Lille Hotel.** Six large, simply furnished rooms make up the second floor of this friendly *lille* (little) hotel. Flowery curtains frame small windows that overlook the garden below. Dating from 1865, the building once housed the offices of Ærø's farmer's journal. It later became a boardinghouse. On the bottom floor are a popular restaurant and bar, both of which draw a daily crowd of regulars (reservations are essential for the restaurant). Paintings of ships and schooners hang on the walls, and a collection of old porcelain coffee- and teapots lines the shelves. A brick-floor terrace opens up in summer, and from here you can catch glimpses of the sea through the trees. The Danish menu includes fried plaice topped with butter sauce and pork fillet with tomatoes, mushrooms, and a white-wine cream sauce. The snug bar is decorated with a ship's wheel and lanterns. ⊠ *Smedeg. 33, DK–5970* 🖼️🛗 *62/52–23–00* ⊕ *www. det-lille-hotel.dk* 🗐 *6 rooms without bath* ♿ *Restaurant* ☰ *MC, V.*

$$$ 🖼️ **Hotel Ærøhus.** A half-timber building with a steep red roof, the Ærøhus looks like a rustic cottage on the outside and an old, but overly renovated, aunt's house on the inside. Hanging pots and slanted walls characterize the public areas, and pine furniture and cheerful duvets keep the guest rooms simple and bright. The garden's five cottages have small terraces. ⊠ *Vesterg. 38, DK–5970* 🖼️ *62/52–31–68* 🛗 *62/52–21–23* ⊕ *www.aeroehus.dk* 🗐 *67 rooms, 56 with bath* ♿ *Restaurant, bar, some pets allowed* ☰ *V.*

¢ 🖼️ **Pension Vestergade 44.** Rising over Ærøskøbing's main street are two superbly maintained patrician homes. Standing side by side, they are mirror images of each other, built by two ship captains, brothers, who wanted to raise their families in identical surroundings. One of the homes has been converted into this small hotel that has been lovingly restored by its owners, a friendly British-German couple, to recapture all of the building's former charms. A clawfoot iron stove heats up the breakfast room that overlooks a sprawling back garden with clucking chickens who lay the eggs for breakfast. White lace curtains frame the windows and an antique wooden plate rack displays blue-and-white English porcelain dishes. The beautifully appointed rooms, each with its own color scheme, have naturally sloping floors and vintage wooden towel racks laden with fluffy, bright-white towels. If you want to pedal around town, they'll lend you a bike. ⊠ *Vesterg. 44, DK 5970* 🖼️ *62/52–22–98* 🗐 *6 rooms without bath* ♿ *Dining room.*

Nightlife & the Arts

Of Ærøskøbing's few bars, one of the most popular is **Arrebo** (⊠ Vesterg. 4 🖼️ 62/52–28–50), with yellow walls, wooden tables, and local art on the walls. On weekends it hosts live music, from blues to rock to jazz. A bell dangles at one end of the bar, and in the sailor tradition, whoever rings it must buy the whole bar a round of drinks.

Shopping

Ærøskøbing is sprinkled with a handful of craft and gift shops. Unfortunately, there are virtually no more bottle-ship makers on the island. Instead, the labor-intensive curiosities are made in Asia and modeled on original ærø bottle-ship designs. For souvenir bottle-ships, head to Kolorit (E Moseager 3 P 62/52–25–21), a small gift shop crammed with Danish mementos.

Marstal

★ ⑫ *10 km (6 mi) southeast of Ærøskøbing, 40 km (25 mi) south of Svend-borg, 84 km (52 mi) south of Odense. From Svendborg it's a one-hour ferry ride to Ærøskøbing; from Langeland it's a 45-min ferry ride to Marstal.*

Southeast of Ærøskøbing, past a lush landscape of green and yellow hills rolling toward the sea, is the sprightly shipping town of Marstal. From its early fishing days in the 1500s to its impressive rise into a formidable shipping port in the 1700s, Marstal's lifeblood has always been the surrounding sea. At its seafaring height, in the late 1800s, Marstal had a fleet of 300 ships. During this heady time, the Marstal government couldn't expand the harbor fast enough to accommodate the growing fleet, so Marstal's seamen took it upon themselves to extend their port. Working together in the winter season, they built the 1-km (½-mi) stone pier—still in use today—by rolling rocks from the fields, along the ice, and onto the harbor. They began in 1835 and completed the pier in 1841.

Today Marstal is home port to 50 vessels, from tall-masted schooners to massive trawlers. Much of the town's activity—and its cobbled streets—radiates from the bustling port. A nautical school, first established in the 1800s, is still going strong, with more than 150 students. In a nod to its seafaring heritage, the Marstal harbor is one of the few places in the world still constructing wooden ships.

Marstal's winding streets are dotted with well-preserved skippers' homes. **Maren Minors Hjem** (Maren Minor's Home) was once the genteel abode of successful Marstal seaman Rasmus Minor, who eventually settled in the United States. The house has been carefully restored inside and out to look just as it did in the 1700s, including vintage art and furniture. Opening hours vary from year to year, so check with the tourist office. ✉ *Teglg. 9* ☎ *62/53–24–25* ✉ *Free* ☉ *June–Aug., Tues.–Sun. 11–3.*

Spread out over three buildings, the sprawling **Marstal Søfartsmuseum** (Marstal Maritime Museum) offers a rich and fascinating account of Marstal's formidable shipping days. Thirty-five showrooms are jam-packed with maritime memorabilia, including more than 200 ship models, 100 bottle-ships, navigation instruments, and a collection of maritime paintings by artist Carl Rasmussen. He was born in Ærøskøbing and made his name painting Greenland sea- and landscapes. Wandering the museum is like exploring a massive ship: step aboard large-scale decks and hulls and command the gleaming ship's wheels like a Marstal captain. Mind your head as you climb up and down the steep ship stairs that connect many of the rooms. "Back on land," you can duck into the low-ceiling parlors of a skipper's house, meticulously reproduced with period furnishings. Long-time museum director and Marstal historian Erik B. Kromann is a font of maritime information, and will enthusiastically take you on a tour of the museum if you ask. The museum shop is bursting with nifty gifts, including key chains made from maritime rope knots. ✉ *Prinsensg. 1* ☎ *62/53–23–31* ⊕ *www.marmus.dk* ✉ *DKr 40* ☉ *July, daily 9–8; June and Aug., daily 9–5; May and Sept., daily 10–4; Oct.–Apr., Tues.–Fri. 10–4, Sat. 11–3.*

Where to Stay & Eat

¢ ✕⌨ **Marstal.** Mere paces from the waterfront is this homey locals' favorite, with wooden ceilings, dim lighting, and a ship's wheel on the wall. The homestyle Danish dishes include minced steak with peas, potatoes, and béarnaise sauce, and smoked salmon served with asparagus and scrambled eggs. Another favorite is mussels and bacon on toast. The cozy bar draws a friendly pre- and post-dinner crowd of dockworkers. Above the restaurant are eight very basic rooms, none with bath, and two with partial views of the harbor. ✉ *Dronningestr. 1A, DK–5960*

🖃 *62/53–13–52* ⊕ *www.hotelmarstal.dk* ⊷ *8 rooms without bath* ⚲ *Restaurant, bar* ⊟ *MC, V* ⊘ *Closed Sept.–May.*

$ 🖫 **Ærø Strand.** On the outskirts of Marstal lies this holiday hotel that caters to the island's summer tourists. Blond-wood and dark-blue tones adorn the comfortable rooms. In the center of the hotel are a heart-shape pool and, for the after-hours crowd, a popular nightclub disco. ⊠ *Ege-hovedvej 4, DK–5960* 🖃 *62/53–33–20* 🖶 *62/53–31–50* ⊕ *www.hotel-aeroestrand.dk* ⊷ *100 rooms with bath, 20 suites* ⚲ *Restaurant, tennis court, indoor pool, gym, sauna, nightclub* ⊟ *AE, DC, MC, V.*

Nightlife & the Arts

Marstal's night scene is sedate, but when locals want a beer they head to the informal **Café Victor** (⊠ Kirkestr. 15 🖃 62/53–28–01), with its yellow walls and a brass-lined bar. Here you can also tuck into simple Danish dishes, such as fillet of sole with french fries.

Shopping

The maritime paintings of Marstal artist Rita Lund are popular throughout the island, gracing the walls of several restaurants and decorating the sunny sitting rooms of the ferries that shuttle between Svendborg and Ærø. For a further look, visit Rita Lund's **Galleri Humlehave** (⊠ Skoleg. 1 🖃 62/53–21–73) which, appropriately enough, is near the Marstal harbor. Her extensive collection includes paintings of crashing waves, ships at sea, and Ærø during the four seasons.

Funen & the Central Islands A to Z

BIKE TRAVEL

With level terrain and short distances, Funen and the Central Islands are perfect for cycling. A bike trip around the circumference of the main island, stopping at the series of delightful port towns that ring Funen like a string of pearls, is a wonderful way of spending a few days. The Odense tourist office has a helpful map of cycle routes in and around Odense. You can rent bikes through City Cykler in Odense or at several hotels around the islands. Contact Fyntour for longer cycling tour packages that include bike rental, hotel accommodations, and a half-board (breakfast and one meal) meal plan.

🔝 **City Cykler** ⊠ Vesterbro 27, Odense 🖃 66/12–97–93 ⊕ www.citycykler.dk. **Fyntour** ⊠ Svendborgvej 83–85, DK–5260 Odense 🖃 66/13–13–37 🖶 66/13–13–38 ⊕ www. fyntour.dk.

BUS TRAVEL

Buses are one of the main public-transportation options in the area. Timetables are posted at all bus stops and central stations. Passengers buy tickets on board and pay according to the distance traveled. If you plan on traveling extensively by bus, ask at any bus station about a 24-hour bus pass, which cuts costs considerably. Contact Fynbus for more information about routes between cities. Odense Bytrafik runs the bus system within Odense.

🔝 **Fynbus** ⊠ Odense Bus Station 🖃 63/11–22–33 🖶 63/11–22–99. **Odense Bytrafik** (Odense City Transport) 🖃 65/51–29–29 🖶 66/19–40–27.

CAR TRAVEL

From Copenhagen, take the E20 west to Halsskov, near Korsør, and drive onto the Great Belt bridge, which costs about DKr 250 per car. You'll arrive near Nyborg, which is 30 minutes from either Odense or Svendborg.

The highways of Funen are excellent, and small roads meander beautifully on two lanes through the countryside. A trip around the circumference of the island can be done in a day, but stopping for a night or two at one of the enchanting port towns can be fun, and offers the chance to meet some of the locals. Traffic is light, except during the height of summer in highly populated beach areas.

EMERGENCIES

For fire, police, or ambulance anywhere in Denmark, dial 112. Lægevagten is the service for house calls, but will also dispatch an ambulance in case of emergencies. Trained phone personnel are generally able to judge whether a house call would be sufficient. The doctor's visits are made according to a priority list, with serious illnesses and sick children at the top of the list. Falck is the emergency road service, for towing vehicles in trouble or in case of accidents.

🚩 **Falck** ☎ 70/10-20-30 ⊕ www.falck.dk. **Lægevagten** (Emergency Doctor) ☎ 65/90-60-10 4 PM–7 AM. **Odense University Hospital** ⊠ Søndre Blvd. 29, Odense ☎ 66/11-33-33. **Ørnen Apoteket** ⊠ Vesterg. 80, Odense ☎ 66/12-29-70.

TOURS

Few towns offer organized tours, but check the local tourist offices for step-by-step walking brochures. The Hans Christian Andersen Tours are full-day tours to Odense that depart from Copenhagen's Rådhus Pladsen. (Six of 11 hours are spent in transit.) Call ahead because departure days and times may vary. The two-hour Odense tour departs from the local tourist office. Contact Fyntour or Odense Tourist Office for details about prices and times of tours. Most itineraries include the exteriors of the Hans Christian Andersen sites and the cathedral and the guides are generally more than willing to answer questions about the area or Denmark as a whole. Odense Tourist Office also offers one-hour tours of the Italian Gothic Odense City Hall. Inside is a long memorial wall commemorating famous Funen citizens. The local calendar of events often presents interesting activities at the city's sites, so it would be wise to call one of the tourist offices to inquire about any events.

🚩 **Fyntour** ⊠ Svendborgvej 83–85, Odense ☎ 66/13-13-37 ⊕ www.fyntour.dk. **Odense Tourist Office** ⊠ Vesterg. 2, Odense ☎ 66/12-75-20 ⊕ www.odenseturist.dk.

TRAIN TRAVEL

Direct trains from Copenhagen's main station depart for the 90-minute trip to Odense's train station about hourly from 5 AM to 10:30 PM every day. The Odense station is central, close to hotels and sites. Large towns in the region are served by intercity trains. The Nyborg–Odense–Middelfart and the Odense–Svendborg routes are among the two most important. You can take the train to Odense direct from Copenhagen Airport.

RESERVATIONS A reservation, which is required during rush hour, costs an additional DKr 20.

🚉 **DSB Train Booking and Information** ☎ 70/13-14-15 ⊕ www.dsb.dk.

VISITOR INFORMATION

For central Odense, the Odense Eventyrpas (Adventure Pass), available at the tourism office and the train station, affords admission to sites and museums and free city bus and train transport. The cost for a 48-hour pass is DKr 150; for a 24-hour pass, DKr 110.

🚉 **Assens Touristbureau** ✉ Tobaksgaarden 7, DK-5610 Assens ☎ 64/71-20-31 🖷 64/71-49-39 ⊕ www.visit-vestfyn.dk. **Egeskov Touristbureau** ✉ Egeskov 1, DK-5772 Kværndrup ☎ 62/27-10-46 🖷 62/27-10-48. **Fyntour** ✉ Sivmosevænget 4, DK-5260 Odense ☎ 66/13-13-37 ⊕ www.fyntour.dk. **Faaborg Touristbureau** ✉ Banegårdspl. 2A, DK-5600 Faaborg ☎ 62/61-07-07 🖷 62/61-33-37 ⊕ www.visitfaaborg.dk. **Kerteminde Touristbureau** ✉ Strandg. 1B, DK-5300 Kerteminde ☎ 65/32-11-21 🖷 65/32-18-17 ⊕ www.kerteminde-turist.dk. **Langeland Touristforeningen** ✉ Torvet 5, DK-5900 Rundkøbing ☎ 62/51-35-05 🖷 62/51-43-35 ⊕ www.langeland.dk. **Marstal Touristbureau** ✉ Havneg. 5, DK-5960 Marstal ☎ 62/52-13-00 🖷 62/53-25-17 ⊕ www. arre.dk. **Nyborg Touristbureau** ✉ Torvet 9, DK-5800 Nyborg ☎ 65/31-02-80 🖷 65/31-03-80 ⊕ www.nyborgturist.dk. **Odense Touristbureau** ✉ Vesterg. 2, DK-5000 Odense ☎ 66/12-75-20 🖷 66/12-75-86 ⊕ www.odenseturist.dk. **Sydfyns Touristbureau** ✉ Centrumpl. 4, DK-5700 Svendborg ☎ 62/21-09-80 🖷 62/22-05-53 ⊕ www. visitsydfyn.dk. **Ærø Touristbureau** ✉ Vesterg. 13, DK-5970 Ærøskøbing ☎ 62/52-13-00 🖷 62/52-14-36 ⊕ www.arre.dk.

South
Jutland

4

Updated by
Bruce Bishop

This easily accessible area of the peninsula has almost been forgotten by many travelers. On the surface, it doesn't seem to have the flashy attractions or striking natural wonders of other regions, but if you look a bit deeper, you'll find the rural charm and unbridled nature you'd expect of a "road less traveled." It's pretty easy to get here, too: you can hop a train in Copenhagen and be in Kolding, the first major town of the region, in a little over two hours. From there you can meander farther south to Tønder, and work your way clockwise to Rømø, Esbjerg, and the island of Fanø. All in all, this area is a delight for the independent traveler who enjoys exploring towns and villages that aren't largely visited by native English-speakers.

Hunters first inhabited Denmark, in southern Jutland, some 250,000 years ago. You can see flint tools and artifacts from this period locked away in museums, but the land holds more stirring relics from a later epoch: after 1,000 years, Viking burial mounds and stones still swell the land, some in protected areas, others lying in farmers' fields, tended by grazing sheep.

At times there's almost a self-consciousness from the Danes in southern Jutland regarding their geographic area bordering northern Germany. Perhaps it's the flip-flops of historical treaties with that country, or 2005's 60th anniversary of the end of World War II, but for all intents and purposes southern Jutland and Germany now share a very peaceful, undefended border. It wasn't always so, of course—between 1864 and 1920 southern Jutland was a part of Germany, and the latter country did occupy Denmark in World War II. Many locals, especially in the southeast, speak a dialect that other Danes find difficult to understand. At times, in southern Jutland, it can seem as if there is more in common with Germany than with the rest of the country.

But Danish pride prevails, and many residents will tell you this is the most fiercely patriotic part of Denmark. The red-and-white Danish flag flies proudly over pedestrian streets in many towns, and supermarkets sell the image of the flag on napkins, plastic glasses, and paper plates, as it is used in abundance for all joyful celebrations, from birthday parties to confirmation receptions.

When you visit the southeast, be ready for acres of pastureland, with horses and sheep farms alongside postcard-perfect towns boasting castles and palaces from days gone by. Cyclists safely ride in their own lanes alongside highways, lending a civilized, peaceful air to the region. In the southwest, islands in the Wadden Sea impress with their expansive beaches and rich seafaring histories, while the oldest town in Denmark (Ribe) competes for attention from one of the newest (Esbjerg).

WHAT IT COSTS In Danish Kroner				
$$$$	**$$$**	**$$**	**$**	**¢**
RESTAURANTS over 180	141–180	121–140	90–120	under 90
HOTELS over 1,500	1,200–1,500	1,000–1,200	700–1,000	under 700

Restaurant prices are for a main course at dinner. Hotel prices are for two people in a standard double room, including service charge and tax.

Kolding

❶ *71 km (44 mi) northwest of Odense (via the Little Belt Bridge), 190 km (119 mi) west of Copenhagen.*

Kolding is an interesting world city that screams "design." It's the home of the Danish School of Art & Design, as important to this country as the Parsons School of Design is to the United States, or the Ontario College of Art & Design is to Canada. It's also a link between other Scandinavian cities (Malmö, Sweden, is 250 km [155 mi] away and Hamburg, Germany, is only 240 km [150 mi] away). The city is home to 63,000 residents and is the sixth-largest town in Denmark. It is near the country's second-largest international airport at Billund.

Indeed, Kolding is a place to begin any adventure in Jutland, whether you choose to travel southward on the peninsula or north. The city itself is a pleasing blend of old and new, with a historical center of cobbled streets and brightly painted half-timber houses that give way to industrial suburbs. But what seems to attract many visitors is the Trapholt Museum of modern Danish art, including furniture design and changing exhibits by international artists. Complementing this museum is, oddly, the Koldinghus, an imposing stone structure from the Middle Ages that overlooks the city, and which itself has won a couple of international design awards in this century.

Koldinghus, a massive structure that was once a fortress, then a royal residence in the Middle Ages (and the last royal castle in Jutland), is today a historical museum. The Danish king Erik Glipping (1259–86) first built a castle here at this important crossing to defend the southern frontier of the realm, and although there are no visible traces of this, recent archaeological evidence proves it to be so. Much later, King Christian III and Dorothea established the reformation in Denmark and had the first Protestant chapel in the country built in the southwest corner of the castle. In the winter of 1808, during the Napoleonic Wars, Spanish soldiers set fire to most of it while trying to stay warm. The place was in ruins, and by 1830, even Hans Christian Andersen spoke in favor of preserving and protecting the site. It wasn't until the 1970s that any serious restoration began, and new foundations were laid in the cellars of the south and east wings. The ruined parts of the castle were preserved, in order to showcase the knowledge about the history of the castle structure. The restoration work was awarded the "Europa Nostra" prize in 1993 for "magnificent restoration work and an imaginative architectural adjustment." Now, the whole castle serves as an important museum, with wings devoted to Romanesque and Gothic church art and sculpture, military history, furniture, ceramics, and silversmithing from 1550 to the present. The building has been used by members of the royal family for exclusive special events. Concerts take place every Thursday night. There is also a popular café, and gift shop. ✉ *Rådhusstr.* ☎ *76/ 33–81–00* ⊕ *www.koldinghus.dk* 🗐 *DKr 50* ☉ *Daily 10–5.*

Southern Jutland is a larger area than it seems on a map, and encompasses two coasts, a border with Germany, and two islands offshore. To make the most of your three days, try not to overdo it, as you'll miss the slow pace and easy nature of this area and its people.

If you have
3 days

After reaching ❶ **Kolding** by car, train, or bus, allow yourself a day to see the city's sights; be sure not to miss Koldinghus and the Trapholt Museum for Modern Art. Shopping is good here, so stop by a few shops before leaving for ❼ **Ribe,** where you can relish its quaint beauty and historic flavor. The next day, find your way to Esbjerg and take a ferry to ❾ **Fanø** to experience island life, both in Nordby and Sønderho.

Fodor'sChoice
★
Just east of town is the **Trapholt Museum for Moderne Kunst** (Trapholt Museum of Modern Art), one of Denmark's largest—and most highly acclaimed—modern art museums outside Copenhagen. Rising over the banks of the Kolding Fjord, this sprawling white complex has been artfully incorporated into its natural surroundings, affording lovely views of the fjord and parkland from its floor-to-ceiling windows. An extensive collection of 20th-century Danish paintings is displayed in the light-filled galleries; it includes works by Anna Ancher, Ejler Bille, Egill Jakobsen, J. A. Jerichau, Jais Nielsen, Richard Mortensen, Aksel Jørgensen, and Franciska Clausen. A true highlight is the Danish Furniture Museum, inaugurated in 1996, and housed in a specially designed annex that is accessed via a circular ramp topped by a skylight. The superbly displayed collection includes the largest assemblage of Danish-designed chairs in the world, offering a unique historical overview of the birth and popularization of Danish furniture design. There are numerous furnishings by prolific designer Hans J. Wegner, including a rounded, blond-wood chair called "The Chair." The museum keeps its furniture storage room open to the public, so you can peruse the entire collection even when it's not officially on display. The Danish ceramics collection, one of the largest in Denmark, is also well worth a look, featuring works by Thorvald Bindesbøll and one-of-a-kind ceramics by Axel Salto, whose pieces often resemble living organisms. Famous designer Arne Jacobsen's summer cottage was moved to Trapholt and opened on its grounds in the summer of 2005, which garnered much interest from Danes and design aficionados. Café Trapholt serves coffee, beverages, and light meals, including a delicious luncheon plate, Frokosttallerken, for DKr 150. The gift shop also offers nice local and international art and design-related gifts. ⊠ *Æblehaven 23* ☎ *76/30–05–30* ⊕ *www. trapholt.dk* ⊒ *DKr 50* ☉ *Daily 10–5.*

Where to Stay & Eat
★ **$$$$**   ✕ **Admiralen.** Across from the harbor is this elegant seafood restaurant, with pale yellow tablecloths, white walls, and blue-suede chairs. It

serves excellent fish dishes, including grilled salmon with spinach and steamed lemon sole with scallops. Pigeon with mushrooms, apples, and a basil gravy is another option. ⊠ *Toldbodeg. 14* ☎ *75/52–04–21* ⊕ *www.admiralen.dk* ☐ *AE, DC, MC, V* ⊘ *Closed Sun.*

$$$ ✕⊡ **Radisson SAS Hotel Koldingfjord.** This impressive neoclassical hotel has mahogany floors and pyramid skylights. Not surprisingly, its safe location and luxurious surroundings have been used by the prime ministers of the European Union countries for meetings. It's five minutes from town and faces the Kolding Fjord and 50 acres of countryside. The rooms vary in size (with 39 in a separate annex), but all have pale-wood furnishings and bright prints. The motto of the excellent French-Danish restaurant is "good food is art"; expect well-presented seafood dishes, as well as intriguing vegetarian options. ⊠ *Fjordvej 154, DK–6000 Strandhuse* ☎ *75/51–00–00* ⊟ *75/51–00–51* ⊕ *www.koldingfjord.dk* ⇝ *134 rooms, 9 suites* ⌂ *Restaurant, tennis court, indoor pool, sauna, billiards, bar* ☐ *AE, DC, MC, V.*

★ **$$** ✕⊡ **Saxildhus Hotel.** This oh-so-Danish property, with gables, black-painted beams, and clunky antiques in its hallways and guest rooms, celebrated its centenary in 2005. Just steps from the train station, this has long been Kolding's premier hotel. Its rooms come in a range of styles, some with mahogany four-poster beds and others with more contemporary furnishings. The basement restaurant, Restaurant Saxen, serves top-notch Danish dishes, with live music on Sunday. The Hotel's other restaurant, Latin, serves breakfast and dinner (with surprisingly good pizzas, one being ample for two people). ⊠ *Jernbaneg. 39, Banegård-spl., DK–6000* ☎ *75/52–12–00* ⊟ *75/53–53–10* ⊕ *www.saxildhus.dk* ⇝ *80 rooms, 7 suites* ⌂ *Restaurant, bar, Wi-Fi, some pets allowed, no-smoking rooms* ☐ *AE, DC, MC, V.*

Nightlife & the Arts

In the heart of town, on Lilletorv (Little Square), is the stylish and amiable **Den Blå Café** (⊠ Slotsg. 4 ☎ 75/50–65–12 ⊕ www.denblaacafe.dk), with British and American rock and blues music playing to a backdrop of film posters. In the afternoons, locals sidle up to the picture windows overlooking the square and enjoy coffee and warm baguette sandwiches or chips and guacamole. In the evening, beer and cocktails flow freely, and on weekends there's live jazz on the terrace. The café is open until midnight Monday through Wednesday and until 2 AM Thursday through Saturday.

There are three dance clubs in town. Four DJs spin the latest pop hits at **Crazy Daisy** (⊠ Jernbaneg. 13 ☎ 75/54–16–88 ⊕ www.crazydaisy.dk). There are also movie nights and other theme parties. This club is very popular and attracts an all-ages crowd. The **Pit Stop** (⊠ Jernbaneg. 54 ☎ 75/50–96–60 ⊕ www.pitstopkolding.dk) offers mainly live rock, though the focus on electronic music has been growing. It's smaller than Crazy Daisy, but just as lively. **Tordenskiold** (⊠ Akseltorv 2B ☎ 75/30–73–13 ⊕ www.tordenskiold.nu) is a two-floor dance club popular with a younger crowd (every Thursday night is "College Night").

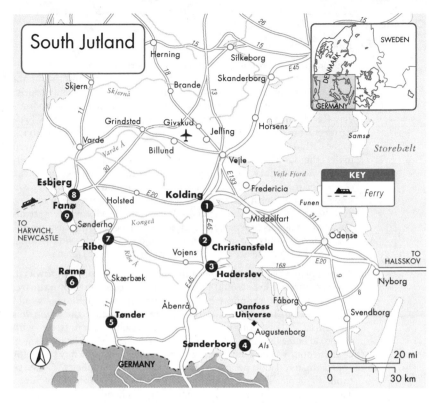

Shopping

Shopping can be a delight in this design-conscious city, with several stores offering famous designer lines in clothing and home interiors. Stores in the city are open from 10 to 6 Monday through Thursday, 10 to 10 Friday, and 10 to 2 PM on Saturday. A shopping center at Skovvangen 42 has later hours on Monday, Thursday, Friday, and Saturday, as do the interior-design stores **Inspiration** and **White Dreams,** which conveniently both have branches in the Skovvangen 42 shopping center. **Furiosa** (⊠ Blæsbjergg. 2A ☎ 75/50–88–87) is the best store in Kolding for interior design.

Fine designer apparel can be found at **Fancy** (⊠ Helligkorsg. 22 ☎ 75/52–01–88), **Frk. Himmelblå** (⊠ Slotsg. 17 ☎ 75/50–78–55), and **Margit** (⊠ Søndertorv 17 ☎ 75/54–11–05).

Kolding's town center is a jumble of walking streets dotted with clothing and jewelry stores and ice-cream shops. The two-story **Bahne** (⊠ Sønderg. 9 ☎ 75/50–56–22) sells all the big names in Danish design, from Stelton and Georg Jensen tableware to functional wooden furniture made by the Danish design firm Trip Trap.

Christiansfeld

2 *15 km (9 mi) south of Kolding.*

This unique small town (population: 800) is rural Denmark at its quietest. It deserves more visitors, as its history is unusual and the inhabitants are true survivors, but as it stands, you might be the only tourist in town should you choose to visit. It was founded in 1773 as a Moravian (Brødremenigheden in Danish) community—an evangelical Christian sect from what is now the Czech Republic that can be traced back to the early 1400s. The Moravian people were almost totally destroyed in the religious wars of 1618 to 1648, and the remaining members scattered; over a century later, King Christian VII of Denmark signed the concession that gave the Moravian Church permission to establish a town in what is now South Jutland. The agreement was generous in its day, as although Denmark was officially Lutheran, the Moravians were allowed free religious practice, tax concessions, freedom from customs duties, their own court, no military service, and cash to help with building projects. Today there are only 385 Moravians in all of Denmark.

A town plan was drawn up along the same lines as Moravian towns in other countries. There would be two parallel streets united by a square, the **Church Square,** around which the most important buildings would be constructed. Today, this Church Square is identical to the way it was built in 1773, lined with linden trees; the straight, austere streets with the broad homes are also the same. The church itself, which has the largest church room without supporting columns in Denmark, has space for approximately 1,000 people, and is striking in its simplicity. The large room is completely white, without an altar, baptismal font, or pictures. The only decorations are the old hand-forged chandeliers, dating from 1776. They are still lowered by rope, and candles are lighted when needed. Besides Sunday service, the church is used for choir and band recitals. ⊠ *Lindeg. at Lysestøbervej* ✆ *Free* ☉ *June–Sept., daily 10–1.*

God's Acre, or the Moravian cemetery, is also worth noting. It is in the town's northeastern corner, and the Sisters of the congregation are buried on one side; the Brethren on the other. All grave markers are alike, as a symbol that all members are alike in death. All the graves have been preserved since 1773, and the site is characterized by simplicity and order.

Christiansfeld is also famous in Europe and in culinary circles worldwide for being the home of a very tasty cinnamon-and-honey cake (*honningkager*), first introduced in 1783. The bakery, **Brødremenighedens Bageri,** sells these treats that the Danish royal family orders for its daily teatime. ⊠ *Lindeg. 36* ✆ *74/56–13–43* ☉ *Weekdays 6 AM–5:30 PM, weekends 6 AM–4 PM.*

Where to Stay

$–$$$ ☷ **Tyrstrup Kro.** This inn on the outskirts of Christiansfeld is a rural oasis and is as Danish as you can get. The inn was built in 1655, and much has been done to preserve the original appearance of the building. Rooms are light and airy, with faux 17th-century furnishings and views of the farmlands. Some guest rooms are in an adjoining building, which architecturally blends in well with the original inn and overlooks the same verdant fields. The large whirlpool tubs are a welcome surprise in all rooms. The dining room is excellent, serving traditionally Danish and nouvelle cuisine. ⊠ *Tyrstrup Vestervej 6, DK–6070* ☎ *74/56–12–42* 📠 *74/ 56–19–70* ⊕ *www.tyrstrupkro.dk* 🛏 *12 rooms, 8 suites* ♿ *Restaurant, meeting rooms* 🚪 *MC, V* 🍴 *BP.*

¢–$ 🏠 **Brødremenighedens Hotel.** A marble slate outside this hotel lists when every Danish king since 1773 (the year it opened) has visited. Inside, photos and souvenirs from the monarchy abound. The hotel began a slow, extensive renovation in 2005, and once the costly project is completed the place should be a small showpiece. (It's open during renovations.) This is a comfortable, clean, and quirky spot. Don't expect five-star service or many in-room amenities, but do expect typical Danish hospitality. The fair-sized rooms are comfortable and overlook the main street. ⊠ *Corner of Lindeg. and Kongensg.* ☎ *74/56–17–10* 🛏 *10 rooms* ♿ *Restaurant, bar* 🚪 *No credit cards.*

Haderslev

③ *27 km (17 mi) south of Kolding, 63 km (39 mi) northeast of Tonder*

This small market city is off the beaten track from the run-of-the-mill tourism centers of the region and therefore doesn't suffer from overwhelming summer crowds. Haderslev would make a good base of operations if you plan on meandering throughout the fjord area, and it has its own attractions as well.

Like many places in this country, Haderslev is old, having been given the rights to become a market town in 1292. In 1525 Duke Christian (later to be King Christian III) introduced the teachings of Martin Luther to Haderslev. As it was the first place in Scandinavia where this happened, the city was called the "Wittenberg of the North" (Wittenberg was the famous university where Luther studied, as did Shakespeare's Hamlet).

Haderslev cathedral, **Our Lady's Church**, became a cathedral in 1920, after being rebuilt several times since the 13th century. The building's beautiful Gothic windows and interiors are worth a visit, and downstairs, behind the altar, are vestments worn by church ministers designed by the current Queen of Denmark, Margrethe. They are on display in glass cases. The steeple towers of the cathedral can be seen far above the roofs in the city. A touching tradition happens every Friday at noon. This is when a music ensemble parades through the town to honor the members of the Haderslev Regiment who were killed in World War II. The parade begins at the barracks at 11:45 and arrives at the cathedral at noon. In the memorial chapel in the cathedral, a page is turned in the regiment's memorial book, and then the parade returns to the barracks.

Walks around the old town are arranged daily from June to August. There are many beautiful gabled homes in the heart of the city from the 16th and 17th centuries that have been preserved, and they continue to be occupied. Contact the Haderslev Tourist Office for times.

The most notable museum in Haderslev, the **Ehlers Collection,** began as a private collection of Danish pottery, and has grown to be the best exhibition of ceramics from the Middle Ages to around 1940 in northern Europe. It's in a house that in itself is noteworthy: it was built in 1557 by a craftsman who was working for Duke Hans the Older, who was commissioning a new castle east of town. In 1976, the house underwent a restoration, and several rooms were found to have painted murals on panels that had been hidden behind 11 layers of wallpaper and 6 layers of paint for 300 years. ⊠ *Slotsg. 20* ☎ *74/53–08–58* ▨ *Free* ☯ *Closed Mon.*

A popular attraction is a ride on the **paddle steamer *Helene,*** with roundtrip departures Tuesday through Sunday from May to September. The leisurely sail takes you from Haderslev (right next to the tourist office) to the island of Åro and to Årosund. You can get off in either place, and then take a bus back to the boat. The whole sojourn will occupy four hours of your day, but it's a good way to see the area. Timetables and tickets are available at the Haderslev Tourist Office.

Sønderborg

❹ *90 km south of Kolding, 75 km south of Christiansfeld*

This town of 30,000 is the center of what is marketed as a "holiday region" of the country—indeed, there are four castles in this area alone. It's deep in southeast Jutland, and has its own airport and train and bus stations. It's the obvious base for a visit to the island of Als, Denmark's seventh largest, which is connected by two bridges from Sønderborg (and a car ferry just north of the town). Als will perhaps become better known now that Danfoss Universe has opened here. This unique theme park has been built by the country's largest heating and air-conditioning enterprise, and aims to teach children (and adults) about the forces of nature, technology, and human attributes.

If you use Sønderborg as a base, you can also visit Gråsten, Broager, and Augustenborg, along with Als. This is lovely countryside, with fields upon fields of canary yellow rapeseed blossoming in May, and sheep and horses in quiet pastures. Græsten is mainly known for its castle, which is used as a summer residence for the royal family. The beautiful surrounding park is open to the public when the royals are not there. (It is generally closed for three weeks around the end of July to mid-August.) Broager has an unusual church worth visiting, as it's the only small-town church in Denmark with two spires, reputed to be a memorial to sisters who were Siamese twins. Augustenborg's beautiful late 18th century castle is now a psychiatric hospital, but its chapel and park are open to visitors.

Southern Jutland was part of Germany between 1864 and 1920, and because of this the art nouveau movement flourished in Sønderborg, whereas in other parts of Denmark the preference was for a traditional Arts and Crafts style. Sønderborg is a wonderful spot for a walking tour, admiring the buildings constructed between 1905 and 1915. A brochure explaining the route is available from the local tourist office.

The **Museum at Sønderborg Castle** is well worth a look, as it offers a wonderful array of artifacts outlining southern Jutland's history and exhibitions on the building's history itself. Dating from 1250, this castle has always been a stronghold, and was even used as a royal prison in the 1500s, when it was one of the most heavily guarded castles in the kingdom. During World War I the German authorities interned Danish partisans from South Jutland in the castle, and at the end of the Second World War Danish authorities interned regional German partisans there. Today the castle has the most intact royal chapel preserved from the time of Reformation in Europe. To enjoy the castle in a unique way, take part in the guided Ghostwalking Tours, which take place on Monday and Wednesday nights at 10 PM from June 1 to August 29. Admission is DKr 65 and tickets can be purchased at the Sønderborg Turistbureau. ⊠ *Sønderbro 1* ☎ *74/42–25–39* ⊕ *www.sonderborgslot. dk* ☜ *Dkr 30* ⊙ *May–Sept., daily 10–5; Oct.–Mar., weekdays 1–4.*

Gråsten Palace Gardens, a summer home of the royal family, isn't quite as sumptuous as you might expect, but it is an enjoyable place for a walk—when the royals aren't in residence. Originally used as the late Queen Mother Ingrid's home between 1935 and her death in 2000, the gardens are a testament to her passion for horticulture and her love for flowers and plants. As far as interiors go, only the chapel of the palace is open to the public; details on opening times (which vary) are available from the local tourist office. ⊠ *Banegården, Kongevej 71, Gråsten* ☎ *74/ 65–09–55* ⊕ *www.visitflensborgfjord.com* ☜ *Free* ⊙ *Varies by season; call tourist office for updates.*

Augustenborg Palace (from 1761) was designed according to the baroque ideals of close contact between nature and architecture. Imposing, and striking in yellow and blue, the building is impressive and the gardens are well kept and stunning. The building had served as a residence for the Augustenborg dukes until the last one left in 1848. The gatehouse contains a small exhibition (open daily) about the history of the palace, the town, and the ducal family, all of which are entwined. There's an unusual chapel within the palace—the altar, pulpit, and organ are all placed on top of one another. Enquire at the tourism office regarding a tour of the chapel and the small museum; the building is now a psychiatric hospital and most of the premises is off-limits to tourists, though you are able to walk around the grounds. ⊠ *Augustenborg Tourist Office, Storegade 28, Augustenborg* ☎ *74/47–17–20* ⊕ *www.visitaugustenborg.com* ☜ *Free* ⊙ *Grounds May–Sept., daily.*

Most non-Danes may not be aware of Danfoss, but it has been Denmark's industrial leader in heating and cooling Scandinavian homes and businesses for decades. It's also the benefactor of **Danfoss Universe,** which opened in May 2005, next to the headquarters. Danfoss Universe is a 10-acre park with more than 150 activities for children—and curious adults. The park is built around the Blue Cube, a 75-foot-high pavilion from EXPO 2000 in Hannover, Germany. The Blue Cube is reminiscent of a giant ice cube, especially since water continuously trickles down the cube's outside walls. Inside the cube, there are exhibits on nature's more violent and awe-inspiring phenomena (volcanoes and glaciers, for example).

Outside the cube, the park is divided into three main areas, including an indoor museum about the history of the Danfoss company. The Outdoors Park has a ton of activities, from water-based interactive games to robotics. Explorama, an indoor area, invites visitors to play with the concepts of creativity and intelligence. This is perhaps the most "adult" part of the park, with interactive exhibits on everything from basic human emotions to intuition and ESP.

The Explorama building, the museum, Café Spisekammeret, and the unique gift shop (do take a look) are open year-round. ⊠ *Mads Patent Vej 1, Nordborg, Als* ☎ *74/88–74–88* ⊕ *www.danfossuniverse.com* ⊞ *DKr 110* ⊙ *May–Oct., daily 10–6 (July until 8 PM.*

Where to Stay & Eat

$$$–$$$$ ✕ **Pascal Vinothek & Brasserie.** Black leather chairs are arranged in front of white walls hung with large Pop Art paintings at this stylish restaurant and wine bar in downtown Søderborg. At dinner you'll get good-sized portions of steak, fish, and shellfish, all local and very fresh. If you find a wine you really like, you can purchase a bottle to take with you. This restaurant is relatively new to the scene, so although service is good, it's not quite polished—yet. ⊠ *Rådhustorvet 5, Sønderborg* ☎ *74/42–38–80* ▤ *DC, MC, V.*

★ **$$–$$$$** ✕ **Skipperkroen Als.** This restaurant may be the second-most obvious reason to make a stop in Augustenborg, after seeing the palace. It's on the marina, and you can always stop by for coffee and cake or an icy Danish beer on the terrace if you don't want to commit to a whole meal. The dining room is at once elegant and cozy, with crisp white linens blending in with the modern Danish decor. Pricey prix-fixe meals are featured at dinner (venison in a red currant sauce is a good choice), but you can get a traditional Danish luncheon platter of herring, smoked salmon, prawns, pâté, and cheese, for a very reasonable DKr 125. ⊠ *Langdel 6D, Augustenborg* ☎ *74/47–10–84* ▤ *AE, DC, MC, V* ⊙ *Closed Jan.*

$ ⊞ **Baltic Hotel.** This beautifully restored hotel from the 1800s is in the village of Høruphav, which is a 15-minute drive from Sønderborg. (Høruphav is easy to find; there is good signposting on the road from Sønderborg toward Augustenborg.) The guest rooms are plush, and most have an easterly ocean view. Meals are well worth having at the hotel's restaurant, with two and three courses. Weekend packages are available in summer. ⊠ *Havbo 29, Sydals, DK–6470* ☎ *74/41–52–00* ▤ *74/41–53–33* ⊕ *www.hotel-baltic.dk* ⤶ *8 rooms, 2 suites* ⚘ *Restaurant, bar* ▤ *DC, MC, V* ⏺ *BP.*

$–$$ ⊞ **Ballebro Færgekro.** This inn, overlooking the calm waters of the Als fjord, seems like a location for an Ingmar Bergman film. Mists hover over the water; a gingerbread-style house is surrounded by verdant, broad lawns. It's idyllic and slightly mysterious. The inn is operated by an affable young couple, Peter and Tina Philipp, and the country-inspired guest rooms are very comfortable, with large bathrooms and quality amenities. A traditional Danish breakfast of cold cuts, cheeses, fresh breads, and jellies is served at your table on a three-tiered tray, which is a nice change from the more standard buffets found elsewhere. This inn is a perfect spot for a romantic getaway—and it's steps from the car ferry that takes you on a five-minute ride to Als. ✉ *Færgevej 5, Blans, Sønderborg, DK–6400* ☎ *74/46–13–03* 🖨 *74/46–13–09* ⊕ *www.ballebro. dk* 🛏 *10 rooms, 1 suite* ⚭ *Restaurant* ☰ *AE, DC, MC, V* ⭐ *BP.*

Tønder

❺ *105 km (66 mi) southwest of Kolding, 195 km (122 mi) southwest of Århus.*

Just 4 km (2½ mi) north of the German border, the historic town of Tønder has long been closely allied with its southern neighbor. In 1864 Tønder was annexed by Germany. After Germany's defeat in World War I, plebiscites were held in the area, and Tønder chose to become reunited with Denmark. Nevertheless, Tønder is still home to a small but important German community, with a German kindergarten, school, gymnasium, newspaper, and library.

Tønder received its official municipal charter in 1243, making it Denmark's oldest municipality. Amble back in time among the winding cobbled streets in the heart of town, where half-timber gabled houses, many with intricately carved doors, lean up against small, old-fashioned shops.

The town is surrounded by low-lying marshes, and has been subject to major floods throughout its history. To combat the floods, a series of protective dikes was built in the 16th century. The result was double-edged: though Tønder was now safe from the sea, it also lost its natural harbor and waterways and, most importantly, its shipping industry. So, the town turned its sights inward, to the Tønder women's sewing rooms, and built itself up as the "lace capital of the world." In the 18th century, lace making became Tønder's most lucrative export. Throughout town are the stately gated homes once owned by successful lace merchants.

Tønder comes vibrantly alive in the last week of August for the **Tønder Folk Music Festival** (☎ 74/72–46–10 ⊕ www.tf.dk), which has been drawing folk music lovers from all over the world since 1974. Big names and local acts perform everything from blues, zydeco, and gospel to the more traditional Irish, Scottish, and American folk tunes. Reserve hotel rooms well in advance, as the town fills up to capacity during this time. There is no all-in-one ticket to the whole Tønder Festival; tickets are sold separately for each concert. The venues vary in size and ambience. There are seats at all the events, with the exception of one or two, which have both seats and standing room.

Founded in 1923, the **Tønder Museum** has amassed an impressive collection of South Jutland arts and crafts. The extensive lace exhibit includes delicate doilies and baptismal gowns. In another room, intricate silverware is displayed alongside antique furnishings. A highlight is the collection of hand-painted glazed Dutch tiles brought back by sailors during the 17th and 18th centuries. The tiles served as ballast for the ships, and were then used to decorate their homes. Tønder's old water tower, connected to the museum via a glass corridor, houses the world's largest collection of chairs designed by Tønder native Hans J. Wegner, one of Denmark's best-known furniture designers. The 130-foot tower with eight sun-drenched decks is the ideal showroom for Wegner's chairs and furnishings, which range from a rope and ash-wood circle chair to his Y-chair, made of beech wood with a plaited paper yarn seat. The skylit top deck, above which sits the old water-tower lantern, displays a massive circular table designed by Wegner's daughter. Around the table sit 25 of Wegner's most popular chair, a rounded blond-wood design that he called simply "The Chair," which brought Wegner worldwide recognition, particularly in the United States, after both Kennedy and Nixon each sat in one during a television interview. Settle into one and enjoy the 360-degree views of Tønder's red rooftops and surrounding green marshland that unfold to the sea. If you're in the market for some Tønder lace, you can buy some in the small museum store. ⊠ *Kongevej 51* ☎ *74/72–89–89* ⊕ *www.tondermuseum.dk* ⊠ *DKr 20* ☉ *June–Aug., daily 10–5; Sept.–May, Tues.–Sun. 10–5.*

Lace lovers will be richly rewarded at the **Drøhses Hus,** a well-preserved 1672 town house with exhibits of lace and lace making. In summer, lace makers often work their trade inside the house. ⊠ *Storeg. 14* ☎ *74/ 72–49–90* ⊠ *DKr 20* ☉ *Apr.–Dec., weekdays 10–5, Sat. 10–1.*

The **Zeppelin and Garnisonsmuseum** showcases the famous "blimps" or zeppelins of the early 1900s (at which time there was a German naval airship base here). In 1920, when South Jutland was back in Danish possession, it became a Danish garrison. On display are pictures, documents, and many other items explaining this dramatic period of 20th-century Danish history. ⊠ *Gasværkvej 1* ☎ *74/72–72–54* ⊕ *www.zeppelin- museum.dk* ⊠ *DKr 25* ☉ *May–Oct., weekends noon–5.*

Where to Stay & Eat

$$$–$$$$
Fodor'sChoice
★

╳⌂ **Schackenborg Slotskro.** Stay at this inn, and you can say that while in Denmark, you were a guest of the Danish royal family. This elegant hotel is the official royal inn of Schackenborg Castle, the next-door residence of Prince Joachim. The prince's former wife, Princess Alexandra, personally decorated the rooms in rich blues, greens, and reds; each has a large, sparkling bathroom and views of the castle. Suites have work areas, living rooms, and hot tubs. The inn's highly acclaimed restaurant serves superb Danish-French cuisine, including beef tournedos, marshland lamb, and an eel appetizer with new potatoes. It's possible in summer to sit outside in the picturesque garden, admiring the Alexandra roses. The castle and inn are 4 km (2½ mi) west of Tønder, in the small village of Møgeltønder. Though the castle is not open to the public, you can roam about the lush grounds that are surrounded by a moat. In addition, Møgeltønder's narrow cobbled main street, lined with lime trees, rose gardens, and lovely brick and half-timber houses, has been rightfully named "Scandinavia's most beautiful village street." ⊠ *Slotsg. 42, DK–6270 Møgeltønder* ☎ *74/73–83–83* 🖶 *74/73–83–11* ⊕ *www. slotskro.dk* ⊸ *25 rooms, 2 suites* ♿ *Restaurant, bar, some pets allowed, no-smoking rooms* ▤ *AE, DC, MC, V.*

DANISH LACE

THE ART OF MAKING LACE has been a part of the Tønder region since the techniques were introduced to the country in the 1500s. Denmark had strong commercial ties with Holland at the time, and it is supposed that because of this the lace-making techniques came to Tønder. The art reached its zenith in the 1700s, and it is estimated that up to 15,000 girls and women plied their craft in this municipality alone. The term "lace maker" was only applied to married women, but girls began learning the craft from the age of five, and were apprenticed to adult lace makers.

Danish lacemaking is intricate, with the use of four needles and special bobbins, and often has flowing designs. The background mesh is made from twisted threads and a heavy gimp outlines the motifs. This lace also incorporates decorative filling stitches including a "honeycomb" effect and others. You may

find that many local Danish museums, from small to large, display headresses adorned with Tønder lace, as it was part of the wardrobe of a well-to-do farmer's wife in the 19th century. These days, lacemaking is a fine art around the world, still taught to children in 18 European countries, Russia, the USA, and Canada.

Every third year an international festival of lace making is held in Tønder; the next one is June 1–3, 2007. Stands from many countries sell everything associated with lace making, including antique lace, books, patterns, yarn, bobbins, and even computer programs. Contact **Tønder Lace** (⌖ Foreningen Kniplingsfestival, Postboks 35, DK–6270, Tønder ☎ 74/72–28–84 ⊕ www.kniplings-festival.dk) for more info on the festival. Accommodations can be booked directly on the festival's Web site.

$ ✕⌂ **Hotel Tønderhus.** This family-owned and -operated hotel is a five-minute walk from the train station in the center of town. The newer buildings have modern, large guest rooms in shades of brown and beige, many with balconies and Wi-Fi. Older rooms have large bathtubs, but are decorated in a more traditional way. The hotel has several tastefully furnished dining rooms that offer a wide selection of smørrebrød and fish dishes. Full dinners of traditional Danish cuisine are also offered. ⊠ Jomfrustien 1 ☎ 74/72–22–22 ⎙ 74/72–05–92 ⊕ www.hoteltoenderhus.dk ➷ 58 rooms, 4 suites ⚐ Restaurant, billiards, bar, some pets allowed, no-smoking rooms ▤ AE, DC, MC, V ﾝ◎ｲ BP.

Sports & the Outdoors
Biking trails crisscross Tønder's lush and flat countryside. The tourist office has helpful cycling maps that detail the bike routes in the area. You can rent bikes at **Top Cycler** (⊠ Jernbaneg. 1C ☎ 74/72–18–81).

You may not have traveled all the way to Denmark to go bowling, but the **Bowler Inn** (⊠ Ribelandevej 56 ☎ 74/72–00–11 ⊕ www.hotelbowlerinn.dk/uk/) has 10 lanes (2 for children, and 2 for playing skittles, the original form of bowling), single and double guest rooms that are soundproofed, a restaurant, and pub. Who would have thought?

If the weather is dull while you're in the city, try swimming, working out, tennis, or squash in the **Tønderhallerne Leisure Center** (⊠ Søndre Landevej 4-6 ☎ 74/72–28–26 ⊕ www.tonderhallerne.dk). The prices and opening times vary, so call before dropping by.

Shopping

Since 1671 **Det Gamle Apotek** (The Old Pharmacy; ⊠ Østerg. 1 ☎ 74/72–51–11) has dispensed medicine to Tønder's townspeople. In 1989 the pharmacy was converted into a Danish gift and crafts center, but the entire building, both inside and out, was left intact. The beautifully carved front entranceway opens onto a vintage interior lined with pharmaceutical artifacts and medicine jars. Craft items for sale include antique stationery and pens, and handmade candles, glassware, and ceramics. From March to September the cellar bursts with Danish Christmas items, from tree decorations and festive paper cutouts to elves and angels. This is a big import-export company and many items from here are found in Copenhagen stores.

Rømø

❻ *34 km (21 mi) northwest of Tønder, 30 km (19 mi) southwest of Ribe.*

The lush island of Rømø has one of Denmark's widest beaches, which unfurls along the island's sunny western coast and has protected areas for windsurfers, horseback riders, nudists, and dune-buggy riders alike— space for everyone, it seems. Rømø has just 850 permanent residents, but masses of vacationing German and Danish families increase this number tenfold in summer. Indeed, it's a haven for campers, cyclists, and budget vacationers. A causeway crosses green fields and marshy wetlands to connect Rømø to the mainland. Many birds live here, feeding off the seaweed and shellfish washed up by the tides. Summer houses dot the island; most of Rømø's services and accommodations are in and around the village of Havneby, 8 km (5 mi) south of the causeway, and in the camping and shopping complex of Lakkolk, in the west.

The 18th century was a golden age in Rømø's seafaring history, when more than 50 local sailors were appointed captains of Dutch and German whaling expeditions to Greenland. Upon their return, the newly prosperous captains built lavish farmsteads, such as **Kommandørgård** (Captain's House), in Toftum, 2 km (1 mi) north of the causeway. Part of the Danish National Museum, this stately, thatch-roof–and–brick farmhouse dating from 1874 has been meticulously restored, with opulent period furnishings including brass-lined chests and marble-top tables. Blue-and-white glazed Dutch tiles cover the walls, alongside hand-painted rococo panels and doors. ⊠ *Juvrevej 60, Toftum* ☎ 74/75–52–76 ⊕ *www.natmus.dk* ▧ *DKr 20* ۞ *May–Sept., Tues.–Sun. 10–6; Oct., Tues.–Sat. 10–3.*

Just north of the Captain's House, in the tiny village of Juvre, is a **whale jawbone fence** built in 1772. Lacking wood and stone, villagers constructed this fence from the whalebones that Rømø captains brought back from Greenland.

Off the main road south of the causeway rises the whitewashed, 18th-century **Rømø Kirke** (Rømø Church), dedicated to St. Clemens, the patron saint of fisherman and sailors. Inside are several hand-painted ship models. The churchyard gravestones, brought back by Rømø captains, are made of Greenlandic stone and carved with depictions of ships. ⊠ *Havnebyvej 152* ☎ *No phone* ☯ *Tues.–Fri. 8–4.*

Where to Stay & Eat

Though there are plenty of campgrounds and bed-and-breakfasts on the island, it's sadly lacking in any great restaurants. Outside of your hotel's dining room, your options will be limited to grocery stores and fast food.

$ ✕☷ **Hotel Færgegaarden.** In the costal village of Havneby, this holiday hotel has basic rooms with white bedspreads and flowery pillows. The cozy maritime-theme restaurant, with a brick fireplace, Dutch-tile walls, and model ships, serves simple Danish-French fare, including fried plaice with butter sauce. ⊠ *Vesterg. 1, DK–6792 Havneby* ☎ *74/75–54–32* ☏ *74/75–58–59* ⌨ *35 rooms* ᕻ *Restaurant, pool, bar* ☰ *AE, DC, MC, V.*

$–$$ ☷ **Hotel Kømmandørgården.** This sprawling resort-style vacation and conference complex gives you the option of a standard hotel room, an apartment, or even a log cabin. The resort is by the Rømø Family and Horse Park, and has great views of the Wadden Sea and the marshland. You certainly won't get bored here: Icelandic horses are available for rides, and the Wellness Center is a fully equipped spa with some unusual features (a "Tepidarium" is a small room incorporating light and sound therapy to presumably rid your mind of toxins). It's a busy, cheery place, filled with families and/or conventioneers. Every unit has a terrace or balcony. ⊠ *Havenybyvej 201, Mølby, DK–6792* ☎ *74/75–51–22* ⊕ *www.kommandoergaarden.dk* ⌨ *40 rooms, 40 apartments and cabins* ᕻ *3 restaurants, 2 pools, spa, billiards, horseback riding, bar, playground, meeting rooms* ☰ *DC, MC, V* ⍾ *BP.*

¢ ☷ **Danhostel, Rømø Vandrerhjem.** If you want to spend a few days on the island without breaking the bank, this pleasant hostel is an option. It's located in an old captain's building from the mid-18th century. The walls in the main building are decorated with Dutch tiles along with original Rømø skirting boards. Breakfast costs extra (DKr 47), as does linen rental (DKr 50) if you don't have your own, and you must have a YHA card to register. Check availability on the Web site. ⊠ *Lyngvejen 7, Mølby, DK–6792 Rømø* ☎ *74/78–98–98* ☏ *74/75–51–87* ⊕ *www.danhostel. dk/romo* ⌨ *19 shared rooms, 6 with bath* ᕻ *Bicycles, lounge, laundry facilities, playground, some pets allowed* ☰ *No credit cards* ☯ *Closed Nov.–Feb.*

Ribe

★ **❼** *60 km (36 mi) southwest of Kolding, 150 km (103 mi) southwest of Århus.*

In the southwestern corner of Jutland, the country's oldest town is well worth the detour for its medieval center preserved by the Danish National Trust. As you stroll around, note the detailed doors and facades of the buildings, and the antique streetlights. From May to mid-September a night watchman circles the town, recalling its history and singing traditional songs. If you want to accompany him, gather at the main square at 10 PM.

Only 4,000 people live in the old part of Ribe, and a guide from the tourist office might tell you that it has always been a "live and let live" place, perhaps due to the fact that there were no dikes built here until 1912, and, therefore, the town has always been under the threat of flooding. When you walk through the town, built on both sides of the river, you'll see many half-timber buildings with wooden pegs: between 1580 and 1650 this type of architecture was popular after a massive fire had destroyed many domiciles. Bricks, laid out in zigzag patterns, were placed between the timbers to help stop drafts. At 31 Mellemdammen (one of the pedestrian streets) you'll see a very pleasant half-timber home, but the astonishing thing is the plaque that is affixed to the outside wall: it lists the names of every family who has lived there since 1487.

The **Ribe Domkirke** (Ribe Cathedral) stands on the site of one of Denmark's earliest churches, built around AD 860. The present structure, which dates from the 12th century, is built of a volcanic tufa stone, transported by boats from quarries in Cologne, France, said to be for the exclusive use of the devil. The 14th-century brick bell tower once clanged out flood and fire warnings to Ribe's citizens, and today affords sweeping views of the town's red-slate rooftops and surrounding marshes. ⊠ *Torvet 15* ☎ *75/42–06–19* ⊕ *www.ribe-domkirke. dk* ⊠ *DKr 12* ☉ *Apr. and Oct., Mon.–Sat. 11–4; May–June and mid-Aug.–late-Sept., Mon.–Sat. 10–5; July–mid-Aug., Mon.–Sat. 10–5:30; Nov.–Mar., Mon.–Sat. 11–3. Hrs vary Sun. year-round.*

The **Ribes Vikinger** (Ribe Viking Museum) chronicles Viking history with conventional exhibits of household goods, tools, and clothing. There's a multimedia room with an interactive computer screen where you can search for more Viking information in the form of text, pictures, and videos. ⊠ *Odinspl.* ☎ *76/88–11–22* ⊕ *www.ribesvikinger. dk* ⊠ *DKr 55* ☉ *Apr.–June and Sept.–Mar., Tues.–Sun. 10–4; July and Aug., Tues.–Sun. 10–6.*

Take Bus 57 (confirm with the driver) from the railway station across the street from the Ribes Vikinger. The bus travels 2 km (1 mi) south and arrives at the **Viking Center,** an outdoor exhibit detailing how the Vikings lived day-to-day, with demonstrations about homes, food, and crafts. ⊠ *Lustrupvej 4, Lustrupholm* ☎ *75/41–16–11* ⊕ *www. ribevikingecenter.dk* ⊠ *DKr 65* ☉ *May, June, and Sept., weekdays 10–3:30; July and Aug., daily 11–5.*

Where to Stay & Eat

¢–$$ ✕ **Sælhunden.** The 400-year-old canal-side "Seal Tavern" can seat up to 60 people, but it feels smaller, and its coziness draws both wayfarers and locals. The only seal mementos left are a few skins and pictures, but you can still order a "seal's special" of cold shrimp, sautéed potatoes, and scrambled eggs or an old Danish favorite of fat strips of pork served with cream gravy and boiled potatoes (only served on Wednesday in winter). Console yourself in summer with *rød grød med fløde* (red porridge with cream); the pronunciation of this dessert—which defies phonetic spelling—is so difficult that Danes get a kick out of making foreigners try to say it. In summer, you can sit outside by the river or in the courtyard. ⊠ *Skibbroen 13* ☎ *75/42–09–46* ⊕ *www.saelhunden. dk* ▤ *DC, MC, V.*

$$–$$$ ✕▦ **Hotel Dagmar.** The Hotel Dagmar is poised to please the hearts of **Fodor's**Choice those wanting a comfortable trip back in time. The hotel, originally built ★ in 1581 by a city alderman, eventually became an inn by 1800. Although city ordinances prohibit such modern conveniences as an elevator, some contemporary touches are apparent. (At this writing, wireless Internet was only available in the lobby, but they're planning to add this service to the rooms.) For a hotel of this vintage, standard rooms are quite comfortable (though not lavish), and some have canopied beds. The cheap amenities in the bathrooms are a bit of a surprise, but shouldn't detract from the hotel's merits overall. The restaurant is fantastic—seasonal menus, where one can choose between two- and six-course set menus (between DKr 325 and DKr 565), or excellent à la carte choices, make this dining room perhaps the best in town. The scallops topped with a sweet-potato crisp and surrounded by vichyssoise is an excellent appetizer, and choosing the North Sea fresh fish of the day in a lobster sauce is a smart idea for the main course. House wines by the half bottle are reasonably priced, and a further good selection of vintages from France, Spain, and Italy should satisfy any discriminating palates. A cellar restaurant-bar, Vœter-kœderen (Watchman's Cellar) is swanky, but can be smoky, as is the case in many Danish bars. Live music and dancing take over the dining room later on weekends, and weekend golf or gourmet packages are also available. The hotel is next door to the local tourist bureau and across the street from the 900-year old cathedral. ⊠ *Torvet 1, DK–6760* ☎ *75/42–00–33* ▤ *75/42–36–52* ⊕ *www.hoteldagmar.dk* ⊷ *48 rooms* ♿ *Restaurant, cable TV, Wi-Fi, bar, meeting room, some pets allowed* ▤ *AE, DC, MC, V.*

$$–$$$ ▦ **Ribe Byferie.** Here's a concept embraced by Europeans but rather unfamiliar to many North Americans: visit a historic city like Ribe, and rent a contemporary two-bedroom town house, buy the groceries you need at Super Brugsen or Føtex (the local big supermarkets), and enjoy all your modern amenities in a condominium-like environment. Each unit has at least one bedroom (the two-bedroom units come with two bunk beds), a living room, dining room, fully equipped kitchen and terrace—but forget about fantastic views. On-site are laundry facilities, saunas, Internet access at 1 DKr per minute (this adds up!), a recreation room, and more. The permanent photo exhibit on the second floor of the main building is by Jacob A. Riis, a local Ribe son, who photographed the seamier side of New York City in the 1890s. This place is friendly and spotless. Renters receive free entrance to the popular Ribe Swimming Baths, which has waterslides and other activities. ⊠ *Damvej 34, DK–6760* ☎ *79/88–79–88* ▤ *79/88–79–98* ⊕ *www. ribe-byferie.dk* ⊷ *94 units* ♿ *Kitchens, sauna, laundry facilities, Internet room* ▤ *DC, MC, V.*

$ 🏨 **Den Gamle Arrest.** Spend the night in the clink at "The Old Jail," a simple yet cozy hotel housed in what was Ribe's main jail from 1893 to 1989. The artist-owner has done a brilliant job of modernizing the cells into comfortably habitable rooms, while preserving all the prison details. The cells, which used to house five prisoners, have been creatively refashioned into single and double rooms with lofts in which the bed can be stored during the day. The tiny windows, once covered with mesh-like gratings so that prisoners couldn't see outside, now offer glimpses of blue sky. The original prison gates, with iron bars and padlocks, still serve as the entrances into the hallways. The prison dungeons have been converted into a sprawling gift shop with handmade Danish crafts, from inventive candles and glassware to hundreds of Christmas decorations. The former guardroom, which opens onto the prison yard–turned–terrace, is now a popular clothing store with exclusive fashions by Danish designers. ⊠ *Torvet 11, DK–6760* ☎ *75/42–37–00* ⊕ *www.dengamlearrest.dk* ☞ *11 rooms, 2 with bath* ♢ *Café, shop.*

¢   🏨 **Danhostel Ribe.** In the town center, this plain, redbrick hostelry has six- and four-bed family rooms arranged in clusters of two, each with its own private bath and toilet. There are also double rooms with private bath and eight four-bed rooms with completely private facilities. They are functional and childproof, with pine bunks and industrial carpeting. A kitchen is available. ⊠ *Ribehallen, Skt. Pedersg. 16, DK–6760* ☎ *75/42–06–20* ▣ *75/42–42–88* ⊕ *www.danhostel-ribe.dk* ☞ *152 beds, 38 rooms with bath* ♢ *Cafeteria* ▭ *No credit cards* ◔ *Closed Dec. and Jan.*

¢   🏨 **Weis Stue.** For very reasonable prices, you can spend a night in a half-timber inn that dates back to 1600, with an original interior from 1704. It's a bit like Robin Hood meets Hamlet in Denmark, and this small place is loaded with character and atmosphere. Climb about a dozen steep, narrow stairs to the second floor to find your single or double room, which probably has a wardrobe or other furniture that's at least 250 years old. The bedrooms (no TVs or other contemporary add-ons) share two bathrooms; two more washrooms are on the main floor next to the pub/restaurant. The location is excellent, adjacent to the Hotel Dagmar and directly across from the tourist office and Ribe Cathedral. Weis Stue is owned by Hotel Dagmar, so you can probably be assured of quality food in the restaurant here—at prices that are much easier on the wallet. ⊠ *Torvet 2, DK–6760* ☎ *75/42–07–00* ▣ *75/41–17–95* ⊕ *www. weisstue.dk* ☞ *8 rooms without bath* ♢ *Restaurant, pub* ▭ *AE, DC, MC, V* ⦿ *BP.*

Shopping

Antikgaarden (⊠ Overdammen 5 ☎ 75/41–00–55) has a varied collection of Danish antiques, including old Royal Copenhagen plates. **Idé Butik Aps** (⊠ Overdammen 4 ☎ 75/42–14–14) sells Danish crafts ranging from paper cutouts and glassware to figurines of Danish *nisser* (elves). For amber jewelry, head to **Rav I Ribe** (⊠ Nedderdammen 32 ☎ 75/42–03–88), one of the largest amber purveyors in town.

Kvickly (⊠ Seminarievej 1 ☎ 75/42–11–00 ⊕ www.kvickly.dk/ribe ◔ Tues.–Sat.) is a popular Danish "groceteria," market, butcher, bakery, and clothing store, and only one of six such establishments on Jutland. A family restaurant is located on the top floor.

Esbjerg

8 *35 km (22 mi) northwest of Ribe, 145 km (90 mi) southwest of Århus.*

Esbjerg's appropriate motto is "alive and kicking," and for this relatively new Danish city (founded in 1868 as an export harbor for the west coast of the country), it works. It may, however, not be on everyone's must-see list in southwestern Jutland for that very reason. As a busy port, with ships arriving and departing on a daily basis, it's party central for the visiting sailors and merchant marines. However, this city is also the best way to get to the island of Fanø, so it's therefore an important stop. It also has a performing arts center, **Musikhuset Esbjerg** (⊠ Havneg. 18 ☎ 76/10–90–10 ⊕ www.mhe.dk) designed by Jan Utzon, the son of Jørn Utzon, who won acclaim for designing the Sydney Opera House. Indeed, the same type of ceramic tile that has been used in Australia adorns the exteriors of this light and airy 1,100-seat center. Everything from exhibitions to fashion shows to the musical *Lord of the Dance* (extended into 2006) is showcased here.

There is a pleasant mishmash of architectural styles in town, including stately turn-of-the-20th-century brick government buildings. The fortified **water tower** (⊠ Havneg. 22 ☎ 75/12–78–11) was erected in 1897, and its castlelike appearance was much influenced by the medieval building Haus Nassau in Nuremburg, Germany. Climb to the top (admission is DKr 10) for splendid views of the city and the sea. Reigning over the central square is a statue of Christian IX, the reigning monarch when Esbjerg was founded.

Esbjerg is also proud of having the country's second-longest pedestrian street (after Copenhagen's Strøget), Kongenstrade. It was the first street in Europe to have neon lighting, in 1949. There's a wide variety of shops and boutiques offering their wares, as well as restaurants and pubs. It can be quite crowded on Saturdays.

The highlight at the **Esbjerg Museum** is its amber collection, one of the largest in Denmark. The west coast of Jutland is well known for being rich in amber. Detailed exhibits trace the history of amber along the Jutland coast over a whopping 10,000-year period. ⊠ *Torveg. 45* ☎ *75/ 12–78–11* ⊕ *www.esbjergmuseum.dk* ☒ *DKr 30, free Wed.* ⊙ *June–Aug., daily 10–4; Sept.–May, Tues.–Sun. 10–4.*

The **Esbjerg Kunstmuseum** (Esbjerg Art Museum) showcases a fine collection of Danish contemporary art starting in 1910, including works by Richard Mortensen. Innovative temporary exhibits feature up-and-coming Danish artists, and have included a retrospective of Danish mobile art and avant-garde sculptures and installations. ⊠ *Havneg. 20* ☎ *75/ 13–02–11* ☒ *DKr 40* ⊙ *June–Dec., daily 10–4.*

The **Fiskeri-og Søfartsmuseet** (Fisheries and Maritime Museum) is a good place to take children, as it has two aquariums and a "sealarium," where seals found in Danish waters can be viewed in an outdoor pool with underwater windows. (They are fed daily at 11 and 2:30.) The exhibits on the history of Danish sea fisheries from 1880 to 1940 are educational, but the open-air display of actual ships and maritime environments of previous ages will probably be more interesting to most. ⊠ *Tarphagevej 2* ☎ *76/12–20–00* ⊕ *www.fimus.dk* ⬚ *DKr 85* ◷ *Sept.–June, daily 10–5; July and Aug., daily 10–6.*

Get a sailor's-eye view of Esbjerg and Fanø by getting on board the **MS Sønderho** in July and August for a 90-minute cruise. You depart from the second dock in the fishing harbor of Esbjerg or at Nordby Havn in Fanø. Don't worry about booking a round-trip ticket in advance, as it's not allowed—you must buy your ticket when you embark. You also can't buy anything on board, but are welcome to bring your own food or drink. There is an additional cruise at 5:30 PM on Wednesday, when there is a good likelihood of spotting seals ☎ *33/15–15–15* ⬚ *DKr 70* ◷ *Cruises Mon.–Thurs. at 11 and 1 from Esbjerg (3:20 PM from Fanø).*

One of Esbjerg's most striking sights is the giant whitewashed sculpture by Danish artist Svend Wiig Hansen entitled **Menesket ved Havet** (*Man Meets Sea*), depicting four 19-foot-tall men staring solemnly out to sea. It has been said that it evokes the mood of a temple or acropolis, or, a reminder of the mysterious stone figures on Easter Island. In clear weather the figures can be seen from a distance of 10 km (6 mi).

Where to Stay & Eat

$–$$$$ ✕ **Restaurant Gammelhavn.** This airy pavilion-style restaurant is right on the harbor front, and offers everything from brasserie food (sandwiches start at DKr 65) to gourmet dinners (a four-course meal would be about DKr 400). You can always stop by in mid-afternoon for coffee and cake, as well. ⊠ *Brittaniavej 3* ☎ *76/11–90–00* 🖃 *DC, MC, V*

$$$ ✕ **Sand's Restauration.** Founded in 1907, this warm, dimly lighted restaurant is one of Esbjerg's oldest. The traditional Danish menu of pork dishes and steaks continues to be popular with locals and tourists alike, and there is a new three-course menu every month. The original owners collected more than 50 works of art by west Jutland artists, which cover the walls. ⊠ *Jyllandsg. 32* ☎ *75/12–02–07* ⬚ *75/45–47–70* 🖃 *AE, MC, V* ◷ *Closed Sun.*

$–$$ 🏨 **Hotel Britannia.** Formerly a Best Western property, this '60s-style, slightly institutional-looking hotel has seen better days, but the promise of a five-year refurbishment plan under new ownership that began in mid-2005 and a terrific dining room still make it worthy of consideration. Guest rooms have fared a bit better than the public areas, and are large with extremely comfortable beds; some rooms overlook the town square. In fact, the location of the Britannia makes it very appealing for both the tourist and business traveler. (The city's tourist office is just a stone's throw away.) Its Restaurant Green Garden impresses with three prix-fixe menus: one all seafood, one five-course gourmet, and one with fresh market products. The sirloin steak with glazed onions in a red wine sauce is top-notch. The other place to eat, a pleasant brasserie-bar, serves a good breakfast, which is also included in the room rate. ⊠ *Torvet* ☎ *75/13–01–11* ⬚ *75/45–20–85* ⊕ *www.britannia.dk* 🛏 *79 rooms* ♿ *Restaurant, café, bar* 🖃 *DC, MC, V* ¶◎ *BP.*

¢–$ ⌑ **Palads Cab Inn.** In the heart of Esbjerg is this budget hotel affiliated with the popular Cab—Inn Copenhagen chain. The rooms, though the standard motel type, were refurbished in 2005. Breakfast is served in a colossal, high-ceiling dining room that once served as a ballroom. ⊠ *Skoleg. 14, DK–6700* ☎ *75/18–16–00* 📠 *75/18–16–24* ⊕ *www. cabinn.dk* 🛏 *107 rooms* ⟠ *Cafeteria, cable TV, in-room broadband, bar, no-smoking rooms* ⊟ *AE, DC, MC, V* ⫶⨀⫶ *BP.*

Nightlife & the Arts

Pubs dot Esbjerg's main drag, Skolegade. In the center of town is the friendly restaurant-bar **Dronning Louise** (⊠ Torvet 19 ☎ 75/13–13–44), named after Queen Louise, the wife of Christian IX. The bar has red-leather chairs and a wall lined with bookshelves. In the upstairs club a DJ spins dance tunes on Friday and Saturday nights. Esbjerg locals flock to the live Saturday-afternoon jazz sessions that start at 1 PM. In summer the jazz is performed on a terrace that faces the main square. The adjoining restaurant serves light lunches (burgers, club sandwiches, and chicken wings) and a Danish dinner menu of meat and fish dishes.

Fanø

❾ *30 km (19 mi) northwest of Ribe, plus 12-min ferry from Esbjerg; 153 km (96 mi) southwest of Århus, plus 12-min ferry from Esbjerg.*

In the 19th century this tiny island had an enormous shipbuilding industry and a fleet second only to Copenhagen's. The shipping industry deteriorated, but the proud maritime heritage remains. Today Fanø is a summer oasis for legions of Danes and other northern Europeans. Silky sand beaches unfold along the west coast, buffered by windswept dunes and green reeds. Cars are allowed on the beach, and it's well worth taking a ride along the flat sandy coast between the ferry port in Nordby, Fanø's capital, and the traditional town of Sønderho, in the south. Spinning along the white sandy expanse is like crossing a desert; only the dark blue sea off in the distance reminds you of your island whereabouts. The beach is so level and wide that the military used to train here. In the off-season, when summer visitors have packed up and returned home, the Fanø shore becomes a tranquil retreat, hauntingly silent save for the rustle of reeds and the far-off squawk of a bird.

The old-fashioned village of Sønderho, 13 km (8 mi) south of Nordby, has tiny winding lanes and thatch-roof cottages decorated with ships' relics, figureheads, painted doors, and brass lanterns. You may even see people wearing the traditional costumes, especially on Sønderhodag, a town festival held on the third Sunday in July.

Fanø's annual kite festival, held in mid-June, draws scores of aficionados who fill the sky with hundreds of their colorful, swooping kites.

The **Fanø Maritime and Costume Museum** is an interesting stop to see how life was on the island in the 19th century, when it boasted the largest fleet of ships after Copenhagen. Family life was difficult with husbands being away for long periods of time, and the women had to rear the children as well as farm the land. The costumes here are originals, and photographs and antiques give a good glimpse into the seaman's life at home and aboard the ships. Ask at the desk for an English brochure that will explain all the exhibits. ⊠ *Hovedgaden 28* ☎ *75/16–22–72* ☒ *DKr 20* ◯ *May–Sept., Mon.–Sat. 11–4; Oct.–Apr., Mon.–Sat. 11–1.*

The **Fanø Kunstmuseum** (Fanø Art Museum) exhibits the work of artists who have painted on the island over the past 100 years. The original museum opened in 1922 in a grocer's shop that now serves as the entrance. The art collection's purpose is to exhibit art that visualizes the past and present of the island in the Wadden Sea. ⊠ *Nord Land 5, Sønderho* ☎ *75/16–40–44* ☒ *DKr 20* ◯ *Apr.–Nov., Tues.–Sun. 2–5.*

The oldest golf course in Denmark (established 1901), **Fanø Golf Links,** is also a genuine links course (i.e. characterized by its seaside location, built on sandy earth, and with the type of vegetation also found on the traditional Scottish links courses). Many holes have "blind strokes," also found in Scotland, as the green is hidden behind the dunes. Several of the tees are on the tops of the dunes, from which there is a view of the North Sea. Fanø Golf Weeks, held the last two weeks of July, is the biggest and oldest open golf tournament in the country. Contact the company ahead of your visit to inquire on entry rules and fees. ⊠ *Golfvejen 5* ☎ *76/66–00–77* ⊕ *www.fanoe-golf-links.dk.*

Where to Stay & Eat

To get an idea of where the locals throw back a few brews, stop by **Hjørnekroen** (⊠ Hovedgaden 14 ☎ 75/16–22–62 ⊕ www.hjoernekroen. dk), which is a true pub with live music, billiards, and darts—it feels a bit like a Danish version of the TV show *Cheers.*

$$$ ✕ **Restaurant Hos Apel.** Located directly behind the Fanø Krogaard hotel, this little restaurant features fish specialties, including the very popular *bakskuld,* a smoked and salted flat fish glazed with butter. ⊠ *Hovedgaden 25* ☎ *75/16–11–44* ☐ *No credit cards* ◯ *Closed Oct.–Apr.*

★ **$–$$** ✕ **Café Nanas Stue.** This half-timber farmhouse restaurant dating from 1854 doubles as the Fanø Flisemuseum (Fanø Tile Museum). The walls and old-fashioned wooden cupboards are lined with glazed Dutch tiles brought back by Danish sailors from the 17th to 19th centuries. The handmade tiles, characteristic of most Fanø homes, are usually blue and white, and depict everything from Bible stories and ships at sea to frolicking children. The restaurant is a favorite among locals, who gather around the wooden tables to tuck into traditional Danish fare, including smørrebrød and pepper steak topped with a cognac sauce. Round out the meal with a taste of their specialty drink, a potent aquavit flavored with orange, vanilla, or coffee beans. In summer, local musicians perform traditional Fanø folk music on the violin, guitar, bagpipe, and harmonica. Inquire at the tourist office for a schedule. ⊠ *Sønderland 1* ☎ *75/16–40–25* ⊕ *www.nanas-stue.dk* ☐ *AE, MC, V* ◯ *Closed Mon. Aug.–Sept.; closed Mon.–Thurs. Oct.–May.*

★ **$$$** ✕☐ **Sønderho Kro.** A member of the Relais & Chateaux collection of small hotels, this thatch-roof inn built in 1722 in the heart of Sønderho is one of Jutland's finest. Its charm has been preserved with painted doors and beamed ceilings, and mahogany floors and new carpeting were laid in 2003. Rooms are jazzed up with four-poster beds, elegant tapestries, and gauzy curtains. The French-Danish restaurant serves excellent seafood, with set menus less expensive on weeknights. ✉ *Kropl. 11, DK–6720 Sønderho* ☎ *75/16–40–09* 🖷 *75/16–43–85* ⊕ *www. sonderhokro.dk* ⇆ *14 rooms* ⟨ *Restaurant, some pets allowed* ⊟ *AE, DC, MC, V* ☉ *Closed Feb. and weekdays Nov.–Jan.*

$ 🏨 **Fanø Krogaard.** About a block away from the Nordby ferry dock is this small hotel which feels very local; kind of a neighborhood place where relatives of the islanders might stay when visiting for a family celebration. It does have history, though: it was built in 1664, and is one of the country's oldest inns to have received a royal warrant. All the guest rooms are about the same size, decorated in a nautical theme. Ask for Room 1, which has the best view of the harbor area; Room 11 is a larger junior suite, also with a sea view. A busy terrace bar rocks in summer, with live music on Saturday. ✉ *Langelinie 11, DK–6720* ☎ *75/16–20–52* 🖷 *75/16–23–00* ⊕ *www.fanokrogaard.dk* ⇆ *17 rooms* ⟨ *Restaurant, bar* ⊟ *V.*

¢–$ 🏨 **Kromanns Fiskerestaurant & Hotel.** It's easy to dismiss the unassuming seafood-only restaurant of this establishment, but above it are four cheery, large double guest rooms, complete with DVD players, balconies, and, for no apparent reason, giant teddy bears. There's a sink in each room for washing up, and very modern shared bathrooms down the hall. It's a reasonably priced option on this end of the island, where rates tend to be steep. ✉ *Sønderho* ☎ *75/16–44–45* 🖷 *75/16–43–26* ⇆ *4 rooms* ⟨ *Restaurant, café, bar* ⊟ *No credit cards.*

South Jutland A to Z

AIRPORTS & TRANSFERS
Billund Airport, 2 km (1 mi) southwest of downtown, is the largest in Jutland and on the arrival end of flights from major European, Scandinavian, and Danish airports. It's a good alternative to Copenhagen Airport if you are flying in from another European city and want to arrive in the center of Jutland.

🛈 Info **Billund Airport** ☎ 76/50–50–50 ⊕ www.billund-airport.com.

TRANSFERS From Billund Airport there are buses to Esbjerg and Kolding. Buses leave for Esbjerg roughly every half hour from 6 AM to 8 PM daily. Buses to Kolding leave the airport regularly from 6:30 AM to 9:45 PM.

It's 60 km to Esbjerg and 41 km to Kolding, so taking a regular taxi is a very expensive option. Limousines are actually a better option if you don't want to take the bus; they can be ordered from Give Taxa in Billund up to three hours in advance.

🛈 **Give Taxa** ☎ 75/35–35–06 ⊕ www.billundgivetaxa.dk.

BIKE TRAVEL
Probably the best tourism guide to help you cycle in the south and southeastern part of Jutland is from the area's tourism office. (See ⊕ www. cycling.sydjylland.com.) The whole peninsula has scores of bike paths, and many highways also have cycle lanes. Keep in mind that distances

feel much longer here than elsewhere in the country, and that even a few humble hills are a challenge for children and novice cyclists. The center of this area is distinguished by long subglacial stream trenches, large forests, and lakes; and the southeast has typical fjord landscapes and old market towns. Basically, there is a network of more than 2,500 km (1,550 mi) of bicycling routes, containing over one-fifth of all the bike routes in Denmark.

In South Jutland you may want to choose one of the special routes. The newest to open in May 2005 is along the Danish-German border: 130 km (56 mi) that weave through the varied landscapes and cultural aspects of both countries. Every 3 km (2 mi) you'll pass an information display that has a map and information about the uniqueness of that area. Currently a free guidebook on this route is available in Danish and German only. For more information, go to ⊕ www.graenseruten.dk.

Package holidays for cyclists are offered by the Haderslev Tourist Office and include accommodation, daily breakfast, maps, baggage assistance, and access to a service hotline. Trips last from four nights to seven nights. The costs, which do not include bike rental, are from DKr 2,150 to DKr 3,550 (per person, double occupancy). Bikes usually rent for about DKr 300 per week or DKr 50 per day.

🚩 **Haderslev Tourism Information Office** ⊠ Honnørkajen 1, DK-6100 Haderslev ☎ 74/52-55-50 ⊕ www.cycling.sydjylland.com.

BOAT & FERRY TRAVEL
Scandinavian Seaways links England's Harwich to Esbjerg.
🚩 **Scandinavian Seaways** ☎ 79/17-79-17 Esbjerg, 33/42-30-00 Copenhagen ⊕ www.dfdsseaways.dk.

BUS TRAVEL
Bus and train travel inside Denmark are made more convenient through Bus/Tog Samarbejde, a comprehensive route and schedule information source. Bus tickets are usually sold on board the buses immediately before departure. Ask about discounts for children, senior citizens, and groups.

Intercity buses are punctual and slightly cheaper but slower than trains. You can buy tickets on the bus and pay according to destination. For schedules and fares, call the local tourist office, as a network of different bus companies covers the peninsula. As there are several bus companies in the country, and often you have to take a ferry, or a train, your best bet in planning an itinerary in South Jutland is to go to ⊕ www.rejseplanen.dk, which will allow you to type in your departure point and arrival point, and will calculate the best way to get there, buses included. Should you want to go by bus only to the north, get on one of the Thinggaard buses in Esbjerg, which will take you all the way to Frederikshavn, with stops in Viborg (north-central) and Aalborg (north). A one-way ticket between Esbjerg and Frederikshavn costs around DKr 245.

Abildskou buses travel between Kastrup Airport on Zealand to Ebeltoft and Århus, in Jutland, but this is more the central part of the peninsula (the train and bus stations in Århus have connections to points south).

The trip lasts about 3 hours and 45 minutes, similar to the train; a one-way ticket is DKr 230.

Schedules for most bus travel within towns are posted at all bus stops, and fares are usually about DKr 15.

🇩Abildskou ⊠ Graham Bellsvej 40, Århus ☎ 70/21-08-88 ⊕ www.abildskou.dk. **Bus/ Tog Samarbejde** ⊕ www.rejseplan.dk. **Thinggaard Bus** ☎ 70/10-00-20 ⊕ www. thinggaard-bus.dk.

CAR TRAVEL

Although train and bus connections are excellent, sites and towns in Jutland are widely dispersed, and the peninsula is best explored by car. Whether you decide to take speedy, modern highways or winding old roads, traffic is virtually nonexistent.

Getting around Denmark these days is much easier than in the past, thanks to bridges that connect the kingdom to both Sweden and the Continent; that said, it's best to confirm all passage with either a local tourist board or FDM before setting out, to avoid confusion caused by ferry mergers and discontinued routes. Although there are several ferry connections to other parts of Denmark and Europe, most travelers drive north from Germany, or arrive from the islands of Zealand or Funen. Ferry prices can get steep, and vary according to the size of the vehicle and the number of passengers.

From Copenhagen or elsewhere on Zealand you can drive the approximately 110 km (69 mi) across the island, then cross the world's second-longest suspension bridge, the Storebæltsbro (Great Belt Bridge), to Knudshoved. You then drive the 85 km (53 mi) across Funen and cross from Middelfart to Fredericia, Jutland, over the Lillebæltsbro (Little Belt Bridge). There are more choices, since two bridges link Middelfart to Fredericia. The older, lower bridge (2 km [1 mi]) follows Route 161, whereas the newer suspension bridge (1 km [½ mi]) on E20 is faster. Driving is at a leisurely pace between the small towns of southern Jutland. You won't see many other vehicles, but there are very few passing lanes, so take extreme care when passing.

🇩FDM ☎ 70/11-60-11.

EMERGENCIES

For ambulance, fire, or police anywhere in Denmark, dial 112. You can contact local pharmacies in Kolding, Haderslev, or Sønderborg for information on emergency doctors.

🇩Aalborg ⊠ Budolfi Apotek, Alg. 60 ☎ 98/12-06-77. **Århus** ⊠ Løve Apoteket, Store Torv 5 ☎ 86/12-00-22. **Kolding** ☎ 75/72-78-78 for medical emergencies, 75/53-96-96 for dental emergencies. **Sønderborg Jernbane Pharmacy** ⊠ Jernbanegade 10 ☎ 74/ 42-35-02

SPORTS & THE OUTDOORS

CANOEING Tønder and the surrounding area may have the best canoeing in the south. You can rent a canoe for one day or several days and paddle along the scenic river system. Contact Tønder Kanoudlejning for more information; note that at this writing, the Web site is only in Danish.

🇩Tønder Kanoudlejning ☎ 74/72-42-50 ⊕ www.vidaa-kano.dk.

FISHING   The fishing (mostly referred to in Denmark as "angling") season is between April 1 and October 31. A 90-km (81-mi) river system awaits in the Tønder area, for example, on the Vidåen River. You must have a fishing license, available at all post offices, for the day or by the week. Check with the local tourist office where you are staying for complete details.

TOURS
Guided tours are few and far between, although some local tourism offices do provide them. Check with the individual city tourism offices for tips, reservations, and brochures that describe walking tours and scenic routes.

TRAIN TRAVEL
DSB makes hourly runs from Copenhagen to Jutland, and Kolding is an obvious choice to begin exploring the southern part of the peninsula. The trip takes only 2 hours and 10 minutes. There are a variety of train passes that can be purchased outside Denmark for use in the country, such as ScanRail and Eurail. A one-way trip from the main station in Copenhagen to Kolding's main station is DKr 269.
⌘ DSB ☎ 70/13–14–15 ⊕ www.dsb.dk.

VISITOR INFORMATION
⌘ South and Southeast Jutland Tourist Information ☎ 75/83–59–99 🖶 75/83–45–67 ⊕ www.visitsouth-eastjutland.com. **Esbjerg** ✉ Skoleg. 33 ☎ 75/12–55–99 🖶 75/12–27–67 ⊕ www.visitesbjerg.com. **Fanø** ✉ Færgevej 1, Nordby ☎ 75/16–26–00 🖶 75/16–29–03 ⊕ www.fanoeturistbureau.dk. **Haderslev Tourist Office** ✉ Honnørkajen 1 ☎ 74/52–55–50 ⊕ www.haderslev-turist.dk. **Kolding** ✉ Akseltorv 8 ☎ 76/33–21–00 🖶 76–33–21–20 ⊕ www.visitkolding.dk. **Ribe** ✉ Torvet 3 ☎ 75/42–15–00 🖶 75/42–40–78 ⊕ www.ribetourist.dk. **Rømø** ✉ Havnebyvej 30 ☎ 74/75–51–30 🖶 74/75–50–31 ⊕ www.romo.dk. **Sønderborg Turistbureau** ✉ Rådhustorvet 7 ☎ 74/42–35–55 ⊕ www.visitsonderberg.com. **Tønder** ✉ Torvet 1 ☎ 74/72–12–20 🖶 74/72–09–00 ⊕ www.visittonder.dk.

Central Jutland

5

WORD OF MOUTH

"We rented a house near Århus one summer. You must definitely see the museum that houses the bog man—astounding! We also loved the beaches and the fact that in many towns the town crier sang the town's news every night at sundown, which was often 11 PM."

—StCirq

Updated by
Bruce Bishop

THE CENTRAL PART OF DENMARK'S GRAND PENINSULA includes Billund, the heartland of the country; the Danish Lake District, the stuff of summer dreams with lakes and rivers meandering into each other; and the youthful city of Århus, Denmark's second largest.

Billund is literally the center of the country and a figurative embodiment of the fun-loving soul of the Dane—it's the home of the world-famous Legoland. On the west coast is Ringkøbing, a centuries-old town and county that has a strip of land called Holmsland, which sits between the Ringkøbing fjord and the North Sea, with calm waters on one side, rough surf on the other.

Almost directly across the peninsula on the east coast is Ebeltoft, which has well-preserved houses, cobblestone streets, and interesting shops, with several featuring glass artists. A bit farther inland the Danish Lake District starts with Silkeborg, a peaceful little town where the phrase "traffic jam" is completely unknown. This area has more lakes than anywhere else in the country, including Denmark's third-largest, Mossø; the longest river in Denmark, the Gudenå, intersects this district.

Slightly north of Silkeborg is Viborg, with its medieval town center, nearby limestone mines, and wonderful canoeing. Randers, also in the east-central area of Jutland, has its off-the-beaten track charms, including a huge biosphere zoo/rain forest, and, well, the largest Elvis Presley museum outside the United States.

Rounding out central Jutland is Århus, where old and new mix effortlessly, nightlife is de rigueur, and the art scene flourishes.

WHAT IT COSTS In Kroner				
$$$$	**$$$**	**$$**	**$**	**¢**
RESTAURANTS	over 180	141–180	121–140	90–120	under 90
HOTELS	over 1,500	1,200–1,500	1,000–1,200	700–1,000	under 700

Restaurant prices are for a main course at dinner. Hotel prices are for two people in a standard double room, including service charge and tax.

Billund

❶ *101 km (63 mi) southwest of Århus.*

Billund is the site of Denmark's second-biggest tourist attraction outside Copenhagen: Legoland. The son of the founder of the Lego Company, Godtfred Christiansen, invented the Lego toy brick in Billund in 1949; today the Lego Company employs 8,000 people (3,000 of whom work in Billund). Over the years the company has manufactured more than 375 billion Lego bricks, all of which trace back to the modest facilities of the family home which still stands on Main Street here. Billund has grown exponentially with the Lego success, and today boasts its own international airport (constructed by Lego and then given to the community) and a large community center (also donated by Lego). However, outside of Legoland there's not much to keep you here—the

Numbers in the text correspond to numbers in the margin and on the Central Jutland map.

If you have
3 days
You may want to base yourself in **Århus ⑦** and make your way around the area from there. Take in that city and all its sights, including the new modern art museum, and then find your way to **Billund ①** the next morning to experience Legoland on your second day. Then get to **Silkeborg ⑤** if you want to immerse yourself in a peaceful river ride, or head to **Randers ⑥** instead and take in the biosphere and have dinner at Hotel Randers. Get back to Århus that night, have one last nightcap in one of the city's many bars or pubs, and leave the next morning by noon.

5

---

bank in town is larger than the town hall, and you're in and out of the little metropolis before you know it.

Fodor'sChoice
★

At the amazing **Legoland** everything is constructed from Lego bricks—45 million of them. Among its incredible structures are scaled-down versions of cities and villages from around the world ("Miniland"), with working harbors and airports; the Statue of Liberty; a statue of Sitting Bull; Mt. Rushmore; a safari park; and Pirate Land. Grown-ups might marvel at toys from pre-Lego days, the most exquisite of which is Titania's Palace, a sumptuous dollhouse built between 1907 and 1922 by Sir Neville Wilkinson for his daughter. The 18 rooms and salons contain hand-carved mahogany furniture, and 3,000 tiny works of art and miniatures from around the world.

Some of the park's newer attractions are more interactive than the impressive constructions. The Falck Fire Brigade, for example, allows a family or group to race eight mini fire engines. The Power Builder Robots allow children and adults to sit inside robots as they program their own ride. Another high-tech perk: parents can feel safe if their child wanders off by renting a Kidspotter wristband, a device connected to a rented mobile phone that allows you to find your child quickly within the large park.

The Lego empire has expanded: the company built other parks in Windsor, England (near London), in 1996; in Carlsbad, California, in 1999; and in Günzburg, Germany, in 2002. Danes maintain that theirs, the original, will always be the best. The park also has a massive theme building–ride–restaurant extravaganza that's much better experienced than described. It all takes place within the massive Castleland, where guests arrive via a serpentine dragon ride. Most everything inside is made of the ubiquitous bricks, including the wizards and warlocks, dragons, and knights that inhabit it. At the Knight's Barbecue, waiters in Middle Ages garb hustle skewered haunches of beef, "loooong sausages," and typical fare of the period.

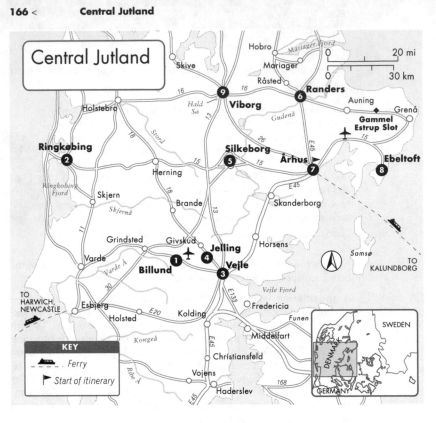

Due to the popularity of this attraction, lines at the entrance can be quite long; however, they do move relatively fast and seem to be well organized. ⊠ *Normarksvej 9* ☎ *75/33–13–33* ⊕ *www.legoland.dk* ⊠ *DKr 185* ☉ *Apr., May, Sept., and Oct., weekdays 10–6, weekends 10–8; June and late Aug., daily 10–8; July–mid-Aug., daily 10–9.*

Sculpturepark Billund is a lovely park, leading from Legoland to the town center, and taking about a half hour to walk. There are 10 permanent sculptures positioned along the path, created by some of Denmark's leading sculptors, and six new and different ones are added each summer. Benches are scattered throughout, making it a nice spot for an impromptu picnic. ⊠ *Across from Legoland Village* ⊠ *Free* ☉ *Daily.*

Where to Stay & Eat

$ ✕ **The Highlander.** If being in a theme park all day puts you in the mood for a good Scotch (or just a beer), head over to this popular pub. The grub is also reminiscent of Scotland's, with UK standards such as fish-and-chips. There's live music on Thursday and Saturday. ⊠ *Rådhuscentret 3* ☎ *75/35–44–22* ⊟ *MC, V.*

$$$–$$$$ ☷ **Hotel Legoland.** It may be a bit pricier than area hotels, but Hotel Legoland is inside Legoland Village, and your room rate includes two days' admission to the park, breakfast, and access to Legoland through the hotel, so you avoid the long lines at the park entrance. The colorful guest rooms overlook all the action. This hotel is beyond kid-friendly: pictograms outside each room help children identify which room they are in, bathrooms are kid-friendly, and rooms include the requisite Legos for kids of all ages to play with. The restaurant serves surprisingly good meals, and, at lunch, a children's buffet is also available. The fitness center is one of the best of any hotel in Jutland, perhaps necessarily installed for harried parents and the many conventioneers who also frequent the hotel. ⊠ *Aastvej 10, DK–7190* ☎ *75/33–12–44* 🖷 *75/ 35–38–10* ⊕ *www.hotellegoland.dk* 🛏 *176 rooms* ♨ *Restaurant, bar, pool, gym, meeting rooms* ☰ *AE, DC, MC, V* ⦿ *BP.*

$$–$$$$ 🔲 **Hotel Propellen.** Very close to the airport (and to Legoland), this stylish hotel is owned by the Danish Air Pilots Union; hence the name. Rooms are tastefully furnished, if not as fun as Hotel Legoland. There is a special summer menu in the restaurant, including an all-you-can-eat ice-cream bar. Note that there's a DKr 30 discount if you pay in cash. ⊠ *Nordmarksvej 3, DK–7190 Billund* ☎ *75/33–81–33* 🖷 *75/35–33–62* ⊕ *www.propellen.dk* 🛏 *91 rooms, 3 suites* ♨ *Restaurant, indoor pool, sauna, billiards, Ping-Pong, bar, playground, meeting rooms* ☰ *AE, DC, MC, V* ⦿ *BP.*

$–$$ 🔲 **Hotel Svanen.** This is a basic motel-style establishment, but recent refurbishments have left its rooms fresher and more modernized (free Wi-Fi) than you'd expect. There are very good weekend specials, which include dinner. It's within walking distance of Legoland. ⊠ *Nordmarksvej 8, DK–7190 Billund* ☎ *75/33–28–33* 🖷 *75/35–35–15* ⊕ *www.hotelsvanen. dk* 🛏 *50 rooms* ♨ *Restaurant, bar, playground* ☰ *DC, MC, V* ⊗ *Closed Dec. 22–Jan. 2* ⦿ *BP.*

Ringkøbing

❷ *35 km (22 mi) north of Esbjerg, 100 km (62 mi) west of Århus*

Though it's a pretty medieval town, founded in the 13th century, Ringkøbing's claim to fame is purely thanks to Mother Nature. A thin strip of land, Holmsland, separates the calm waters of the Ringkøbing Fjord with the rough-and-tumble North Sea. If you climb Troldbjerg Hill (by following wheelchair-friendly pathways), you will end up admiring the view over Hvide Sande, Ringkøbing Fjord, and the North Sea, all at the same time.

The shallow waters of the fjord and the best wind statistics in Denmark make it the windsurfing capital of central Jutland. The North Sea's winds are not mild, thereby helping this sport immeasurably, as well as attracting all styles of surfing, including freestyle, free ride, racing, and kite.

The county of Ringkøbing is known for its cultural pursuits. Holstebro is home to the Odin Theatre and the Peter Schaufuss Ballet, which is the only Danish ballet company outside Copenhagen. The ballet company puts on what is known as "dansicals," which are musicals with dance and movement instead of singing.

The well-kept and preserved town center can be a relaxing place to visit, particularly in summer, when jazz concerts take place outdoors. Trendy boutiques and cafés line the square, which is dominated by the parish church with the tourist office next door.

Ringkøbing Church is the oldest building in town, dating back to the 14th century, with a unique feature and its own controversy, of sorts. The tower is broader at the top than at the bottom, perhaps the result of an architectural slight-of-hand. In 1995–96 major renovations of the interior and restoration of all historic furnishings took place. The church elders felt, according to one local historian, that the centuries-old oil painting of Christ with his Apostles was too "dull," so they purchased a new painting—a semiabstract—by artist Arne Hagen Sørensen, which depicts the hand of God cradling civilization. Then, in another bold move they bought a beautiful crystal-and-glass baptismal font designed by the same artist and sculpted by Per Hebesgaard. Both painting and font are proudly displayed at the front altar, which is to some an exciting nod to contemporary Danish design, and to others, an affront to the historic interior of the church. The original painting is still on display, but just not as prominently. The organ from 1654 is preserved, but is now used almost exclusively for the summer concerts that are a permanent feature of the town's music life. ⊠ *Town Sq.* ☎ *97/32–02–17* ⊙ *Daily 10–5.*

If you have a penchant for local history and archaeology, stop by the **Ringkøbing Museum**, where you will also find an extensive collection on arctic explorer Mylius Eriksen. ⊠ *Kongevejen 1* ☎ *97/32–16–15* 🖃 *Dkr 30* ⊙ *Mid-Jun.–Aug., daily 11–5; Sept.–mid-Jun., Mon.–Thurs. 11–4, weekends 1–4.*

Gallery Lodberg is a bit outside town, but here you can get a flavor of a local artist's interpretation of west Jutland and its scenic vistas. In oil paintings and watercolors, Svend Lodberg magically re-creates the beauty of the area. ⊠ *Borkvej 14* ☎ *97/33–00–21* ⊕ *www.s-lodberg. dk* ⊙ *Mon.–Sat. 10–5.*

Where to Stay & Eat

$–$$$
Fodor'sChoice
★

✕🖃 **Hotel Fjordgården.** This friendly hotel, a 10-minute walk from the town square into a residential neighborhood, is probably the best bet for both food and lodging in this area. Built in the mid-1960s, the hotel is remarkably up-to-date with large rooms sleeping up to four; new abstract Danish paintings adorning the public areas and rooms; and a pool complex keeps both kids and adults happy. The restaurant serves a small selection of à la carte dishes and a daily menu with two to four courses and wine pairings (at a separate cost). The cream of cauliflower soup with a flan of scallops, and the pork fillet stuffed with guinea fowl are standouts. Some French wines can be purchased by the half bottle. ⊠ *Vesterkær 28* ☎ *97/32–14–00* 🖶 *97/32–47–60* ⊕ *www. hotelfjordgaarden.dk* ⇋ *98 rooms* ♨ *Restaurant, Wi-Fi, pool, hot tub, sauna, bar, meeting rooms* ▤ *AE, DC, MC, V* ℟ *BP.*

$
🖃 **Hotel Ringkøbing.** This is supposed to be the second-oldest building in town—it's certainly the most central. The half-timber building has an English-style pub, the Watchman's Pub, so named for the night watchmen who regale people with song between 10 PM and midnight.

A few of the rooms are in this main building, while other, newer ones are in a building a few doors away. An inviting patio spills out into the square and the general feeling is more that of an inn, rather than a hotel. ☒ *Torvet 18* ☎ *97/32–00–11* 🖹 *97/32–18–72* ⊕ *www.hotelringkobing. dk* ⊷ *30 rooms* ⚇ *Restaurant, bar* ☰ *MC, V* ⦿ *BP.*

Vejle

❸ *40 km (25 mi) east of Billund, 73 km (46 mi) southwest of Århus.*

Vejle is beautifully positioned on a fjord on the east coast, amid forest-clad hills. It's a bustling little city and has its own art museum, a terrific pedestrian street for shopping, and quick access to the countryside. You can hear the time of day chiming on the old **Dominican monastery clock**; the clock remains, but the monastery long ago gave way to the town's imposing 19th-century city hall.

In the town center, at Kirke Torvet, is **Skt. Nikolai Kirke** (St. Nicholas Church). In the left arm of the cross-shape church, lying in a glass Empire-style coffin, is the body of a bog woman found preserved in a peat marsh in 1835; she dates from 500 BC. The church walls contain the skulls of 23 thieves executed in the 17th century. ☒ *Kirke Torvet* ☎ *75/ 82–41–39* ⊙ *May–Sept., weekdays 9–5, Sat. 9–noon, Sun. 9–11:30.*

Where to Stay

$$$$ 🏨 **Munkebjerg Hotel.** Seven kilometers (4½ mi) southeast of town and surrounded by a thick beech forest and majestic views of the Vejle Fjord, this elegant hotel attracts guests who value their privacy. Beyond the rustic lobby, rooms furnished in blond pine and soft green overlook the forest. There are also two top-notch French-Danish restaurants and a swank casino. ☒ *Munkebjergvej 125, DK–7100* ☎ *75/42–85–00* 🖹 *75/72–08–86* ⊕ *www.munkebjerg.dk* ⊷ *7 rooms, 2 suites* ⚇ *3 restaurants, cafeteria, tennis court, indoor pool, gym, sauna, bar, casino, meeting room, some pets allowed, no-smoking rooms* ☰ *AE, DC, MC, V.*

$ 🏨 **Park Hotel.** The Park is centrally located and offers very spacious rooms considering its small stature. The pleasant service caps off an overall enjoyable experience, and ensures return visits from its patrons. A bountiful breakfast is included in the price, and the restaurant is good though perhaps a bit thin on variety. ☒ *Orla Lehmannsg. 5, DK–7100* ☎ *75/ 82–24–66* 🖹 *75/72–05–39* ⊕ *www.park-hotel.dk* ⊷ *32 rooms* ⚇ *Restaurant, bar, some pets allowed* ☰ *AE, DC, MC, V.*

Nightlife

The casino at the **Munkebjerg Hotel** (☒ Munkebjergvej 125 ☎ 75/ 72–35–00) has blackjack, roulette, baccarat, and slot machines.

Jelling

❹ *10 km (6 mi) northwest of Vejle (via Rte. 18), 83 km (52 mi) southwest of Århus.*

Two 10th-century burial mounds mark the seat of King Gorm and his wife Thyra here. Between the mounds are two **Runestener** (runic stones), one of which is Denmark's certificate of baptism, showing the oldest known figure of Christ in Scandinavia. The inscription explains that the stone was erected by Gorm's son, King Harald Bluetooth, who brought Christianity to the Danes in 960. This is where the power of the Danish king and state developed between 200 and 1000 A.D.

The most scenic way to get to Jelling is via the **vintage steam train** that runs from Vejle in summer. The journey passes through the striking Grejsdal Valley, the longest gorge in Denmark. The train's engine is from a 1920 branch-line train, and the cars are from 1898 to 1916. Call the tourist office for schedules.

Silkeborg

⑤ *60 km (38 mi) north of Jelling, 43 km (27 mi) west of Århus.*

At the banks of the River Gudenå begins Jutland's Lake District. Stretching southeast from Silkeborg to Skanderborg, the area contains some of Denmark's loveliest scenery and most of its meager mountains, including the 438-foot **Himmelbjerget,** at Julsø (Lake Jul), 15 km (10 mi) southeast of Silkeborg. You can climb the narrow paths through the heather and trees to the top, where an 80-foot tower stands sentinel. It was placed there on Constitution Day in 1875 in memory of King Frederik VII.

In the past few years, conventioneers from medical and other professions, perhaps fatigued with always meeting in Copenhagen, have "discovered" Silkeborg, partly due to the new Radisson SAS Hotel here. Therefore, this town has become as progressive as it is scenic, with a convention center, restaurants, a multiplex cinema, and lively bars lining the river's edge. Across the water is a shopping area with 200 specialty stores that bustles during the day. On Saturday it turns into the largest marketplace in central Jutland, and often has jazz concerts.

Indeed, in late June jazz-lovers from all over Europe come to celebrate Silkeborg's **Riverboat Jazz Festival** (☎ 86/80–16–17 ⊕ www.riverboat. dk), with live jazz performed on indoor and outdoor stages over four days. Jazz styles are varied: New Orleans, Dixieland, swing, street parade, gospel, big band, and jam sessions. Although concerts are scattered throughout the town, four large tents—harborside, on Bindslevs Plads, and on the main square—comprise the main stages; concerts in these tents are always free. Each year the program includes at least 65 bands and solo artists from Denmark and the rest of the world. Attendance is consistent at 40,000–45,000 people, so be sure to reserve lodgings in advance.

The best way to explore the Lake District is by water, as the Gudenå winds its way some 160 km (100 mi) through lakes and wooded hillsides down to the sea. Take one of the excursion boats or the world's last coal-fired paddle steamer, *Hjejlen,* which departs in summer (mid-June through August) from Silkeborg Harbor. Since 1861 it has paddled its way through narrow stretches of fjord, where the treetops meet overhead, to the foot of the Himmelbjerget. ⊠ *Havnen* ☎ *86/82–07–66* ⊕ *www.hjejlen.com* ⊠ *DKr 100.*

If you're at all interested in **canoeing,** either for a day or week, this is definitely an area in which to do it. Check out the information available at the local tourist office. (*See* Central Jutland A to Z)

The **Silkeborg Museum** is not only the oldest building in the town, dating from 1767, it houses the city's main attractions: the 2,400-year-old Tollund Man and Elling Girl, two bog people preserved by the chemicals in the soil and water. Discovered in 1950, the Tollund Man remains the best-preserved human face from the Iron Age. He was killed by strangulation—the noose remains around his neck—with a day's worth of stubble that can still be seen on his hauntingly serene face. The Elling Woman or Girl was found in 1938 about 200 feet from where Tollund Man came to light 12 years later. Elling Woman was wrapped in a sheepskin cape, and another covered her legs and feet. She was also hanged with a leather thong, which left a V-shaped furrow that is clearly visible in her neck. Her death occurred in the pre-Roman Iron Age, between 350 and 100 B.C. The museum also showcases trades made famous in the area, such as clog and wheel making, and pottery and papermaking. It also has a fine collection of old Danish glass, a café, and a gift shop. ⊠ *Hovedgårdsvej 7* ☎ *86/82–14–99* ⊕ *www.silkeborgmuseum. dk* ▣ *DKr 40* ⊗ *May–mid-Oct., daily 10–5; mid-Oct.–Apr., Wed. and weekends noon–4.*

A little less grisly and much more eclectic is the **Silkeborg Museum of Art,** which holds Danish artist Asger Jorn's collection of more than 5,000 works by 150 international artists, including Max Ernst, Picabia, Le Corbusier, and many Danish contemporaries, such as Bjerke Petersen, Carl-Henning Pedersen, and Egill Jacobsen. Jorn's own works number around 100, in various mediums (paintings, ceramics, drawings, and graphics). ⊠ *Gudenåvej 7-9* ☎ *86/82–53–88* ⊕ *www.silkeborgkunstmuseum.dk* ⊗ *Apr.–Oct., daily 10–5.*

The **Art Centre Silkeborg Spa** only used to be a spa; now it's a gallery devoted to modern art with changing exhibitions (2005 exhibits featured works by Thai and Korean artists). However, people sometimes come here just for the serene location by Ørnsø Lake. The park, which contains a few sculptures, is always open, even if the center is closed. ⊠ *Gjessøvej 40* ☎ *86/81–63–29* ⊕ *www.silkebordbad.dk* ▣ *DKr 45* ⊗ *Centre May–Sept., Tues.–Sun. 10–5.*

One of the everyday things in life we often take for granted is paper, the focus of Silkeborg's **Papirmuseet Bikuben** (Paper Museum), which is in the former town mill where handmade paper was made. The museum shows why Silkeborg was put on the map as a paper-producing town in 1846; has exhibits on watermarks and molds and machine-made paper; and explains how pulp is made into paper. You can even make your own— what else?—paper. ⊠ *Smedebakken 1* ☎ *86/85–45–64* ⊕ *www. papirmuseet.dk* ▣ *DKr 20* ⊗ *July and Aug., daily noon–5.*

At the **Aqua Ferskvands Akvarium** (Aqua Aquarium), which is the largest freshwater aquarium in northern Europe, you can see beavers, otters, freshwater fish, and other animals in re-creations of their natural habitat. ✉ *Vejlsøvej 55* ☎ *89/21–21–89* ⊕ *www.aqua-ferskvandsakvarium. dk* ☜ *DKr 75* ⊙ *Mid-June.–mid-Sept., daily 10–6.*

Where to Stay & Eat

$$$–$$$$ ✗ **Aalekroen.** Also known as Onkel Peters Hus (Uncle Peter's Place), this spot is noted for its house specialties, fried eel and seafood. The grilled meat dishes are also excellent. This old inn stands at the shore of a scenic lake. ✉ *Julsøvænget 5* ☎ *86/84–60–33* ⊕ *www.aalekroen.dk* ☜ *Reservations essential* ▤ *AE, DC, MC, V* ⊙ *Closed Mon.*

★ $$$–$$$$ ✗▣ **Radisson SAS Hotel Silkeborg.** This is the newest business-class hotel in the country to open outside Copenhagen, and it's deserving of its rapid, excellent reputation. The hotel has been constructed within the main building of the old paper mill on the bank of the river, and is connected to a convention center (Jysk Musik & Teaterhus). Rooms are soothing, with slate-gray and warm yellow tones and relaxing views of the river. The lobby areas, including a swanky bar, have been decorated by Botikken, a popular retail design store, in a minimalist, very Scandinavian look. The Riverside Restaurant, also on the main floor, is thought to be Silkeborg's trendiest dining spot, and the food does not disappoint (though service should be a bit more attentive and polished). The prix-fixe dinner menu changes daily, and half bottles of excellent wines can be ordered. Note that rates are substantially lower on weekends. ✉ *Papirfabrikken 12, DK–8600 Silkeborg* ☎ *88/82–22–22* 🖶 *88/82–22–23* ⊕ *www.radisson.dk* ⇄ *86 rooms, 5 suites* ☜ *Restaurant, in-room broadband, bar, meeting rooms* ▤ *AE, DC, MC, V.*

Randers

6   *73 km (45 mi) from Silkeborg; 35 km (21 mi) from Århus.*

There's something about Randers that makes you want to return to it, to explore further, to discover what makes its people tick. It's the sixth-largest city in the country, with 60,000 people, and yet it comes across as a bit of a small town—in all the right ways. You may hear people refer to it as Crown Jutland (Kronjylland)—a term used by Danish writers and poets of the 18th century, when they wrote about all the beautiful estates that the king owned in the area.

Back in 1302 Randers was granted its municipal charter by King Erik Menved, and since then it's been an important commercial trading center. Streets dating back to the Middle Ages are now pedestrian areas, dotted with many half-timber houses, specialty shops, and outdoor cafés. If you're in town on the first Saturday of the month, be prepared for music, singing, and entertainment in the streets.

If you were to ask someone from Copenhagen what he or she knows about Randers, you might hear it's where 13 highways meet, where there are an inordinate number of beautiful women, where salmon is plentiful, and where gloves are made. And one more thing—isn't it where that big Elvis museum is located?

One of the biggest attractions to be built in Jutland in the past 25 years is located in Randers on the bank of the river Gudenå. The **Randers Regnskov**

(Tropical Zoo) opened in 1996 under the patronage of Princess Alexandra. It has three biospheres, or glass domes, under which a complete zoological garden grows and thrives, complete with indigenous animals from the rain forests of Asia, Africa, and South America. It's almost like invading the territory of these 450 plant species and 200 animals, especially since many of the latter are not in cages or behind glass. And it's pretty exceptional to be able to see an aardvark, a sloth, a lemur, a Jaco parrot, a dwarf marmoset, and numerous other members of the animal kingdom, all in one place. Wear light clothing—temperatures inside the domes are exactly that of a real rain forest. Ask about feeding times. Note that no pets or baby carriages are allowed. The zoo is technically wheelchair accessible, but navigating can be difficult in places. ⊠ *Tørvebryggen 11* ☎ *87/10–99–99* ⊕ *www.randers-regnskov.dk* ⊠ *DKr 95* ⊗ *Mid-June–mid-Aug., daily 10–6; mid-Aug.–mid-June, weekdays 10–4, weekends 10–5.*

Yes, there really is an **Elvis Unlimited Museum** in Randers. And, it's the largest Elvis memorabilia spectacle outside Graceland. Henrik Knudsen, the owner and fan extraordinaire, says that his interest in Elvis's music began in 1977 (when he was 13), at the time of Presley's death, and he hasn't stopped collecting and selling since. He even arranges Elvis tribute concerts in the United States and Denmark. Now, with five full-time employees in this two-story, 2,000-item Elvis department store, much business is done worldwide via the Internet, but in the actual museum one might feel like it's either very cool or very disturbing to see so much Elvis ephemera (including all 75 record album covers, and one of those jumpsuits from the early '70s). ⊠ *Underværket, Stemannsgade 9C* ☎ *86/42–96–96* ⊕ *www.elvispresley.dk* ⊠ *DKr 20* ⊗ *Weekdays 10–5:30, Sat. 10–2.*

The **Randers Kunstmuseum** (Randers Museum of Art) proves that Elvis isn't the end-all, be-all of the city's cultural offerings. Its collection begins with Danish work from 1800 and continues thereafter, including masterpieces from the Danish "golden age" to provocative contemporary pieces. One of the highlights is Icelandic artist Tróndur Patursson's incredible mirror installation, called Cosmic Room, where your image goes on forever. ⊠ *Kulturhuset, Stemannsgade 2* ☎ *86/42–29–22* ⊕ *www.randerskunstmuseum.dk* ⊠ *DKr 30* ⊗ *Tues.–Sun. 11–5.*

You don't need a tour guide in Randers if you want to get a great feel for the old town—just follow the **Star Route** (⊠ Randers Turistbureau, Tørvebryggen 12 ☎ 86/42–44–77 ⊕ www.visitranders.com), which is 15 strategically placed plaques in the shape of stars in the sidewalks (or pedestrian streets) that point you to places of cultural and historical interest. The route is only 2½-km (1½-mi) long, and it's accessible to wheelchairs; it runs in a circuit, so you can start and finish wherever you want. Make sure you pick up a brochure in English (which explains all the stars/sites) from the local tourist office before you begin your walk.

Where to Stay

$–$$$ 🏨 **Hotel Randers.** Without any doubt, this hotel has become a reason to
Fodor'sChoice   visit Randers in and of itself, because of its history, charm, comfort, and
★   great service. This is the epitome of the great, family-owned and -op-

erated hotel, where tradition, character, and quiet pride have endeared the place to everyone from Danish monarchs to world-weary travelers. It opened in 1856, and Hans Christian Andersen was an early guest. In 1956 Paul Gauguin's son, sculptor and artist Jean René Gauguin, decorated the main dining room and created four ceramic sculptures of mythological figures for the hotel, which are still in the dining room today. The stories are endless: during the German occupation Danish resistance fighters hid seven machine guns and ammunition behind false walls in the basement bar, which weren't discovered until 1970 when the bar was being refurbished. The art deco decor in the lobby, guest room No. 311, and the restaurant look as if they belong in a museum, and they probably do. All the guest rooms are roomy, and have elegant wall coverings and artwork. The included breakfast in the stunning Banquet Room with its 1927 decor and Venetian chandeliers may be worth the price of the room alone. But what mostly affects the visitor and guest here is the love the owner, Sonja Mathisen, has for the hotel. As she tells visitors, "We do not modernize, but renovate so that we can keep the soul of the hotel." ⊠ *Torvegade 11* ☎ *86/42–34–22* ⧉ *86/40–15–86* ⊕ *www. hotel-randers.dk* ⇝ *67 rooms, 12 suites* ⌂ *Restaurant, bar, meeting rooms* ▤ *AE, MC, V* ⟦◎⟧ *BP.*

Århus

❼ *40 km (24 mi) east of Silkeborg.*

Århus is Denmark's second-largest city, and, with its funky arts and college community, one of the country's most pleasant. Cutting through the center of town is a canal called the Århus Å (Århus Creek). It used to run underground, but was uncovered a few years ago. Since then, an amalgam of bars, cafés, and restaurants has sprouted along its banks, creating one of Denmark's most lively thoroughfares. At all hours of the day and night this waterfront strip is abuzz with crowds that hang out on the outdoor terraces and steps that lead down to the creek.

The VisitAarhus tourist office has information about the **Århus Passport,** which includes passage on buses, free or discounted admission to the 12 most popular museums and sites in the city, and tours. A one-day pass is DKr 97, a two-day pass is DKr 121, and a seven-day pass is DKr 171. The passport is also available for purchase at hotels, campgrounds, marinas, the youth hostel, and the Kommune Information at City Hall (Rådhus).

The town comes most alive during the first week of September, when the **Århus Festival** (☎ 89/40–91–91 ⊕ www.aarhusfestuge.dk) begins, combining concerts, theater, and art exhibitions with beer tents and sports. The **Århus International Jazz Festival** bills international and local greats in early or mid-July. In July the **Viking Moot** draws aficionados to the beach below the Museum of Prehistory at Moesgård. Activities and exhibits include market booths, ancient defense techniques, and rides on Viking ships.

The **Rådhus** is probably the most unusual city hall in Denmark. Built in 1941 by noted architects Arne Jacobsen and Erik Møller, the pale Norwegian-marble block building is controversial, but cuts a startling figure when illuminated in the evening. Go to the Kommune Information booth next to the tower entrance to obtain multiride tickets and passport tourist tickets, and to get information on everything connected with traveling by bus in Århus. That office is open from 10 to 5:30 (☎ 89/40–10–10). ⌧ *Park Allé* ☎ *89/40–67–00* ⌦ *City hall DKr 10, tower DKr 5* ☉ *Guided tours (in Danish only) mid-June–early Sept., weekdays at 11; tower tours weekdays at noon and 2.*

Rising gracefully over the center of town, the **Århus Domkirke** (Århus Cathedral) was originally built in 1201 in a Romanesque style, but was later expanded and redesigned into a Gothic cathedral in the 15th century. Its soaring, whitewashed nave is one of the longest in Denmark. The cathedral's highlights include its chalk frescoes, in shades of lavender, yellow, red, and black, that grace the high arches and towering walls. Dating from the Middle Ages, the frescoes depict biblical scenes and the valiant St. George slaying a dragon and saving a maiden princess in distress. Also illustrated is the poignant death of St. Clement, who drowned with an anchor tied around his neck. Nonetheless, he became the patron saint of sailors. Climb the tower for bird's-eye views of the rooftops and thronged streets of Århus. ⌧ *Bispetorv* ☎ *86/20–54–00* ⊕ *www.aarhus-domkirke.dk* ⌦ *Tower DKr 10* ☉ *Jan.–Apr. and Oct.–Dec., Mon.–Sat. 10–3; May–Sept., Mon.–Sat. 9:30–4.*

Århus's 13th-century **Vor Frue Kirken** (Church of Our Lady), formerly attached to a Dominican abbey, has an eerie but interesting crypt church rediscovered in 1955 and dating from 1060. One of the oldest preserved stone churches in Scandinavia, the vaulted space contains a replica of an old Roman crucifix. ⌧ *Frue Kirkepl.* ☎ *86/12–12–43* ⊕ *www.aarhusvorfrue.dk* ☉ *Jan.–Apr., daily 10–2 (Sat. to noon); May–Sept., daily 10–4 (Sat. to 2); Oct.–Dec., daily 10–2 (Sat. to noon).*

★ Don't miss the town's open-air museum, known as **Den Gamle By** (Old Town). It's the only three-star museum outside Copenhagen. Its 75 historic buildings, including 70 half-timber houses, a mill, and millstream, were carefully moved from locations throughout Denmark and meticulously re-created, inside and out. Actors portray people from times past. You can explore the extensive exhibits, and then have a pint in the Beer Cellar or coffee and cake in the garden. ⌧ *Viborgvej 2* ☎ *86/12–31–88* ⊕ *www.dengamleby.dk* ⌦ *DKr 45–DKr 75 depending on season and activities* ☉ *June–Aug., daily 9–6; Apr., May, Sept., and Oct., daily 10–5; Jan., daily 11–3; Feb., Mar., Nov., and Dec., daily 10–4. Grounds always open.*

ARoS Århus Kunstmuseum, the city's newest art museum, was an immediate hit when it opened in April 2004, and 340,000 people passed through its doors in its first nine months of opening. The museum was designed by the Danish architectural firm of Schmidt, Hammer & Lassen and encompasses 19 floors. It may look on the outside like a huge, red, brick cube, but inside it's much more inviting. You're free to wander around in the foyer and go to the café, or browse in the gift shop, or you can buy a ticket to view the four main galleries. To go from one gallery to the next you must cross a footbridge that allows excellent views of the city below. On the top floor there is a restaurant as well as a rooftop patio—a photographer's dream. The art, of course, is paramount, and comprises the museum's own collection of more than 9,000 works dating from 1770 to the present, as well as internationally known visiting exhibits. The unofficial symbol of the museum has turned out to be the giant and lifelike fiberglass sculpture *Boy* by Ron Mueck. ⊠ *Aros Allé 2* 🕾 *87/30–66–00* ⊕ *www.aros.dk* 🖃 *DKr 60* ⊙ *Tues. and Thurs.–Sun. 10–5, Wed. 10–10.*

The **Steno Museum** or the Danish Museum for the History of Science and Medicine, is a culturally based historical museum regarding the development of these two disciplines. Featured among many exhibits over three floors are a medicinal herb garden with 350 different plants, a planetarium seating 57, an operating theater, old x-ray machines, and some of the first Danish calculators from the 1950s. It is located at the southernmost end of the university campus, a short walk from the city center. ⊠ *C. F. Møllers Allé, Bldg. 100* 🕾 *89/42–39–95* ⊕ *www.stenomuseet. dk* 🖃 *DKr 40* ⊙ *Tues.–Fri. 9–4, weekends, 11–4.*

Kvindemuseet I Danmark (Women's Museum in Denmark) has been around since 1984, and is one of a few of its kind in the world. The permanent exhibition, Women's Lives from Prehistoric to Present Times, paints a broad picture of birth, work, learning, and everyday life. The attractive building, originally a town hall from 1857, also contains a nice café. ⊠ *Domkirkeplads 5* 🕾 *86/13–61-44* ⊕ *www.womensmuseum. dk* 🖃 *DKr 30* ⊙ *June–Aug., weekdays 10–5, weekends 11–5; Sept.–May, Tues.–Fri. 10–4, weekends 11–4.*

Just south of the city is **Marselisborg Slot** (Marselisborg Castle), the palatial summer residence of the royal family. The changing of the guard takes place daily at noon when the queen is staying in the palace. When the royal family is away (generally in winter and spring), the palace grounds, including a sumptuous rose garden, are open to the public. Take Bus 1, 8, or 19. ⊠ *Kongevejen 100* 🕾 *No phone* ⊕ *www.kongehuset. dk* 🖃 *Free.*

In a 250-acre forest south of Århus is the **Moesgård Forhistorisk Museum** (Prehistoric Museum), with exhibits on ethnography and archaeology, including the famed Grauballe Man, a 2,000-year-old corpse so well preserved in a bog that scientists could determine his last meal. In fact, when the discoverers of the Grauballe Man stumbled upon him in 1952, they thought he had recently been murdered and called the police. The Forhistorisk vej (Prehistoric Trail) through the forest leads past Stone- and Bronze Age displays to reconstructed houses from Viking times. ⊠ *Moesgård Allé (Bus 6 from center of town)* 🕾 *89/42–11–00* ⊕ *www.moesmus.dk* 🖃 *DKr 45* ⊙ *Apr.–Sept., daily 10–5; Oct.–Mar., Tues.–Sun. 10–4.*

If you are in Århus with children, or simply wish to enjoy a young-at-heart activity, visit the provincial **Tivoli Friheden,** with more than 40 rides and activities, attractive gardens, and restaurants. Pierrot the Clown entertains, and concerts are given by contemporary artists. ⊠ *Skovbrynet* 🕾 *86/14–73–00* ⊕ *www.friheden.dk* 🖃 *DKr 55; rides* cost extra ⊘ *Call or check Web site as opening times vary greatly throughout summer.*

Where to Stay & Eat

$$$–$$$$ ✕ **Restaurant Margueritten.** Tucked into a cobbled courtyard, this cheery restaurant is housed in former stables, which accounts for the low wood-beam ceiling. Well-worn wooden tables and tan walls round out the warm atmosphere. Contemporary Danish fare includes guinea fowl stuffed with tiger shrimp and marinated in tandoori and yogurt, and chicken breast served with Italian ham. In summer the back garden is open all day. ⊠ *Guldsmedg. 20* ☎ *86/19–60–33* ▭ *AE, DC, MC, V* ⊘ *No lunch Sun.*

$$–$$$$ ✕ **Seafood.** Just south of town is Marselis Harbor, a bustling little sail-
Fodor's Choice boat cove surrounded by waterfront restaurants and cafés that draw big
★ crowds on sunny summer weekends. Here you'll find Seafood, one of the best seafood restaurants in Århus. Its signature dish, which draws moans of delight from diners, is a seafood bouillabaisse heaped with tiger prawns, squid, Norwegian lobster, and mussels, and served with aioli on the side. Other dishes include oven-baked catfish with asparagus and warm ginger butter. The restful interior has light-blue walls. ⊠ *Havnevej 44, Marselisborg* ☎ *86/18–56–55* ▭ *AE, DC, MC, V* ⊘ *Closed Sun. Sept.–Apr.*

★ **$$–$$$$** ✕ **Bryggeriet Sct. Clemens.** At this popular pub you can sit among copper kettles and quaff the local brew, which is unfiltered and without additives, just like in the old days. Between the spareribs and Australian steaks, you won't go hungry, either. ⊠ *Kannikeg. 10–12* ☎ *86/13–80–00* ⊕ *www.bryggeriet.dk* ▭ *AE, DC, MC, V.*

$$$ ✕ **Prins Ferdinand.** Sitting on the edge of Old Town, and right next to the entrance of Den Gamle By, this premier Danish-French restaurant is named after the colorful Århus-based Prince Frederik (1792–1863), who was much loved despite his fondness for gambling and carousing about town. Here elegant crystal chandeliers hang over large round tables with crisp linen tablecloths and ceramic plates created by a local artist. Vases of sunflowers brighten the front room. Grilled turbot is topped with a cold salsa of radishes, cucumber, and dill. Cabbage, foie gras, and new potatoes accompany a venison dish. A daily vegetarian option is offered, and might include grilled asparagus with potatoes, olives, and herbs. ⊠ *Viborgvej 2* ☎ *86/12–52–05* ⊕ *www.prinsferdinand.dk* ▭ *AE, DC, MC, V* ⊘ *Closed Sun. and Mon.*

$$$ ✕▭ **Philip.** Occupying a prime spot along the canal, this hotel offers an original—but pricey—concept in lodging. Eight former studio apartments have been converted into luxury suites, each outfitted in its own sumptuous style. Suites have original white wood-beam ceilings, elegant wooden furniture imported from France and Italy, huge gleaming bathrooms, and views of the canal. The plush restaurant, with dark hardwood floors and brass candleholders, serves a blend of cuisines that may include cannelloni stuffed with Serrano ham, Danish feta, and crayfish served with truffles and new potatoes. ⊠ *Åboulevarden 28, DK–8000* ☎ *87/32–14–44* 🖶 *86/12–69–55* ⊕ *www.hotelphilip.dk* ⇋ *8 suites* ⚎ *Restaurant, bar* ▭ *DC, MC, V* ⊘ *Closed Sun.*

★ $$$$ ⊡ **Hotel Royal.** In operation since 1838, Århus's grand hotel has welcomed such greats as musicians Artur Rubinstein and Marian Anderson. Well-heeled guests enter through a stately lobby appointed with sofas, modern paintings, and a winding staircase. Rooms vary in style and decor, but all have velour and brocade furniture and marble bathrooms. ⊠ *Store Torv 4, DK–8100* ☎ *86/12–00–11* 🖷 *86/76–04–04* ⊕ *www. hotelroyal.dk* ⇱ *98 rooms, 7 suites* ⚭ *Restaurant, cafeteria, sauna, bar, casino, some pets allowed* ⊟ *AE, DC, MC, V.*

$ ⊡ **Hotel Guldsmeden.** Small and intimate, this hotel with a personal touch is housed in a renovated 19th-century town house. The soothing rooms are dressed in cool greens and yellows and have teak shelves; two have claw-foot tubs. The sunny garden blooms with flowers in summer, and the outdoor terrace is just the spot to enjoy the organic breakfast of fruit, muesli, toast, and marmalade. The owners also have a penthouse apartment, fully equipped for four, by the waterfront; it's a short walk away. ⊠ *Guldsmedg. 40, DK–8000* ☎ *86/13–45–50* 🖷 *86/ 13–76–76* ⊕ *www.hotelguldsmeden.dk* ⇱ *26 rooms, 20 with bath; 2 suites* ⚭ *Bar, some pets allowed* ⊟ *AE, DC, MC, V.*

¢ ⊡ **Danhostel Århus.** As in all Danish youth and family hostels, the rooms here are clean, bright, and functional. The secluded setting in the woods near the fjord is downright beautiful. Unfortunately, the hostel can get a bit noisy. Guests may use the kitchen. ⊠ *Marienlundsvej 10, DK–8100* ☎ *86/16–72–98* ⊕ *www.aarhus-danhostel.dk* ⇱ *138 beds in 30 shared rooms, 11 with private shower* ⚭ *Dining room* ⊟ *AE, MC, V* ☺ *Closed mid-Dec.–mid-Jan.*

Nightlife & the Arts

There's no better time to visit Århus than during the 10-day **Århus Festival Week** in early September, when jazz, classical, and rock concerts are nonstop, in addition to drama, theater, and dance.

The state-of-the-art **Musikhuset Århus** (Århus Concert Hall; ⊠ Thomas Jensens Allé 2 ☎ 89/40–40–40) has a splendid glass foyer housing palm trees and a fine Danish-French restaurant. The concert hall showcases theater, opera, ballet, and concerts of all kinds, from classical music to rock. In summer it often hosts free musical and theater performances on its outdoor stages; ask at the tourist office for a schedule.

As in most other towns, the local dance clubs come and go with remarkable frequency; stop by at a local café for the latest on what's happening. A prime spot to start—and perhaps end—your night is along the Århus Å, which is thronged with bars and cafés.

BARS & LOUNGES **Café Brasserie Svej** (⊠ Åboulevarden 22 ☎ 86/12–30–31 ⊕ www.svej. dk), on the canal, is a popular meeting spot for drinks and quiet chats in its Viennese-inspired decor. The friendly **Café Jorden** (⊠ Badstueg. 3 ☎ 86/19–72–22) has a brass-and-wood bar and a heated outdoor terrace with a red awning. Students and young professionals mix with the chatty bar staff, who like to sing along to the pop and rock classics.

★ The **Café Under Masken** (Under the Mask Café; ⊠ Bispeg. 3 ☎ 86/ 18–22–66), next door to the Royal Hotel, is the personal creation of Århus artist Hans Krull, who also designed the unique iron sculptures that grace the entrance to the hotel. The surreal bar is crammed with every type of mask imaginable, from grinning Balinese wooden masks to black-and-yellow African visages. Pygmy statues and stuffed tropical birds and fish line the shelves. Everything was collected by Krull and other bar patrons. The back wall is one long aquarium filled with exotic fish. As the bar manager puts it, "Everyone's welcome. This bar is a no-man's-land, a place for all the 'funny fish' of the world." If that's not enough of a draw, consider that the drink prices are the lowest in town, and more than 30 kinds of beer are on offer. It's open nightly until 2 AM.

Carlton (⊠ Rosensg. 23 ☎ 86/20–21–22) is a classy bar and restaurant, presided over by a carousel horse. Sip cocktails in the front bar-café, or dine on contemporary Danish fare in the dining room. The **Cockney Pub** (⊠ Maren Smeds Gyde 8 ☎ 86/19–45–77 ⊕ www.cockneypub.dk) is just that, and a bit more. It offers an exclusive line of beers and a wide selection of whiskeys. It was awarded the Cask Marque medal in 2004, "for pubs which serve the perfect pint." The **Hotel Marselis** (⊠ Strandvejen 25 ☎ 86/14–44–11) attracts a varied crowd to its two venues: the **Beach Club,** with danceable rock and disco, and the more elegant **Nautilus** piano bar. Delighting committed smokers everywhere (it advertises to them specifically), **Ris Ras Filliongongong** (⊠ Mejlg. 24 ☎ 86/18–50–06 ☉ Daily noon–2 AM), a self-described "sitting-room" with a major selection of beers, is never empty. **Sidewalk** (⊠ Åboulevarden 56–58 ☎ 86/18–18–66) has a large waterfront terrace that draws crowds on warm nights; in the equally lively interior you can sip cocktails at the long bar or graze on tapas and light meals, including hummus with olives and salad topped with soy-roasted chicken and spinach pasta.

LIVE MUSIC & **Fatter Eskil** (⊠ Skoleg. 25 ☎ 86/19–44–11 ⊕ www.fattereskil.dk ☑ Ad-
DANCE CLUBS mission varies) has live music five nights a week, featuring pop, rock, funk, soul, blues, and jazz. **Lion's Pub** (⊠ Rosensg. 21 ☎ 86/13–00–45) showcases live jazz on Friday night (mid-August through May) in its downstairs club, which is lined with black-and-white photos of jazz greats. A small stage faces several long tables that fill up with toe-tapping jazz aficionados. **Sams Bar** (⊠ Klosterg. 28 ☎ 86/13–21–31 ⊕ www.samsbar.dk ☉ Thurs. 9–3, Fri. and Sat. 9–5) is the dance club of choice at the moment, offering current Euro pop and old disco tunes. Happy "hour" is on Thursday from 9 PM to 3 AM and Friday and Saturday from 9 PM to 1 AM. One of Denmark's largest and most talked-about music venues, **Train** (⊠ Toldbag. 6 ☎ 86/13–47–22 ⊕ www.train.dk ☉ Thurs.–Sat until 5 AM), has seen the likes of Iggy Pop, Bryan Ferry, and John Hiatt, among many others, take the stage since its opening in 1998. Its sister property, **Kupé** (⊕ www.kupelounge.dk) is another popular bar with great music.

CASINO The **Royal Hotel** (⊠ Store Torv 4 ☎ 86/12–00–11), the city's casino, offers blackjack, roulette, baccarat, and slot machines.

Shopping

With more than 800 shops and many pedestrian streets (Strøget, Fredericksgade, Sct. Clemensgade, Store Torv, and Lille Torv), this city is a great place to play havoc with your credit cards. As befits a student town, Århus also has its "Latin Quarter," a jumble of cobbled streets around the cathedral, with boutiques, antiques shops, and glass and ceramic galleries that may be a little less expensive. In Vestergade street, you can turn on Grønnengade and stroll along Møllestien to see its charming old homes.

The Fredericksbjerg quarter, which includes the streets Bruunsgade, Jægergårdsgade, and Fredericks Allé, is called the larder of the city because there are so many specialty food shops here. There's also a shopping center, Bruun's Galleri.

At the **Bülow Duus Glassworks** (✉ Studsg. 14 ☎ 86/12–72–86) you can browse among delicate and colorful glassworks from fishbowls to candleholders. While there, visit Mette Bülow Duus's workshop and witness the creation of beautiful glassware. **Folmer Hansen** (✉ Sønderg. 43 ☎ 86/12–49–00) is packed with Danish tableware and porcelain, from sleek Arne Jacobsen–designed cheese cutters, ice buckets, and coffeepots to Royal Copenhagen porcelain plates. For the best selection of Georg Jensen designs, head to the official **Georg Jensen** (✉ Sønderg. 1 ☎ 86/12–01–00 ⊕ www.georgjensen.com or www.damask.dk) store. It stocks Jensen-designed and -inspired watches, jewelry, table settings, and art nouveau vases. The textile designs of Georg Jensen Damask, in a separate department, are truly beautiful.

Ebeltoft

❽ *45 km (28 mi) east of Århus.*

Danes refer to Ebeltoft—a town of crooked streets, sloping row houses, and crafts shops—as Jutland's nose. The Glass Museum in Ebeltoft houses a highly regarded international collection of contemporary works in glass, and from April through October you can watch beautiful vases, bowls, and tumblers being made in the museum's workshop. In the middle of the main square is Ebeltoft's half-timber **Det Gamle Rådhus** (Old Town Hall), said to be the smallest town hall in Denmark. Dating from 1789, it served as the town hall until 1840; today it is an annex of the Ebeltoft Museum, with historical exhibits displayed in its traditionally decorated rooms. The mayor still receives visitors here, and couples come from all over Denmark to be married in the quaint interior.

Near the town hall is the **Ebeltoft Museum,** which holds the Siamesisk Samling (Siamese Exhibit), a motley collection of Thai artifacts—from silks and stuffed lemurs to mounted tropical insects—brought back by explorer and Ebeltoft local Rasmus Havmøller. The museum also encompasses the nearby well-preserved dye-works factory, where the Ebeltoft peasants had their wool dyed until 1925. In summer, dyeing demonstrations are often held. ✉ *Juulsbakke 1* ☎ *86/34–55–99* 🖰 *DKr 25 (includes town hall)* ⊘ *June–Aug., daily 10–5; Sept.–mid-Oct., Apr., and May, Sat.–Thurs. 11–3; mid-Oct.–Dec., Feb., and Mar., weekends 11–3.*

Danish efficiency is on display beside the ferry at the **Vindmølleparken,** one of the largest windmill parks in the world. Sixteen of them on a curved spit of land generate electricity for 600 families. ✉ *Færgehaven* ☎ *86/34–12–44* 🖰 *Free* ⊘ *Daily.*

You can't miss the frigate *Jylland,* dry-docked on the town's main harbor. The renovation of the three-masted tall ship was financed by Danish shipping magnate Mærsk McKinney Møller, and it's a testament to Denmark's seafaring days of yore. You can wander through to examine the bridge, gun deck, galley, captain's room, and the 10½-ton pure copper-and-pewter screw. Don't miss the voluptuous Pomeranian pine figurehead. ⊠ *Strandvejen 4* ☎ *86/34–10–99* ⊕ *www.fregatten-jylland. dk* ⊡ *DKr 70* ⊘ *Mid-June–Aug., daily 10–7; Apr.–mid-June, Sept., and Oct., daily 10–6; Nov.–Mar., daily 10–5.*

The small, light, and airy **Glasmuseet Ebeltoft** is on the Ebeltoft harbor, a perfect setting for the collection, which ranges from the mysterious symbol-laden monoliths of Swedish glass sage Bertil Vallien to the luminous gold pavilions of Japanese artist Kyohei Fujita. Once a customs and excise house, the museum has a glass workshop where international students come to study. The shop sells functional pieces, art, and books. The museum stages six to nine separate exhibitions each year, presenting the latest trends in glassmaking, and from April to October glassblowers can be seen at work in the glassblowing studio. In July, on Thursday evenings, you can enjoy a social hour during "Glass-Wine-Art": advance reservations are necessary. On Wednesday afternoons also in July, another event called "Close to Hot Glass" allows you to create your own little work of art (this is an extra DKr 75). ⊠ *Strandvejen 8* ☎ *86/34–17–99* ⊕ *www.glasmuseet.dk* ⊡ *DKr 40* ⊘ *Jan.–June and Aug.–Dec., daily 10–5; July, daily 10–7.*

Where to Stay & Eat

★ **$$$$** ✕▥ **Molskroen.** Perched on the coast northwest of Ebeltoft, in a sunflower-yellow, half-timber manor house from 1923, is this swanky inn and restaurant. The ample rooms are tastefully decorated in cool tones with four-poster beds and Bang & Olufsen televisions. The large, gleaming bathrooms, done up with designer fixtures, could easily grace the pages of an interior-design magazine. Half the rooms overlook the water. Acclaimed young chef Jesper Koch heads the restaurant, which serves fine French fare with an imaginative twist. Roasted duck is stuffed with apricots, figs, and dates and drizzled in a sauce of rum and raisins. Marinated cod sashimi comes with mussels and dill salad. Four brightly colored original Warhol prints of famous queens—including Queen Margrethe, of course, and Queen Nomi of Swaziland—lend a dazzling touch to the blond-wood floors and pale orange walls. Large picture windows overlook the lush garden, through which a path winds to the private beach. The adjoining sitting room is perfect for a post-dinner brandy and cigar in front of the fireplace. ⊠ *Hovedg. 16, DK–8400* ☎ *86/36–22–00* 🖶 *86/36–23–00* ⊕ *www. molskroen.dk* ⊟ *18 rooms, 3 suites* ⚹ *Restaurant, beach, bar* ⊟ *AE, DC, MC, V* ⊘ *Restaurant closed Mon.–Tues. Oct.–Mar.*

Viborg

⑨ *22 km (36 mi) north of Silkeborg, 66 km (41 mi) northwest of Århus.*

Viborg dates back at least to the 8th century, when it was a trading post and site of pagan sacrifice. Later it became a center of Christianity, with monasteries and an episcopal residence. It has no fewer than 16 museums (with interests ranging from psychiatry to cycling) and eight different churches ranging in age from 25 to 900 years old. It's worth a stop if you're looking for a slower-paced town that still has a few attractions.

The 1,000-year-old **Hærvejen,** the old military road that starts near here, was once Denmark's most important connection with the outside world; today it lives on as a bicycle path. Legend has it that in the 11th century King Canute set out from Viborg to conquer England; he succeeded, of course, and ruled from 1016 to 1035. You can buy reproductions of a silver coin minted by the king, embossed with the inscription "Knud, Englands Kong" (Canute, King of England).

Built in 1130, Viborg's **Domkirke** (cathedral) was once the largest granite church in the world. Only the crypt remains of the original building, which was restored and reopened in 1876. The dazzling early-20th-century Biblical frescoes are by Danish painter Joakim Skovgard. ⊠ *Sct. Mogensg. 4* ☎ *87/25–52–50* ☒ *Free* ⊙ *June–Aug., Mon.–Sat. 10–5, Sun. noon–5; Apr., May, and Sept., Mon.–Sat. 11–4, Sun. noon–4; Oct.–Mar., Mon.–Sat. 11–3, Sun. noon–3.*

Where to Stay & Eat

$$$ ✕ **Brygger Bauers Grotter.** A former brewery dating from 1832, this cozy, cavernous underground restaurant has arched wooden ceilings, old paintings depicting Viborg history, and beer barrels lining the back wall. The contemporary Danish menu includes a hearty beef stew served with rice, and chicken breast stuffed with Gorgonzola. ⊠ *Sct. Mathiasg. 61* ☎ *86/61–44–88* ☐ *MC, V.*

$$$ ▥ **Palads Hotel.** This large hotel near the center of town has ample, simply furnished rooms done up in a rose decor. A third of the rooms are designed for longer stays and have kitchenettes. ⊠ *Sct. Mathiasg. 5, DK–8800* ☎ *86/62–37–00* ☐ *86/62–40–46* ⊕ *www.hotelpalads.dk* ↬ *99 rooms, 19 suites* ♧ *Some kitchenettes, sauna, bar, some pets allowed, no-smoking rooms* ☐ *AE, DC, MC, V.*

Central Jutland A to Z

AIRPORTS & TRANSFERS

Central Jutland has hubs in Århus and Billund, which handle mainly domestic and European traffic. Billund Airport, 2 km (1 mi) southwest of the city's downtown, is the larger of the two, and on the arrival end of flights from major European, Scandinavian, and Danish airports. Århus airport has regular flights to Copenhagen, Gothenburg, Stockholm, Oslo, and London, as well as charters to southern Europe. 🛪 Airports **Århus Airport** ☎ 87/75–70–00 ⊕ www.aar.dk. **Billund Airport** ☎ 76/50–50–50 ⊕ www.billund-airport.dk.

TRANSFERS   Hourly buses run between Århus Airport and the train station in town. The trip takes around 45 minutes and costs DKr 80. There is also a scheduled bus service (Bus 212) between Århus Airport and Randers and Ebeltoft. The bus timetable is independent of flight arrivals and departures, so call ahead for availability (☎ 96/12–86–22). Tickets are sold on the bus. Accepted currencies are Danish or Norwegian crowns, U.S. dollars, British pounds, and euros; Visa and MasterCard are also accepted. A taxi ride from the airport to central Århus takes 45 minutes and costs well over DKr 300.

From Billund Airport there are buses to Århus (Radisson SAS Hotel, DKr 130), Esbjerg, Kolding, Vejle, Odense, and the Hotel Legoland, near the airport. The bus to Hotel Legoland is free and operates weekdays from 6:15 AM to 11:30 PM, Saturday from 6:30 AM to 5:30 PM, and Sunday from 11 AM to 11:30 PM. It's only a five-minute drive. See the timetable at www.bll.dk.

BIKE TRAVEL
Cycling in Central Jutland is a special treat. The landscape is perfect for cyclists—varied but generally flat and easy to find your way around. The detailed cycle maps of Ringkøbing County lets you put together your own route through the region. Indeed, there are a total of 61 cycling and hiking routes in central and western Jutland. For a list of bicycle routes, check out ⊕ www.ringkobingfjord.dk or ⊕ www.cykelvandreture.dk.

BOAT & FERRY TRAVEL
More than 20 ferry routes still connect the peninsula with the rest of Denmark (including the Faroe Islands), as well as England, Norway, and Sweden, with additional connections to Kiel and Puttgarden, Germany, the Baltics, Poland, and Russia. For most ferries you can get general information and make reservations by calling FDM (Danish Motoring Association). For direct Zealand to Jutland passage, you can take a car-ferry hydrofoil from Zealand's Odden to Ebeltoft (45 minutes) or Århus (1 hour). You can also take the slower, but less expensive, car ferry from Kalundborg (on Zealand) to Århus (2 hours, 40 minutes). Both ferries travel five times daily on weekdays, and slightly less often on weekends. For ferry schedules and information, call Mols-Linien.
🚩 FDM ☎ 70/11-60-11. Mols-Linien ☎ 70/10-14-18 🖷 89/52-52-90 ⊕ www.molslinien.dk.

BUS TRAVEL
Bus and train travel inside Denmark are made more convenient through Bus/Tog Samarbejde, a comprehensive route and schedule information source. Bus tickets are usually sold on board the buses immediately before departure. Ask about discounts for children, senior citizens, and groups.

Århus Public Transport offers one-day tickets, valid for 24 hours, allowing the bearer to travel on all buses in the city and county of Århus, which also includes transfers on buses in Randers, Silkeborg, and Grenaa. Schedules for bus travel within towns are posted at all bus stops, and fares are usually about DKr 15.

Abildskou Bus 888 has up to nine daily departures between Århus Bus Station and Copenhagen's Valby Station, with direct connections to Copenhagen Airport. The trip takes about 3 hours and 45 minutes, similar to the train; a one-way ticket is DKr 230. These buses go on the

Mols-Linien ferries, and the company also has three weekly departures from Århus to Berlin.

🏛**Abildskou** ✉ Graham Bellsvej 40, Århus ☎ 70/21-08-88 ⊕ www.abildskou.dk. **Århus Public Transport** ✉ Kommuneinformationen City Hall (Tower Entrance) ☎ 89/40-10-10 ⊙ Weekdays 10-5:30. **Bus/Tog Samarbejde** ⊕ www.rejseplan.dk.

CAR TRAVEL

Although train and bus connections are excellent, sites and towns in Jutland are widely dispersed, and the peninsula is best explored by car. Whether you decide to take speedy, modern highways or winding old roads, traffic is virtually nonexistent.

Getting around Denmark these days is much easier than in the past thanks to bridges that connect the kingdom to both Sweden and the Continent; that said, it's best to confirm all passage with either a local tourist board or FDM before setting out, to avoid confusion caused by ferry mergers and discontinued routes. Although there are several ferry connections to other parts of Denmark and Europe, most travelers drive north from Germany, or arrive from the islands of Zealand or Funen. Ferry prices can get steep, and vary according to the size of the vehicle and the number of passengers.

From Copenhagen or elsewhere on Zealand, you can drive the approximately 110 km (69 mi) across the island, then cross the world's second-longest suspension bridge, the Storebæltsbro (Great Belt Bridge), to Knudshoved. You then drive the 85 km (53 mi) across Funen and cross from Middelfart to Fredericia, Jutland, over the Lillebæltsbro (Little Belt Bridge). There are more choices, since two bridges link Middelfart to Fredericia. The older, lower bridge (2 km [1 mi]) follows Route 161, whereas the newer suspension bridge (1 km [½ mi]) on E20 is faster.

If you need to rent a car, Europcar/Østergaard Biler is the largest and oldest car-rental business in the country, with 40 outlets nationwide.

🏛**Europcar** ✉ Sønder Allé 35, 8000 Århus C ☎ 89/33-11-11 ⊕ www.europcar.dk. **FDM** ☎ 70/11-60-11.

EMERGENCIES

For ambulance, fire, or police anywhere in Denmark, dial 112. You can contact local pharmacies in Århus for information on emergency doctors.

🏛 **Århus pharmacy** ✉ Løve Apoteket, Store Torv 5 ☎ 86/12-00-22. **Århus Kommunehospital** ☎ 87/31-50-50 emergency room, 86/20-10-22 doctor off-hours, 40/51-51-62 dentist off-hours, 86/12-00-22 pharmacist off-hours.

SPORTS & THE OUTDOORS

CANOEING The Silkeborg Turistbureau publishes an excellent brochure on canoeing in that area, on the Gudenå River. It includes information on how to pack a canoe; regulations for canoeing on the river and lakes; and lists of camps and tent sites along the river, including phone numbers and prices. Most important is the description of package trips that are available, including the Family Tour, Pioneer Tour, and the Luxury Tour. After reserving one of the trips (from three to six days), all you need do is show up at the desired starting point, where the canoes and equipment will be waiting for you. The daily distance will have been determined beforehand and accommodation will have been booked.

❼ Silkeborg Turistbureau ☎ 86/82-19-11 🖷 86/81-09-83 ⊕ www.silkeborg.com.

FISHING For the past 24 years the same four friends from England have been fishing in the Silkeborg region on their vacation—surely an excellent endorsement for angling opportunities in the region. The Lake District is a great place for fishing—more than 15 popular species of fish can be found here. License requirements vary, and package tours are also available; contact any local tourist office for details.

TOURS
Guided tours are few and far between, although some local tourism offices do provide them. Check with the individual city tourism offices—especially the one in Århus—for tips, reservations, and brochures that describe walking tours and scenic routes.

TRAIN TRAVEL
DSB makes hourly runs from Copenhagen to Århus (3½ hours). The trip includes train passage across the Storebæltsbro between Korsør, on west Zealand, and Nyborg, on east Funen. A one-way trip from Copenhagen to Århus is about DKr 292. For long trips, the DSB trains are fast and efficient, with superb views of the countryside. Smaller towns do not have intercity trains, so you have to switch to buses once you arrive.

❼ DSB ☎ 70/13-14-15 ⊕ www.dsb.dk.

VISITOR INFORMATION
At the Århus tourist office, check out the Århus Pass, which includes bus travel, free or discounted admission to museums and sites, and tours.

❼ Århus ✉ Park Allé 2 ☎ 89/40-67-00 ⊕ www.visitaarhus.com. **Ebeltoft** ✉ Strandvejen 2 ☎ 86/34-14-00 ⊕ www.visitdjursland.com. **Jelling** ✉ Gormsg. 23 ☎ 75/87-13-01 🖷 75/82-10-11 ⊕ www.visitvejle.com. **Mid-Jutland** ⊕ www.midtjylland.dk. **Randers Turistbureau** ✉ Tørvebryggen 12, DK-8900 ☎ 86/42-44-77 🖷 86/40-60-04 ⊕ www.visitranders.com. **Ringkøbing Tourist Association** ✉ Torvet, Postboks 21 ☎ 70/22-70-01 🖷 97/32-49-00 ⊕ www.ringkobingfjord.dk. **Silkeborg** ✉ Åhavevej 2A ☎ 86/82-19-11 🖷 86/81-09-83 ⊕ www.silkeborg.com. **Vejle** ✉ Banegårdspl. 6 ☎ 75/72-31-99 ⊕ www.visitvejle.com. **Viborg** ✉ Nytorv 9 ☎ 87/25-30-75 🖷 86/60-02-38 ⊕ www.viborg.dk/turisme.

North Jutland

6

WORD OF MOUTH

"One full day is enough for Skagen unless you are lucky to visit on a warm day; then you might want to [spend] some extra time on the beach. The town is very small, but it has some nice crafts and jewelry shops and art galleries. Old Skagen town is a good place to be at sunset."

—fun4

Updated by
Bruce Bishop

YOU'RE AT THE END OF THE LINE, HERE, SO TO SPEAK—North Jutland is the very tip of northern Denmark, where the railway ends and seaside adventures begin. Tourism officials boast that in this region you can explore 55 million years of history within a range of 100 km (60 mi). The two main places to visit in North Jutland are Aalborg, an old city with Ice Age and Viking roots nearby, and Skagen, a seaside town once known for its fishing culture and now better known for its tourism industry. Aalborg is brimming with life and possibilities, with restaurants that rival those in Copenhagen. Skagen is more peaceful, and it has broad beaches and spectacular sunsets. Oh, and there are more hours of sunshine in North Jutland than in any other part of the country—all the better for exploring the small communities that fan out around Skagen.

WHAT IT COSTS In Danish Kroner				
$$$$	**$$$**	**$$**	**$**	**¢**
RESTAURANTS over 180	141–180	121–140	90–120	under 90
HOTELS over 1,500	1,200–1,500	1,000–1,200	700–1,000	under 700

Restaurant prices are for a main course at dinner. Hotel prices are for two people in a standard double room, including service charge and tax.

Aalborg

❶ *80 km (50 mi) northeast of Viborg, 112 km (70 mi) north of Århus.*

The gentle waters of the Limfjord cut off the top segment of Jutland completely. Perched on its narrowest point is Aalborg, Denmark's fourth-largest city, which includes the youthful Aalborg University, founded in 1974. Aalborg's began, in 692, as the gateway between north and mid-Jutland. It was granted a municipal charter in 1342, and the Limfjord has been crucial to the city's economy since the heyday of the herring industry. Until 1879 a ferry and pontoon bridge provided the link between the north and south parts of the city; a bridge came in 1933, and then a 1,900-foot-long tunnel was built in 1969.

Overall, the city is a charming combination of new and old; twisting lanes filled with medieval houses and, nearby, broad modern boulevards. Its restaurants and cuisine offerings just seem to be getting better and better, and do not take a backseat to any other city in Jutland.

Aalborg's harbor is a busy place, with ships bound for Bornholm, Norway, Iceland, the Faroe Islands, Ireland, and Britain. (Aalborg Portland is probably the most important company on the waterfront. It makes cement from the thick chalk bed that lies underneath the city, mixes it with sand from the mouth of the Limfjord, and exports 50% of its annual cement output of 2.7 million tons to 70 countries worldwide.)

In many parts of the world, Aalborg is identified more as a brand—a brand of schnapps, that is: the clear, potent liquor many Danes enjoy with herring. Since **Danish Distillers/De Danske Spritfabrikker** bought Harald Jensen's still in 1883, the city's name has been linked with aquavit, and the world-famous schnapps still carries the name of Aalborg.

You can take part in a two-hour guided tour of the plant, with a tasting and a stop at the company store. ⊠ *C. A. Olesens Gade 1* ☎ *98/12–42–00* ⊕ *www.aalborgsnaps.dk* 🖃 *DKr 40* ⊙ *Mid-May–Aug., Mon. and Sat. 10 AM and 2 PM.*

The baroque **Budolfi Kirke** (Cathedral Church of St. Botolph) is dedicated to the English saint. Eight cocks crow the hour from four identical clock faces on the tower. The stone church, replacing one made of wood, has been rebuilt several times in its 800-year history. It includes a copy of the original spire of the Rådhus in Copenhagen, which was taken down about a century ago. The money for the construction was donated to the church by a generous local merchant and his sister, both of whom, locals say, had no other family on which to lavish their wealth. The main entrance is at the west end of the cathedral, but admittance is from Algade through the porch, which is a former Catholic chapel, where symbols of the four evangelists can be seen on the cross vaulting. Inside the main church, take note of the altar from 1689 and the pulpit, built in 1692. ⊠ *Gammel Torv.*

Next to Budolfi Kirke is the 15th-century **Helligåndsklosteret** (Monastery of the Holy Ghost). One of Denmark's best-preserved monasteries—and perhaps the only one that admitted both nuns and monks. It is now a home for the elderly. The building was erected in several stages during the 15th century and the beginning of the 16th century, and coincidentally, the duties of the first nuns and monks were to look after the sick and aged. During World War II the monastery was the meeting place for the Churchill Club, a group of Aalborg schoolboys who became world famous for their sabotage of the Nazis—their schemes were carried out even after the enemy thought they were locked up. ⊠ *C. W. Obels Pl., Gammel Torv* ☎ *98/12–02–05* ⊙ *Guided tours mid-June–mid-Aug. daily at 1:30.*

★ The local favorite landmark is the magnificent 17th-century **Jens Bang Stenhus** (Jens Bang's Stone House), built by the wealthy merchant Jens Bang in 1642. It was rumored that because he was never made a town council member, the cantankerous Bang avenged himself by caricaturing his political enemies in gargoyles all over the building and then adding his own face, its tongue sticking out at the town hall. The five-story building has been the home of Aalborg's oldest pharmacy for more than 300 years. Note that the Aalborg tourist office is directly across the street. ⊠ *Østeråg. 9.*

In the center of the old town is **Jomfru Ane Gade,** named, as the story goes, for an aristocratic maiden accused of being a witch, then beheaded. Now the street's fame is second only to that of Copenhagen's Strøget. Despite the flashing neon and booming music of about 30 discos, bars, clubs, and eateries, the street attracts a thick stream of pedestrian traffic and appeals to all ages. Halfway down the street there is a large three-story building in neoclassical style with pilasters. It was built in 1813, and from 1848 to 1889 it housed the Aalborg Cathedral School. Go through the gate into the old schoolyard to see the restored gymnasium and a warehouse now converted into the Jomfru Ane Theatre.

The only Fourth of July celebrations outside the United States blast off in nearby **Rebild Park,** a salute to the United States for welcoming some 300,000 Danish immigrants. The tradition dates back to 1912.

Just north of Aalborg at Nørresundby (still considered a part of greater Aalborg) is **Lindholm Høje,** a Viking and Iron Age burial ground where stones placed either in the shape of a ship or in triangles denote where men were buried; oval and circular groups of stones show where women were buried. In total, there are about 682 graves dating from AD 400 to shortly before AD 1000. The whole site was found during a major excavation between 1952 and 1958, and it also revealed parts of a Viking village and a "newly" plowed field. The village had been functional for about 200 years, between AD 700 and AD 900. The Vikings had moved to Jutland about 15,000 years ago, after the ice had melted, but at the end of the Viking era this area became buried under drifting sand and was thereby preserved until modern times. Grazing sheep now act as natural lawn mowers. There's a museum at the bottom of the hill that chronicles Viking civilization. The original archaeological finds (pottery, bones, traces of handicrafts, and so on) are displayed next to large murals, maps, and texts. Upon entering, ask for an English translation of the displays in the museum. On the premises are a nice gift shop, featuring Viking-style jewelry, and a café.

The **Viking Drama** (☎ 98/17–33–73 ⊕ www.geocities.com/vikingespil ☒ Dkr 70) is a musical and dramatic performance about the daily lives of the Vikings, held on the grounds of Lindholm Høje. It's performed in Danish, but the music, singing, dancing, and costumes don't need any translation. The show is performed mid-June through early July only at 7 PM on weekdays, 4:30 and 11 PM on Saturday, and 4:30 on Sunday. ⊠ *Vendilavej 11* ☎ *96/31–04–28* ☒ *Burial ground free, museum DKr 30* ☉ *Easter–mid-Oct., daily 10–5; mid-Oct.–Easter, Tues.–Sun. 10–4.*

The blocky marble-and-glass structure of the **Nordjyllands Kunstmuseum** (North Jutland Museum of Modern Art) was designed by architects Alvar and Elissa Aalto and Jacques Baruël. The gridded interior partition system allows the curators to tailor their space to each exhibition, many of which are drawn from the museum's permanent collection of 20th-century Danish and international art. On the grounds there are also a manicured sculpture park and an amphitheater that hosts occasional concerts. ⊠ *Kong Christians Allé 50* ☎ *98/13–80–88* ⊕ *www. nordjyllandskunstmuseum.dk* ☒ *DKr 30* ☉ *Easter–mid-Oct., daily 10–5; mid-Oct.–Easter, Tues.–Sun. 10–4.*

The **Aalborg Historical Museum** contains the well-preserved underground ruins of a medieval Franciscan friary, including a walled cellar and the foundations of the chapel. Enter via the elevator outside the Salling department store. Another favorite attraction is the Renaissance chamber Aalborgstuen, which features furniture and glassware from the 16th and 17th centuries. ⊠ *Alg. 48* ☎ *96/31–04–10* ⊕ *www.aahm.dk* ☒ *DKr 30* ☉ *Thurs.–Sun. 10–5.*

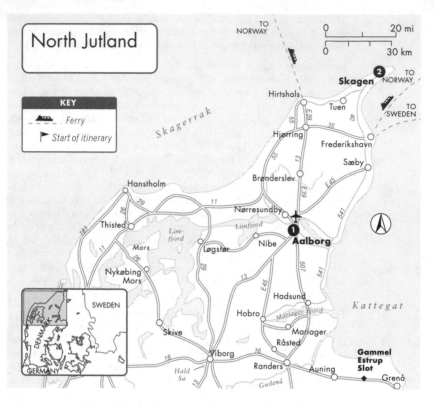

Aalborg Maritime Museum includes a visit aboard the submarine *Springeren* or the torpedo boat *Søbjørnen*, and a look at Queen Margrethe's Prinsesse-jollen, a dinghy she learned to sail when she was still a crown princess. All the exhibits depict what life is like at sea, in the port of Aalborg, and at the shipyard. ☒ *Vestre Fjordvej 81* ☎ *98/11–78–03* ⊕ *www.aalborgmarinemuseum.dk* ☒ *Dkr 65* ⊙ *May–Aug., daily 10–6.*

Ⓒ **Tivoliland** is a spring and summer amusement park that boasts as its prime attraction the hair-raising Boomerang roller coaster—the biggest roller coaster in Scandinavia—which whips you through narrow bends and loops, both forward and backward. ☒ *Karolinelundsvej 40* ☎ *98/ 12–33–15* ⊕ *www.tivoliland.dk* ☒ *Admission DKr 50; rides extra* ⊙ *May and Jun., daily noon–8; Jul., daily 11–9; late-Mar. and Apr., daily noon–7.*

Where to Stay & Eat

$$$$ ✕ **Mortens Kro.** The chef-owner of Mortens Kro, Morten Nielsen, is a celebrity in these parts, having hosted many TV shows and authored three books (one of which is amply illustrated with Danish beauties sensually enjoying Chef Nielsen's cuisine). The food here is a delight, both visually and gastronomically. The menu changes monthly, but a starter might be steamed white asparagus with leeks in a mousseline sauce, with herbs and freshly shelled shrimp. A main course could be free-range veal tenderloin from North Jutland, marinated in basil and served with slow-baked small tomatoes and the ubiquitous new potatoes. The sleek interior was designed by an art director well known in the Swedish film industry (she did Bergman's *Fanny and Alexander)*. Every inch of the restaurant is thoughtfully designed, even the washrooms—they're equipped with waterfalls and nature sound effects emanating from invisible speakers. A DJ spins Euro jazz on Friday and Saturday evenings. Jackets aren't required, but a "business casual" look is a good way to go. ⊠ *Mølleå Arkaden* ☎ *98/12–48–60* ⊕ *www.mortenskro.com* ⩔ *Reservations essential* ⊟ *DC, MC, V* ⊘ *Closed Sun.*

\$\$\$\$ ✕ **Rosdahl's Restaurant, Food Market, and Wine Shop.** This one-stop-shopping homage to food and beverage is in an old sugar warehouse just steps from the Limfjord. To pick up picnic items, stop by the fresh-food market every Saturday between 9:30 and 2:30, or, for a more formal repast, the à la carte and prix-fixe menus from the restaurant will be sure to please. The cuisine is definitely French-inspired—even the cheeses sold in the market are from the big Rungis market outside Paris. ⊠ *Strandvejen* ☎ *98/12–05–80* ⊟ *DC, MC, V* ⊘ *Closed Sun.*

\$\$–\$\$\$\$ ✕ **Isbryderen Elbjørn.** Having dinner or lunch on an icebreaker ship isn't typical, even for Jutland, but this floating restaurant and glassworks is nothing if not unique. Meals in the dining room can be pricey, but lunch (and Denmark's largest assortment of schnapps) is available at more reasonable prices in the ship's Aquavit Lounge. A museum tells the history of the *Elbjørn* and what life was like on board, and you can also step into the glassblower's workshop, where all the glassware and table service for the restaurant is handmade. Reservations are recommended for dinner in the main dining room. ⊠ *Strandvejen 6B* ☎ *43/42–34–34* ⊟ *AE, DC, MC, V.*

¢–\$\$\$ ✕ **Søgaards Bryghus.** Microbreweries normally aren't upscale, but this brew house is a cut above the rest. The spotless interior; piping hot food from the kitchen; attractive glassware, brass, and exposed brick; and lots of smiles make this pub special. It serves great food, like barbecued ribs, steaks, and fries; it even has its own in-house butcher shop. Tasting and tours can also be arranged, and if you're in Aalborg for a couple of days you can buy a liter of your favorite homemade brew in a Danish-designed bottle and return for refills. At this writing, the entrepreneur behind the brewery was planning to open up 12 guest rooms next door by summer 2006; in keeping with the hops theme, there will beer taps in each room. ⊠ *C. W. Obels Pl. 1A* ☎ *98/16–11–14* ⊕ *www. soegaardsbryghus.dk* ⊟ *MC, V.*

★ ¢–\$\$ ✕ **Duus Vinkjælder.** Most people come to this cellar—part alchemist's dungeon, part neighborhood bar—for a drink, but you can also get a light bite. In summer enjoy smørrebrød; in winter sup on grilled specialties such as *biksemad* (a meat-and-potato hash), and the restaurant's special liver pâté. ⊠ *Østeråg. 9* ☎ *98/12–50–56* ⊟ *DC, V* ⊘ *Closed Sun.*

\$\$\$ ⊞ **Helnan Phønix.** In a central and sumptuous old mansion, this hotel is popular with vacationers as well as business travelers. The rooms are luxuriously furnished with plump chairs and polished, dark-wood furniture; in some the original wooden ceiling beams are still intact. The

Brigadier restaurant serves excellent French and Danish food. ☒ *Vester-bro 77, DK–9000* ☎ *98/12–00–11* 🖷 *98/10–10–20* ⊕ *www.helnan.dk* ⇗ *219 rooms, 2 suites* ⚴ *Restaurant, gym, bar, meeting room, some pets allowed, no-smoking rooms* ≡ *AE, DC, MC, V.*

$–$$$ 🏨 **Hotel Hvide Hus.** This Best Western property is one of the city's few "high-rises," at 15 stories; the bright rooms have balconies overlooking Kildepark. It's a 5-minute walk to the train station diagonally across the park, or a 10-minute walk to the city center. Breakfasts in the top-floor Restaurant Kilden are more than adequate, and it's worth checking out the daily dinner specials in the same room—meals are well presented in a relaxed atmosphere with a wonderful view of the city. Weekend rates are very reasonable. ☒ *Vesterbro 2, DK–9000* ☎ *98/13–84–00* 🖷 *98/13–51–22* ⊕ *www.hotelhvidehus.dk* ⇗ *196 rooms, 2 suites* ⚴ *Restaurant, bar, meeting rooms* ≡ *AE, DC, MC, V* �🍽 *BP.*

Nightlife & the Arts

BARS & WINE CELLARS   Consider a pub crawl along the famed **Jomfru Ane Gade,** wildly popular for its party atmosphere and rock-bottom drink prices, which are much lower than anywhere else in Denmark. Opt for the house drink of the night (usually a Danish beer), and you'll often pay one-third of the normal cost. There's much variety in music and ambience, so if one place doesn't fit your mood, maybe the one next door will.

Dimly lighted and atmospheric, **Duus Vinkjælder** (☒ Østeråg. 9 ☎ 98/12–50–56) is extremely popular, one of the most classic beer and wine cellars in all of Denmark. It's an obligatory stop for anyone who wants a taste of Aalborg's nightlife. **L. A. Bar** (☒ Jomfru Ane Gade 7 ☎ 98/11–37–37) is a chatty, American-style bar. **Rendez-Vous** (☒ Jomfru Ane Gade 5 ☎ 98/16–88–80) has a pleasant outdoor terrace with black and brown wicker chairs. Thursday through Saturday it opens its upstairs dance floor, which attracts 18- to 25-year-olds with standard disco. **Spirit of America** (☒ Jomfru Ane Gade 16 ☎ 98/12–47–55) is a good spot to catch an international soccer match on the bar's big-screen TV.

CASINO   The city's sole casino is at the **Radisson SAS Limfjord Hotel** (☒ Ved Stranden 14–16 ☎ 98/16–43–33).

LIVE MUSIC & DANCE CLUBS   **Gaslight** (☒ Jomfru Ane Gade 23 ☎ 98/10–17–50) plays rock and grinding dance music to a young crowd. **Le Bar Bat** (☒ Jomfru Ane Gade 25 ☎ 98/13–32–41) offers live music Thursday through Saturday. **Pusterummet** (☒ Jomfru Ane Gade 12 ☎ 98/16–06–39) is open during the day, but turns into a dance club on Friday and Saturday. **Rock Caféen** (☒ Jomfru Ane Gade 7 ☎ 98/13–66–90) is for serious rock-and-roll lovers, with live music most nights. **Rock Nielsen** (☒ Jomfru Ane Gade 9-11 ☎ 98/13–99–29) is a rock-and-roll dance club where disco music would most likely never be heard!

Skagen

❷ *88 km (55 mi) northeast of Aalborg, 212 km (132 mi) north of Århus.*

For over a century, Skagen (pronounced *skane*), a picturesque area where the North Sea meets the Baltic Sea, has been a favorite destination of well-off travelers, artists, and architects. This 600-year old market town on Jutland's windswept northern tip has long pebbly beaches and huge open skies. Sunsets are tremendous events, so much so that idlers on the beach stop and applaud. Its main industry has traditionally been fishing, but tourism now seems to be eclipsing that. Cruiseship passengers on a day visit, school groups, families, cyclists, and couples looking for a romantic getaway can all be seen anytime in Skagen, though it's never truly overrun with visitors. Prices can be considerably less expensive before June 15 and after October 15.

Skagen is also well known for its annual folk and bluegrass festival, held annually the last weekend in June since 1971. Acts from as far away as Australia and New Zealand perform in venues all over town. For more information, check out ⊕ www.skagenfestival.dk. And if you happen to be there on Midsummer Eve (June 23), be prepared for a massive beach bonfire and thousands of people gathering around town to celebrate the warm, sunny weather.

As parking is difficult, especially in the summer months, consider renting a bicycle. Like everywhere else, there are no steep hills, and motorists are used to looking out for cyclists when there are no separate bicycle paths. One good rental shop, Skagen Cykeludleejning, is next to the train station; it rents regular bicycles for DKr 75 per day.

The 19th-century Danish artist and nationally revered poet Holger Drachmann (1846–1908) and his friends, including the well-known P. S. Krøyer and Michael and Anna Ancher, founded the Skagen School of painting, which sought to capture the special quality of light and idyllic seascapes here. They and their contemporaries mostly enjoyed depicting everyday life in Skagen from the turn of the 20th century until ★ the 1920s, and you can see their efforts on display in the **Skagen Museum.** It's a wonderful homage to this talented group of Danes, and you'll become mesmerized by some of the portraits, which seem more like a photographic collection of days gone by. Some of the more famous canvases may be on loan at museums throughout the world, but do try to visit, even if you're only in Skagen for a half day. The museum store offers the best selection in town of posters, postcards, and other souvenirs depicting the Skagen paintings. ⊠ *Brøndumsvej 4* ☎ *98/44–64–44* ⊕ *www.skagensmuseum.dk* 🖼 *DKr 60* ⊙ *June–Aug., daily 10–6; May and Sept., daily 10–5; Apr. and Oct., Tues.–Sun. 11–4; Nov.–Mar., Wed.–Fri. 1–4, Sat. 11–4, Sun. 11–3.*

Michael and Anna Ancher are Skagen's—if not Denmark's—most famous artist couple, and their meticulously restored 1820 home and studio, **Michael og Anna Ancher's Hus** (Michael and Anna Ancher's House), is now a museum. Old oil lamps and lace curtains decorate the parlor; the doors throughout the house were painted by Michael. Anna's studio, complete with easel, is awash in the famed Skagen light. More than 240 paintings by Michael, Anna, and their daughter, Helga, grace the walls. ⊠ *Markvej 2–4* ☎ *98/44–30–09* ⊕ *www.anchershus.dk* 🖼 *DKr 40* ⊙ *May–Sept., daily 10–5 (until 6 late June–mid-Aug.); Apr. and Oct., daily 11–3; Nov.–Mar., weekends 11–3.*

Fodor'sChoice Danes say that in Skagen you can stand with one foot on the Kattegat,
★ the strait between Sweden and eastern Jutland, the other in the Skagerrak,
the strait between western Denmark and Norway. It is possible to do
this, but by no means go swimming here—it's very dangerous. The
point is so thrashed by storms and roiling waters that the 18th-century
Tilsandede Kirke (Sand-Buried Church), 2 km (1 mi) south of town, is
completely covered by dunes.

Even more famed than the Buried Church is the west coast's dramatic
Råbjerg Mile, a protected migrating dune that moves about 33 feet a year
and is accessible on foot from the Kandestederne.

Where to Stay & Eat

There are 24 hotels and boarding homes, two youth hostels, seven
campsites, and a wide range of summer homes in the Skagen area. Pri-
vate-yacht owners can dock in one of two marinas. Restaurants are numerous, and look out for reasonably priced luncheon specials at some
of the smaller downtown hotels.

A tip: If you are staying at a site with any kind of kitchen facility, such
as a holiday home, the main supermarket, Merko, on Doggerbanke 2,
between Skagen and Old Skagen, is the place to pick up supplies. It's
open daily until 9 PM.

$$–$$$$ ✕ **Skagen Fiske Restaurant.** Located on the waterfront, this place at first
seems very unassuming, but it actually faces one of the two marinas that
dock private yachts—in summer the restaurant's terrace is the place to
see and be seen by the denizens of these vessels. On the ground floor a
sand floor (over wood) greets you in the restaurant's pub; upstairs, the
blue-and-white restaurant might reminder you of a warehouse attic, but
this is Danish chic, and that's Russian abstract art on the walls. (Gothic-
letter signs on the very low door frames say in Danish, "Duk eller suk,"
which means "Duck your head or sigh.") Upstairs or down, the Pandestegte
fiskefrikadelier (fish cakes) are a must-try. Made from three Nordic fish
and gently creamed with herbs and potatoes, they may be the restaurant's
most popular item. Wash them down with a frosty Danish beer or lemon
soda. Pub menu items are more reasonably priced, but the dining room
upstairs is a real night on the town. Note that there's no dress code, but
you'll want to put on your best casual chic threads. Reservations are rec-
ommended. ✉ *Fiskehuskaj 13* 🕾 *98/44–35–44* ⊕ *www.skagen-
fiskerestaurant.dk* ▤ *AE, DC, V* ☉ *Closed Nov. and Jan.*

$$$–$$$$ ✕▦ **Ruths Hotel.** This is definitely the grande dame of Old Skagen, orig-
inally built by Emma and Hans Christian Ruth. It faces westward to
the sea and oozes over a century of history, recalling when wealthy city
folk would take a ferry from Copenhagen to nearby Frederikshavn and
then a carriage or train to Skagen to enjoy the good life in summer. It
has been completely rebuilt with modern facilities, and its main restau-
rant, Ruth's Gourmet, is operated by Chef Michel Michaud, known for
heading up the kitchens at such renowned venues as Kong Hans in Copen-
hagen. (The only drawback is that you have to call ahead at least a month
in advance for a reservation!) There is also a brasserie that serves local
delicacies prepared by any of Chef Michaud's 17 cooks. Rooms are typ-

JUL-TIDE IN DENMARK

T COULD BE THE BLANKET *of snow on thatched roofs, or the dancing flames of candles flickering behind frosted window panes. It might be the pungent aroma of roast goose wafting from the kitchen, or perhaps the giggling group of rosy-cheek children in red clogs catching snowflakes in their mittens. If Denmark is the land of all that's cute and hygellig (the catch-all Danish term for cozy), then a Danish Christmas (Jul) just about epitomizes the country's charm.*

It is on December 1 that Danish children are permitted to open the first little window on their advent calendars, a signal that the Christmas season has officially begun. A seasonal staple, the colorful advent calendar (also called Nativity calendar) has 25 windows, behind which lie a Christmas scene and, more importantly, a chocolate. The calendar culminates on December 25th, usually with a depiction of the birth of baby Jesus—and the largest chocolate of the lot.

The Danes' penchant for home decoration blossoms during the holidays. Delicate paper cutouts of snowflakes and reindeer dangle from ceilings. Wreaths heavy with berries hang on front doors, and red and white candles set living rooms aglow.

As any Danish child knows, when you can't find a sock, or if the milk suddenly spills as if an invisible hand pushed it, then it means that the mischievous Christmas nisser (elves) are up to their tricks again. Pranksters at heart, the nimble nisser can wreak havoc on a household—that is, unless they're left a bowl of porridge or some other Christmas goodie, which Danish kids make sure to do. And what goodies to choose from— candy stores and bakeries are bursting with marzipan of all shapes and sizes, drizzled with chocolate and sprinkles in every hue of the rainbow. The windows are piled high with glistening wienerbrød, *Denmark's decadent, flaky pastry—often oozing with creamy fillings—that knows no equal.*

Christmas is officially celebrated on the evening of December 24. Families gather 'round the table for a Christmas feast, which may be roast duck or goose stuffed with oranges or prunes, or pork roasted in its own juices. No Danish meal is complete without the omnipresent rød kål, boiled, vinegary red cabbage, and kartofler (potatoes). The choice for dessert is unanimous: the Christmas meal always ends with riz à l'amande, a thick and creamy rice pudding. Hidden within its fluffy folds is an almond, and whoever finds it receives a gift—and, some believe, good luck for the rest of the year.

A properly decorated Danish Christmas tree is a sight to behold, bedecked in handmade decorations—from gold-paper angels to brightly painted wooden figures—and strung (but of course) with miniature Danish flags. Purists still decorate their trees with white candles, which are lighted for the next phase of the evening. Dancing around the tree, the perfect antidote to falling into a post-feast stupor, is the bonding highlight of the night. Family and guests hold hands and skip and sway around the tree, singing Danish carols. All worries and differences are forgotten as they engage in this refreshingly primary act of sharing, just as generations have before them. The circle breaks when the children can't bear the temptation a moment longer and scamper over to the gifts piled high under the tree. This is when a Danish Christmas ends like any other: kids sitting among reams of ribbons and ripped paper, while the adults sip their spiked eggnog, remembering when happiness was what you got for Christmas.

ically lavish, in an understated way, and all have balconies or terraces and Swedish-made DUX beds; some have hot tubs. The Wellness Centre provides regular spa and beauty treatments, as well as some forms of laser cosmetic surgery. ⊠ *Hans Ruths Vej 1* ☎ *98/44–11–24* 🖷 *98/ 45–08–75* ⊕ *www.ruths-hotel.dk* ☞ *14 rooms, 12 suites* ⚷ *2 restaurants, in-room broadband, indoor pool, gym, spa, sauna, steam rooms, meeting rooms* ☰ *AE, DC, MC, V.*

$$–$$$ ✕▣ **Strandhotellet.** Also in Old Skagen, this bright and romantic hotel is the perfect foil to the wild, windy sea- and sandscapes nearby. Built in 1912, it's filled with gently curved wicker furnishings, painted woods, and original art. The guest rooms are painted in pastels, and are reminiscent of those from a country estate—a country estate that just happens to have Bang & Olufsen flat-screen televisions. The staff is friendly and accommodating, though in the off-season they may leave at 10 PM (returning the next morning to prepare a handsome Continental breakfast, of course). Sømærket, a restaurant next door operated by the same owner, is a steak house under the watchful eye of famous French Chef Michel Michaud, who is employed by Ruths Hotel around the corner. It's open only between April and October. ⊠ *Jeckelsvej 2, DK–9990* ☎ *98/44–34–99* 🖷 *98/44–59–19* ⊕ *www.strandhotellet.glskagen.dk* ☞ *15 rooms, 13 suites, 2 houses* ⚷ *Restaurant, café, Wi-Fi, lounge, meeting room* ☰ *AE, DC, MC, V.*

$–$$$ ✕▣ **Plesner Hotel & Restaurant.** This appealing hotel is just a three-minute walk from the train station. Ulrik Plesner, a famous local architect responsible for many buildings in Skagen, designed this one as well, and his portrait graces the upper landing on the first floor. Rooms are all bright and airy, with nice color schemes of blue, green, or rose. All have a private bath; the newer rooms (21 and 22) have French windows. Rooms in the hotel's annex, although smaller, are charming and have little terraces. There are no phones or elevator, but there are TVs, and the place is spotless. The dining room has popular lunch specials, though note that it's only open from June 16 to August 14. ⊠ *Holstvej 8, DK–9990* ☎ *98/44–68–44* 🖷 *98/44–36–86* ⊕ *www.hotelplesner.dk* ☞ *24 rooms, 2 suites* ⚷ *Restaurant; no room phones* ☰ *MC, V* ⦿ *BP.*

$ ✕▣ **Brøndums Hotel.** A few minutes from the beach, this 150-year-old gabled inn is furnished with antiques and Skagen School paintings, and although it's still charming, it is definitely showing its age. The very basic guest rooms in the main building are old-fashioned and include wicker chairs, Oriental rugs, and four-poster pine beds. The annex rooms are more modern, but most rooms do not come with a private bath. There is no elevator. But if you don't mind a great deal of flowery wallpaper and little to no handicapped access, the hotel has lots of character and history, and is a bit like stepping back in time. (If you don't stay overnight here, do drop by for a coffee or a meal to admire the artwork.) The fine French-Danish restaurant, where the Skagen School often gathered, has a lavish cold table (a series of plates with cold items: cheeses, cold cuts, pickles, marinated herring, cold meatballs). Brøndums Hotel became associated with the Skagen School early on: Anna Ancher was the daughter of Eric Brøndum, the hotel proprietor. ⊠ *Anchersvej 3, DK–9990* ☎ *98/44–15–55* 🖷 *98/45–15–20* ⊕ *www.broendums-hotel.dk* ☞ *46* *rooms, 13 with bath ᓬ Restaurant, bar, meeting room, some pets allowed ☰ AE, DC, MC, V.*

Shopping

Skagen's artistic heritage and light-drenched landscapes continue to draw painters and craftspeople, meaning you'll find better-than-average souvenirs in town. The pedestrian street in town has a fascinating and intimate shopping atmosphere with stores as fine as those you'd see in Copenhagen. For colorful, innovative handblown glass, for example, head for **Glaspusterblæser** (⊠ Sct. Laurentii Vej 33 ☏ 98/44–58–75), a large glassblowing workshop housed in what was once Skagen's post office. The amber store and workshop **Ravsliberen I Skagen** (⊠ Sct. Laurentii Vej 6 ☏ 98/44–55–27) sells top-quality amber jewelry, including pieces with insects trapped inside. You can buy miniature replicas of figureheads, ships' "guardian angels," at **Trip Trap** (⊠ Sct. Laurentii Vej 17A ☏ 98/44–63–22), a branch of the popular Danish home-decorating chain.

North Jutland A to Z

AIRPORTS & TRANSFERS

Northern Jutland's regional hub is in Aalborg. Flights to Aalborg from Copenhagen are less than one hour and there are several flights a day. The airport is 5 km (3 mi) from the city center.

🛈 Airport **Aalborg Airport** ☏ 98/17–11–44 ⊕ www.aal.dk.

TRANSFERS Taxi and bus routes connect Aalborg Airport with the city. A taxi costs around DKr 175 and takes roughly 20 minutes. Nordjyllands Trafikselskab has buses connecting the airport to towns near Aalborg, and the company Flybusnord runs routes to Sæby and Frederikshavn.

🛈**Flybusnord** ☏98/43–30–00 ⊕www.flybusnord.dk. **Nordjyllands Trafikselskab** ☏98/11–11–11 ⊕ www.nordjyllandstrafikselskab.dk.

BIKE TRAVEL

North Jutland is ideal for a bicycle holiday, and whether you choose to travel along the coastline, go inland, or explore the islands of Mors or Læsø, the area has plenty of quiet roads, disused railway lines, bicycle paths, and signposted routes, which allow you to enjoy the region by bicycle without worrying about cars. The North Jutland tourism Web site can help you choose between 14 different cycling holidays, with packages available from Zig Zag around the Limfjord to Seven Days by the North Sea.

🛈 Visit **Nord** ☏ 96/96–12–00 ⊕ www.visitnord.dk.

BOAT & FERRY TRAVEL

There are ferries from Göteborg (3¼ hours), on Sweden's west coast, and Oslo, Norway (10 hours), to Frederikshavn in the northeast. Call Stena Line for both. There are bus and train connections to Aalborg from the ferry ports of Hirtshals and Frederikshavn every hour. The Norwegian Fjordline, which carries passengers to Norway's fjord region (Egersund, Stavenger, Haugesund, and Bergen) offers bus transport from Hanstholm (in northeast Jutland) to Aalborg for their passengers.

The Color Line ferries also sail between Hirtshals and Norwegian ports.
🔢 **Color Line** ☎ 99/56-20-00 ⊕ www.colorline.dk. **Fjordline** ☎ 97/96-30-00 ⊕ www.
fjordline.com. **Stena Line** ☎ 96/20-02-00 ⊕ www.stenaline.com.

BUS TRAVEL

Bus and train travel inside Denmark are made more convenient through
Bus/Tog Samarbejde, a comprehensive route and schedule information
source. Bus tickets are usually sold on board the buses immediately before departure. Ask about discounts for children, senior citizens, and groups.

Thinggaard buses traverse Jutland from north to south, between Frederikshavn and Esbjerg, with stops in Aalborg and Viborg; a one-way
ticket between Frederikshavn and Esbjerg costs around DKr 245.

Long-distance bus routes from Aalborg to Copenhagen (5 hours) are
available through Abildskou buses or from Aalborg to Esbjerg (3 hours)
through Thinggaard Express.

Schedules for most bus travel within towns are posted at all bus stops
and fares are usually about DKr 15.
🔢 **Abildskou** ⊠ Graham Bellsvej 40, Århus ☎ 70/21-08-88 ⊕ www.abildskou.dk. **Bus/
Tog Samarbejde** ⊕ www.rejseplan.dk. **Thinggaard Bus** ☎ 70/10-00-20 ⊕ www.
thinggaard-bus.dk. **Thinggaard Express** ⊠ Jyllandsg. 8B, Aalborg ☎ 98/11-66-00
⊕ www.expresbus.dk.

CAR TRAVEL

Although train and bus connections are excellent, sites and towns in Jutland are widely dispersed, and the peninsula is best explored by car.
Whether you decide to take speedy, modern highways or winding old
roads, traffic is virtually nonexistent.

It is 275 km (175 mi) on the highway from the German/Danish border
in southern Jutland to Aalborg in the north. From Aalborg, it is only
60 km (38 mi) to the ferries in Frederikshavn or 70 km (44 mi) to Hirtshals.

EMERGENCIES

For ambulance, fire, or police anywhere in Denmark, dial 112. You
can contact local pharmacies in Aalborg for information on emergency
doctors.
🔢 **Aalborg pharmacy** ⊠ Budolfi Apotek, Alg. 60 ☎ 98/12-06-77.

SPORTS & THE OUTDOORS

CANOEING   Canoeing is not quite as popular in the north of the peninsula, as there
are many other sea-related sports available. However, the Sindal Turistbureau does offer one canoeing trip. (Sindal is inland, in the center
of Vendsyssel, where you'll find Denmark's northernmost beech forest.)
Starting in Ilbro, this canoeing trip allows you to paddle past Sønder-
skov, Sindal, Mosbjerg, the old electricity plant at Bindslev, and Uggerby.
Basic overnight accommodation is available.
🔢 **Info Sindal Turistbureau** ⊠ Jernbanegade 8, DK-9870 Sindal ☎ 98/93-66-93 ⊕ www.
sindal-tourist.dk.

FISHING   North Jutland, especially the "top of Denmark," offers dozens of fishing (or angling, as the Danes call the sport) opportunities for groups,

couples, or individual arrangements. Contact Toppen af Danmark to arrange trips.

🚺 Toppen af Danmark ⊠ Scandiatorv 1, DK-9900 Frederikshavn ☎ 98/42-31-49 ⊕ www.toppenafdanmark.dk/gb.

TOURS
Guided tours are few and far between, although some local tourism offices do provide them. Check with the individual city tourism offices for tips, reservations, and brochures that describe walking tours and scenic routes.

TRAIN TRAVEL
DSB makes hourly runs from Copenhagen to Frederikshavn, in northern Jutland, stopping in Aalborg (4¾ hours) along the way. The trip includes train passage across the Storebæltsbro between Korsør, on west Zealand, and Nyborg, on east Funen. A one-way trip from Copenhagen to Frederikshavn is about DKr 320. For long trips, the DSB trains are fast and efficient, with superb views of the countryside. Smaller towns do not have intercity trains, so you have to switch to buses once you arrive.

🚺 DSB ☎ 70/13-14-15 ⊕ www.dsb.dk.

VISITOR INFORMATION
🚺 Aalborg ⊠ Østeråg. 8 ☎ 98/12-60-22 🖶 98/16-69-22 ⊕ www.visitaalborg.com. **North Jutland Tourist Office** ⊕ www.visitnord.dk. **Skagen** ⊠ Sct. Laurentii Vej 22 ☎ 98/44-13-77 🖶 98/45-02-94 ⊕ www.skagen-tourist.dk.

Bornholm

WORD OF MOUTH

"Bornholm is grand! It is a wonderful place, with a great history. I fell in love with the place as a teen, and it continues to hold a special place in my heart!"

—Danna

Updated by
Bruce Bishop

CALLED THE PEARL OF THE BALTIC for its natural beauty and winsomely rustic towns, Bornholm, 177 km (110 mi) southeast of Zealand, is geographically unlike the rest of Denmark. A temperate climate has made this 588-square-km (235-square-mi) jumble of granite bluffs, clay soil, and rift valleys an extravagance of nature. Rich plantations of fir bristle beside wide dunes and vast heather fields; lush gardens teem with fig, cherry, chestnut, mulberry, and blue-blooming Chinese Emperor trees; and meadows sprout 12 varieties of orchids. Denmark's third-largest forest, the Almindingen, crowns the center; the southern tip is ringed with some of Europe's whitest beaches.

During the Iron and Bronze ages, Bornholm was inhabited by seafaring and farming cultures that peppered the land with burial dolmens and engravings. From the Middle Ages to the 18th century, the Danes battled the Swedes for ownership of the island, protecting it with strongholds and fortified churches, many of which still loom over the landscape. Bornholm's unique round churches—whitewashed splendors topped with black conical roofs—are a sight to behold. Considered to be some of the finest examples of Scandinavian medieval architecture, the churches imbue the island landscape with a lovely, stylized simplicity.

Today Bornholmers continue to draw their livelihood from the land and sea—and increasingly from tourism. Chalk-white chimneys rise above the rooftops, harbors are abob with painted fishing boats, and in spring and summer fields blaze with amber mustard and grain.

Few people come to Bornholm to stay indoors. Long, silky beaches, gentle hills, and lush forests make this a summer haven for walking, hiking, and swimming—particularly for families, many of whom take their summer vacations by packing provisions and children onto bikes, and cycling throughout the island.

Bornholm is famous throughout Scandinavia for its craftspeople, especially glassblowers and ceramicists, whose work is often pricier in Copenhagen and Stockholm. In the center of each town (especially Gudhjem and Svaneke) you can find crafts shops and *værksteder* (workshops). When you're on the road, watch for KERAMIK signs, which direct you to artists selling from home.

WHAT IT COSTS In kroner				
$$$$	**$$$**	**$$**	**$**	**¢**
RESTAURANTS over 180	141–180	121–140	90–120	under 90
HOTELS over 1,500	1,200–1,500	1,000–1,200	700–1,000	under 700

Restaurant prices are for a main course at dinner. Hotel prices are for two people in a standard double room, including service charge and tax.

Rønne

▶ ❶ *190 km (120 mi) southeast of Copenhagen (7 hrs by ferry from Køge or 3 hrs from Ystad, Sweden).*

Bornholm's capital, port, and largest town is Rønne, a good starting point for exploring northward or eastward. East of Nørrekås Harbor on Laksegade is an enchanting area of rose-clad 17th- and 18th-century houses, among them the tile-roof **Erichsens Gård** (Erichsen's Farm), from 1806. The home of the wealthy Erichsen family, whose daughter married the Danish poet Holger Drachmann, it includes paintings by Danish artist Kristian Zahrtmann, period furnishings, and a lovely garden. ⊠ *Lakseg. 7 ☎ 56/95–87–35 ⊕ www.bornholmsmuseer.dk/erichs ☜ DKr 30 ⊗ Mid-May–mid-Oct., Mon.–Sat. 10–5.*

Near Store Torv, the main square, is the **Bornholm Museum,** which puts on local geological and archaeological exhibits in addition to regular displays of more than 4,500 pieces of ceramics and glass. The museum also displays 25 18th-century Bornholmure (Bornholm Clocks), as characteristic of the island as smoked herring. In 1744 a Dutch ship was wrecked on Bornholm, and the English grandfather clocks it carried became the models for the island's clocks. ⊠ *Skt. Mortensg. 29 ☎ 56/95–07–35 ⊕ www.bornholmsmuseum.dk ☜ DKr 35 ⊗ Apr.–June, Sept., and Oct., daily 10–5; July and Aug., daily 10–5.*

Bornholm has long been recognized for its beautiful ceramics. **Hjorths Fabrik** (Hjorth's Factory), founded in 1859 by ceramicist Lauritz Hjorth, is one of Bornholm's oldest ceramics factories, and is today a "working ceramics museum." Follow the "route of clay" through the old factory and workshops, from the mixer and the kiln to the painting and decorating rooms. Along the way you see the ceramicists at work, casting, glazing, decorating, and firing, and you can observe how a lump of raw clay slowly takes shape on the potter's wheel, blossoming into a lovely vase or bowl. (Note that the ceramicists take a lunch break from about noon to 1.) The museum displays ceramics made at Hjorths factory since 1859, from Greek Revival pieces of the mid-1800s to ceramic apothecary jars from 1930–50. Many of the ceramic pieces dating from the mid- to late 1900s were made by Ulla and Marie Hjorth, sisters of the factory's founder. The museum shop sells a wide range of Hjorth ceramics, from its distinctive stoneware to old-fashioned pharmacy jars. ⊠ *Krystalg. 5 ☎ 56/95–01–60 ⊕ www. bornholmsmuseer.dk/hjorths ☜ May–Oct. DKr 30; Nov.–Apr. DKr 10 ⊗ May–Oct., Mon.–Sat. 10–5 (factory closed Sat.); Nov.–Apr., weekdays 1–5, Sat. 10–1 (exhibits and shops only).*

Where to Stay & Eat

★ $$$ ✕ **Fyrtøjet.** Overlooking the Strøget, this bright and spacious restaurant offers an ample dinner buffet with soup, salad, a selection of fish dishes (usually smoked salmon and cod), and beef. The lunchtime herring and fish buffet is a hit with summer crowds, as is the restaurant's inviting interior of pale yellow walls, blue tablecloths, and wooden floors. The house specialty is *granitbøf,* a hefty slab of beef served on a heated Bornholm granite-and-iron tray. While the beef is cooking on the hot gran-

Bornholmers don't have a lot of positive words for material goods, but when it comes to expressing nature, the language is abundant. Bornholm, dubbed the Sunshine island, generally has a better climate than the rest of Denmark, so a bicycle can make a great form of transportation if you are so inclined; if not, these tours can be accomplished in a car, as well. Moreover, bringing a tent for beachside camping allows you more time to explore the beautiful coastline as well as the lush inland forests of the island. If you are pressed for time, you should choose between the north and east coasts, rather than trying to cram it all in on a whirlwind tour. If you have a week, a full island loop with excursions inland is more feasible.

7

Numbers in the text correspond to numbers in the margin and on the Bornholm map.

If you have 3 days

Begin day one in **Rønne ❶** ⌐, where you will have arrived by ferry. Beforehand, you should choose to explore either the island's north or east coast. If you decide on the north coast, hop on your bike early and peddle up to the fortress ruins of **Hammershus ❷**, where you will continue on to **Hammeren ❸** and end your lengthy day in 🏨 **Allinge ❹**. Spend the next day at **Gudhjem ❺**, giving yourself plenty of time to see the sights and sample the local smoked herring. On the third day cycle back to Rønne, heading home through the **Rø Plantage ❻**. If you're up for it, you could make a small detour (10 km) to visit **Østerlars ❼** to see the largest traditional church on Bornholm.

If you should wish to go eastward from Rønne, aim for 🏨 **Svaneke ❽** on the first day, stopping in the forest at **Almindingen ❿** to rest your legs. On the second day move on to **Neksø ❾**; stock up on food and drink and spend the rest of the day on the southern beaches swimming and tanning. On the third day follow the southern shoreline back to Rønne.

If you have 6 days

From **Rønne ❶** ⌐, follow the northern three-day route laid out above as far as 🏨 **Gudhjem ❺**, where you should spend your second night. Swing by the **Rø Plantage ❻** on your way to **Østerlars ❼**, and on to 🏨 **Svaneke ❽**, where you will spend two nights, taking the fourth day for an excursion to the woods at **Almindingen ❿**. On the fifth day drive to **Neksø ❾** for a quick stopover, then look for a perfect strip of sand along the shore between Snogebæk and Pedersker, where you can while away the afternoon. Either stay and camp there or return to Svaneke for its hotel accommodations. On the sixth and last day, turn west toward Rønne, driving through **Åkirkeby ⓫** to view the island's oldest church and to **Nylars ⓬**, where you'll see another round church typical of the island's architecture.

ite, it's flambéed with whiskey. You pour the accompanying cold sauce (usually béarnaise) over the meat when it's suitably done. The former owner patented this unique tray. ⊠ *Store Torveg. 22* ☎ *56/95–30–12* ⊕ *www.fyrtoejet.dk* ⊟ *AE, DC, MC, V* ⊗ *No lunch Jan.–Mar.*

$–$$ ✗ **Rådhuskroen.** With exposed timbers, comfortable armchairs, and close-set tables, this restaurant provides a softly lit change from Rønne's busy streets. The menu highlights substantial beef dishes such as pepper steak with wine and cream sauce, but you can also choose from a couple of local fish specialities—try the poached Baltic salmon or grilled fillet of sole, both served with lobster sauce. ⊠ *Nørreg. 2* ☎ *56/95–00–69* ⊟ *AE, DC, MC, V.*

★ ¢–$$$ ✗ **Strøgets Spisehûz.** When the hunger pangs hit, Rønne locals head for this friendly, family-owned restaurant at the end of Strøget. The hearty Danish fare includes beef with cognac sauce and potatoes, and smoked salmon sprinkled with lemon. The mood is casual, with hanging plants, little Danish flags, paper napkins, and pink and purple curtains. ⊠ *Store Torveg. 39* ☎ *56/95–81–69* ⊟ *MC, V* ⊗ *Closed Mon.*

$$$ ▦ **Radisson SAS Fredensborg.** Along a curve of forest near a small beach, this hotel sets the island's standard for luxury. The glass-and-tile lobby is spare and sunny, the staff pleasant and eager. The dozen ample apartments have full kitchens, and guest rooms have modern furniture and balconies overlooking the sea. The rustic restaurant, De Fem Ståuerne, serves traditional French-Danish food. Guests have use of the pool at Hotel Griffen. ⊠ *Strandvejen 116, DK–3600* ☎ *56/90–44–44* ⊟ *56/90–44–43* ⊕ *www.bornholmhotels.dk* ⌲ *72 rooms, 4 suites, 12 apartments* ⚲ *Restaurant, room service, tennis court, hot tub, sauna, bar, meeting room, some pets allowed, no-smoking rooms* ⊟ *AE, DC, MC, V.*

$$ ▦ **Hotel Griffen.** One of Bornholm's largest and most modern hotels is just off a busy street near the Rønne harbor. Three stories tall with plenty of windows, it has wonderful views—the sea on one side and Rønne on the other. Rooms have every modern convenience. Guests may use the tennis facilities at the Radisson. ⊠ *Nordre Kystvej 34, DK–3700* ☎ *56/90–42–44* ⊟ *56/90–42–45* ⊕ *www.bornholmhotels.dk* ⌲ *142 rooms, 2 suites with bath* ⚲ *Restaurant, room service, cable TV, indoor pool, sauna, bar, dance club, meeting room, some pets allowed, no-smoking rooms* ⊟ *AE, DC, MC, V.*

¢ ▦ **Sverres Hotel.** Near the harbor in a building dating from 1850, this cheery hotel has simple, clean rooms. Enjoy a morning meal in the sunny breakfast room. Contented guests have covered the walls with artwork and drawings; the former owner, a jazz musician, sounded his own note by leaving behind his collection of jazz memorabilia. ⊠ *Snellemark 2, DK–3700* ☎ *56/95–03–03* ⊟ *56/95–03–92* ⊕ *www.sverres-hotel.dk* ⌲ *20 rooms, 10 with bath* ⚲ *Dining room* ⊟ *AE, DC, MC, V.*

¢ ⚴ **Galløkken Camping.** This site is just a short walk from the Rønne center, near an old military museum. The open grounds are surrounded by a perimeter of trees. The shower and cooking facilities are good. ⊠ *Strandvejen 4, DK–3700 Rønne* ☎ *56/95–23–20* ⊕ *www.gallokken.dk* ⚲ *Kitchen, playground, laundry facilities, flush toilets, drinking water, showers, general store.*

1

Fresh & Smoked Seafood
Fishing has been a major industry in Bornholm since the Middle Ages, when inhabitants fished large quantities of herring in the Baltic Sea and preserved it by means of drying and salting. In recent years times have been hard, but the island is still famous for its seafood. Some of the best herring in the country comes from the waters around Bornholm and the locals have their own special recipes for pickling or curing the fish. Salmon and cod are also prevalent; inquire about local specialties. The northern and eastern coasts are dotted with fishing harbors and most of them have a local smokehouse with an excellent selection of fish. After the day's catch has been brought in and cleaned, the fish are taken to the smokehouse and hung side by side on large spears in smoking chambers above red-hot alderwood for eight or nine hours. A number of smokehouses double as informal eateries, or there will be a vendor nearby. A local specialty is called Sol over Gudhjem (Sun over Gudhjem, named for the town where the first smokehouse was built in 1886), a smoked herring served with raw egg yolk, radishes, and onions on rye. Another item to try is smoked herring eaten Bornholmer style, which is taking the fish by the tail, holding it above your mouth, and eating the whole thing, starting with the head.

Hiking
In contrast to the rest of Denmark, Bornholm is hilly and rugged. Marked trails crisscross the island, including three 4-km (2½-mi) hikes through the Almindingen Forest and several more through its Ekkodalen (Echo Valley). The northern coastline is beautiful but a rocky and more strenuous walk. Ask for a map, routes, and tips from any tourism office. The *Bornholm Green Guide*, available in shops and tourism offices, offers suggestions for walking and hiking tours.

Swimming
Beach worshipers thrive in Bornholm. The swimming and sunning are best in the south, between Pedersker and Snogebæk, where the dunes are tall and the beaches wide. Dueodde beach, blanketed in fine, white sand, unfolds along Bornholm's southern edge. As elsewhere in Denmark, topless bathing is common and nude bathing is tolerated.

Nightlife & the Arts
Bornholm's nightlife is limited to a handful of discos and clubs in Rønne, which open and close frequently as tastes change. For live jazz on weekends, head for the atmospheric **Doctor Jazz** (⊠ Snellemark 26 ☎ no phone), outfitted with an ample stage surrounded by round tables and jazz instruments hanging on the walls. At the ever-popular **O'Malley Irish Pub** (⊠ Store Torveg. 2 ☎ 56/95–00–16) a friendly crowd of locals and tourists mingles with frothy pints in hand.

Shopping
Bornholm is famous for its quality ceramics, and Rønne, as the island's capital city, offers the widest variety. The island's history of ceramics

starts in 1773 when ceramicist Michael Andersen established a factory in Rønne. Today, his legacy lives on at the large factory-turned-shop **Michael Andersen Bornholmsk Keramik** (⊠ Lille Torv 7 ☎ 56/95–00–01 ☉ weekdays 10–5:30, Sat. 10–3) on a small square near the center of town. The shop's wide selection includes the distinctive *krakelering* ceramics, where the surface of the ceramics is covered with a web of tiny black lines that give the pieces a cracked look. Ceramicists still work in the back studio, and the store sells a range of ceramics.

The distinctive clocks, or Bornholmures, sold on the island are all handmade and hand painted with round (or sometimes rectangular) faces. The new-style clocks have a modern touch: on the hour they play classics such as Mozart or Verdi and some even sound the hour with Stephen Sondheim or Andrew Lloyd Webber. Antique versions are the costliest, with prices from DKr 10,000 to DKr 80,000 and up. A handmade custom clock costs DKr 37,000 on average. Reproductions modeled on original clocks are custom-made by **Bornholmerure** (⊠ Torneværksvej 26 ☎ 56/95–31–08).

You can pick up unusual gifts and one-of-a-kind clothing made of handprinted textiles at **Bente Hammer** (⊠ Nyker Hovedg. 32 ☎ 56/96–33–35).

Hammershus

★ ❷ *8 km (5 mi) north of Jons Kapel, 30 km (19 mi) north of Rønne.*

The **fortress of Hammershus,** now in ruins, was once northern Europe's largest stronghold. The hulking fortress was begun in 1255 by the archbishop of Lund (Sweden), and became the object of centuries of struggle between Denmark and Sweden. In 1658 Danes under Jens Kofoed killed its Swedish governor, and the castle was given back to Denmark. Used until 1743, it was quarried for stone to fortify Christiansø and that island's buildings. The government finally intervened in 1822, and the site is now a mass of snaggle-toothed walls and towers atop a grassy knoll. Occasionally concerts and other performances are held here. ✉ *Free.*

Nightlife & the Arts

Special events don't happen nearly often enough, but check with Bornholm's **Main Tourist Office** (☎ 56/95–95–00 ⊕ www.bornholminfo.dk) to see if any are planned at or near Hammershus. The ruins add a spectacular dimension to classical music and the performing arts.

Hammeren

❸ *5 km (3 mi) north of Hammershus, 36 km (23 mi) north of Rønne.*

This knuckle of land jutting from the island's northern tip is nearly separated from the island by a deep rift valley and the Hammer Sø (Hammer Lake). Despite constant Baltic winds, rare plants and trees grow on the warm, granite-scattered Hammeren (the Hammer), including radiant anemones. Look across the water south of the tip to the stone formation known as the Camel Heads.

> **need a break?**

A little more than 3 km (2 mi) southeast of Hammeren is **Madsebakke,** the largest collection of Bronze Age rock carvings in Denmark. They are presumed to be ceremonial carvings, which ancient fishermen and farmers hoped would bring good weather and bountiful crops. The most interesting of them depicts 11 ships, including one with a sun wheel, an ancient type of sun dial.

Allinge

❹ *3 km (2 mi) east of Madsebakke, 21 km (13 mi) north of Rønne.*

In Allinge and its twin town Sandvig you'll find centuries-old neighborhoods and, particularly in Allinge, half-timber houses and herring smokehouses sprouting tall chimneys. Just south is a wood that the islanders call **Trolleskoven** (Trolls' Forest). Legend says that fog comes from the brew in the troll's kitchen and that when the trolls are brewing something they leave their little abodes under the cover of fog to wander the forest looking for trouble. The most mischievous is the littlest troll, Krølle Bølle, who has become a mascot of sorts for Bornholm. His likeness is everywhere—especially in souvenir shops.

Where to Stay

$–$$ ⊡ **Strandhotellet.** Romantic charm is the draw at this venerable hotel,
Fodor'sChoice built in 1895 and refurbished in 1992. It's on a corner across from the
★ harbor. A white arched entry leads into a stone-and-whitewashed lobby.
Rooms are furnished in plain beech furniture with woolen covers and
pastel colors. ⊠ *Strandpromenaden 7, DK–3770 Sandvig* ☎ *56/48–03–14*
🖶 *56/48–02–09* ⊕ *www.strandhotellet.dk* ⤳ *52 rooms, 1 suite with
bath* ⚲ *Restaurant, bar* ⊟ *MC, V.*

¢ ⚠ **Sandvig Familie Camping.** Pleasantly close to the beach, most of the
camping sites here have a view of the water. The large kitchen and bathing
facilities are well maintained. ⊠ *Sandlinien 5, DK–3770* ☎ *56/48–04–47
or 56/48–00–01* ⚲ *Kitchen, playground, showers* ⊙ *Closed Nov.–Mar.*

**need a
break?**

Eight kilometers (5 mi) southeast of Allinge along the coastal path are
the grottoes and granite cliffs of the **Helligdomsklipperne** (Cliffs of
Sanctuary), which contain a well-known rock formation best seen
from the boats that sail the nearby waters in summer. In the Middle
Ages, people used to visit these waters, believing that they had
healing powers—hence the name. The **Helligdomsklipperne boat**
(☎ 58/48–51–65) departs several times daily in the summer from the
Gudhjem harbor. The round-trip costs DKr 60. Just southeast of the
Helligdomsklipperne, a pastoral coastal path leads to the tiny,
preserved **Døndalen Forest.** Its fertile soil bears a surprising
profusion of Mediterranean vegetation, including fig and cherry trees.
During rainy periods look for a waterfall at the bottom of the dale.

Gudhjem

★ ❺ *18 km (11 mi) east of Allinge, 33 km (21 mi) northeast of Rønne.*

At the height of summer, Gudhjem (God's Home) is perhaps the most
tourist-packed town on Bornholm. Tiny half-timber houses and gift shops
with lace curtains and clay roofs line steep stone streets that loop around
the harbor. The island's first smokehouses still produce alder-smoked
golden herring.

★ ☕ Walk down Brøddegade, which turns into Melstedvej; here you'll find
the **Landsbrugs Museum** (Agricultural Museum) and Melstedgård, a
working farm. The farm includes the well-kept house and garden of a
19th-century family who lived here. Notice the surprisingly bright colors used on the interior of the house, and leave time to visit the old shop
where you can buy locally produced woolen sweaters, wooden spoons,
and even homemade mustard. ⊠ *Melstedvej 25* ☎ *56/48–55–98* ⊕ *www.
bornholmsmuseer.dk/melstedg* 🎫 *DKr 35* ⊙ *Mid-May–June and
Sept.–Oct. 22, weekdays and Sun. 10–5; July and Aug., daily 10–5.*

Just up the hill from Gudhjem's waterfront is the **Oluf Høst Museet,** with
a collection of paintings by Bornholm artist Oluf Høst, including his
series of a whitewashed Bornholm farm called Bognemark, which he depicted with glowing splashes of oranges and reds from the setting sun.
Høst and other modernist Bornholm artists are well known for their abil-

ity to capture Bornholm's natural light. The museum is in Høst's home, which he built in 1929 out of two fisherman's cottages and lived in until his death in 1966. It's easy to see why Høst found artistic inspiration here. At the top of the house's leafy, rock-strewn garden are lovely views over the colorful cottages of Gudhjem. ⊠ *Løkkeg. 35* ☎ *56/ 48–50–38* ⊕ *www.ohmus.dk* ✉ *DKr 45* ☉ *May–mid-June, Tues.–Sun. 11–5; mid-June–Sept., daily 11–5.*

off the beaten path

BORNHOLMS KUNSTMUSEUM – If you follow the main road, Hellidomsvej, out of Gudhjem in the direction of Allinge/Sandvig, you'll come to Bornholm's art museum, an excellent example of the Danes' ability to integrate art, architecture, and natural surroundings. Built by the architectural firm of Fogh and Følner in 1993, with an extension added in 2003, the white-painted brick, granite, and sandstone building surrounds a thin stream of "holy" trickling water that exits the building and leads the visitor to a walkway and overlook above the Helligdomsklipperne. Throughout, the walls of the museum are punched with picture windows overlooking nearby grazing cows and the crashing Baltic: a natural accompaniment to the art. Most of the works are by Bornholmers, including a body of modernist work by Oluf Høst, Karl Esaksen, and Olaf Rude. The museum also displays some sculpture and glass, as well as a survey of more historical paintings. Check out the restaurant and shop. ⊠ *Hellidomsvej 95* ☎ *56/48–43–86* ⊕ *www. bornholms-kunstmuseum.dk* ✉ *DKr 35* ☉ *May, Sept., and Oct., Tues.–Sun. 10–5; June–Aug., daily 10–5; Nov.–Apr., Tues. and Thurs. 1–5, Sun. 10–5.*

CHRISTIANSØ – A 45-minute boat ride northeast from Gudhjem will bring you to the historic island of Christiansø. Though it was originally a bastion, the Storetårn (Big Tower) and Lilletårn (Little Tower) are all that remain of the fort, built in 1684 and dismantled in 1855. The barracks, street, and gardens, for which the earth was hauled here by boat, have hardly changed since that time. They remain under the jurisdiction of the defense ministry, making this a tiny tax-free haven for its 100 inhabitants. Nearby, the rocky, uninhabited island of **Græsholmen** is an inaccessible bird sanctuary—the only place in Denmark where the razorbill and guillemot breed.

Where to Stay & Eat

¢–$ ✕ **Café Klint.** Locals flock to this red, half-timber harborside restaurant, where the portions of down-home Danish fare are generous and the prices are low. Dishes include smoked salmon with spinach, fillet of sole with remoulade, or a plate heaped with different kinds of herring. In summer, tables are set out on the terrace. In winter the restaurant changes its name to Vinter Klint (Winter Klint), and you can't get cozier than sitting in the low-ceiling dining room, surrounded by pine-green walls, and perhaps warmed by a glass or two of the house wine. ⊠ *Ejnar Mikkelsensvej 20* ☎ *56/48–56–26* ▭ *MC, V.*

$–$$ ✕◫ **Jantzens Hotel.** Founded in 1872, this bright-yellow building with white shutters and wrought-iron balconies is Gudhjem's oldest hotel. The front windows face the sea, and the backyard gives way to a sunny, idyllic terrace and rose garden. Much of the hotel has been lovingly restored, with an eye to recapturing its turn-of-the-20th-century ambience. Rooms are outfitted with hardwood floors, pale green walls, and rattan furniture. The balconies have views over Gudhjem's yellow and red houses, clustered against a backdrop of the blue Baltic. The bathrooms are small and basic, but all rooms are equipped with a refrigerator. The hotel's interior is still a work in progress; so far half the rooms have been restored, so ask when booking. What was once a pavilion and tea terrace is now utilized by the restaurant, Andi's Kokken, which includes on its French-Danish menu such dishes as mussels in a mild curry sauce with capers, and venison with shallots and mushrooms. Dessert might be fresh blueberries, hand-picked by the chef from the nearby fields. The restaurant is closed Mondays and November through April. ✉ *Brøddeg. 33, DK–3760* ☎ *56/48–50–17* 🖷 *56/48–57–15* ⊕ *www. jantzenshotel.dk* ⛟ *18 rooms with bath* ⚎ *Restaurant, some pets allowed (fee)* ▭ *MC, V* ⊙ *Closed Nov.–Apr.*

¢ ◫ **Danhostel Gudhjem.** In a half-timber 100-year-old former manor house, this hostel in the middle of Gudhjem offers single- to eight-bed rooms of standard pine bunks and industrial carpeting. There are six kitchens available for use. The hostel also has rooms in several houses within the village (with common kitchens and baths), which tend to be quieter than the main house. ✉ *Løkkeg. 7, DK–3760* ☎ *56/48–50–35* 🖷 *56/48–56–35* ⊕ *www.danhostel-gudhjem.dk* ⛟ *50 rooms with shared bath* ⚎ *Restaurant, laundry facilities* ▭ *MC, V.*

Shopping

Baltic Sea Glass (✉ Melstedvej 47 ☎ 56/48–56–41), on the main road just on the outskirts of town, offers high-quality, bright, and imaginative decanters, glasses, candlesticks, and one-of-a-kind pieces, including an old-fashioned contraption to catch flies. In town, see the delicate porcelain bowls of **Per Rehfeldt** (✉ Salenevej 1 ☎ 56/48–54–13). Unique, hand-thrown ceramic work is available from and by **Julia Manitius** (✉ Holkavej 12 ☎ 56/48–55–99).

Rø Plantage

❻ *6 km (4 mi) southwest of Gudhjem, 24 km (15 mi) northeast of Rønne.*

Rø Plantation is dense forest that serves as a quiet foil to the hubbub of Gudhjem. A century ago it was a heather-covered grazing area, but after stone dikes were erected to keep the cattle out, spruce, pine, larch, and birch were cultivated. The cool refuge now consists largely of saplings and new growth—the result of devastating storms in the late '50s and '60s.

Rø Golfbane (✉ Spellingevej 3 ☎ 56/48–40–50) has won various European and Scandinavian awards for its natural beauty—and challenges. Its 18 holes are set close to the coastal cliffs and have views of the sea. It has a pro shop and a restaurant.

Østerlars

❼ *5 km (3 mi) east of Rø Plantage, 22 km (14 mi) northeast of Rønne.*

Fodor's Choice ★ The standout attraction here is the **Østerlars Kirke.** The largest of the island's four round churches, it was built in about 1150; extensions, including the buttresses, were added later. Constructed from boulders and slabs of limestone, the whitewashed church was part spiritual sanctuary, part fortification, affording protection from enemy armies and pirates. Inside is the island's only painted tympanum, with a faded image of a cross and decorative foliage. Several Gothic wall paintings—including depictions of the Annunciation and Nativity—have survived from the 1300s. ✉ *Gudhjemsvej 28* ☎ *56/49–82–64* 🖃 *DKr 10* ⊙ *May–mid-Oct., Mon.–Sat. 9–5; in July, also open Sun. 1–5.*

> **off the beaten path**

KIRSTEN CLEMANN'S CERAMIC STUDIO – Bornholm, with its Baltic Sea location and wide-open skies, has been drawing artists to its shores for the past century. Kirsten Clemann has been here for several decades, creating her fanciful, one-of-a-kind ceramic designs in a clay-spattered studio adjoining her home, just west of the small, blink-and-you'll-miss-it town of Østermarie, 5 km (3 mi) southeast of Østerlars. As Clemann tells it, it took awhile to be accepted into the island community, but now her pieces are proudly displayed in restaurants and craft shows across Bornholm—and across the globe. Clemann works out of her pleasantly chaotic studio, where she creates turtles, hens, birdbaths, and delicate, floating ceramic balls for ponds. She usually works with the colors blue and rose. Clemann's large, unique reliefs are often snapped up by German buyers; the pieces may depict rows of dancing women twirling their umbrellas, or be covered with protruding glazed ceramic fish heads, inspired by a display at a fish market. Clemann's other passion is her garden, which is teeming with blooming bushes and flowers and is strewn with her ceramic creations. Call ahead. ✉ *Almindingensvej 84, 2½ km (1½ mi) west of Østermarie* ☎ *56/47–27–05.*

Svaneke

❽ *21 km (13 mi) east of Østerlars, 49 km (31 mi) northeast of Rønne.*

The coastal town of Svaneke, Denmark's easternmost settlement, is an enchanting hamlet of 17th- and 18th-century houses, winding cobbled streets, and a harbor sliced from the rocky earth. Once a fishing village, it is now immaculately preserved and the site of a thriving artists' community.

Bornholm's smoked herring is famous throughout Scandinavia, and no visit to the island is complete without sampling it for yourself—preferably in the manner of the Danes, who eat it outside on a sunny terrace, with a cold Carlsberg in hand. For more than 35 years, Hjorth Hansen has been smoking herring at **Hjorths Røgeri** (Hjorth's Smokehouse), 2 km (1 mi) south of Svaneke. Every morning at 6 AM, Hjorth hauls in big baskets of elmwood, lights a fire, and begins smoking the fresh herring, tending to the fire with a long pole wrapped with rags at one end. Five hours later, he serves up plates of warm, smoked herring in the adjoining terrace. Hjorth works from late April to October. The best time to watch him in action is around 10 AM, in the last hour of the smoking process. ✉ *Brugsebakken 18, Årsdale* ☎ *56/49–61–10* ☉ *Late Apr.–Oct.*

Where to Stay & Eat

¢–$$ ✕ **Bryghuset.** Microbreweries are a new concept in the land of Carlsberg, but the idea is catching on, and Svaneke's Bryghuset (Brew House) is one of the first. All the beer is brewed on the premises, in a massive copper brew kettle linked by piping to the kitchen. The menu is based on the concept that food should compliment the beer. The house specialty is Bryggerben ("Brewer's bone"), a messy, finger-licking plate of spareribs smothered in barbecue sauce, which can be enjoyed at one of the long wooden tables set under the beam ceilings or on the large summer terrace. Also on offer is a platter of Christiansø herring served with egg, rye bread, and butter. At Easter and Christmas, try the stronger festive brew. ✉ *Torvet 5* ☎ *56/49–73–21* ⊟ *MC, V* ☉ *Closed Jan.*

$$ ✕▣ **Siemsens Gaard.** Built in a 270-year-old merchant house, this U-shape hotel with a gravel-courtyard café overlooks the harbor. The inside is cushy with sofas below severe black-and-white prints and antiques. The rooms are varied, but all have stripped pine and soft colors, and all are no-smoking. The bright, modern restaurant serves French-Danish food, with a menu of 75 dishes—from club sandwiches to smoked Baltic salmon to smørrebrød. The restaurant is closed from November to May. ✉ *Havnebryggen 9, DK–3740* ☎ *56/49–61–49* ⊕ *www. siemsens.dk* ⇆ *51 rooms with bath* ⚲ *Restaurant, café, some pets allowed, no-smoking rooms* ⊟ *AE, DC, MC, V.*

Shopping

Stroll through the boutiques in the central Glastorvet in Svaneke. Among them is the studio of **Pernille Bülow** (✉ Glastorvet, Brænderigænget 8 ☎ 56/49–66–72), one of Denmark's most famous glassblowers. Her work is sold in Copenhagen's best design shops. Even if you buy directly from her studio, don't expect bargains, but do expect colorful, experimental work.

Neksø

❾ *9 km (5½ mi) south of Svaneke, 48 km (30 mi) northeast of Rønne.*

Neksø (or Nexø) bustles with tourists and locals who shop and live around its busy harbor, lined with fishing boats from throughout the Baltics and Eastern Europe. It might seem like a typical 17th-century town, but it was rebuilt almost completely after World War II, when the Russians bombed it to dislodge stubborn German troops who refused to surrender—three days after the rest of Denmark had been liberated. The Russians lingered on the island until April 1946.

Wander down to the harbor to find the **Neksø Museum,** housed in a mustard-yellow building that was once the town's courthouse. The museum has a fine collection of fishing and local history exhibits and maritime memorabilia. ⊠ *Havnen* ☎ *56/49–25–56* ⊕ *www.bornholmsmuseer. dk* ⊒ *DKr 35* ⊘ *May–Oct., Tues.–Sun. 10–4.*

The **Andersen Nexøs Hus** contains photographs and mementos of Danish author Martin Andersen Hansen (1909–55), who changed his last name to Nexø after his beloved town. A complicated man and vehement socialist, he wrote, among other works, *Pelle the Conqueror,* set in Bornholm at the turn of the 20th century, when Swedish immigrants were exploited by Danish landowners. The story was turned into an Academy Award–winning film. ⊠ *Ferskesøstr. 36* ☎ *56/49–45–42* ⊕ *www.bornholmsmuseer.dk/manexo* ⊒ *DKr 20* ⊘ *Mid-May–Oct., weekdays 10–4, Sat. 10–2.*

Where to Eat

$$–$$$ ✕ **Tre Søstre.** Facing Nexø's bustling harbor, this spacious restaurant, housed in a converted storage warehouse, is named after a 19th-century Danish ship *The Three Sisters,* a model of which hangs on the wall. The creatively decorated interior (right down to the plates and the candlesticks) pays tribute to Bornholm's artists. The lavender, pale-orange, and sea-green vases of Svaneke glassblower Pernille Bülow grace the window sills, providing a bright and delicate contrast to the restaurant's rustic furnishings. Hanging from the ceiling is a playful, blue-and-green ceramic fish, created by long-time Bornholmer Kirsten Clemann. The Danish menu includes grilled salmon with spinach and hollandaise sauce, and fried scampi flavored with cognac, garlic, and curry. Occasionally, jazz concerts are performed here. ⊠ *Havnen 5* ☎ *56/49–33–93* ⊟ *AE, DC, MC, V* ⊘ *Closed Sept.–May.*

Shopping

For exquisite woodwork see **Bernard Romain** (⊠ Rønnevej 54 ☎ *56/ 48–86–66*).

Almindingen

⑩ *23 km (14 mi) west of Neksø, 27 km (17 mi) northeast of Rønne.*

The lush Almindingen, Denmark's third-largest forest, is filled with ponds, lakes, evergreens, and well-marked trails, and it blooms with lily of the valley in spring. Within it, the oak-lined **Ekkodalen** (Echo Valley)—where children love to hear their shouts resound—is networked by trails leading to smooth rock faces that soar 72 feet high. At the northern edge, near the road to Østermarie, once stood one of Bornholm's most famous sights: seven evergreens growing from a single trunk. The plant succumbed to old age in 1995, but you may still be able to see the remains of its curious trunk.

Sports & the Outdoors

HIKING Check with the tourist board for a map showing three 4-km (2½-mi) hikes through the Almindingen Forest and several more through its Echo Valley. The *Bornholm Green Guide,* available in shops and tourism offices, offers walking and hiking routes.

Åkirkeby

⑪ *5 km (3 mi) south of Almindingen, 16 km (9 mi) east of Rønne.*

Åkirkeby is the oldest town on the island, with a municipal charter from 1346. The town's church, the **Åkirke,** is Bornholm's oldest and largest, dating from the mid-12th century. Though it is not one of the more typical round churches, its walls and tower were well suited for defense. The altarpiece and pulpit are Dutch Renaissance pieces from about 1600, but the carved sandstone font is as old as the church itself. ✉ *Torvet* ☎ *56/97–41–03* 🎫 *DKr 10* ⊙ *Mon.–Sat. 10–4.*

Nylars

⑫ *8 km (5 mi) west of Åkirkeby, 9 km (6 mi) east of Rønne.*

Like the Østerlars church, the round **Nylars Kirke** dates from 1150. The chalk paintings from the Old Testament on its central pillar are the oldest on the island, possibly dating from 1250. Even older are the runic stones on the church's porch. Both are of Viking origin. ✉ *Kirkevej* ☎ *56/ 97–20–13* 🎫 *Free* ⊙ *Mid-May–mid-Sept., weekdays 9–5.*

Bornholm A to Z

AIRPORTS

Bornholm's airport is 5 km (3 mi) south of Rønne at the island's southwestern tip.

Cimber Air has six flights a day to Copenhagen (three per day on weekends); the trip lasts 35 minutes and costs about DKr 750. ✈ **Bornholms Lufthavn** ☎ 56/95–26–26 ⊕ www.slv.dk/bornholm. **Cimber Air** ☎ 56/ 95–11–11 ⊕ www.cimber.dk.

BIKE TRAVEL

Biking is eminently feasible and pleasant on Bornholm, thanks to a network of more than 200 km (125 mi) of cycle roads, including an old railway converted to a cross-island path. The network is made up of paths, forest tracks, quiet roads, and marked cycle lanes on main roads. The cycle routes are marked by green and blue signs. Today Bornholm has one of the best and most beautiful cycle networks in northern Europe.

Rentals of sturdy two-speeds and tandems are available for about DKr 50 a day at more than 20 different establishments all over the island—near the ferry; at the airport; and in Allinge, Gudhjem, Hasle, Pedersker (near Åkirkeby), Rønne, Svaneke, and most other towns. ✈ Bike Rentals **Bornholms Cykeludlejning** ✉ Nordre Kystvej 5, Rønne ☎ 56/ 95–13–59. **Cykel-Centret** ✉ Sønderg. 7, Rønne ☎ 56/95–06–04.

BOAT & FERRY TRAVEL

The Bornholmstrafikken car ferry is Bornholm's "lifeline" to the rest of Denmark, with the Køge–Rønne service, which allows you to travel from Køge to the island overnight (travel time is 6½ hours). There is one departure nightly.

With the opening of the Øresund Bridge between Copenhagen and Malmö, *Bornholmstrafikken* has increased its ferry departures from Ystad, which lies 57 km (36 mi) southeast of Malmö. There are two to four departures from Ystad to Rønne daily, on either the high-speed ferry (1 hour, 20 minutes), or the conventional ferry (2½ hours). There are up to nine departures a day during the peak season.

Nordbornholms Turistbureau (North Bornholm Tourist Board) is the agent for a summer ferry that links Neu Mukran and Fährhafen Sassnitz on the island of Rügen in Germany. Scandlines, a competing company, offers passage aboard the ferry to Fährhafen Sassnitz. Prices vary according to the number of people traveling and the size of the vehicle. There is also a boat between Swinoujscie, Poland and Rønne (7 hours); call Polferries in Poland.

◢ **Bornholmstrafikken** ☎ 56/95-18-66 ⊕ www.bornholmferries.dk. **Nordbornholms Turistbureau** ☎ 56/48-00-01 ⊕ www.bornholmsbookingcenter.dk. **Polferries** ✉ Norgesvej 2 Rønne ☎ 56/95-10 69, 48/943-552-102 in Poland ⊕ www.polferries. com. **Scandlines** ☎ 33/15-15-15 ⊕ www.scandlines.dk.

BUS TRAVEL

The Bornholmerbussen (Bornholm Bus) No. 866 runs from Copenhagen's main station, travels across the Øresund Bridge to Malmö, in Sweden, and then continues to Ystad, where it connects with a ferry to Rønne. The trip takes around three hours. Buses depart two to four times daily, usually once in the morning and several times in the afternoon and evening. Call Bornholmerbussen for more details.

Though bus service is certainly not as frequent as in major cities, there are regular connections (with BAT, see below) between Bornholm towns. Schedules are posted at all stations, and you can usually pick one up on board. The major bus routes have an hourly service, and all buses depart from Rønne. In peak season an additional service also operates around the coast. The timetable is coordinated with ferry arrivals and departures.

◢ **BAT** (Bornholm Municipality Traffic Company) ☎ 56/95-21-21 ⊕ www.bat.dk. **Bornholmerbussen** ✉ Yderholmen 18 DK-2750 Ballerup ☎ 44/68-44-00 ⊕ www. bornholmerbussen.dk.

CAR RENTAL

Rønne's Hertz agency is near the ferry arrivals and departures area. The Avis branch is also nearby.

◢ **Avis** ✉ Snellemark 19, Rønne ☎ 56/95-22-08. **Hertz** ✉ Munch Petersens Vej 1, Rønne ☎ 56/91-00-12.

CAR TRAVEL

There are excellent roads on the island, but be alert for cyclists and the occasional cow-crossing.

EMERGENCIES

The general emergency number for ambulance, accident, or fire anywhere in Denmark is 112.

◢ **Bornholm's Central Hospital** ✉ Sygehusvej, Rønne ☎ 56/95-11-65. **Rønne Apotek** (Rønne Pharmacy) ✉ Store Torveg. 12, Rønne ☎ 56/95-01-30.

SPORTS & THE OUTDOORS

FISHING Cod, salmon, and herring fishing are excellent in season, though better from a boat than from shore. There are unique experiences in autumn, winter, and spring: massive releases of salmon fry from the Salmon Hatchery in Nexø and the deep water around the island provide perfect conditions and ensure good salmon fishing in the Baltic. Licenses cost DKr 25 per day, DKr 75 per week, and DKr 100 per year. Contact the tourist office for details and information on charter trips.

TOURS

Klippefly can arrange a 20- to 40-minute aerial tour in a Cessna or Piper plane that covers either the entire coast or the northern tip.

The BAT (Bornholm Municipality Traffic Company) offers some inventive summer tours. All are available Tuesday through Friday, from mid-July until early August. All begin at the red bus terminal at Snellemark 30 in Rønne at 10 AM and cost DKr 110. (You can also buy a 24-hour bus card for DKr 110, or a five- or seven-day card for DKr 390, good for both the regional buses and the tours.) Tour prices do not include some DKr 5–DKr 10 admissions or lunch at a herring smokehouse. The five-hour tour aboard the Kunsthåndværkbussen (Arts and Crafts Bus) includes stops at glass, pottery, textile, and silver studios. In summer, different studios are visited each day. The Havebussen (Garden Bus) visits sights that illustrate the ways in which the island's exquisite flora and fauna are being preserved. The Veteranbussen (Veteran Bus), a circa World War II Bedford, connects some of Bornholm's oldest industries, including a clockmaker, water mill, and Denmark's last windmill used for making flour.

From mid-June to mid-September, boats to the Helligdomsklipperne (Sanctuary Cliffs) leave Gudhjem at 10:30, 1:30, and 2:30, with extra sailings from mid-June to mid-August. Call Thor Båd.

You can visit the Ertholmene archipelago near Bornholm, which is better known as Christiansø, the name of the biggest island in the group. King Christian V's old fortress stands on Christiansø today almost as it did when the fortress was built in 1684, and offers an exciting historical experience. Boats to Christiansø depart from Svaneke at 10 AM daily year-round; May to September daily at 10:20 from Gudhjem, and at 1 from Allinge; and between mid-June and August an additional boat leaves Gudhjem weekdays at 9:40 and 12:15. The cost is DKr. 160. Call Christiansø Farten for additional information.

🚍 **BAT** (Bornholm Municipality Traffic Company) ☎ 56/95-21-21 ⊕ www.bat.dk. **Christiansø Farten** ✉ Ejnar Mikkelsensvej 25, Gudhjem ☎ 56/48-51-76 ⊕ www. christiansoefarten.dk. **Klippefly** ✉ Søndre Landevej 2, Rønne ☎ 56/95-35-73 ⊕ www. bornholmerguiden.dk/klippefly. **Thor Båd** ✉ Melstedvej 17, Gudhjem ☎ 56/48-51-65.

TRAIN TRAVEL

A DSB Intercity train travels two to five times a day from Copenhagen's main station, across the Øresund Bridge to Malmö, and then to Ystad, where it connects with a ferry to Rønne.

🚍 **DSB** ☎ 70/13-14-15 ⊕ www.dsb.dk.

VISITOR INFORMATION
The main tourist office in Rønne operates a Web site with area listings.
🔳 **Bornholm Tourist Office** ✉ Nordre Kystvej 3, DK-3700 Rønne ☎ 56/95-95-00 🖷 56/
95-95-68 ⊕ www.bornholminfo.dk. **Allinge-Nordbornholms Turistbureau** ✉ Kirkeg.
4, DK-3770 Allinge ☎ 56/48-00-01 🖷 56/48-00-20 ⊕ www.bornholmsbookingcenter.
dk. **Åkirkeby** ✉ Torvet 2, DK-3720 Åkirkeby ☎ 56/97-45-20 🖷 56/97-58-90 ⊕ www.
sydborn.dk. **Gudhjem** ✉ Åbog. 9 DK-3760 Gudhjem ☎ 56/48-52-10 🖷 56/48-52-74.
Hasle ✉ Havneg. 1 DK-3790 Hasle ☎ 56/96-44-81 🖷 56/96-41-06 ⊕ www.hasle-
turistbureau.dk. **Nexø** ✉ Søndre Hammer 2A DK-3730 Nexø ☎ 56/49-70-79 🖷 56/
49-70-10 ⊕ www.nexoe-dueodde.dk. **Svaneke** ✉ Storeg. 24, DK-3740 Svaneke ☎ 56/
49-70-79 🖷 56/49-70-10 ⊕ www.nexoe-dueodde.dk.

UNDERSTANDING DENMARK

DENMARK AT A GLANCE

Fast Facts

Name in local language: Kongeriget Danmark (Kingdom of Denmark)
Capital: Copenhagen
National anthem: Civil: *Der er et Yndigt land* (*There is a Lovely Land*); Royal: *Kong Christian* (*King Christian*)
Type of government: Constitutional monarchy
Administrative divisions: Metropolitan Denmark: 14 counties (amter; singular: amt) and 2 boroughs (amtskommunder; singular: amtskommune). The Faroe Islands and Greenland are part of the Kingdom of Denmark and are self-governing overseas administrative divisions.
Independence: First organized as a unified state in the 10th century; became a constitutional monarchy in 1849.
Constitution: Original constitution adopted June 5, 1849; major overhaul to constitution on June 5, 1953 allowed for a unicameral legislature and a female chief of state.
Legal system: Civil law system; judicial review of legislative acts; accepts compulsory ICJ jurisdictions, without reservations.
Suffrage: 18 years of age; universal
Legislature: Unicameral People's Assembly or Folketinget (179 seats, including 2 from Greenland and 2 from the Faroe Islands; members elected by popular vote on the basis of proportional representation to serve four-year terms).
Population: 5.4 million
Population density: 326 people per square mi
Median age: Male 38.6, female 40.4

Life expectancy: Male 75.3, female 80
Infant mortality rate: 4.6 deaths per 1,000 live births
Literacy: 100%
Language: Danish, Faroese, Greenlandic (an Inuit dialect), German (small minority), English (Denmark's predominant second language)
Ethnic groups: Scandinavian, Inuit, Faroese, German, Turkish, Iranian, Somali
Religion: Evangelical Lutheran 95%, other Protestant and Roman Catholic 3%; Muslim 2%
Discoveries & Inventions: Current concept of atomic structure (the Bohr model): Niels Bohr; theory that light has finite velocity: Olaus Roemer; first modern star catalog: Tycho Brahe; tape recorder (magnetic steel tape): Valdemar Poulsen; subatomic quantum theory: Niels Bohr; LEGO toy bricks; microscope

American Danish can be doughy, heavy, sticky, tasting of prunes and is usually wrapped in cellophane. Danish Danish is light, crisp, buttery and often tastes of marzipan or raisins; it is seldom wrapped in anything but loving care.
                    R. W. Apple, Jr.

Beer is the Danish national drink, and the Danish national weakness is another beer.
                    Clementine Paddleford

Something is rotten in the state of Denmark.
                    William Shakespeare, *Hamlet*

Geography & Environment

Land area: 43,090 square km (16,640 square mi), about twice the size of New Jersey

Coastline: 7,310 km (4,540 mi) along the North Sea, Baltic Sea, and Denmark Strait (*Skagerrak* and *Kattegat*)

Terrain: Low and flat to gently rolling plains
Islands: Denmark consists of 406 islands–82 of which are inhabited–and the peninsula of Jutland, which borders Germany
Natural resources: Chalk, fish, gravel and sand, limestone, natural gas, petroleum, salt, stone

Natural hazards: Flooding: some areas are protected from the sea by a system of dikes.
Environmental issues: Air pollution, principally from vehicle and power-plant emissions; nitrogen and phosphorous pollution of the North Sea; drinking and surface water pollution from animal wastes and pesticides

Economy

Currency: Danish krone (DKr)
Exchange rate: 6.2 Danish kroner = $1
GDP: 1.08 trillion Danish kroner ($174.4 billion)
Per capita income: 199,000 Danish kroner ($32,200)
Inflation: 1.4%
Unemployment: 6.2%
Workforce: 2.87 million
Debt: 134.3 billion Danish kroner ($21.7 billion)
Economic aid: 10.1 billion Danish kroner ($1.6 billion)
Major industries: Chemicals, food processing, iron, machinery and transportation equipment, nonferrous metals, iron
Agricultural products: Barley, dairy products, pork, potatoes, sugar beets, wheat
Exports: 452.2 billion Danish kroner

($73.1 billion)
Major export products: Chemicals, dairy products, fish, furniture, machinery and instruments, meat and meat products
Export partners: Germany 16.9%; Sweden 14%; United Kingdom 6.9%; United States 5.4%; France 5.2%; Netherlands 5.1%; Norway 4.8%
Imports: 392.7 billion Danish kroner ($63.5 billion)
Major import products: Chemicals, consumer goods, grain and foodstuffs, machinery and equipment, raw materials and semimanufactures for industry
Import partners: Germany 22.9%; Sweden 12.4%; Netherlands 7.6%; France 5.6%; United Kingdom 5.4%; Norway 5%; Italy 4.3%

Political Climate

Denmark is a part of the European Union but does not use the euro. The country has also opted out of the European defense cooperation and issues concerning certain justice and home affairs.
Danish citizens enjoy a high standard of living. The government's objectives include streamlining the bureaucracy, further privatizing state assets, and

confronting a future decline in the ratio of workers to retirees.

How absurd men are! They never use the liberties they have, they demand those they do not have. They have freedom of thought, they demand freedom of speech.

Søren Kierkegaard, Danish philosopher

Did You Know?

- An orally transmitted Danish story written down in the late 12th century was the inspiration for William Shakespeare's *Hamlet*.

- Denmark's monarchy has endured for more than 1,000 years.

- The band Aqua, which performed the song *Barbie Girl,* is from Denmark

- Denmark has ruled England, Norway, Finland, Iceland, Ireland, parts of the Virgin Islands, Tranquebar in India, parts of the Baltic coast, and what is now northern Germany.

- Wine is consumed in 93% of Danish homes, the highest level of consumption in the world.

- Denmark has the highest per capita candy consumption in the world.

- Charles Schulz's *Peanuts* comic strip is called *Radishes* in Denmark.

- The Danes use ketchup on spaghetti.

- In Denmark, a Danish pastry is called *wienerbrød,* or "Vienna bread."

THE UTTERLY DANISH PASTRIES OF DENMARK

I BELIEVE ABOVE AND BEYOND every gastronomic specialty a country offers, there is one, just one, perfect, delicious bit or bite or drop of something or another that sums up everything the country is and ever has been. As a transplanted American living in Denmark, I long thought the country's perfect bite was the smørrebrød, or open-face sandwiches: they are practical, well designed, and small—in essence everything Denmark is. Over time, however, I have revised my theory. Today, I believe that divine bite can be found in the pastries, the Danish pastries.

Take a stroll through Copenhagen, and before long you'll have to make an effort to pass up the bakeries, to steel yourself not to try one of the flaky sweets. But then again, why should you? A Danish pastry is effortlessly elegant, unobtrusively hedonistic, and often packed with a surprise—an edible metaphor of the Danish experience.

Imagine this: you are walking through Copenhagen, and you happen to meander off Strøget, the store-crammed and remarkably congested pedestrian spine. Immediately, you notice the pace of the city slows. Antiques shops sidle up to cafés while, a block away, rows of half-timber houses lined with thick squares of convex windows wiggle to nowhere. At the tip of Gammel Strand, literally the old beach, you spy a lone fisherwoman in worn shawls and a head scarf hawking live eel and smoked herring. You wind back to La Glace, more than 150 years old and purported to be the oldest confectionery shop in Copenhagen. Decorous ladies in aprons serve you a dainty china pot of coffee and light, crisp, and exceedingly Danish pastries.

Not just any sweets these—not French, nor Austrian—and certainly not those suspicious-looking pillows of white dough injected with red stuff you chance to order in the United States, but the real McCoy, made in the same way since the 19th century. It makes me wonder why the Danes don't lay claim to the name, and insist upon it as an *appellation d'origine*.

The first time I had a Danish pastry at the source was 14 years ago, when the Dane of my affections (my husband today) introduced me to Copenhagen. A late night of debauchery had turned into an early-morning amble, when Jesper and his best friend, Jan Erik, assured me that pastries would cure all of our ails. Though most bakeries don't open until 6 AM, Jan Erik went to a side door and rapped on its top window. Shady conversation with a young, flour-dusted blade ensued, and paper bags and cash were quickly exchanged. (I was never clear if it was law or legend, but in those days, most Danes believed the police enforced regular shopping hours.) Prize in hand, we strolled to Peblinge Sø, one of the city's lakes, where we sat on a bench, drank from a carton of milk, and ate several flaky pastries topped with nuts and sugar icings and filled with marmalades and creams. As the sun rose, defining the ducks, swans, and occasional heron, I felt enormously happy just to be there.

Those who record such events mark the birth of the Danish pastry sometime at the end of the 19th century, when Danish bakers went on strike, demanding money rather than room and board as payment for their work. Their employers replaced them with Austrian bakers, who brought with them the mille-feuille, or puff pastry, which they learned to make from the French. Once the Danes were back at work, they adopted the Continental dough, making it their own by adding yeast and sweet fillings.

It was a tradition at the time (and to a lesser degree today) for Danish bakers to travel abroad to add to their repertoire. This pastry cross-pollination helps explain why the yeast-risen puff pastry is called *Kopenhagener Geback,* literally "Copenhagen bread," in Austria, and Danish pastry in America. Ironically, the yeast-risen pastries are still called *wienerbrød,* or Vienna bread, in Denmark.

What makes Danish pastries special is the production process, which for most bakers is still done by hand. Essentially, the dough—milk, flour, eggs, butter, sugar, and yeast—is made, then chilled. It is then rolled into a rectangle, and, unapologetically, a slab of margarine or butter is put on the center third. The two ends of the dough are folded over the butter, and the process is repeated three times, until there are 27 layers in all.

Once the dough has been rolled and chilled, it is finally shaped into pretzel forms (called *kringle*), as well as braids, squares, triangles, fans, combs, swirls, pinwheels, horns, crescents, and wreaths, and filled with *remonce,* the stupefyingly rich butter, sugar, and nut (or marzipan) combination. The word "remonce" only sounds French; since it was very fashionable in 19th-century Denmark to give things French-ified names, a Danish baker is said to have invented the word. Ask for it in Paris, and, no doubt, you will be met with bewilderment.

In addition to the remonce, Danish bakers also fill their pastries with raisins, fruit compotes, and vanilla and—to a lesser degree—chocolate custards. As Gert Sørensen, the chief baker and owner of Konditoriet in Tivoli, says, "The final product should be crisp on the outside, juicy on the inside."

He should know: as one of the country's most respected pastry chefs, he has been educating and enlightening generations of young pastry stars. In fact, not just anyone can be a *konditor,* as they are known in Denmark. The rigorous education takes three years and seven months, and entails basic economics as well as an apprenticeship at a bakery, making wienerbrød daily. Danes are happy to consume the schoolwork, and do so at breakfast, after lunch, or with their afternoon coffee, especially on weekends. Copenhagen alone boasts more than 150 of Denmark's 1,400 bakeries, the latter pulling in the equivalent of $727 million annually, about 20% of which is attributable to wienerbrød. At an average cost of 5 kroner (roughly 91¢), I figure that's close to 30 million pastries a year.

Trying to pick the best of Copenhagen's— let alone Denmark's—pastries is like hunting down France's best truffle. Though Denmark's pastry chefs participate in a number of national and international pastry contests (and consistently rank among the world's best), nearly every Dane has found a bakery within a five-minute cycling radius of home that they claim to be the best in the land. My own allegiance is to the bakery named Bosse, in the neighborhood of Østerbro. I often find my bed-headed self wandering there on Saturday morning to buy a bagful of pastries with names like rum snail, marzipan horn, and my husband's favorite, a rum ball, essentially the sausage of pastries, all the leftover bits rolled together and often covered with chocolate sprinkles. My own favorites include the *spandauer,* a flat swirl of dough centered with vanilla custard, and the marzipan horn, a crispy twirl of pastry rolled up with remonce. Even though these may not be the finest pastries in town, they are the genuine article, and uncommonly Danish.

But, there's much more to Danish pastries than wienerbrød. At La Glace the windows display delicate special-occasion cakes like those for baptisms, trimmed with marzipan pacifiers, cradles, and dolls. From her original 1920 pink, green, and gold tearoom, proprietor Marianne Stagetorn Kolos explains that most guests come for her layer cakes, like the best-selling *Sportskage,* a mound of macaroons, whipped cream, and caramel chunks created and named for a play performed at the nearby Folketeatret in 1891. It's a Danish custom to name confections for events and personalities, but there was a time when ordering a miniature Sarah Bernhardt, a chocolate-truffle-covered macaroon named for the French actress, was an act of courage. During World War II resistance fighters and sympathizers recognized one another by ordering the pastry as a "radio macaroon," since it resembles an old-fashioned radio knob. The name stuck.

Close by, on a quiet cobblestoned courtyard, is the Kransekagehuset, where confectioner Jørgen Jensen makes the marzipan cakes compulsory at any Danish wedding.

Using 1 kilogram marzipan to 400 grams sugar to 200 grams egg whites, Jensen molds the dough into rings of varying sizes. Once baked, they are fashioned into cones or cornucopias, squiggled with white icing, decked with paper decorations, or filled with wrapped candies.

I know the *kransekage* intimately. At our wedding years ago, Jesper and I split the difference in our Italian-Armenian-American-Danish backgrounds, and ordered two cakes, one of which was a kransekage laced with Danish and American flags, and tiny, shiny-paper firecrackers that made a polite little bang.

"It's something special," smiles Jensen. "It's something very Danish."

—Karina Porcelli

THE FEAST BEFORE THE FAST

J ENS PETER NISSEN loves to behold his handiwork smashed to smithereens. "It's a pure delight to see," he says. It begins when youngsters in vividly colored costumes shriek with glee as they bash a wooden baton against the fruits of Nissen's labor. Princesses and pirates swing the baton with all of their might in an attempt to "knock the cat out of the barrel." The loud crack of wood striking wood punctuates the excited cries of the youngsters. One by one, they take a turn until one of the revelers succeeds in splintering the barrel and spilling the goodies inside. The lucky one will become the Cat King or Cat Queen of Fastelavn, the Danish Shrovetide celebration.

Nissen is one of the few remaining coopers who makes barrels for Fastelavn parties, as the art of barrel making has been pushed aside by the importation of cheaper wares. Using resilient beech wood, Nissen crafts several thousand barrels each season. In fact, he has even begun a "green barrel" project. "I can recoup around two-thirds of the staves from local customers and make new barrels," he says. The recycled staves are then reassembled to face the onslaught of costumed kiddies the following Fastelavn.

Fastelavn Sunday, or Shrove Sunday, falls seven weeks before Easter at the time of the second new moon of the year, sometime during February or the first week of March. During this anxious late-winter period before the dawn of spring, agrarian societies saw their stores of food running low and felt considerable apprehension about the growing season to come. Thus, Danish Fastelavn evolved as a fertility rite, mixing practices and beliefs imported from other cultures. Like Carnival, Mardi Gras, and Shrovetide, Fastelavn also provided the final binge before the 40-day Lenten fast preceding Easter.

Centuries ago, Danish peasants gathered for Fastelavn festivities at the larger farms in their region. Provisions were gathered by donation from area farmers, and long days were spent in preparation. Since there was little farm work to be done this time of year, landowners were liberal about allowing free time and the event sometimes lasted for a week. Beer and *akvavit* (the local spirit that tastes like caraway seeds) flowed generously, while pork and pigs' feet often featured in the menus alongside *Æggesøppe* (a concoction of eggs, sugar, and beer) and other baked goods. Behind the gaudy smorgasbords and conspicuous consumption, though, was a strong symbolism, with the ubiquitous and variously cooked egg signifying the holiday's obsession, fertility.

When the day of the feast arrived, people would gather dressed in costumes and ready for a blowout. Usually there was a hag, a ragamuffin, and a jester at each gathering, each playing a predetermined role in the festivities. Bacchus, the Greek god of wine, was a regular (and fitting) figure at most feasts. Some costumes revealed the revelers' "birthday suits," borrowing elements from fertility rites in other countries, where sowing seeds in the nude was thought to ensure a bountiful agricultural year. One common Fastelavn event was a women's footrace where the ladies would hike their skirts and reveal their bare bottoms—all for the sake of a good crop!

In the 16th century Danish rulers and clergy attempted to abolish what they called "the debauchery of Fastelavn." Outcries protesting the sinfulness of the spectacles echoed down through the years, but Fastelavn was too beloved a celebration to stamp out altogether. Although authorities managed to tame the celebrations, and particularly raucous traditions fell by the wayside, the spirit of Fastelavn has survived to the present day.

When Danish children try to "knock the cat out of the barrel," they are in effect jousting. In olden days and even up through the 19th century, a live cat was placed in a barrel suspended on a rope between two houses or trees. Cats, especially black ones, had the misfortune of being considered harbingers of bad luck. Riders on horseback would "tilt the barrel" until it shattered and the unlucky (and often deceased) cat was expelled. The rider who succeeded in liberating the cat would receive a "free ride" for the party or even a reprieve on taxes. Edible goodies gradually replaced the hapless felines, so that today the barrels are filled with an inanimate cargo of fruit, nuts, and sweets.

Outside Copenhagen on the island of Amager, many of the older traditions connected to Fastelavn have been preserved and draw thousands of spectators each year. At Store Magleby, 12 km (7½ mi) from the capital on the outskirts of Dragør, the day-long festivities begin early Monday morning when riders dressed in top hats, white embroidered shirts, and black vests gather to participate in a parade led by flagmen and a carriage full of musicians. The procession winds its way throughout the district where the burghers serve participants hot rum punch. In return, the hosts are toasted for their graciousness with a song.

Later in the day the mounted assembly meets for spectacular tilting of the barrel, as riders take turns steering their steeds under the hoisted cask. The audience gasps as each of the 25 to 30 "knights" swings a beautifully carved baton to whack the barrel at full gallop. The excitement of thundering hooves and gleaming horseflesh draws the imagination back to yesteryear. When the final stave has been bashed, the gathering elects a Barrel King who gets a wreath for his valor and a kiss from the Barrel Queen. The couple then opens the festive Barrel Ball with the first three dances and the revelry extends long into the night.

Traces of other traditions can also be seen in the family's celebration of Fastelavn. Children start the day by looking under their beds, where their parents have placed a *ris,* a small cluster of twigs decorated with colored paper and sweets. The twigs bear significance as an implement of punishment, as mock floggings used to mark the holiday, and their decorations symbolize hopes for a fruitful season ahead. The children then "beat" their parents out of bed with the twigs, singing a song in which they threaten to make mischief unless they are fed. The parents' duty is to then serve the youngsters Fastelavnsboller, a heated sweet bun.

After breakfast the kiddies don costumes ranging from fairy-tale princesses to modern-day superheroes. Many of them rattle coin boxes to get contributions from friends and family, a throwback to the days when the good burghers bore some of the cost of holiday festivities. But, of course, the real highlight of Fastelavn is "knocking the cat out of the barrel," in cobblestone courtyards and lawns on Sunday and again in school the following day. Children can't wait to get into their costumes and take a swipe at the barrel, making it certain that this tradition will live on for years to come.

"It's funny. I'm a fourth-generation cooper," says Jens Peter Nissen, "and my son told me recently that he was interested in becoming a cooper one day."

—Charles Ferro

BOOKS & MOVIES

Books

A History of the Vikings (Oxford University Press, 1984) recounts the story of the aggressive warriors and explorers who during the Middle Ages influenced a large portion of the world, extending from Constantinople to America. Gwyn Jones's lively account makes learning the history enjoyable.

The History of the Danes is a 10-volume chronicle by the 13th-century monk Saxo, containing a fascinating mix of legend and history, and was where Shakespeare allegedly found the inspiration for his Hamlet character. *The Journey of Niels Klim to the World Underground* is probably Ludvig Holberg's most internationally recognized play. He is regarded as the father of Danish literature, and created the Lille Gronnegade Theater at a time when Danish drama hardly existed.

The 19th century was the dawn of the Golden Age of Danish literature, marked mainly by the works of Søren Kierkegaard and Hans Christian Andersen. Kierkegaard was not really recognized in his own time, but rediscovered in the next century. Andersen is too often dismissed as simply a writer of fables, which were really aimed at an adult audience. His travel accounts, poems, plays, and other writings give a broader, and fairer, picture of who the man really was. The works of Karen Blixen (Isak Dinesen) are mostly set in Denmark and are excellent introductions to the country. A good starting point would be Blixen's debut *Seven Gothic Tales*, which was first published in the United States a year before its translation and Danish release in 1935. Blixen was like a literary Janus, simultaneously looking back at outdated traditions and gazing forward toward postmodern literature. The film *Out of Africa*, from Blixen's novel, has become her signature.

Pelle the Conqueror (volumes I and II) by Martin Andersen Nexø is a novel about a young Swedish boy and his father who work on a stone farm in Bornholm under hateful Danish landowners. Henrik Pontoppidan's *The Country of the Dead* is world literature at its finest. Pontoppidan won the Nobel Prize for literature with another Dane, Karl Adolph Gjellerup, in 1917. Johannes V. Jensen is another Nobel Prize recipient. He is probably best known for his epic novel *The Long Journey*, but his *Poems* and the historical-mythical novel *The Fall of the King* demonstrate his outstanding use of language.

Laterna Magica is a novel of the Faroe Islands by William Heinesen, perhaps Denmark's greatest writer since Karen Blixen. Other excellent books on Denmark include: the satirical trilogy by Hans Scherfig—*Stolen Spring, The Missing Bureaucrat,* and *Idealists*; and Wallace Stegner's novel *The Spectator Bird*, which follows a man's exploration of his Danish heritage. Ib Michael's visits to foreign shores, especially Latin America, have a deep influence on his work. He brings this cultural inspiration back to Danish soil in his novel *Prince*.

Much of Carsten Jensen's prose is devoted to lovely travelogues drawn from numerous journeys throughout the world. A good starting point would be *I Have Seen the World Begin,* where he displays his uncanny eye for detail and insight into human behavior. Leif Davidsen was a foreign correspondent for the Danish media before becoming a potboiler best seller. His experiences abroad help draw settings for superb spy novels such as *The Russian Singer* and *Lime's Photograph.* For contemporary Danish poetry, try Jens Christian Grøndahl's collections *Silence in October* or *Lucca.*

In more recent children's literature, Bjarne Reuter's *Buster's World* tells an exciting tale with appeal for all ages. Peter Høeg's acclaimed novel *Smilla's Sense of Snow* is a compulsive page-turner that paints a dark and foreboding picture of Copenhagen and the waters around Greenland; the movie version debuted in 1997.

Fjord Press (Box 16349, Seattle, WA 98116, ☎ 206/935–7376, 🖷 206/938–1991) has one of the most comprehensive selections of Danish fiction in translation of any publisher in the United States. The Danish Literature Council's excellent Web site (www.literaturenet.dk) has a long list of books in translation and author profiles.

Movies

Babette's Feast, which won the Oscar for the best foreign film of 1987, was produced in Denmark. A year later Bille August won Danish cinema another Oscar for *Pelle the Conqueror* and launched his international career. Danny Kaye starred in the 1952 film *Hans Christian Andersen.* In fact, his crooning of "Wonderful Copenhagen" became Denmark's official tourism slogan. In 2005 Denmark celebrated Andersen's 200th birthday. Disney's *The Little Mermaid* is a great way to get your kids interested in Andersen's fairy tales. A more recent film for youngsters is Pia Bovin's *Wallah Be* (2002), a humorous look at a suburban Danish boy who wants to be a Muslim. The film takes a comic approach to a political hot potato of the day.

Pusher (1997) has been called the Danish *Trainspotting* for its hard-driving tempo and director Niclas Winding Refn's portrayal of the drug culture. Refn takes a frightening and unique approach to the whodunit mystery in *Fear X* (2003), starring John Turturro. *Let's Get Lost* (1997) was Jonas Elmer's film debut, in which he effectively stages in black and white the laughter and tears of a group of young friends. Nils Malmros depicts 18th-century life on the Faroe Islands and the love affair between a minister and a young woman twice widowed in *Barbara* (1998).

Søren Kragh-Jacobsen, Lars von Trier, and Thomas Vinterberg cofounded the Dogma Manifesto, one of the boldest cinema experiments ever. The three wrote up a "vow of chastity" to make films with as few props and frills as possible. The results peel away layers of cinematic technique and leave the viewer with a raw view of the subject on screen. Vinterberg's *The Celebration* (1999) turns a family celebration into a nightmare; in *The Idiots* (1999) von Trier examines a perverse grassroots experiment in human nature; and Kragh-Jacobsen takes an off-center perspective of returning home to find love in *Mifune* (1998). Lone Scherfig's *Italian for Beginners* (2000) takes the Dogma concept into the romantic comedy genre. Scherfig stepped onto the international filmmaking stage with the English-language *Wilbur Wants to Kill Himself* (2002), a highly entertaining, warm comedy with a serious bent. Kragh-Jacobsen and Vinterberg both made English-language films in 2003. Kragh-Jacobsen's *Skagerrak* is part of what he calls the "Women's Trilogy" that started with *Mifune.* On their latest outing, two women spend their time pursuing men and liquor, but somehow end up finding direction and meaning for their confused lives. *It's All About Love* is Thomas Vinterberg's millennial fairy tale, a romance, with an unsettling dreamlike atmosphere.

Susanne Bier's *The One and Only* (1999) provided audiences with hilarious romantic comedy that made it the best-selling picture in Danish history. In the same year Ole Christian Madsen gave viewers the stark realism of life for young nonethnic Danes who step outside the law in *Pizza King.* Bier then made a real international breakthrough with her first Dogma venture *Open Hearts* (2002), a tearjerker about personal tragedy and its effects on love. Lars von Trier revived the cinema musical, with a twist, in his *Dancer in the Dark* (2000), a work that won him a number of international awards and nominations. The film was a major victory for Danish cinema and an excellent follow-up to von Trier's *Breaking the Waves* (1997). In another trilogy in the making, director Per Fly investigates the class structure of Danish society and displays an amazing ability to get right down to eye level with the protagonist. *The Bench* (2000) examines the dark alcoholic underclass, and *Inheritance* (2003) follows with a view of upper-class life.

CHRONOLOGY

ca. 10,000 BC Stone Age culture develops in Denmark.

ca. 2,000 BC Tribes from southern Europe, mostly Germanic peoples, migrate toward Denmark.

ca. 1800–500 BC The Bronze Age culture develops in Denmark. Metal tools and weapons are made, and trade with other European countries increases.

ca. 500 BC Migration of Celts across central Europe impinges on Denmark's trade routes with the Mediterranean world. Trade becomes less economically crucial because of the growing use of abundant iron.

ca. 770 AD The Viking Age begins. For the next 250 years, Scandinavians set sail on frequent expeditions stretching from the Baltic to the Irish seas, and even to the Mediterranean as far as Constantinople and to North America, employing superior ships and weapons and efficient military organization.

811 The Eider River is declared the southern border of the Kingdom of Denmark. It remains there for nearly 1,000 years.

830 Frankish monk Ansgar makes one of the first attempts to Christianize Sweden and builds the first church in Slesvig, Denmark.

ca. 940–980 King Harald Bluetooth imposes Christianity on the people of Denmark. In less than a century, virtually the whole population has been converted.

1016–35 Canute (Knud) the Great is king of England, Denmark (1018), and Norway (1028). The united kingdom crumbles shortly after Canute's death in 1035.

1070 Adam of Bremen composes *History of the Archbishops of Hamburg-Bremen,* the first important contemporary source for Danish history.

ca. 1100–1200 The power of the Danish crown grows, and the country becomes dominant in the Baltic region.

1169 King Valdemar, who was acknowledged as the single king of Denmark in 1157 and undertook repeated crusades against the Germans, captures Rugen and places it under Danish rule, signifying the beginning of the Danish medieval empire. It culminates in 1219 when Valdemar marches to Estonia and builds a fortress at Ravel. In 1225 Valdemar, after being kidnapped by a German vassal, is forced to give up all his conquests, except for Rugen and Estonia, in exchange for his release.

ca. 1200 Saxo writes his history of Denmark, the first volume of Danish literature. It is an amazing source of history and legend, and is believed to have inspired Shakespeare to write about the fictitious Danish prince Hamlet.

1282 At a meeting of the Hof, or Danish Parliament, Danish king Erik Glipping signs a coronation charter that becomes the first written constitution of Denmark.

ca. 1340 King Valdemar IV reunites Denmark after a long period of civil unrest.

1370 The Treaty of Stralsund gives the north German trading centers of the Hanseatic League free passage through Danish waters and full control of Danish herring fisheries for 15 years. German power increases throughout Scandinavia.

1397 The Kalmar Union is formed by Queen Margrethe as a result of the dynastic ties between Sweden, Denmark, and Norway; the geographical position of the Scandinavian states; and the growing influence of Germans in the Baltic. Erik of Pomerania is crowned king of the Kalmar Union.

ca. 1417 The center of power shifts from Roskilde to Copenhagen, which becomes the capital of Denmark.

1479 The University of Copenhagen is founded.

1520 Christian II, ruler of the Kalmar Union, executes 82 people who oppose the Kalmar Union in an event known as the "Stockholm bloodbath." Sweden secedes from the Union three years later. Norway remains tied to Denmark and becomes a Danish province in 1536.

1528–36 The Reformation reaches Denmark. Lutheran clergy rapidly gain access to the royal court and spread the religious word. The Reformation brings on civil unrest culminating in the Count's War, in which the nobility wins power. King Christian III declares Lutheranism to be the official religion of the country. Catholic clergy are imprisoned, and Catholic properties and other assets are confiscated.

1534 Count Christoffer of Oldenburg and his army demand the restoration of Christian II as king of Denmark, initiating civil war between supporters of Christian II and supporters of Prince Christian (later King Christian III).

1563–70 Denmark wages war, but fails to reclaim Sweden.

1588–1648 King Christian IV sits on the throne in one of the longest and most influential reigns in Danish history. Prosperity flourishes, despite an unsuccessful war against Sweden. Christian becomes known as the "Building King" for initiating huge construction projects, especially in Copenhagen, where many of his buildings still stand. His lavish spending brings the country to the brink of bankruptcy.

1611–16 During the Kalmar War, Denmark wages a campaign against Sweden in hopes of restoring the Kalmar Union.

1611–60 Gustav II Adolphus reigns in Sweden. Under his rule, Sweden defeats Denmark in the Thirty Years' War and becomes the greatest power in Scandinavia as well as in northern and central Europe.

1660 The Peace of Copenhagen establishes the modern boundaries of Denmark, Sweden, and Norway.

1665 King Frederik III establishes an absolute monarchy.

1754 The Royal Danish Academy of Fine Arts is established.

1762 The Duke of Gottorp becomes czar of Russia and declares war on Denmark. Catherine, the czar's wife, overrules her husband's war declaration and makes a peaceful settlement.

1801–14 The Napoleonic Wars are catastrophic for Denmark economically and politically: the policy of armed neutrality fails, the English destroy the Danish fleet in 1801, Copenhagen is devastated during the bombardment of 1807, and Sweden, after Napoléon's defeat at the Battle of Leipzig, attacks Denmark and forces the Danish surrender of Norway. The Treaty of Kiel, in 1814, calls for a union between Norway and Sweden despite Norway's desire for independence. The Danish monarchy is divided into three parts: the Kingdom of Denmark; the duchies of Schleswig and Holstein; and Iceland, Greenland, and the Faroe Islands.

1810–30 This is the Golden Age of Danish literature and art. Hans Christian Andersen and Søren Kierkegaard make their mark during this period. C. W. Eckersberg influences a generation of artists with his focus on nature.

1849 Denmark's absolute monarchy is abolished and replaced by the liberal June Constitution, which establishes freedom of the press, freedom of religion, the right to hold meetings and form associations, and rule by two chambers of Parliament, which are overseen by the king and his ministers.

ca. 1850–1900 The beginning of the industrial age is heralded by the building of railroads in Scandinavia. The expansion of industrialism draws people to Copenhagen, which has a population of almost 1.5 million by the turn of the 20th century.

1864 Denmark goes to war against Prussia and Austria; the hostilities end with the Treaty of Vienna, which forces Denmark to surrender the duchies of Schleswig and Holstein to Prussia and Austria.

1914 At the outbreak of World War I, Germany forces Denmark to lay mines in an area of international waters known as the Great Belt. Because the British fleet makes no serious attempts to break through, Denmark is able to maintain neutrality.

1917 Danish writer Henrik Pontoppidan is awarded the Nobel Prize for literature.

1918 Iceland becomes a separate state under the Danish crown; only foreign affairs remain under Danish control. Sweden, Denmark, and Norway grant women the right to vote.

1920 Scandinavian countries join the League of Nations.

ca. 1930 The Great Depression brings unemployment to 40% of the organized industrial workers in Denmark. The age of the Social

Democrats begins, and foundations are laid for the welfare state that still exists today.

1939 Denmark and the other Nordic countries declare neutrality in World War II.

1940 Germany occupies Norway and Denmark. Denmark trades basic cooperation with their occupiers in exchange for a degree of self-government.

1949 Denmark, Norway, and Iceland become members of NATO.

1952 The Nordic Council is founded to promote cooperation among the Nordic parliaments.

1973 Denmark becomes a member of the European Union. Queen Margrethe II ascends the throne of Denmark.

1982 Poul Schluter becomes Denmark's first Conservative prime minister since 1894.

1989 The IMAX Tycho Brahe Planetarium opens in Copenhagen, and Denmark becomes the first NATO country to allow women to join front-line military units. Denmark becomes the first country in the world to recognize marriage between citizens of the same sex.

1991 The Karen Blixen Museum opens in Rungstedlund, Denmark.

1992 Denmark declines to support the Maastricht Treaty setting up a framework for European economic union. Denmark wins the European Soccer Championships.

1993 Denmark is the president of the European Union for the first half of 1993. In a second referendum, the country votes to support the Maastricht Treaty, as well as its own modified involvement in it. Tivoli celebrates its 150th year, Legoland celebrates its 25th birthday, and the Little Mermaid turns 80.

1996 Copenhagen is feted as the Cultural Capital of Europe.

1997 Copenhagen's venerable Carlsberg Brewery, one of the largest supporters of the arts in Denmark, celebrates its 150th anniversary.

2000 In a national referendum, Danish voters reject full membership in the European Economic Union by voting against the euro to replace the krone as (inter)national currency. The Øresund Bridge linking Denmark to Sweden opens for rail and motor traffic, connecting Scandinavia to the Continent. Queen Ingrid dies at the age of 90. Swedish by birth and a beloved member of the royal family, her death is mourned throughout the country.

2001 Denmark gets a Liberal-Conservative coalition government after the ruling Social Democrats call for an election. Political campaigning generates a great amount of (sometimes critical) foreign interest as the focal topic of the election is limiting immigration.

2002 Prince Felix is born to Princess Alexandra and Prince Joachim. The first section of the Copenhagen Metro goes into operation. Denmark passes legislation to curb immigration. Denmark occupies the seat of the European Union presidency in the second half of the year. Danish prime minister Anders Fogh Rasmussen gets credit for successfully coordinating the planned expansion of the union from 15 to 25 member nations.

VOCABULARY

	English	Danish	Pronunciation
Basics			
	Yes/no	Ja/nej	yah/nie
	Thank you	Tak	tak
	Thank you	Mange tak	**mahng**er tak
	You're welcome	Selv tak	**sell** tak
	Excuse me (to apologize)	Undskyld	**unsk**-ul
	Hello	Hej	hi
	Hello/Good day	Goddag	go-day
	How do you do?	goddag	go-**day**
	May I introduce . . .?	å jeg presentere . . .	Mo yie pre-sen-teer
	. . . my friend	min ven	meen ven
	. . . my sweetheart	min kæreste	meen **care**-es-te
	. . . my son	min søn	meen sohn
	. . . my daughter	min datter	meen dat-ter
	. . . my mother	min mor	meen mor
	. . . my father	min far	meen far
	. . . my sister	min søster	meen **soes**-ter
	. . . my brother	min bror	meen bror
	. . . my wife	min kone	meen **ko**-neh
	. . . my husband	min mand	meen man
	. . . my boss	min chef	meen shayf
	Good morning (early)	godmorgen	go-**more**-en
	Good afternoon	goddag	go-**day**
	Good evening	godaften	go-**af**-ten
	Good night	godnat	go-nat
	Sleep well	Sov godt	sow gut
	Goodbye	Farvel	fa-**vel**
	See you later	På gensyn	pa **en**-sewn
	See you (casually spoken)	Vi ses	vee sees
	Today	I dag	ee **day**
	Tomorrow	I morgen	ee **morn**
	Yesterday	I går	ee **gore**

Morning	Morgen	**more**-en
Afternoon	Eftermiddag	**ef-tah**-mid-day
Evening	Aften	**af**-dern
Night	Nat	nat

Numbers

1	een/eet	een/eet
2	to	toe
3	tre	treh
4	fire	fear
5	fem	fem
6	seks	sex
7	syv	syoo
8	otte	**oh**-te
9	ni	nee
10	ti	tee
11	elleve	**el**-ver
12	tolv	tol
13	tretten	**tre**-tern
14	fjorten	**fyor**-tern
15	femten	**fem** tern
16	seksten	**sehgs**-tern
17	sytten	**soo**-tern
18	atten	**ah**-tern
19	nitten	**ni**-tern
20	tyve	**tyoo**-ver
30	tredive	**tred**-ver
40	fyrre	**few**-rer
50	halvtreds	hal-**trays**
60	tres	trays
70	halvfjerds	hal-**fyairz**
80	firs	feers
90	halvfems	hal-**fems**
100	hundrede	**hoon**-red-der
1000	tusind	**too**-sin
10,000	ti tusind	tee **too**-sin

Days of the Week & Months

Monday	mandag	**man**-day
Tuesday	tirsdag	**tears**-day
Wednesday	onsdag	**ons**-day
Thursday	torsdag	**tors**-day
Friday	fredag	**free**-day
Saturday	lørdag	**lore**-day
Sunday	søndag	**sin**-day
January	januar	**yan**-oo-are
February	februar	**feb**-oo-are
March	marts	marts
April	april	a-**breel**
May	maj	my
June	juni	yoo-**nee**
July	juli	yoo-**lee**
August	august	ow-**goost**
September	september	sep-**tem**-beh
October	oktober	ock-**toh**-beh
November	november	no-**vem**-beh
December	december	des-**sem**-beh

Useful Phrases

Do you speak English?	Taler du engelsk	te-ler doo in-galsk
I don't speak . . . Danish	Jeg taler ikke . . . Dansk	yi tal-ler **ick** . . . Dansk
I understand	Jeg forstår	yi foh-stoh
I don't understand	Jeg forstår ikke	yi foh-stoh **ick**
I don't know	Det ved jeg ikke	deh **ved** yi ick
I am	Jeg er	yi ehr
American/British	amerikansk/britisk	a-meh-ri-**kansk**/bri-**tisk**
I am sick.	Jeg er syg	yi air **syoo**
Please call	Kan du ringe	can **doo** rin-geh
a doctor	til en læge	til en **lay**-eh
Pharmacy	apotek	a-po-**teek**
Do you have	Har du et	har **doo** eet
a vacant room?	værelse?	varay-l-sa
How much does it cost?	Hvad koster det?	va cos-ta **deh**

It's too expensive.	Det er for dyrt	deh air **fohr** deert
That's inexpensive	Det var billigt	**day** vahr beeleet
How are you?	Hvordan har du det?	vore-dan **ha** do deh
I am fine/well	Jeg har det godt	Yie **ha** de gutt
I am very pleased to meet you.	Det glæder mig at træffe Dem.	Deh **glay**derr mig at **treh**fer dem
My name is . . .	Mit navn er . . .	mid nown air . . .
Where are you from?	Hvor kommer du fra?	Vore **com**-mer doo fra
I am from . . .	Jeg kommer fra . . .	Yie com-mer fra . . .
Where do you live?/ Where are you staying?	Hvor bor du hen?	Vore bore doo hen
How old are you?	Hvor gammel er du?	Vore gam-mel air **do**
Are you going to work today?	Skal du arbejde idag?	Skal doo **are**-buy-da ee-day
I am free	Jeg har fri	Yie har **free**
Beautiful	Smukt	smukt
I'm sorry. I don't like it.	Jeg synes ikke om det	yie **soo**-ners ick om day
Help!	Hjælp	yelp
Can you help me, please?	Vil De være så venlig at hjælpe mig?	vil dee **vay**-rer saw **ven**-lee ad **yel**-per my
Stop!	Stop	stop
I am lost	Jeg er faret vild	yi air **far**-rerd veal
How do I get to . . .	Hvordan kommer yi til . . .	vore-**dan** kom-merjeg til
. . . the train station?	banegarden	**ban**-eh-gore-en
. . . the post office?	postkontoret	**post**-kon-toh-raht
. . . the tourist office?	turistkontoret	too-**reest**-kon-toh-raht
. . . the hospital?	hospitalet	hos-peet-**tal**-let
Does this bus go to . . .	Går denne bus til . . .	**goh** den-na boos til
Where's the bathroom?	Hvor er toilettet?	vor **air** toi-let-it
It's urgent	Det haster	day **hahs**-der
Where is the nearest bank?	Hvor er den nærmeste bank?	vor air den **nair**-mers-der bahnk
Where can I get a taxi?	Hvor kan jeg få en taxa?	vor kahn yie faw een **tahg**-sah

I would like to go to . . .	Jeg skal til . . .	Yie skal til
When?	Hvornår?	vor-**nawr**
On the left	Til venstre	til **ven**-strah
On the right	Til højre	til **hoy**-ah
Straight ahead	Lige ud	lee udth
North	nord	nor
South	syd	sudth
East	øst	ohst
West	vest	vest
What time is it?	Kan du sige mig hvad klokken er?	can do see my vadth **clok**-ken air
It is . . .	Den er . . .	Den air
one, two, three, etc.	et, to, tre, etc.	o'clock
quarter past . . .	kvart over . . .	kvart ower
quarter to . . .	kvart i . . .	kvart ee
half past (literally half before)	halv et, halv to, etc. (N.B. halv et = 12:30, halv to = 1:30 etc.)	hal
big	stor	sdoar
small	lille	liller
early	tidlig	**tid**-lee
late	sen	sayn
It's (too) late	Det er (for) sent	de air (for) **seent**
It's (too) early	Det er (for) tidlig	de air (for) tid-lee
Sorry I'm late	Undskyld jeg kom for sent	**un**-skuld yie com for seent
Do you have time?	Har du tid?	ha do tid
How long will it take?	Hvor lang tid tager det?	vor lahng tid tah de
Would you like to go to the movies?	Skal vi i biografen?	Skal vee ee bee-o-grahf-en
I'd like to go to the movies	Jeg vil gerne i biografen	Yie vil gairn ee bee-o-grahf-en
What would you like to see?	Hvad kun du tænke dig at se?	Vadth koon doo tan-keh die at see
movie	film	feelm
It was a good movie	Det var en god film	de var een go **feelm**
Do you like music?	Kan du lide musik?	can du lee moo-**seek**

Would you like to dance?	Vil du danse med mig?	vil do dan-seh medth mie
I would like to	Det vil jeg gerne	de vil yie **gair**-ne
I like you	Jeg kan lide dig	yie can lee die
I love you	Jeg elsker dig	yie el-skah die
You are cute/pretty	Du er sød	do air **suhdth**
The same to you	I lige måde	ee **lee** mo-deh
Never	aldrig	**ahl**-dree
Maybe	måske	mo-**skee**
Always	altid	ahl-tid
Congratulations	Tillykke	til-**luk**-ka
I'm sorry to hear that (condolences)	Det gøre mig ondt	day goohr my unt
Weather	været **vair**-it	
It's raining/snowing	Det regner/sneer	day **rhine**-er/**snee**-er.
The sun is shining	solen skinner	sol-en **skin**-ner.
It's cold/hot.	Det er koldt/varmt.	day air kolt/varmt.
I'm cold.	Jeg fryser.	yie **froo**-ser.
Do you have an umbrella?	Har du en paraply?	har do een par-a-**ploo**
overcast	overskyet	ower-sku-et
It's windy	Det blæser	day **blay**-ser.

Dining Out

Would you like to have breakfast/lunch/ dinner together?	Skal vi spise morgenmad/ frokost/middag sammen?	skal vee **spee**-sa more en madth/fro-coast/ mid-day sam-men
Are you hungry?	Er du sulten?	air **do** sool tan
I am hungry	Jeg er sulten	yie air **sool**-tan
I am thirsty	Jeg er tørstig	yie air **turss**-tee
What would you like to eat?	Hvad har du lyst til at spise?	vadth ha do loost til at **spee**-sa
Would you like a . . .?	Kunne du tænke dig en . . .?	coo-neh do tan-keh die een
Please bring me . . .	Må jeg få . . .	moh yie foh
Can I have . . .?	Kan jeg få . . .?	kahn yie faw
I'd like some . . .	Jeg vil gerne have . . .	yie vil **ger**-ner **hay**-fisk
Please pass the . . .	Kunne du række mig . . .	koo-neh do raik my

May I have a bit more, please?	Må jeg bede om lidt mere?	moh yie bee om lit meer
I'm a vegetarian	Jeg er vegetar	yie air ve-ge-**tar**
menu	menu	me-**nu**
fork	gaffel	gaf-**fel**
knife	kniv	ka-**new**
spoon	ske	skee
glass	glas	glass
cup	kop	cop
bowl	skål	skoal
plate	tallerken	tal-**air**-ken
napkin	serviet	ser-**veet**
bread	brød	brood
butter	smør	smoor
fish	fisk	fisk
vegetables	grøntsager	**grunt**say-er
salad/lettuce	salat	sal-**ate**
meat	kød	koodth
milk	mælk	malk
pepper	peber	**pee**-wer
salt	salt	selt
sugar	sukker	**su**-kar
water/bottled water	vand/Dansk vand	van/dansk van
ice cream	is	ees
beer	øl	ohl
cup of coffee	kop kaffe	cop **cah**-feh
wine	vin	veen
red wine	rødvin	**roadth**veen
white wine	hvidvin	**vidth**veen
assorted hors d'oeuvre	forskellig hors d'oeuvre	fos-**geh**-lee or-**durvr**
sole	søtunge	**sur**-doanger
trout	ørred	**ur**-rerd
lobster	hummer	**hoa**-mer
crayfish	krebs	krebs
prawns	store rejer	**stoa**-rer **rig**-ger
steak	en engelsk bøf	een **eng**-erlsk burf
lamb	lammekød	**la**-mor-kurd

pork chop	svinekotelet	**sveen**-er-ko-ter-led
chicken	kylling	**kew**-ling
duck	and	ahn
It tastes good	Det smager godt	De smay-ya **gut**
Thank you for the meal (customary etiquette)	Tak for mad	tak for madth
You're welcome	Velbekomme	Vel-be-kom-men
Cheers		Skål skoal
Thank you for the last time we were together (I had a good time)	Tak for sidste	tak for **seest**
It (the occasion) was/ is pleasant/cozy.	Det var/er hyggeligt.	De var/air **hoo**-geh-lee.
The check, please.	Må jeg bede om regningen	mo yie bi om **ri**-ning
Is service included?	Er det med betjening	air day med ber-**tyay**-ning?

INDEX

PHOTO CREDITS

NOTES

NOTES

NOTES

ABOUT OUR WRITERS

Canadian writer **Bruce Bishop,** who was born and raised in Nova Scotia, is still awed that his home province is bigger geographically than the whole country of Denmark. His love affair with Denmark began as an impressionable 18-year-old in the late '70s, when he visited a Danish school buddy. Bruce has been a freelance travel writer since 1994 and a frequent contributor to Fodor's since 1998. He is former president of Travel Media Association of Canada and an award-winning journalist and author. Among his many projects, he currently serves as the travel editor for *The European Reporter,* a biweekly tabloid from Toronto, and a media-relations consultant for his company, Global Travel Communicators.

Nima Adl, a native New Jerseyan, can often be seen jetlagged from the many miles he travels in his waking hours, and the many more he travels in his dreams. His essay on Christiania, an anarchist commune in Copenhagen, was based on the former.